Scripts of Blackness

GLOBAL STUDIES OF THE UNITED STATES

Edited by Jane C. Desmond
and
Virginia R. Domínguez, IFUSS founders

*The International Forum for U.S. Studies (IFUSS) is a research center
for the transnational study of the United States
at the University of Illinois, Urbana-Champaign.*

Scripts of Blackness

Race, Cultural Nationalism,
and U.S. Colonialism in Puerto Rico

ISAR P. GODREAU

UNIVERSITY OF ILLINOIS PRESS
Urbana, Chicago, and Springfield

© 2015 by the Board of Trustees
of the University of Illinois
All rights reserved
Manufactured in the United States of America
1 2 3 4 5 C P 5 4 3 2 1
♾ This book is printed on acid-free paper.

Library of Congress Cataloging-in-Publication Data
Godreau, Isar (Isar P.)
Scripts of blackness: race, cultural nationalism, and U.S. colonialism
in Puerto Rico / Isar P. Godreau.
 pages   cm. — (Global studies of the United States)
Includes bibliographical references and index.
ISBN 978-0-252-03890-7 (hardback : acid-free paper)
ISBN 978-0-252-08045-6 (paper : acid-free paper)
ISBN 978-0-252-09686-0 (ebook)
1. Puerto Rico—Race relations. 2. Puerto Rico—Colonial influence.
3. San Antón (Ponce, P.R.)—Race relations. 4. Ponce (P.R.)—Race
relations. 5. Race—Political aspects—Puerto Rico. 6. Nationalism—
Puerto Rico. 7. United States—Relations—Puerto Rico. 8. Puerto
Rico—Relations—United States. 9. Geopolitics—Puerto Rico. 10.
Geopolitics—United States.
I. Title.
F1983.N4G63   2015
305.80097295—dc23   2014019829

*To my mother, Annie Santiago,
for her wisdom and laughter*

Contents

Acknowledgments ix

Introduction 1

1. Place, Race, and the Housing Debate 31

PART I. BENEVOLENT SLAVERY: DOCILE SLAVES OR FREE PEOPLE OF COLOR

2. Slavery and the Politics of Erasure 65
3. Unfolkloric Slavery: Alternative Histories of San Antón 93

PART II. HISPANICITY: SHADES OF "WHITENESS" BETWEEN EMPIRES

4. Hispanophile Zones of Whiteness 121
5. His-Panic/My Panic: Hispanophobia and the Reviled Whiteness of Spain 147

PART III. RACE MIXTURE: IN THE BLOOD OR IN THE MAKING?

6. Flowing through My Veins: Populism and the Hierarchies of Race Mixture 177

7. Irresolute Blackness: Struggles and Maneuvers
   over the Representation of Community   203

   Conclusion   227

   Notes   243

   References   259

   Index   291

Acknowledgments

This book came to completion thanks to the love and encouragement of my family, colleagues, and friends. Its publication, after more than eighteen years since fieldwork, is a testament of their long-standing enthusiasm. I am particularly grateful to Virginia Domínguez and Jane Desmond for rooting me on and providing such a supportive research environment at the University of Illinois Urbana-Champaign through the International Forum for U.S. Studies (IFUSS) initiative. The opportunity to meet with other IFUSS scholars, present my work, use the wonderful library at UI, and have the great editorial assistance of Dr. Janet Keller contributed immensely to completing this work.

Over the years, the input of colleagues and friends such as Toño Díaz Royo, Juan José Baldrich, Jorge L. Giovannetti, Antonio Lauria, José (Pito) Rodríguez, Lena Sawyer, Patricia Landolt, Ivelisse Rivera Bonilla, Mareia Quintero, and Mariluz Franco helped me make sense of my fieldwork material. The support of Luis Santos while doing fieldwork and his ample knowledge of the island's geography made him an invaluable partner during the 1990s. Years later, keen commentaries offered by friends like Yarimar Bonilla, Hilda Lloréns, Juan Giusti, Aaron Ramos, and especially my dear friend Errol Montes-Pizarro, who has lovingly served as my *víctima inteligente* for ten years, were crucial as I revised the text for publication. I am also thankful for the keen recommendations and enthusiastic response of the two anonymous reviewers, which tremendously improved this work.

Revisions for this book manuscript took place during my current tenure at the University of Puerto Rico at Cayey and had to be reconciled with institutional efforts to build and strengthen the Institute of Interdisciplinary Research there. I was lucky to have a supportive group of deans and co-workers like Vionex Marti, Yajaira Mercado, Neymarí Ramos, Jannette Gavillán, Jessica Gaspar, Noel Caraballo, and many others who understood that I sometimes had to "hide" to write and never questioned the importance of that undertaking. The help of my diligent and sharp research assistant, Sherry Cuadrado, was also crucial for bringing this project to an end. She was my most constant interlocutor during the process of revising the manuscript for publication.

Institutional support for fieldwork also deserves recognition. The Wenner-Gren Foundation, the Research Institute for the Study of Man, the Society for the Psychological Study of Social Issues, the Teresa Lozano Long Institute of Latin American Studies, and the University of Puerto Rico (Presidential Scholarship Program) supported different stages of my fieldwork from 1993 to 2001. I am especially grateful and indebted to the Ford Foundation and the fellows who supported my academic development at different stages of this journey. Thanks to that support, I was able to meet and work with colleagues and anthropologists from many different institutions: the University of California at Santa Cruz, Johns Hopkins University, the University of South Florida, and the University of Texas at Austin. I had the benefit of meeting wonderful professors and senior mentors such as my advisor Lisa Rofel and professors Ana Tsing, Virginia Domínguez, Olga Nájera Ramirez, Ann Kingsolver, Carolyn Martin Shaw, Franklin Knight, Sidney Mintz, Rolph Trouillot, Kelvin Yelvington, and Charles Hale. Sid Mintz, in particular, encouraged me to pay attention to the history of Puerto Rico and of the Caribbean. The historical and political-economy-informed vision that he and scholars like Rolph Trouillot, Sara Berry, and fellow graduate students brought to the graduate program of anthropology at Hopkins had a crucial impact on my approach to questions of race, racism, and national identity in Puerto Rico. Back then, I felt like this framework was at odds with the postmodern and discursive orientation that my base institution (UC Santa Cruz) took to these questions. But I now realize I was quite fortunate to have been exposed to both. I hope the book shows this.

During my fieldwork in Ponce, local government agencies such as the Oficina de Desarrollo Comunal y Eonómico and the Oficina de Ordenamiento Territorial provided crucial information. I am also grateful to Humberto Figueroa, Carmen Rivera, Gary Gutiérrez, and the late Rigín Dapena for sharing their knowledge of Ponce with me, and to Gladys Tormes, who was an invaluable resource at Ponce's Historical Archives. Thanks also to Yarimar Bonilla, Keith B., Lucio Oliveira, David Gasser, and José Calderón for their help with photos and images.

Of course, none of this support would have yielded a book had it not been for the people of San Antón. My greatest debts are to the families and community leaders who took me in to their homes and let me participate in their community activities, answering my questions and accepting my intrusions with hospitality and patience. Most of their names appear as pseudonyms in the book, but I want to give credit for their assistance and thank them individually here. Most of all, I am indebted to the late Doña Judith Cabrera and her daughter María Judith Banchs Cabrera, who first introduced me to the community and who allowed me to spend many afternoons in their yard. It was through the wise eyes of Doña Judith and the committed disposition of her daughter María Judith that I first came to know the barrio. Their trust made it possible for me to do fieldwork in the community, and for that I will always be grateful. I also thank Felícita Tricoche Santiago, her daughters Rosa and Nilda, and her granddaughter Mara for letting me into their homes and for sharing their life histories. Luisa Franceschi, Carlos (Cao) Vélez Franceschi, and their family also shared invaluable information. In addition I thank Paula and her daughter Jeamaly Rivera, who offered invaluable assistance with my archival research in Ponce. I am especially grateful to the *sabia* Librada Roque and the members of her *patio* (María Daisy and the late Inó). Peyo Roque and the late Enrique Montalvo contributed valuable information, as well. The following families also deserve many thanks for their contributions: the Colón Family, especially Luis Colón and Cuto Colón; the Roque family, especially the late Felix Roque Feliciano (Chano) and Eli; the Rentas family, especially María Cancel Rentas and her mother Paula Rentas; the Quiñonez family, especially the late Mariano Quiñonez, his daughter Sonia, and his granddaughter Yaritza; the family of Concepción Muriel; the family of Consuelo Rivera de Jordán, especially her son Berto Ferrer; the family of Elena Torres Renta; and the family of Santos Antoneti. I also wish to thank Cirila Morales, Elba Franceschi, Ottoniel Vélez, and Don Ramón Feliciano for their time and important interviews. Efrain Matos, Agustín Ledeé, Guadalupe Delgado, Willi "el pirata," Cheo, Margarita, Julia, Blanca Nieves, Felo, and many others were also important contributors to this work. Without their knowledge and generosity with their time and ideas, this research would not have been possible.

Finally, I owe this project and many others to the love and support of my family: my parents, Annie Santiago, Michel Godreau, Sara Irrizarry, and the late Eliezer Curet Cuevas; my sisters, Agnes Marie Bosh Irrizarry and Carla Irene Godreau; and my beautiful fifteen-year-old daughter Amanda Nahir, who, over the years, has had to share her mom with the demands of this project. When tasks seem too monumental, Amanda always kept things "real" and in perspective for me. My mother, who consistently supported me, not just with her caring love and good humor but with her intellectual advice, deserves a special mention. I never know if her accomplishments are a product of her incredible resiliency or of her sheer enthusiasm and curiosity . . . in any case, her joy for life is contagious, and the influence has kept me sane. This book is dedicated to her. Responsibility for any errors lies with me and my twenty-three-pound cat, who has sat in all the books, drafts, agendas, and papers I have used while revising this manuscript for publication.

Scripts of Blackness

Introduction

> We demystify myths not to diminish the beauty of myth, but to overcome the idea that identities must be fixed and that human beings are hostages of their culture or prisoners of their physical appearance.
> —Patricia de Santana Pinho

The first time I saw the barrio of San Antón was in 1992 as I looked through car windows from a passenger seat. Antonio (Toño) Díaz Royo, a university professor and good friend of my mother, knew of my interest in racial dynamics and drove me there after suggesting I consider this community of the city of Ponce as a possible field site for research. Ponce is centrally located on the southern coast of Puerto Rico, between the Caribbean Sea and the Cordillera Central mountain range. It is the third-largest *municipio* (county) on the Island, with a population of approximately 185,000. San Antón is one of Ponce's urban low-income barrios (see dot in Map 1) but stands out among them as a bedrock of Puerto Rico's African heritage since important Afro–Puerto Rican musical genres developed there. By contrast, the larger *municipio* of Ponce is known as *la Ciudad Señorial* (the Aristocratic [lit. patrician] City), a title pointing to the wealth of the late nineteenth-century elites who established themselves along its central historic quarter. Although Ponce harbored a large free colored and slave population during the period of slavery, the municipality has a reputation for flaunting the influence of European immigrants who settled there when the city became a commercial conduit for sugar and coffee exports in the nineteenth century. As a young researcher, I wondered about the class and racial hierarchies triggered by the contrast between a renowned black barrio and the "aristocratic city."

Ponce (about two hours' driving distance from the capital city of San Juan) was not foreign to me. I was raised in San Juan, but my mother's side of the family was from Ponce, and when I was a child, we would often visit grandaunts and cousins there during weekends. My grand-aunts, two retired, dark-skinned *mulatas*,[1] lived in Urbanización Los Maestros, an urban housing complex subsidized for public school

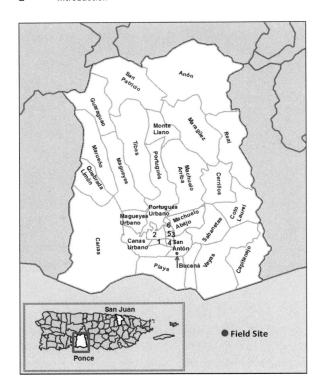

Map 1. Ponce's barrios and field. Map produced by José Calderón Squiabro using combined Census Bureau data from the Census County and County Subdivisions Web site: http://tinyurl.com/ny7wkav http://tinyurl.com/7vcaxm8.

teachers, located about ten minutes by car from San Antón. However, I never went to or heard of the barrio of San Antón during my visits to Ponce. I came to know about the community years later, in the context of undertaking graduate studies.

As a graduate student, living in the United States, I encountered racial discourses that I perceived as more essentializing than the fluid dynamics I experienced growing up in Puerto Rico among family members who described themselves as *black*, *white*, *mulato*, and *trigueño* (brown), and who sometimes called me *jabá* (high yellow), *rubia* (blond), or *colorá* (red), with no apparent intention of creating boundaries among us.[2] I wanted to explore the contrast further. At the same time, I had to consider that my perception of fluidity could be the outcome of the privilege afforded by my middle-class status and looks (I have very curly hair but also light skin and light-colored eyes). Would Puerto Ricans who live in poor black communities also describe "race" as fluid and unessentialized?

As Toño drove me through San Antón, I noticed clusters of wooden houses unevenly distributed along a predominantly unpaved landscape. Two bifurcating narrow streets, a river canal, and two bordering highways roughly outlined this sector. I noticed an abundance of trees, an empty plot of land, and goats and chickens wandering around on patches of dry soil. As we passed a couple of slack wooden structures, Toño mentioned that he had heard that people in San Antón do not demolish their old houses. Instead, they build new ones next to, rather than in place of, older structures. He entertained the possibility of religious or sentimental reasons for this practice, and my gaze turned a bit romantic. The wooden houses, the lack of iron bars protecting windows or balconies, the absence of a distinguishable linear pattern in their arrangement, and the domestic animals, dirt streets, and abundance of trees and grass made San Antón look like a rural pocket in the midst of a surrounding sea of cement homes, highways, traffic lights, chain stores, and fast-food restaurants.

After this first impression, I was quick to follow Toño's lead to do fieldwork here, sparked by contrasts I perceived between Puerto Rico and the United States, between the barrio and my own class/racial positions, and between San Antón and Ponce's aristocratic reputation. Our drive that first day was short, but the wooden houses I saw summoned a romantic image of a premodern Puerto Rico that could easily strike a nationalistic chord among those who believe progress and Americanization are eroding Puerto Rican national identity (see houses in Figures 1a–d[3]). Yet soon I learned that the houses I romanticized had been the objects of residents' complaints for some time. The houses' moth- and termite-ravaged wood, loose floors and walls, leaking ceilings, and lack of sewage systems—along with the fire hazards and problems of access created by clustered and abandoned homes—signaled poverty, underdevelopment, and—according to many residents—administrative abandonment.

Figures 1a–1d. Views of San Antón in 1993. Photos by author.

Residents had actively denounced this abandonment since the 1970s, but not until 1996—an election year—did construction work for a housing project begin.

* * *

In this book I analyze the narratives and discourses that inform the racialization of San Antón as a "black community of Ponce" in the context of discussions and debates that surfaced during the development of this housing project. San Antón is a working-class community constituted by approximately three hundred residents. Although it was a much larger peripheral rural settlement in the nineteenth century, the community was reduced and absorbed by Ponce's urban growth after the 1950s. Residents familiar with the barrio's history link its development to the sugar plantations that flourished nearby during the late nineteenth century, emphasizing the role of skilled laborers. In Ponce, San Antón is also well known as the birthplace of famous artists, musicians, and baseball and basketball athletes. The community, however, is best known in Puerto Rico for its *bomba* and *plena*, two music genres that constitute the most explicit, celebrated link to the Island's African presence (Blanco 1979; Barton 1995; Cartagena 2004). Because of San Antón's reputation as the birthplace of the *plena*, residents of Ponce and Puerto Rico consider the community a traditional site of Afro–Puerto Rican folklore.[4] This folkloric status was actively sustained during the time of my fieldwork in the mid- to late 1990s through festivals and commemorative events organized by community spokesmen in coordination with government agencies in charge of the city's historic and cultural development.

The neighborhood revitalization project of the late 1990s sought to improve housing conditions for residents of San Antón, but also aimed to pay tribute to the barrio's African heritage and cultural contributions. However, government interpretations of the community's traditions and corresponding efforts at preservation did not necessarily correspond to residents' expectations or understandings of their community. While some spokesmen talked about preserving the community's Afro–Puerto Rican traditions, other residents argued the barrio was not really black but mixed, just like any other Puerto Rican community. While the government claimed to be assisting the community in a project dedicated to preserving the cultural roots of their famous barrio, most residents framed demands in terms of improving their modern standard of living, not in terms of gaining cultural recognition as a black or Afro-descendant community. In fact, many residents did not assume a "black" identity, and I never heard anyone describe themselves as *afrodescendiente* or *afropuertorriqueño*. Disagreements over how the housing project should be implemented spurred a controversy that evidenced San Antón residents' and government officials' discrepant expectations about the cultural practices, racial-identity politics, political aspirations, and everyday lives of residents there.

Based on an ethnographic study of this debate and other racialized dynamics in Puerto Rico, in this book I examine the construction of institutional and local representations of blackness as a power-laden, historically informed process that is inherently selective and political, not neutral or natural. My aim, therefore, is not to document the black cultural expressions of San Antón, but to outline the various debates, social hierarchies, and colonial discourses that inform the construction of this community and its residents as "black."

This outlook differs from Herskovitzian approaches that—in searching for African traits in burials, religion, music, dance, and rituals across the Americas— inadvertently tie "blackness" to particular places. Such studies unearthed important cultural continuities between Africa and the Caribbean, yet many portray blackness as a self-evident and geographically contained category found only in specific sectors such as Bahia in Brazil, Oriente in Cuba, El Chocó in Colombia, or Loíza and San Antón in Puerto Rico (Whitten and Torres 1998). I find this "emplacement"[5] problematic, especially when applied to Afro-Latino America and the Caribbean, because by circumscribing blackness to a place, it conveys the sense that blackness is different or exceptional from the context of the larger "mixed" nation, thereby rendering blackness pure and homogenous (Godreau 1999, 2002). Furthermore, while black places and their inhabitants are marked and celebrated for "cultural distinctiveness," the broader national context remains unmarked, implicitly represented as mixed and "not-black."

Moreover, the fact that communities or regions are designated as "black" by outsiders, intellectuals, government officials, cultural educators, or even some community representatives is not tantamount to all or even most residents in such communities adopting such labels.[6] As Mara Loveman (1999) points out, "it is not axiomatic that membership in a category will correspond directly to experienced group boundaries or social identities. The extent to which categories and groups do correspond, and the conditions under which they do so, should be recognized as important theoretical questions that are subject to empirical research" (892).

Attentive to such pitfalls, I question the demarcation of San Antón as a place of "black difference" and examine the historical underpinnings and everyday implications of local processes of race making. In particular, I pay attention to the role that history (as a selective interpretation of the past) plays in the formulation of national ideologies that marginalize blackness and support the construction of San Antón as a place of racial uniqueness or exceptionality.

Here I follow the lead of scholars who have argued that space and place are central to the production of racial constructs and national identities (e.g., Brown 2000; Hartigan 1999; Wade 1993; Appelbaum 1999; Streicker 1997). Jacqueline Nassy Brown, for example, argues that the "local" is not important just as a data collection site that enables the researcher to be specific. How spaces and regions are produced as distinct in the first place deserves our attention. She argues for a "truly ethnographic approach to studying the local," one that would not assume anything about its content, its political uses, the subjectivities it names, and its relations with or to the wider world (Brown 2000, 349).

Because Puerto Rico is a U.S. territory, not an independent sovereign nation, I consider processes of racialization and their emplaced manifestations in San Antón as deeply informed by the geopolitical influence of the United States in the region and by the historical narratives developed to make sense of that influence. Based on this understanding, I develop two main arguments. First, that "race" is a key idiom through which institutions and people construct, interpret, and "defend" Puerto Rican identity in the context of U.S. intervention. And, second, that the selective manner in which blackness gets construed as part of this process is informed by the different formulations of "Puerto Rican nationhood" developed in the context of that colonial relationship. In other words, in this book I document key historical discourses and effects embedded in the formulation of a Puerto Rican "difference" vis-à-vis the United States, through an ethnography of how a particular community in the Island is constructed as "black."

Nation, Race, and Culture in the 1990s

My fieldwork and the neighborhood-revitalization project developed by Ponce's municipal government in San Antón took place primarily during the late 1990s (fieldwork was carried out primarily from 1995 to 1996 and intermittently in 1992, 1998, and 2002). The late 1990s were years of heightened awareness and debate about nationalism, U.S. intervention in the Island, and the question of national identity in Puerto Rico. The debate magnified in 1996, when Carlos Romero Barceló, an ex-governor of Puerto Rico, who advocated U.S. statehood for the Island, publicly declared that Puerto Rico "is not and has never been a nation." The then-governor, Pedro Rosselló, also a pro-statehood leader, added that, although Puerto Ricans constituted a people, his nation is the United States (Torres-Gotay 1996, 16). Those statements provoked public upheaval. Angry callers flooded local radio stations accusing the governor of, at best, ignorance and, at worst, selling out. Public figures appeared on TV to challenge Governor Rosselló and declare that, although Puerto Ricans were U.S. citizens, Puerto Rico was undoubtedly a nation; it had a territory, a language, and a culture, and its people a common heritage. The debate eventually led to the organization of three parallel marches in which thousands mobilized to support their competing goals for the Island: U.S. statehood, political independence, or the defense of a sovereign Puerto Rican cultural—albeit not necessarily political—identity.

The controversy over the Puerto Rican nation not only mobilized members of political parties, but also convened intellectuals. Historian Carlos Pabón, for example, questioned, "What is this thing called the nation? Who defines it? And what are some of its excluding effects?" Borrowing from Foucault, Anderson, Hobsbawn, and Bhabha, Pabón argued that what is at stake is less nationhood than how mechanisms of national discourse are linked to power and knowledge used by elites to exclude "others" from a nation's "imagined" boundaries (Pabón 1995; Pabón 1996, 18). Pabón's statements were praised by some but criticized by scholars who questioned the political effect of his failure to consider the impact of U.S. colonialism on Puerto Rico (Carrión 1993, 1996; Coss 1996). Juan Manuel Carrión, for example, argued that although elites make use of nationalist discourse, the nation is not a simple product of their need to dominate. Nationalism, he argued, is also linked to a sense of solidarity and emotive belonging. Thus, although the concept of "nation-state" is in crisis, the idea of nationalism is not (Carrión 1996, 41).[7]

Alongside these voices, Puerto Rican intellectuals working from U.S. institutions, like Ramón Grosfoguel, Frances Negrón Muntaner, and other contributors to the edited volume *Puerto Rican Jam* (1997), critiqued the pitfalls of framing Puerto Rico's political struggles as a colonial/national dichotomy. This, they argued, privileged the formation of the Puerto Rican nation-state as the cure to all problems, ignoring the Puerto Rican diaspora and the persistence of enduring class, racial, and gender hierarchies not mitigated—and sometimes exacerbated—by nationalism as a political strategy (Negrón-Muntaner and Grosfoguel 1997). Some of these scholars publicly proposed a "radical statehood"—Puerto Rico becoming a U.S. state with activist priorities—as an alternative that could make viable the struggle against U.S. empire in alliance with other discriminated-against minorities (African Americans, Native Americans, and other Latinos) resisting exploitation from "within the belly of the beast" (Duchesne et al. 1997, 30–31). Other scholars also tried to make sense of how there could be cultural nationalism without political nationalism, since most Puerto Ricans imagine themselves as a nation even though few support the constitution of a nation-state (Duany 2002; Dávila 1997).

At the same time that these discussions about nationalism were taking place, a series of initiatives addressing the role of racism and blackness in Puerto Rican society developed in the Island. Related topics were debated publicly in local conferences, newspaper columns, and TV and radio shows.[8] Although these discussions about race and racism did not—as was the case with the controversy over nation—mobilize great numbers of people or materialize into an organized antiracist or black political movement, they did mark a fertile period for the growth of a number of Island-based antiracist initiatives. As Idsa Alegría and Palmira Ríos

(2005) note, "The world-wide explosion at the end of the millennium of ethnic, racial, and political identities contributed largely and unmistakably to the recognition of the existence of deep racial inequalities. This situation favored in Puerto Rico the opening of a greater breach to talk, to debate and to research not only diversity and Otherness but also our racisms" (10).[9]

During these years, small antiracist organizations emerged, such as UMUPUEN (Unión de Mujeres Puertorriqueñas Negras—Collective of Black Puerto Rican Women) and Ilé: organizando para la conciencia-en-acción (Ilé: Organizers for Consciousness in Action). Two important study groups focusing on race formed at the University of Puerto Rico, one of which in 1997 developed into the IPERI Institute (Instituto Puertorriqueño de Estudios de Raza e Identidad—Puerto Rican Institute of Race and Identity Studies). In 1997 and 1999, institutions such as the Lawyer's Guild and the Commission for Civil Rights organized seminars, congresses, and publications on the topics of race and racism. Two exhibits, *La tercera raíz: presencia africana en Puerto Rico* (The Third Root: African Presence in Puerto Rico; 1992) and *Ocho artistas negros contemporáneos* (Eight Black Contemporary Artists; 1996), addressed the issue of racism from artistic perspectives developed within the plastic arts (see Alegría and Ríos 2005). Moreover, the first museum dedicated to African heritage in Puerto Rico, El Museo de Nuestra Raíz Africana (The Museum of Our African Roots), opened in 1999 under the sponsorship of the Institute of Puerto Rican Culture.[10] Concurrently, a number of important books, essays, and special periodical issues about race and racism were published (see Vázquez 1996; Santiago-Valles 1994, 1996; Rivero 2005; Ramos Rosado 1999; Ortiz Lugo 2004[1995]; Comisión de Derechos Civiles 1998; L. M. González 1992; and González and Vega 1990).

At the same time, in Latin America, the 1990s marked unprecedented transformations characterized by the strong militancy of indigenous and Afro-descendant groups. Achievements in the form of land rights, multicultural-education reforms, political representation, and antidiscrimination legislation were gained based on this militancy and Latin American states' recognition of their societies as plurilingual and multicultural, rather than just as mestizo nations (Hale 2002; French 2009; Hooker 2005; Anderson 2009; Paschel 2010). As this shift from state discourses of *mestizaje* to multiculturalism was taking place, neoliberal policies that privatized public services and decentralized the state were on the rise (Hale 2002; Velázques Runk 2012). Charles Hale argues that this co-development is not fortuitous or contradictory. Neoliberal policies support the cultural recognition of ethnic groups while imposing restrictions, third-party arbiters, standards of authenticity, and principles of political participation that do not threaten and, in fact, may even facilitate the neoliberal agenda of trimming down the state (Hale 2002, 2005). At the same time, neoliberal multiculturalism also promotes "culture" as a marketable asset to spur global economic competition and decentralization (Hale 2002; Dávila 2001, 2004). In the Caribbean, such uses of culture became increasingly important for promoting tourism's highly problematic approach to diversity as a profit-making device (Dávila 1997; Scher 2011; Klak and Myers 1998).

In Puerto Rico, neoliberal forms of governance did not and have not been accompanied by a state discourse of multiculturalism, as there is still a strong institutional commitment to the notion of a single Puerto Rican culture (with blended racial heritages). Neither did the Island experience the kind of Afro-descendant militancy or the resulting antiracist or multicultural affirmative-action policies that developed in countries like Brazil, Colombia, Ecuador, Nicaragua, Guatemala, and Honduras (Hanchard 1994; Ng'weno 2007; French 2009; Anderson 2009; Hale 2005; Paschel 2010). However, neoliberal tendencies prevalent during those years, such as decentralization of the state, privatization of services, devolution of responsibilities to multilateral institutions and civic organizations, and the use of culture as a tool for development and marketing (especially in tourism) were evident in Latin America and Puerto Rico alike. An analysis of neoliberalism's impact on the Island is beyond the scope of the present book, but neoliberal forms of governance and the concomitant receptivity to "culture" as a marketable asset in Puerto Rico (Dávila 1997) opened spaces for decentralization and greater recognition of regional and cultural characteristics that municipalities such as Ponce had to offer for the tourist industry.

Housing Traditions in the Aristocratic City

Developed in the 1990s, San Antón's housing project was influenced by all these concurrent public discourses, national debates, and neoliberal and regional policies. In 1991, new legislation passed, allowing municipalities to attain greater autonomy from San Juan's central government, chart their own zoning plans, and establish cultural initiatives and economic strategies, including the marketing of their cultural heritage for international and, especially, local tourism.[11] In 1992, Ponce became the first county to attain such autonomy. The pioneering initiative was supported by a previous $600 million program and public policy known as Ponce en Marcha (Ponce on the Move) (Jolee 1994). The plan became a reality in 1985 with an executive order signed by ex-governor Rafael Hernandez Colón, who made Ponce en Marcha a priority during his term as governor (1985 to 1992), as he was also a *ponceño* (Jolee 1994).[12]

Ponce en Marcha, and the municipal autonomy attained thereafter, was supported by a detailed and comprehensive research-based master plan (Plan de Ordenación Territorial) developed by a team of at least thirteen young, well-educated professionals who, with input from the public, established zoning policies and recommendations for economic, social, and political development (Jolee 1994). The master plan aimed to improve the city's infrastructure, giving priority to revitalizing Ponce's Historic Center and refurbishing historic areas targeted for tourism, and it resulted in Ponce becoming the second-most-important tourist destination in the Island, after San Juan (Resto, 1995; Jolee 1994). It also emphasized the protection of cultural, historical, and ecological resources; the preservation of communities; and the need to make the city walkable, deter urban sprawl, and create mechanisms to ensure community participation in city developments through Juntas de Comunidad, community boards composed of volunteers from Ponce who were residents of different areas within the municipality (Junta de Planificación de Puerto Rico 1992).

Besides having the support of the central administration from 1984 to 1992, the ambitious project was developed—and continued thereafter with scant support and tenacity during the period of my fieldwork—under the leadership of Ponce's charismatic mayor Rafael Cordero Santiago. Cordero Santiago (1942–2004), better known as "Churumba," served as Ponce's mayor for fifteen consecutive years (1989–2004) and was a regional leader of wide popularity. As members of the Partido Popular Democrático (Popular Democratic Party; from here on referred to as the *commonwealth party*), his administration favored commonwealth status that maintained U.S. citizenship but sought greater political autonomy for Puerto Rico. At a regional level, this stance translated into an adamant defense of Ponce's municipal autonomy and cultural legacy vis-à-vis the capital of San Juan.

In terms of tourism, the local commonwealth administration sought to distinguish Ponce from San Juan's overcrowding and urban sprawl, marketing the city as a destination that could offer different cultural assets (Resto 1995). As stated by Ponce's director of tourism:

> Another attribute of Ponce is that it still preserves its *sabor de pueblo* [town flavor], its Puerto Rican tradition. "We are not Americanized," the director of tourism emphasizes. "We still maintain the trips in *coches*, the *vejigantes*, the *bomba* and *plena*, in addition to our rich cuisine, which is excellent and reasonably priced." (Resto 1995, S-6)[13]

The city's development and rehabilitation plan prioritized monumental structures located in the Historic Center of the aristocratic city. However, it also considered the particularities of Ponce's surrounding urban barrios and other areas of historic interest that enhanced the city's appeal. San Antón's housing project was one among other projects developed in these urban barrios, conceived within this autonomous regional framework of preserving Ponce's communities and their distinctive (non-Americanized) characteristics. Prior developments in working-class communities such as La Playa de Ponce, Arenas Betances, and 25 de Enero were also implemented with this perspective. In all of them, the goal was to improve housing and infrastructure without displacing residents and without introducing a "modern" aesthetic that would drastically modify traditional facades. These housing projects were coordinated with government agencies in charge of managing the city's historical and cultural development, such as the local branch of the Institute of Puerto Rican Culture and the Office of Historic Preservation (Centro Histórico) in Ponce.

As a cradle of *bomba* and *plena*, San Antón's housing project received exceptional mid-1990s press coverage celebrating Ponce's progressive outlook and regional pride in its traditions. That sense of national pride as championed by the commonwealth party in Ponce clashed with the central government statehood leadership in power at the time of my fieldwork and its public stance that Puerto Rico was not and had never been a nation. The implementation of the project also coincided with an election year, 1996, in which the pro-statehood party (leading the central government) and the commonwealth party (leading in Ponce) sought reelection. In that context, and after years of Ponce's municipal government investing in works targeted at the "aristocratic" Historic Center, San Antón materialized as an indicator of the commonwealth party's populist defense of Puerto Rican culture, of its poor urban communities, and of the *municipio*'s Afro–Puerto Rican cultural heritage.

This political mobilization of Afro–Puerto Rican traditions in "defense of Puerto Rican culture" vis-à-vis pro-statehood contenders is not unique to Ponce. As Hilda Lloréns and Rosa Carrasquillo (2008) document, Caguas, another stronghold of the commonwealth party with a charismatic mayor (Willie Miranda Marín), also used public funds to fulfill their party's orientation toward Puerto Rican traditions. There, the municipality sponsored a number of sculptures and murals dedicated to Afro–Puerto Rican heritage in 2006 and 2007 (Lloréns and Carrasquillo 2008). In both places, Ponce and Caguas, mayors also mobilized notions of blackness to challenge pro-statehood contenders, asserting their respective *municipios* as autonomous cities at the vanguard of Puerto Rican values.

Ponce's efforts were nevertheless earlier and, in a sense, more groundbreaking, since no other housing project developed in the Island (before or after) has been explicitly designed with the public intent to preserve the Afro–Puerto Rican traditions of a community.[14] There, architects and government planners charted a housing and spatial distribution plan for San Antón that reproduced, in their view, the "traditions" of this black barrio and its families. Yet, as future chapters demonstrate, "San Antón's traditions" did not mean the same thing to everybody. Discrepant ideas of typical, appropriate, or decent living conditions caused controversy among residents, and between residents and the municipal government of Ponce. The debate also evidenced the salience of certain notions about African heritage, U.S. citizenship, and cultural nationalism that, although not completely hegemonic, prevailed during the controversy, compelling people to speak to, for, or against them. Because I argue that Puerto Rico's colonial relationship with the United States is key for understanding how "blackness" was emplaced in San Antón and mobilized during the controversy, some of the historical antecedents of the Island's neocolonial status deserve further explanation.

Blackness in the Non Sovereign Nation

Puerto Rico was a colony of Spain for approximately four hundred years until 1898, when the United States occupied the Island during the course of the Cuban-Spanish-American war. Before that, during the period of Spanish occupation, and especially toward the latter half of the nineteenth century, a strong liberal movement for greater autonomy from Spain emerged in Puerto Rico under the Partido Autonomista (Autonomist Party), whose bastion was Ponce. However, unlike in Cuba, which gained independence from Spain in 1898, Puerto Rican liberal demands did not develop into a strong movement for independence, and in 1898, Puerto Rico passed from one colonial power to another (Scarano 2000).

The U.S. acquisition of Puerto Rico from Spain occurred as the United States emerged as an imperial power on the world stage, drawing into its orbit other territories (the Philippines, Guam, American Samoa, the U.S. Virgin Islands) that posed complex, legal, economic, and social challenges (Rivera-Ramos 2001, 5). In the Reconstruction era, U.S. leaders championed an expansionist project that sought to present the United States as a strong, integrated, democratic nation in the wake of the U.S. Civil War (Pérez 2008). Enticed by the promise of democratic ideals, many Puerto Rican leaders, in turn, believed that the military occupation would lead to an autonomous political arrangement with the United States. Others aspired to the incorporation of Puerto Rico into the Union (Nieto-Phillips 1999, 51). During the early decades of the twentieth century, political parties like the Partido Unión (Union Party) favored U.S. citizenship and greater self-governance for Puerto Rico, while others, like the Partido Republicano (Republican Party) and the Partido Socialista (Socialist Party), called for complete annexation of Puerto Rico to the United States (Pagán 1959). Yet other parties, such as the Nationalist Party (founded in 1922, also in Ponce) and later the Partido Independentista Puertorriqueño (founded in 1946), shared the goal of attaining political independence for the Island, launching strong criticism against the United States for its repressive, exploitative colonial policies and expansionist agenda in the Western Hemisphere.

Transformations ushered in by World War II in the 1940s, including the need to maintain domestic peace and gain access to Puerto Rican cheap labor, combined with local and international pressures to change the overtly colonial relationship between Puerto Rico and the United States. In 1948, Puerto Ricans were able to elect their own governor, and in 1952, a constitution was drafted, ratifying the political status of the Island as an Estado Libre Asociado (ELA—Free Associated State), or commonwealth. Although this status defined Puerto Rico as a non-incorporated territory subject to U.S. federal law, it marked a rupture with traditional colonial practices, ameliorating anti-imperialist sentiments and international pressure against the United States (Negrón-Muntaner and Grosfoguel 1997).

Still, the Island's political relationship with the United States remains conflict-ridden. Puerto Ricans have been U.S. citizens since 1917 and can be drafted for military service, yet Island dwellers cannot vote in the U.S. presidential elections. Both Spanish and English are recognized as official languages, but Spanish is without a doubt the dominant spoken language. The Island governor and Puerto Rican government officials like Ponce's mayor, Rafael Cordero, have authority over some internal and regional affairs, but currency, defense, external relations, communications, the postal service, social security, and interstate commerce are within the jurisdiction of the U.S. federal government. Under commonwealth status, Puerto Ricans elect the country's governor and all other public officials (senate, legislature, and regional representatives), including a U.S. congressional representative who has a voice but no vote. General local elections are held every four years at the same time as U.S. elections.

This ambiguous situation might seem unique. However, Puerto Rico is part of what Yarimar Bonilla (2012) calls the non sovereign Caribbean: a conglomerate of over forty-five societies in the region that are neither independent states nor official colonies. In these societies, the relationship among territoriality, nationality, citizenship, and political power responds more to enduring colonial legacies than to the internationally supported idea that nations should hold supreme authority over their internal affairs. Rather than anomalies, Bonilla argues, these societies exemplify broader challenges to sovereignty faced by many formally independent nation-states (particularly in the global south), the internal affairs of which are shaped by outside interests, supranational organizations, and external nongovernmental actors (lending agencies, the World Bank, global development firms, NGOs, military contractors, and security firms) (Bonilla Ramos 2013).

As a non-incorporated U.S. territory, Puerto Rico can exemplify how powerful external interests and the enduring imperial legacy of the United States shape local discourses of "race" in the region and elsewhere in Latin America. We know that racial discourses in Latin America and the Caribbean are shaped by emergent national discourses that are not so "postcolonial." Ginetta Candelario and Deborah Thomas, for example, demonstrate how U.S. influence and capitalist interests affect contemporary racialization processes and nation-building efforts in the Caribbean (Thomas 2004; Candelario 2000). Metropolitan and U.S. influence upon racial discourses in the region can also be appreciated for the role that multinational corporations (Dávila 1997) and political parties (Yelvington 1997) have played in marketing racial mixture in Latin America and blackness in the Caribbean. Scholars have also explored the role of compromised states and powerful global forces in the production of black commodities, the folklorization of blackness, and the institutionalization of black heritages for tourism in the context of neoliberal multicultural discourses (Guss 1993; Edmonds 2003; Roland 2006; Thomas 2004; Lewis 2000; Matory 2006; Pattullo 1996; Pinho 2010; Paschel 2009; Scher 2011; Gotham 2007). Patricia de Santana Pinho (2010), for example, documents the growing popularity of "roots tourism" in Bahia in Brazil, as Bahia becomes the place where African Americans exchange their "modernity" for the "traditional blackness" of Brazil. Paschel (2009) argues that these and other commercialized aspects of Afro-Brazilian identity can perpetuate the ideology of racial democracy by subsuming a marginalized culture under the flag of nationalism, ignoring the socioeconomic inequalities linked to racism and discrimination faced by the producers of such celebrated cultural expressions.

Racial Scripts

In dialogue with this literature, I expand the present scope of analysis by examining the effects of U.S. colonialism on the construction of what I call "scripts of blackness" in Puerto Rico—that is, dominant narratives and stories that set standards, expectations, and even spatial templates for what is publicly recognized, celebrated, and sponsored as black *and* Puerto Rican. My notion of racial scripts can be seen as a variant of processes described as *racial essentialism*, *stereotyping*, and *stigmatization* (Goffman 1959; Loury 2002; Hall 1980; Gates 1986; Gilroy 1987). However, *racial scripts* as defined here are closely tied to celebratory notions of nationalism developed under the rubric of *mestizaje*, or race mixture. Unlike most forms of stereotyping, which often assign negative qualities to groups, the "scripts of blackness" I analyze essentialize black people and black communities (and define expectations about them) according to attributes presented in the dominant discourses as primarily positive and often celebrated as exceptional qualities of the mixed-race nation.

These scripts often intertwine with other, more overtly negative racial stereotypes. For example, while black people may be shunned as promiscuous and their neighborhoods declared immoral, "scripts of blackness" celebrate the sensual beauty of Puerto Rican *mulata* women and the allure of black communities where visitors can "let themselves go."[15] Although both processes are related to stereotypes, I argue that the "scripts" that frame the representation of blackness are supported by narratives that, from a dominant perspective, exalt the mixed-race nation and its African heritage.

A related concept of "scripts" (also referred to as *schema*) is widely used in psychology, cognitive anthropology, and cognitive linguistics (Casson 1983; Schank and Abelson 1977a, 1977b; Bower et al. 1979; Abelson 1981). Within this tradition, "scripts" describe conceptual abstractions or structures serving as the basis for meaning-making processes. They are cultural norms, story templates, or common lines of argument that orient individuals and help guide their thoughts and actions in particular scenarios, enabling people "to efficiently process new and emergent situations in terms of old familiar ones" (Smith and Yachnes 1998; Vanclay and Enticott 2011).[16] For example, someone who has never visited a chiropractor's office knows what to do there by applying the script of going to a doctor's office, in turn an elaboration of a broader script for visiting a professional office of any kind (Rumelhart and Norman 1988). Such scripts are learned and stored in memory (Bower et al. 1979). According to Edwards (1997), "through repeated exposure to places such as restaurants, or to parents cooking food in the kitchen, or to school lessons, children and adults build mental schemas or models of what the world is like, and what to expect" (143).

In this way, the concept of "scripts" describes frameworks people apply to direct their actions (or even feelings) in prototypical situations understood as instances of a general model (Casson 1983; Hinton et al. 2008).[17] Anthropologists have also referred to scripts in a more general sense as widely shared unwritten rules of a particular society about what is considered "normal" in terms of ways of speaking, thinking, and feeling (Wierzbicka 2005). A script can thus be a conceptual model or story, a set of unspoken behavioral rules, or a widely shared set of ideas prevailing in a given society.

My use of scripts is similar to yet differs from this understanding. It is similar in the sense that I identify frameworks or templates about race widely shared and considered prototypical of what represents a particular racial heritage in Puerto Rico (especially African heritage). These stories or scripts inform expectations and unspoken standards about how people should behave in a particular situation or place (in a black community like San Antón, for example). Like the scripts of cognitive or psychological anthropology, they orient and guide action and talk, in this case about race in Puerto Rico. However, their "sharedness" resides not necessarily on memories or on repeated exposure to situations. The information, rather, is obtained via powerful state-sponsored mediums that—supported by particular constructions of history—filter, silence, domesticate, or simplify people's life experiences, creating normative ideas that can even contradict people's memories or everyday practices. For this reason they are influential but not completely hegemonic. They are constantly challenged and contradicted. Furthermore, while powerful actors and popular media representations mediate the dominant scripts, the public can also manipulate them. Hence the scripts documented here by virtue of association with governmental authority are inherently subject to contestation in everyday practice.

The scripts I refer to in this book are also historically constructed and disseminated through discourses that reproduce racial hierarchies in conversation with and against the United States. This notion is developed further on, but the point to be made here is that unlike trends in the psychologically oriented disciplines, my focus is not on cognitive or thought mechanisms accounting for a script's acquisition or application by individuals. Neither do I attempt to explain how people feel about embodying an essentialized script of blackness, although this affective aspect is important as it impacts self-concept and intersubjective experiences. Racial scripts can be deeply felt, explicitly assumed and embodied. Yet the question I address is how a script is historically constituted, disseminated by powerful actors and institutions, but also challenged or refashioned in everyday experience.

Furthermore, unlike the concept of scripts developed in cognitive disciplines, the scripts I refer to are not tacit features of culture or psychology. They are verbalized, presented in textual or aesthetic form, and often activated in public displays of nation; particularly in national representations that celebrate race mixture. One can find such "scripts of blackness" in festivals, carnivals, folk art, or state-sponsored kiosks where *frituras* (foods), *panderos* (instruments), *vejigante* (masks), and other commodities associated with Afro–Puerto Rican culture are presented or sold. However, I pay particular attention to the ways in which such scripts are inherently linked to places or emplaced. This is because dominant discourses of cultural nationalism often locate these "authentic" products of blackness in specific geographical areas (i.e., the coast), in towns (i.e., Loíza), or in communities (San Antón) where black people and their traditions are said to have "survived" Americanization and modernity—and its by-product: *blanqueamiento*, or whitening.

Scholars have established that management of space via housing and urban policies can create or reinforce class and race distinctions institutionalized through neighborhoods, zoning laws, architecture, and conventions of use (see Gieryn 2000, 474–75). In Puerto Rico, researchers have called attention to how gating and police surveillance reinforce associations among crime, poverty, blackness, and particular urban settings (Santiago-Valles 1995; Dinzey-Flores 2013; Fusté 2010; Rivera-Bonilla 2003, Rivera-Rideau 2013). Zaire Dinzey-Flores's (2013) work in Ponce is particularly relevant, as it explores the simultaneous gating of public multiple-dwelling housing projects (*caseríos*) for the poor and the private gating of single-family-home-owned neighborhoods (*urbanizaciones*) for the rich. She contends that since class distinctions are understood, maintained, and mediated through racial hierarchies, such class-differentiated gating practices frame race in concrete and explicit ways. Quoting Stuart Hall's notion that "race is the modality in which class is lived" (Hall 1980), she argues that urban structures (especially gates) that demarcate where poor people and rich people live in Ponce reify blackness and whiteness in space as separate identities, differentiating between who is safe or dangerous, good or bad, worthy or suspect (Dinzey-Flores 2013, 133–41). Related approaches have examined historical underpinnings of such processes documenting how intellectuals and politicians of the nineteenth century tried to contain and regulate the residents of barrios and shantytowns, describing the black and *mulato* working class, and women in particular, as inherently immoral, lazy, dirty, disorderly, incapable of political agency, and in need of the guidance of the *criollo* elite (see Findlay 1999; Fusté 2010; Hoffnung-Garskof 2011; Rodríguez-Silva 2012).

By contrast, scholars have also documented how music genres, fashions, and vernaculars identified as black and associated with black people in urban areas can also be perceived as quintessentially hip and modern. For example, work by Ana Yolanda Ramos-Zayas (2007) addresses Puerto Rican youth in New Jersey to argue that the performance of "urban blackness" can become a valued marker of being modern and cosmopolitan, and of actually belonging to a city. She states: "For many young Latin American migrants and United States–born Latinos, "becoming American" was not equated with "becoming white," as has been the case for other (mainly European) migrants, but rather with "becoming Black" (Ramos-Zayas 2007, 86),

Ramos-Zayas argues that Puerto Rican youth in Newark are valued by other Latin American youths as the diasporic Latino group "closest to Black" and as those who have the greatest "urban competency" given their U.S. citizenship, English-language skills, and physical proximity to African Americans. On a similar note, Dinzey-Flores (2008) examines the urban spatial aesthetics of reggaetón in Puerto Rico, to argue that the lyrical profile of reggaetón underscores poverty, violence, masculinity, and race (particularly blackness) as vital constructs of an authentically urban experience. In a recent article, Petra Rivera-Rideau (2013) underscores how in Puerto Rico this urban construction of blackness exists alongside folkloric construction of blackness, tracing their different emplacements to the "traditional" town of Loiza and to the *cacerios* associated to urban crime, respectively. She argues that "rather than being integrated into Puerto Rican identity like folkloric blackness, constructions of urban blackness are positioned outside of the parameters of acceptable Puerto Ricanness" (Rivera-Rideau, 624).

San Antón, like other low-income urban neighborhoods and public-housing projects or *caserios*, is similarly profiled as a place of urban blackness, drugs, violence, and crime. However, unlike many such communities, San Antón is also considered folkloric or "traditional." The emplacement of stigmatized and valued constructions of blackness thus occurs simultaneously.[18] Alongside the schema that constructs barrio residents in Puerto Rico as criminal, hostile urban young men with "urban competency" operate national scripts that represent these same places in premodern times, idealizing their black residents as exotic, happy, and rhythmic tradition bearers who still inhabit homogeneous communities and bodies. While the schema of modern blackness tends to be gendered as male and young, the folkloric script tends to be gendered as female and old; one is aggressive, the other hospitable; one materialistic, the other spiritual; one tends to be urban, the other coastal. One schema is nationalistic, insular, and disapproving of "outside" interventions; the other has been incorporated into transnational markets of modern blackness that incorporate different Afro-Diasporic groups (Rivera 2007; Arroyo 2010). Hence, at the same time that urban blackness is associated with mobility and the transnational projection of rap or reggaetón, the folkloric schema privileges communal expressions *in situ* connected to *bomba* and *plena*.[19]

While attentive to how essentialized and coexisting notions of blackness can be fragmented along these lines (modern urban vs. folkloric coastal), I focus on the second folkloric formulation of "scripts" because these have been less examined and, with wide public approval, can almost paradoxically set restrictive expectations and limits upon people and communities racialized as black and exceptional. Scripts of blackness appear in tourist brochures, school textbooks (Godreau et al. 2008), and political discourses produced by representatives of all political parties and ideologies in Puerto Rico: statehood, commonwealth, or independence. These representations even come up in venues produced by people one could consider allied with the communities at issue, such as anthropologists, antiracist activists, and community residents themselves. Consider, for instance, this passage from a recent ethnography by Puerto Rican anthropologist Samiri Hernández, where she reminisces about her first visits to the Puerto Rican town of Loíza:

> ... most people on Loíza's streets were fairly dark skinned. I was enchanted by the local folklore, vibrant colors, loud street music, and dancers moving to the rhythm of the drums. From the open air eateries came the rich smells of *frituras* [fried traditional food], coconuts and fish. I will always remember my first trip to the *ancón* a rustic ferry that had become a symbol of the area. I remember feeling then that Loíza is both unique and yet close, familiar. Little did I know that day at the ancon that years later I would return to Loíza as a researcher to experience the uniqueness of its people again and to find a part of myself still waiting there. (Hernández-Hiraldo 2006a, xi)

Ironically, Hernández-Hiraldo's ethnography challenges religious essentialisms that cast Loíza as a religious anomaly and its residents as practitioners of "witchcraft." She critiques the "disproportionate obsession with Afro–Puerto Rican religion" in Loíza and documents a plurality of religious frameworks and affiliations, particularly the rapid growth of Pentecostalism, charismatic Catholicism that coexists with a wide variety of homegrown temples and churches. Nevertheless, the folkloric representation of blackness she describes as "unique" to *loizeños* remains initially unexamined.

What accounts for the popular adherence to these narratives of Afro–Puerto Rican culture by so many Puerto Ricans? For once, cultural products associated with black folklore are not mere "inventions" of nationalist discourses or multicultural neoliberal markets. They derive from concrete subaltern practices and histories pertinent to Afro–Puerto Rican and working-class communities with whom cultural activists, intellectuals, and practitioners of folklore identify. As such, they can be construed as a counterhegemonic practice or bottom-up manifestation of Puerto Rican culture.[20] Furthermore, these folkloric renditions are thus not just strategic deployments but can be valued and felt as elements of lived experience and identity by people who passionately affirm their sense of national belonging in a context of nonsovereignty (Alamo 2009; Rivera 2007; Cartagena 2004). Moreover, these scripts have persuasive power among folklorists, intellectuals, cultural nonprofit institutions, and even some San Antón residents themselves, because the celebration of black foklore may challenge other practices (institutional and popular) that silence discussions about race, blackness, and racism.

However, what happens when such expressions of Puerto Rican blackness are not just practiced from below but also celebrated and managed from above? Once signs of Afro–Puerto Rican culture have been incorporated (albeit marginally) into official government-sponsored nationalist narratives about Puerto Rico, under what terms and conditions are they voiced or made visible? What makes such indexes of blackness palatable for cultural nationalism? How are these signs of Afro–Puerto Rican folklore incorporated into a story about national identity? And what is lost, silenced, debated, or invented in that process?

I argue that too often, the scripted terms that define the "bottom-up" contributions of Afro–Puerto Ricans to the nation (i.e., their exceptionality, their nostalgia, their rootedness in the blood) are broadly applied, taken for granted, and uncritically celebrated without questioning the terms under which the silence appears to be broken. Metaphors of silence and invisibility have been widely used by scholars (myself included), antiracist activists, and critical people alike to describe how race, racism, and more specifically blackness are ignored, censored, or excluded from dominant constructions of the nation in the Caribbean and Latin America. The literature is quite extensive, but comprehensive treatments of this topic include Robin Sheriff's work on Brazil, "Exposing Silence as Cultural Censorship" (2000), and Ileana Rodríguez-Silva's *Silencing Race: Disentangling Blackness, Colonialism and National Identities in Puerto Rico* (2012). Both examine patterned silences about race at play in the reproduction of racial hierarchies, considering the social function as well as the personal and political investments people have in silencing race. Against the backdrop of cultural censorship described by these and other scholars, the deployment of racial scripts may appear to be "breaking" this silence and unspoken rule of invisibility. Yet, rather than disrupt the silence, I argue that scripts set the terms for how "race" is sanctioned and allowed. They provide an endorsed story, a well-disseminated and legitimated frame that enables notions about blackness, whiteness, and indigeneity to be verbalized, talked about, and made visible without disrupting the social pacts of cordiality or conviviality that sustain racial hierarchies and the taken-for-granted value placed on whitening, or *blanqueamiento*.

Folklore and Scripts

In previous works, I described some of the essentialist outcomes of such processes as the folklorization of blackness (Godreau 2002), arguing that co-opted representations of African heritage often rob communities like San Antón of their complexity and fail to value residents' practices as contemporary phenomena. In this book, I use the more pertinent concept of "scripts" to identify those dominant story templates that seem to be inherently connected to folkloric manifestations but in fact are not. The story that is told about black folklore (the script), I argue, has more to do with national discourses that seek to distinguish Puerto Rico from the United States than with the history or everyday practices of those who produced the cultural manifestation in the first place. My goal is to examine ethnographically the work that such scripts accomplish and their effects in San Antón and elsewhere, and to point out their contemporary and historical inconsistencies.

This critical approach to the management of black folklore within corresponding scripts should not be confused with a general critical or disparaging posture toward Afro–Puerto Rican folklore itself, as if this were a coherent unitary expression to criticize. Afro–Puerto Rican folklore as manifested in the form of carnival masks, music genres, foods, and religious imagery and beliefs can be and has been mobilized to challenge social hierarchies and racism. As Hernández-Hiraldo herself and others have documented, Puerto Ricans in the Island and of the diaspora celebrate practices associated with an African heritage to resist elitist and racist constructions of Hispanicity that often exclude Afro–Puerto Ricans from dominant constructions of the nation (Hernández-Hiraldo 2006a, 28; Alamo-Pastrana 2009; Rivera 2003, 2007). In the context of the Puerto Rican diaspora, folkloric performances and practices have also allowed black and working-class Puerto Ricans living in the United States to gain recognition and even claim moral superiority as "culturally authentic Puerto Ricans" in the face of both U.S. and middle-class or elite Puerto Rican judgments of diasporic Puerto Ricans as assimilated (Ramos-Zayas 2003). Moreover, Afro-Latinos across the Americas have also intentionally drawn on black folklore and notions of cultural-ethnic difference as modes of strategic essentialism to denounce racism, demanding recognition and rights as citizens (French 2009; Hale 2002; Pinho 2010; Anderson 2009; Paschel 2010).

Thus what I call "scripts" is not necessarily tantamount to folklore. While folklore can name a broad, multivalent complex set of sanctioned practices that can simultaneously resist and comply with racial and other social hierarchies, I use "scripts" to call attention to dominant *stories* and ideological templates that frequently frame the institutionalized celebration and exaltation of such folkloric practices and expressions, often emplacing them as unique vis-à-vis a normative, mixed, whitened, and contemporary social background.

Part of my present contribution with this book is to examine the everyday deployment of such scripts and the dominant narratives that have historically supported them, particularly in the context of U.S. intervention in the Island. This endeavor requires paying attention to the political limits and challenges of both colonialism and cultural nationalism and to the everyday practices and political alternatives people formulate to transcend, confront, or deal with them.

The Politics of Colonial Sovereignty: A Racialized Domain

In response to U.S. colonial intervention, Puerto Ricans have mobilized in support of U.S. statehood, independence from the United States, or an improved version of the current commonwealth status. Since the 1960s, these alternatives have been primarily represented by three political parties: the Partido Nuevo Progresista (PNP) or pro-statehood party, the Partido Popular Democrático (PPD) or commonwealth party, and the Partido Independentista Puertorriqueño (PIP) or pro-independence party. Of these, the pro-statehood and commonwealth parties draw the most voters, with the pro-independence party obtaining less than 6 percent of votes since 1960 and less than 3 percent since 2004 (Álvarez Rivera 2013).[21]

According to Ramón Grosfoguel, the rejection of political independence in Puerto Rico must be understood in the context of a modern capitalist world system that maintains a racial and ethnic hierarchy of Western versus non-Western people. Puerto Rican people don't want to endure the socioeconomic conditions of neighboring Caribbean countries that experience the cruel exploitation of the capitalist world system without the metropolitan transfers and the access to metropolitan citizenship that Puerto Ricans receive as a "modern colony" (Grosfoguel 2003, 2). Bonilla documents a similar rejection of political independence in the overseas French departments of Martinique and Guadeloupe, where people prefer formulas of "strategic entanglements" over political independence, to tackle the hegemony of powerful economic interests (Bonilla-Ramos 2010). People from Guadeloupe and Martinique frame demands for better living conditions in histories of economic exploitation and racial inequality resulting from their colonial relationships with France, but they also invoke political rights obtained through affiliation with France as an overseas department (Bonilla-Ramos 2010).

Similarly, Puerto Rico is deeply entangled with the United States, with few opportunities to develop an economy outside the U.S. purview. Furthermore, while an estimated 3,667,084 million people reside on the Island (U.S. Census Bureau 2013), almost 5 million Puerto Ricans are now living in the United States (U.S. Census Bureau 2011; CB Staff 2013). Accordingly, it should come as no surprise that both preferred political parties uphold U.S. citizenship and the preservation of economic ties to the U.S. economy. In future chapters, I distinguish these parties' political agendas and racial maneuvers, but the point to make here is that this study about the racialized dynamics of nation takes place in a context where there is no Puerto Rican national sovereignty, no nation-state, no national citizenship, and where the great majority of "nationals" express no desire to attain these. Is this a problem?

Scholarship on nationalism has emphasized that, despite the certainty with which some historians speak of the rational "origins" of nations, the nation is an imagined, highly ambivalent, and inherently polemical construct everywhere (Anderson 1989; Bhabha 1994; Chatterjee 1986). Partha Chatterjee has pointed out that in the colonial world,

> The polemic is not a mere stylistic device which a dispassionate analyst can calmly separate out of a pure doctrine. It is part of the ideological content of nationalism, which takes as its adversary a contrary discourse—the discourse of colonialism. Pitting itself against the reality of colonial rule—which appears before it as an existent almost palpable, historical truth—nationalism seeks to assert the feasibility of entirely new political possibilities. (1986, 40)

According to Chatterjee, this polemical process of formulating political possibilities is precisely what allows nationalist discourses to come into existence in the colonial world. Puerto Rico's long colonial trajectory—first with Spain, then with the United States—has made the practice of formulating political possibilities a formative, passionate, never-ending force that propels the concept of a national community into existence. The debate about Puerto Rico's political status vis-à-vis the United States has even been called the Island's favorite "national sport." According to some researchers, the resilience of a collective identity among Puerto Ricans after more than five hundred years of colonial rule suggests that, contrary to commonly held assumptions, colonial pressure can strengthen rather than diminish national identity (Morris 1995, 8). Academic, political, and popular opinions overwhelmingly indicate that Puerto Ricans view themselves as a distinct national group with common history, culture, and heritage (Morris 1995; Duany 2002; Dávila 1997). However, this sentiment of nationalist pride and the search for new political possibilities is not necessarily tantamount to a desire for establishing an independent nation-state in Puerto Rico (Morris 1995, 12).

The widespread adherence to U.S. presence in Puerto Rico undermines and complicates traditional liberal premises of nationalist thought that equate "the nation" with the universal search for "liberty," "democracy," "progress," and legitimacy through the nation-state. It does not, however, undermine the power of the nationalist imagination that creates its own domain of sovereignty within colonial society when accepting and even encouraging certain aspects of metropolitan intervention (Chatterjee 1986). In this process, as in other projects of nation making, notions of blood and "race" as carriers of culture become fundamental to notions of belonging. As an important idiom of nation building, I argue that these signs also operate in the not-so-postcolonial context of Puerto Rico as a constitutive element in the creation of what Chatterjee calls the "domain of sovereignty."

To return to a question posed previously, then, the reason that studying racialized dynamics of nation makes sense in a context like Puerto Rico is that it can reveal how race becomes instrumental for the nationalist imagination constructed in opposition to—or at least in conversation with—colonial power. Chatterjee qualifies this process of constructing a national sense of "difference" as one that operates in two distinct, albeit related, domains: the material and the spiritual. He states:

> The material is the domain of the 'outside,' of the economy and of state-craft, of science and technology, a domain where the West had proved its superiority and the East had succumbed. In this domain, then, Western superiority had to be acknowledged and its accomplishments carefully studied and replicated. The spiritual, on the other hand, is an 'inner' domain bearing the 'essential' marks of cultural identity. The greater one's success in imitating Western skills in the material domain, therefore, the greater the need to preserve the distinctness of one's spiritual culture. (Chatterjee 1996, 217)

Chatterjee mentions language, performative practices in drama, the novel, and the family as areas that have fallen within this spiritual domain and that nationalism transforms in the course of its journey. The ultimate goal, according to the author, is to fashion a "modern" national culture that is nevertheless not Western. This project is relevant for Puerto Rico and has direct bearing on the way in which race has been imagined as part of this inner, spiritual domain. In fact, the distinctiveness of Puerto Rican culture is often said to emanate from the qualities afforded by the mixture of its three distinct racial components: the Spanish, the *Taíno* Indian, and the African in a process of fashioning a "modern" national culture that is not North American (of the United States).

Puerto Rico's colonial situation fuels this understanding and the ideological distinction between a racially mixed, seemingly harmonious Puerto Rican "us" and a deeply segregated U.S. "Other." Academically, the effects of this antagonistic posture are evident in a general tendency among Puerto Rican scholars to assume that race and color are "foreign"—irrelevant, if not divisive—topics of analysis. Puerto Rico's colonial situation fosters these silences and the understanding that race can divide, disintegrate, or weaken the struggle to maintain a national identity. Writer Juan Manuel Carrión, for example, asks,

> Are we going to replace the integrating myths with the ripping counter-myths of racial resentments? We would then be like them [meaning the United States], with their ethnic and racial divisions and conflicts . . . (Carrión 1993, 11)
>
> What the national project of Puerto Rico does not need is to accentuate its racial fissures. What it needs is to emphasize the links of solidarity that give it life. (Carrión 1993, 13)

Puerto Rican scholars who have argued otherwise and insisted on writing about racism have often been accused of imposing U.S. notions upon the Puerto Rican context or of partaking in intellectual imperialism.

This ideological deployment of a local fluid and mixed reality versus a supposedly foreign U.S. racist one is not unique to Puerto Rico (for a similar argument in Brazil, see Bourdieu and Wacqant 1999). Brazil's principal ideologue of racial nationalism, Gilberto Freyre (1977), developed the ideology of racial democracy explicitly in contrast with the United States and even while studying in the United States under the mentorship of Franz Boas (Healey 2000, 101). His notion of Brazil as a racial democracy was in turn consolidated by U.S. activists, writers, and intellectuals who saw in Brazil an alternative to the racist oppression they experienced in the United States (Fry 2000, 90). Besides Freyre, other ideologues of racial democracy in the Americas, like Martí in Cuba and Muñoz Marín in Puerto Rico, also construed their corresponding versions of racial democracy and racial mixture in explicit comparison with the United States and in diasporic dialogue with U.S. institutions and thinkers (see Yelvington 2006; Fry 2000; Andrews 1996).

Recent scholarship has questioned the generally established distinction portrayed since then between the United States and the continuum model of race mixture that Brazil and Latin America more broadly represent. The literature highlights racist dynamics that respond more to a binary rationale of exclusion—often associated with the United States—than to the fluid logic of racial mixture and upward mobility often attributed to Brazil and to Latin American race relations (see Hernández 2013; Goldstein 1999; Sheriff 2000; Vargas-Ramos 2005; Hanchard 1994; for a similar argument about Cuba, see Helg 1997). Tanya Kateri Hernández (2013), for example, examines how even though few formal laws supported racial segregation after emancipation in Latin America, customary law and the state systematically regulated, sustained, and institutionalized racial subordination in key areas such as immigration, police surveillance, spatial segregation, political underrepresentation, education, and unemployment across the region. Still, the region posits itself as racially innocent in comparison to the United States. This denial of racism, argues Hernández, operates in conjunction with the notion that true racism can be found only in the formal Jim Crow type of racial segregation of the United States (Hernández 2013, 3–4). In conversation with this literature, I argue that nationalist ideologies in Puerto Rico and the various "scripts" of blackness they promote do not operate independently of the United States. They are rather reinforced by the politics of colonial nation building historically fostered by Puerto Rico's relationship with the metropolis. In fact, I argue that contemporary renderings of harmonious race relations in Puerto Rico and the "fixity" of the scripts of blackness depend upon the ideological influence of the United States.

This does not mean that the United States is the only important vector of difference. Haiti, the English Caribbean, Cuba, and more recently the Dominican Republic have played key roles in the construction of Puerto Rico's racial nationalisms. Contrasts drawn between Puerto Rico and these societies have varied in saliency at different historical moments and at times rival the United States for advancing particular claims.[22] However, such contrasts, while important, are not privileged here. This is partly because of the practical need to limit the object of study, but also because I aim to contribute to scholarship that examines the United States as a geopolitical imperial entity, exploring how U.S. commodities, cultural practices, people, and ideas circulate and have an impact around the Western Hemisphere, especially in countries directly impacted by its expansionist agenda.

Anthropologists, for whom questions of empire were present at the outset of the discipline, have underscored the need to conduct ethnography on the contemporary effects of U.S. colonialism, expansionism, and military presence in the world (see Lutz 2006; Kaplan and Pease 1993). Catherine Lutz notes that, while a rich literature on the global effects of U.S. empire has emerged, there is little attention to the ethnographic details of those projects (2006, 594). For example, Latin American scholars such as Aníbal Quijano (2000) and Walter Mignolo (2000) have inspired macro-level analysis—including Puerto Rican contributions—of the "coloniality of power" as a contemporary global pattern of Western domination where capitalism, racism, imperialism, and patriarchy mingle (Santiago-Valles 2003, 2005; Laó-Montes 1997, 2008–9; Grosfoguel et al. 1997; Grosfoguel 2003, 2008). Here, I provide a micro-level analysis of effects that U.S. imperialism and Puerto Rican colonial nationalism have on everyday constructions of blackness, whiteness, and mixture by attending to details of how racialized identities are produced and of their concrete effects and vicissitudes on the ground. Thus, while not directly concerned with U.S. history, U.S. international relations, or even the U.S. mainland, I analyze the historical legacies and contemporary effects of U.S. overseas imperialism by studying ethnographically how race is formulated in one of "its territories." My goal, then, is to analyze the cultural and historical manifestations of racial discourses and scripts as people develop and deploy them within this matrix of imperial power. The question is how does this happen? And how can one trace the effects of such racial discourses ethnographically?

Discursive Pillars of the Racialized Domain of Sovereignty: An Organizational Matrix

In this book I trace such effects at two different discursive levels. One is the level of scripts, which provide storied templates about particular racial heritages. A second, broader level is that of national discourses that support and grant historic legitimacy to the more specific racial scripts deployed, partly because they are formulated against the United States. At this broader level, I identify three important discourses about the Puerto Rican nation that have played key roles in mapping racial nationalism crafted in relationship to the United States. These discourses, in turn, inform the scripts that layer dominant representations of blackness and other racialized identities in everyday interactions. These broader national narratives are: (1) discourses about "benevolent" slavery (as opposed to the "harsh" form of slavery of the United States); (2) discourses about Hispanicity and Spanish whiteness of the nation (as opposed to Anglo whiteness of the United States); and (3) discourses about race mixture (as opposed to the "purity" of white/black races found in the United States). I maintain that these three nationalist ideologies mediate powerful racial scripts, set limits, and kindle debates about what is celebrated as "black," "white," "Indian," or "mixed" in Puerto Rico. All three narratives of nation, I also argue, strategically essentialize the U.S. Other in carving out that "inner domain of sovereignty" that Chatterjee writes about. In that process, problematic renditions of race position Puerto Rico as a different, sometimes also "morally superior" nation vis-à-vis the United States. Moreover, narratives about benevolent slavery, Hispanicity, and race mixture are also strategically deployed to characterize the nation as well equipped, fit to assume its political destiny vis-à-vis the United States—no matter which destiny that might be—statehood, commonwealth, or independence. Furthermore, I theorize them as discursive tactics that attempt to whiten the majority while making blackness palatable for celebratory displays of national identity.

While recognizing that such construction of the Puerto Rican nation can reproduce racial hierarchies, I also look at their contradictory effects. On this issue, Carlos Alamo-Pastrana (2009) argues that too much emphasis on the essentialist practices of the state and other powerful actors can render invisible subaltern expressions and alternative propositions about race, class, and gender that take place concurrently and alongside official renderings of blackness:

> Understanding these essentialist constructions from a limited frame that only see [sic] discourses about Blackness rooted in nostalgic historical representations as part of a larger dominant discourse of cultural nationalism . . . limits an appreciation of how such renderings also provide an outlet for the inclusion of productive and valuable conversations about the relationship between history and race on the island. Labeling the employment of Blackness through traditional state-sanctioned cultural outlets as exclusively being *just* an essentialist representation empowers the state to function as the hegemonic arbiter of the history of blackness on the island. (Alamo-Pastrana 2009, 581)

Attentive to this criticism, I highlight the contested and contradictory nature of these dominant national narratives and the scripts they support by organizing this volume into a first chapter and three subsequent sections that focus on the three dominant narratives (i.e., benevolent slavery, Hispanicity, and race mixture). To highlight their contested nature, chapters included under each section are organized in pairs. The first of the pair establishes the historical underpinning and ethnographic manifestation of the dominant discourse crafted vis-à-vis the United States from a critical perspective. The following chapter focuses on a concrete challenge, identifying cracks, ethnographic inconsistencies, or forms of political resistance launched at that particular national narrative and the scripts supported by it. In these alternative propositions, the United States may appear as an ally or model (rather than as a vector of difference) or not be mentioned at all. Challenges I take up may be more or less articulate: political movements, artistic performances, or subtle features of everyday practices not necessarily verbalized as "alternatives" but just as what people do.

Challenges are also complex and can simultaneously question one script while reproducing or accommodating another. Hence, I do not pretend to suggest that people resist the dominant discourses in some romanticized or coherent fashion. This would undermine dynamics of complicity, individualism, internalized racism, compromise, or even cooperation that everyone partakes of to survive, lest they fall exhausted from conceiving life as a constant battlefield of domination and subordination.[23] Nevertheless, this organizational strategy of first explaining and contextualizing the dominant narrative and then focusing on dynamics that do not quite fit the mold allows me to illustrate distinct effects that these three discourses and corresponding scripts provoke when people employ and challenge them in the same situation.

Another reason to organize the book according to each of these narratives is that each national discourse (benevolent slavery, Hispanicity, and race mixture) surfaced most prominently at a different historical moment, provoking different kinds of dialogues with and against the United States. Hence, the book draws substantially from historical material as I identify the political conditions and historical factors shaping the different racial discourses produced about the Puerto Rican "nation" and their contestations.

Gilroy, as well as Omi and Winant, has underscored the importance of taking such historical considerations seriously when addressing questions of racial formation in relationship to nationalism. For Gilroy (1987), "Nationhood is not an empty receptacle which can be simply and spontaneously filled with alternative concepts according to the dictates of political pragmatism. The ideological theme of national belonging may be malleable to some extent but its links with the discourses of classes and races and the organizational realities of these groups are not arbitrary. They are confined by historical and political factors" (55).

For Omi and Winant, too, the concept of racial formation must attend to preexisting historical, political, and economic transformations that alter racial identities and meanings, placing constraints and limits on people's present struggles to transform them (1986, 64–67). With this notion in mind, each of the book's three parts make reference to a particular time period in order to elucidate the historical and political factors that make some narratives about race and nation more viable than others.

Since the chapters in each of the three parts draw on my ethnography about the housing project, the chapter following this introduction (Chapter 1) provides a detailed ethnographic account of the housing controversy. Here, I place particular emphasis on the racial and spatial coordinates that informed debate over its implementation, pointing to the problematic and contested deployment of scripts of nostalgia, homogeneity, matrifocality, harmony, and unchanging traditions that marked San Antón as an exceptional place of racialized difference. In the three parts following the first chapter, I expand on and situate this information in historical and theoretical perspectives by looking at the housing development through the discursive lenses of benevolent slavery, Hispanicity, and race mixture.

The section on benevolent slavery (Part I) explores how this discourse bolstered folkloric scripts about San Antón that cast the community—and blackness in general—as an exceptional, geographically contained, and fading element of Puerto Rican national identity. First, I trace this discourse in Chapter 2 to scholarly writings of the 1940s, 1950s, and 1960s primarily developed by historians who claimed that slavery in the colonies of Catholic Spain (namely Puerto Rico and Cuba) was "soft" compared to the type of slavery that developed in the colonies of Protestant powers such as in the English Caribbean or the United States (Blanco 1942; Díaz-Soler 1981; Tannenbaum 1947). I illustrate the connection between this discourse's trivialization of slavery at the national level of Puerto Rico and its concomitant exaggeration of slavery at the level of San Antón. In Chapter 3, I challenge this dominant narrative by combining historical information about free people of color in San Antón with residents' interviews about the history of plantation slavery and sugar cane in Ponce. By presenting an alternative, non-scripted history of the community, I seek to take into account its complexities and the organizing categories most relevant for residents themselves.

Chapters 4 and 5 constitute Part II and focus on Hispanicity as a key counter-concept for the construction of blackness as an exception. Here I explore how Spain was marshaled (and contested) as marker of cultural whiteness at the turn of the century and in the ethnographic present. In Chapter 4, I trace this idea to narratives developed during the 1930s that exalted the influence of Spain in Puerto Rican culture in order to counteract the political and economic colonial encroachment of the United States. I explore some of the ethnographic continuities of this discourse and its impact on the timing, zoning policies, and architectural scripts used by Ponce's municipal government to mark San Antón a "historic site." Chapter 5 documents challenges to Hispanophilia from the turn of the century and in the ethnographic present. Here I explore the Hispanophobia of U.S. colonial officials and of those working-class Puerto Ricans who supported annexation to the United States at the turn of the twentieth century. For both of these groups, Spain represented a backward, antidemocratic influence and—albeit for different reasons—a suspect source of whiteness. Here again I identify continuities with the ethnographic present in negative renditions of Spain (and of Hispanic whiteness) that surfaced during my fieldwork in Ponce and Puerto Rico.

The next and final section of the book (Part III) explores how previous narratives about Hispanic whiteness as a "cultural attribute" complement the construction of blackness as a "biological trace," facilitating "scripts" that represent African heritage as an impulsive, raw, spontaneous, kinesthetic quality that flows in the blood of all Puerto Ricans. In Chapter 6, I discuss how such scripts of blackness developed in tandem with discourses of race mixture that supported populist forms of governance and cultural policies in the 1940s and 1950s, and I describe their more contemporary deployment in San Antón. In Chapter 7, I illustrate the challenges to such scripts by documenting how the showcasing of black folklore in San Antón requires work and ideological maneuvering. I present debates among residents over who controls the representation of San Antón's African heritage (evidencing that it is far from a natural flow), as well as controversies between residents and government officials over housing. In these debates, residents did not follow state expectations about their "race" but even deployed Native American and Taíno scripts to get their points across.

All these chapters foreground the ethnography of how racial scripts and nationalist discourses operate in historical analysis by combining archival and secondary historical sources with contemporary material and field notes that elucidate their everyday effects. Finally, in the conclusion, I summarize the theoretical contributions of this project in dialogue with approaches to *mestizaje* in Afro-Latin America and to the global study of the United States and its colonizing effects.

Overall, the chapters aim to call attention to the selective, problematic effects and contested processes through which scripts of blackness and other racial scripts are selectively celebrated, deployed, and emplaced in Puerto Rico. The book is an invitation to consider this complexity and to challenge the limits that racial scripts about blackness can place upon the cultural practices that people in San Antón and elsewhere can claim as authentic and eligible for sponsorship or recognition. As the epigraph opening this introduction indicates, "We demystify myths not to diminish the beauty of myth, but to overcome the idea that identities must be fixed and that human beings are hostages of their culture or prisoners of their physical appearance" (Pinho 2010, 10). With the present book, I seek to overcome precisely those ideas by calling attention to the silences that national scripts produce and by demonstrating how people subvert them, complicate them, and sometimes employ them unexpectedly to their advantage in their everyday lives and in the context of U.S. empire.

CHAPTER 1

Place, Race, and the Housing Debate

In the fifth-grade classroom of the public elementary school where I volunteered in Ponce, students were asked to build a representation of an Aztec city. The teacher explained that people of different classes occupied the city: traders, soldiers, priest, politicians, and slaves. "Who lived in the houses made of straw?" she asked.[1] "Poor people," a student answered. "And in the cement ones?" "Rich people," said a couple of students in unison. After a brief discussion, the teacher divided the students and instructed two groups to build a barrio. One student said, "I'm going to build San Antón!" The teacher described the Aztec barrios and how to make them: "The barrios are where poor people live . . . You've got to build houses with straw roofing and clay walls . . . Each barrio has a sowing field, houses, and people. The other groups will build a marketplace, and the others will build temples."

* * *

Scholars of Latin America have underscored the importance of spatial dynamics and core-periphery hierarchies based on race, class, and "national representativeness" as assigned to regions (Wade 1993; Appelbaum 1999; Rahier 1998; Streicker 1997). Researchers have also examined the racialization of residential areas in cities, documenting the ways segregation produces ethnic enclaves, race-based subcultures, or "white habitus" (Hartigan 1999; Ramos-Zayas 2003, 2007; Bonilla-Silva et al. 2006; Dinzey-Flores 2013).

In the classroom I visited in Ponce, third graders learned spatial coordinates of class and the subordinate place of barrios through the use of wood, straw, and clay. This elementary school was located in Urbanización Constancia and served youngsters from San Antón and surrounding urban neighborhoods. Urbanización Constancia is a middle-class neighborhood built in 1960 in what used to be the eastern sector of San Antón before a series of modernizing projects (including the construction of Constancia) divided and significantly reduced San Antón (Mills-Bocachica 1993). During my stay in Ponce, I rented a small apartment in this neighborhood just across the street from San Antón. (Map 2 shows San Antón in relationship to Constancia.)[2]

Urbanizaciones like Constancia are an integral part of the changes that accompanied the economic shift from an agrarian to an industrial economy in Puerto Rico during the 1940s and 1950s. By the late 1950s, they were the model for private home ownership (Rivera-Bonilla 2003; Dinzey-Flores 2013). Cement houses in Constancia (which was once a cane field) are designed with garage space for a car and an area for a washer and dryer. They follow a linear configuration along streets arranged in an asphalt grid. The complex has a recreational area, a baseball field, two basketball courts, a playground, a community center, and a Catholic church. Save one basketball court, no such facilities existed in San Antón at the time of my fieldwork, and, as mentioned earlier, infrastructure was lacking. Furthermore, the need for protection against crime, made visible in the iron bars in windows

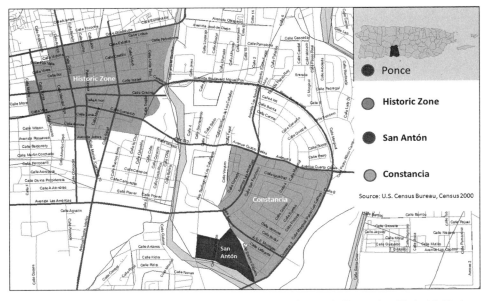

Map 2. Ponce's Historic Zone, the barrio of San Antón, and *urbanización* Constancia. Map produced by José Calderón Squiabro using combined Census Bureau data from the Census Block Maps Web-site: http://tinyurl.com/n3d5f4t and http://tinyurl.com/7vcaxm8.

and doors of houses in Constancia, distinguished it from the wooden and mostly ungated structures of San Antón.

Ironically, the area lacking bars (San Antón) was marked as unsafe. Distinction between safe and unsafe spaces became particularly prevalent during the late 1980s and early 1990s, when Puerto Rico seemed to be "drowning in a crime wave" linked to drug trafficking (Dinzey-Flores 2013, 15). Sensationalistic print and TV media coverage of crime activity, combined with policies targeted at urban poor neighborhoods and especially *caseríos* (public housing complexes), constructed black neighborhoods and particularly black youth in urban areas as the main target of police surveillance against which a "decent" Puerto Rican middle class and whiter identity was affirmed (Dinzey-Flores 2013; Santiago-Valles 1996; Fusté 2010). As mentioned in the introduction, San Antón is also construed against the violent and delinquent schema of this "urban blackness." A middle-aged *ponceña* I met at the airport, for example, exclaimed: "*¡Ay Virgen!*" (Oh, mother of God!) while pressing one hand to her chest, when I told her I had lived near San Antón during my fieldwork. While there, I also witnessed an unannounced police raid conducted with the mounted guard and a heavy display of police vehicles, including the canine unit. At least twenty police officers blocked the main entrance of the community with rifles and firearms on a Friday afternoon (October 11, 1996) while a helicopter overhead shone a spotlight on the residences. Police conducted violent searches against young men in the community during the almost two-hour raid. No one was arrested, and the police found no drugs or arms. No such interventions took place in Constancia during my fieldwork.

San Antón residents criticized these interventions and people who stereotype the community as "dangerous" because of the illicit activities of a few. Other community members, like Carlos "Cao" Vélez Franceschi, the director of the *bomba* and *plena* musical group Los Guayacanes de San Antón, also question the stark division people make between the two adjacent residential areas. Cao lived in Constancia and said:

> I've never been outside of San Antón. Remember that Constancia was the cane field of San Antón. My aunts still live in San Antón, my family, I mean I've always made my life in San Antón and I live next door in Constancia. . . . I mean, Constancia is nothing other than part of San Antón. It was San Antón's cane field. We moved to Constancia around 1971, my mother, my brother—we had already started playing professional baseball. It wasn't a drastic change, because I had the same friends. I played baseball in San Antón. I didn't change my ways, my friends, because, like I said, one is so close to the other. The baseball park that we, the baseball players of San Antón, use is in Constancia, because we still don't have a baseball park here. I mean, that sharing that bond was never interrupted; and it's never going to be interrupted, because we have strong roots that unite us to San Antón. And I believe

that I can be wherever I can be, and my spirit and my soul will keep on being in San Antón. Simple . . . that's the way it is.

Still, group distinctions and the privileges attached to class and racial identities often become naturalized and marked through the spatial structures and neighborhoods people inhabit (Dinzey-Flores 2013, 133–41; De Certeau et al. 1998). Thus, although San Antón residents visited the Catholic church, convenience store, baseball park, and elementary school located in Constancia, there were clearly distinct social implications associated with living in a barrio or in an *urbanización*. Luis "Cuto" Colón, a local candidate for the pro-statehood party who was born and raised in San Antón, commented:

> There are some stereotypes . . . If a young barrio woman gets pregnant, she's degenerate, a sexual whatchamacallit. [*Hesitation.*] Well, they even call her a prostitute. A young girl from an *urbanización* . . ."No! No! She made a mistake!" I mean, look at these two things. And so, a young man from San Antón goes to ask permission to visit a girl . . . at her home. [And they ask him,] "Where are you from? From San Antón! Umm let me think about it, I'll let you know later." Then a boy from an *urbanización* comes along with a whole bunch of bad ways, "No! No! That's so-and-so's son." . . . That's the way it is; we're in Puerto Rico. *La gente se mide más, no por el valor del ser humano, y sí por el de dónde viene y lo que representa . . . o sea de acuerdo al sitio donde venga.* [People measure others not by their value as human beings, but by where they come from and what that represents . . . meaning according to (the) place they come from.]

Maria Judith Banchs Cabrera, a teacher and community leader who grew up in San Antón, says she was made aware of this stigma attached to place from an early age:

> At the beginning I saw myself as a person who was equal to others. But later I realized that there were very marked differences socially . . . people called San Antón a barrio [*with a pejorative tone*]. And I asked myself, "Why do people call it a barrio?" Why do they call Constancia an *urbanización*? What is the difference between one and the other?" Well, the houses that were there, next to us, which are the *urbanizaciones*, were arranged in linear fashion, had services we did not have . . . They planted their trees in a linear fashion in a very stylish way. Us, our trees are, as we say, wild. Besides that, people dressed differently—and isn't it a curious thing that the place where they lived used to be part of the place where I was born. Yet *they* were called *urbanización* and *we* were called barrio [*she laughs sarcastically*]. Then the curious thing is that when you analyze the term barrio in relationship to who you are, you realize that people slowly define who you are, and sometimes that definition does not have anything to do with who you think you are. And you say, "But my

God, does that mean that the place where you come from defines how you will be, how you will behave, and how you really are?" I say this because I have heard a lot of people who don't know I am from San Antón say, "People there are stupid little black folk, and well . . . the majority are drug addicts, prostitutes, burglars—people who don't have manners, who don't know how to speak well . . ." All that forms part of coming from a barrio. And one has to fight against all that . . . because others have already programmed things so that you will only get to a certain point. If you go beyond that, you'll be considered a rebel. You are a person who likes to make trouble. You are controversial, you are *una negrita atrevida, una afrontá* [a defiant little black woman, a loudmouth]. All these things come to delineate how you will project yourself in the future and in your life. In other words, this is more profound, being from a barrio is more profound than saying "barrio San Antón."

Maria Judith's compelling statements illustrate that racism is not just a structural force, but also a personal one that carries meanings and affects life chances in ways that are emotionally experienced. The stigma of place she describes informed her own personal struggle for upward mobility against barriers that are not just set in the landscape, but that are, as she says, "more profound," becoming internalized and ingrained in one's sense of self.

Urbanizaciones endow their dwellers with a different set of personal assets and social expectations. Originally intended to replace *arrabals*, or slum habitations, they stand for modernity and for a "decent" way of living (Joplin 1988, 256; Dinzey-Flores 2007). Notions of *dignidad* (dignity) and respectability acquired through ownership and nuclear family arrangements are also fundamental meanings of *urbanización* houses (Joplin 1988, 258). Their widespread emergence in Puerto Rico responds not only to post-1940 industrialization developments in Puerto Rico, but also to the desires of a then-expanding upwardly mobile class whose taste, food habits, and leisure options became more and more Americanized.

Despite their general correlation with progress, *urbanizaciones* vary and serve different socioeconomic sectors. Constancia was not a high-end complex. The cost of a house there in the 1990s could range from seventy thousand to one hundred thousand dollars.[3] Located in the south-central part of Ponce, Constancia has a population primarily composed of teachers and employees of the service and government sector. My landlords, for example, were a couple in their late fifties who worked for the government. He was a recently retired lawyer and she a public school principal. They lived on the first level and I on the second level of a two-story cement house.

One day, as I left the house to walk to San Antón, my landlord told me he regretted the fact that Constancia could not expand all the way into San Antón. He believed San Antón should not continue to exist as a separate entity from the *urbanización* and said he failed to understand why people insisted on preserving the barrio as it was. He disagreed with the local commonwealth government's preservationist plans and argued that, although there still might be some old people in San Antón who preserve the traditions of the *bomba* and *plena*, the majority of the young people who live there have nothing to do with that tradition. They should not be seen as any different from Constancia.[4] Then, to illustrate the advantages of integration, he established a pedagogical analogy about the benefits of mainstreaming "slow" kids with normal kids in the classroom. San Antón, he argued, could also be slowly mainstreamed into the "modern" normality of Constancia.

Emplaced Race

Besides representing San Antón as dangerous, "backward," and different from the "mainstream," people also distinguished Constancia from San Antón in terms of race. In formal conversations, however, this distinction was rarely made by calling the barrio *negro* (black) explicitly. Rather, people spoke of *bomba* and *plena*, "traditions," or "deep cultural roots," or used other racially oriented terms that indirectly suggested blackness. For example, one of my neighbors—an English teacher and father of four—compared San Antón to the color of his dark brown pants when talking to two Italian tourists who were visiting me. He said, "In Puerto Rico everybody is mixed. You can see that down there [*pointing to San Antón*] there are about three hundred people who are of 'this color' [*pointing to his dark pants*], and here [*meaning Constancia*] there is everything. And here, in my house, we are of all colors, there are *prietos* [blacks] of my color."

Then Rita, his wife, jested—"*prietas rubias*" (blond blacks) as she laughed at her self-description. (Her hair was dyed blond and she often changed her haircolor.)[5]

During the conversation, Tavín described me as blond, and I added that I was *jabá* (roughly translated as "high yellow"). Tavín, however, disagreed with my self-description, because according to him *jabá* meant "black," and I was not black. He said, "Because you don't have the lips nor the nose that go all the way to over here"—and he made a wide-open gesture with his hand. "Because there are people that *are* black even if they are of your color." He used his father as an example, saying to my Italian friends that his father had light skin like me and *el pelo malo* (bad hair). Then I said in a pedagogical tone, "*Rizo*" (curly), to call attention to the pejorative connotation of the term *bad hair*. Rita looked at Tavín and said in a teasing tone: "*Rizo*, Tavín, *rizo* . . . learn!" Tavín obediently replied in a litany, "*Rizo*," but later turned to me and said, "No, but he had bad hair, you know," and he made a claw-like gesture placing his hands above his hair. He said his mother, on the other hand, was *prieta como yo, pero con el pelo lacio, lacio como ella* (black like me [i.e., like Tavín] but with straight hair, straight like hers [one of the Italian tourists]).

Discrepancies such as this are frequent in Puerto Rico and elsewhere in the Caribbean and Latin America, as people assign different meanings to the same racial term or change classifications depending on their interpretation of hair texture and other features that can sometimes override skin-tone as criteria (Wade 1993; Godreau 2008b; Lancaster 1991; Alexander 1977; Drummond 1980; Harris 1970; Hoetink 1985; Khan 1993; Sanjek 1971; Skidmore 1974). Hence, even though I preferred the term *jabá*, Tavín disagreed because I did not have enough black phenotypic features to qualify as black, just my curly hair, which according to him did not have the tightness of the coils needed to warrant calling someone *jabao* or *jabá*.[6] Hence, I might have *pelo rizo*, but his father, who was really *jabao*, had "*pelo malo*."

Such terms and their specificities are as commonplace as the taken-for-granted racial hierarchies that make people interpret black features as ugly or "bad." And while terms with clear pejorative connotations like *pelo malo* are used naturally as descriptors, the term *negro* is avoided. For these same reasons, people often use euphemisms such as *de color* (colored) or *trigueño*[7] (brown), or alternative terms such as *prieto* to soften the taken-for-granted negative connotation of *negro*.[8] People also stammer, laugh, hesitate, or look for comparisons in the dark colors of clothing or in the complexion of someone present in order to avoid the stigma and the social hazards of describing someone as black (Godreau 2008b). In this case, Tavín's explanation to my Italian friends about San Antón did not explicitly name the community as "black" but effectively located it on the extreme pole of a color continuum, similar to the color of his dark brown pants. Meanwhile, he positioned Constancia as mixed and diverse—just like his family.

I often came across similar descriptions that distinguished San Antón from the racial "standard" of other neighborhoods considered more "mixed." For example, the day after the Million Man March organized by Louis Farrakhan to call attention to the economic and social problems black men face in the United States (the march was held October 16, 1995), I asked an older man sitting in the plaza if he thought a similar civil rights event could take place in Puerto Rico. According to him, that could never happen because *los puertorriqueños no son de color* (Puerto Ricans aren't colored). "We're eighty percent white... Where do you find blacks? In San Antón, it's the only place," he said.

As inaccurate as this man's remark might seem, his depiction of Puerto Ricans as being 80 percent white was supported by the 2000 census results, in which only 8 percent of Puerto Ricans declared themselves black, while an overwhelming majority, 80.5 percent, identified as white only—a percentage that surpasses the number of people classified as white in the United States by 5.4 percent (U.S. Census Bureau 2000b, 2000e).[9] Such results evidence the social currency of the ideology of *blanqueamiento* (whitening) and the erasure of African ancestry in everyday identification practices across all of Puerto Rico (Franco Ortiz 2010; Rodríguez 2008).[10]

Practices of racial identification in Ponce were similar to those reported for the Island, as a majority of residents there, 83.6 percent, identified themselves as white, while 5.3 percent identified as black (U.S. Census Bureau 2000c). Results, however, vary considerably when comparing San Antón to Constancia. While 91 percent of residents in Constancia identified themselves as white in 2000 (n = 2,479), only 24 percent of residents in San Antón classified themselves as such (n = 73). Similarly, while only 5 percent of Constancia residents classified themselves as black (n = 139), 65 percent of San Antón residents classified themselves as black (n = 201) (U.S. Census Bureau 2000a). This does not mean, however, that "blackness" was unambiguously affirmed in San Antón. Just as the man I interviewed in Ponce's plaza referred to San Antón as the only black community in Puerto Rico, some residents in San Antón referred to one specific family in the community as "*los negros*," as if this were the only black family there. Others located blackness somewhere else, beyond San Antón. As a middle-aged woman from the community told me: "The majority of people here in San Antón are not *black* black. We are mixed. If you want to study black people, you should go to Loíza, *ahí sí que son bien negritos* (people are really black there)."

Of course, not everyone in the community agreed with this characterization. Doña Judith Cabrera, a tall, black, slender woman in her sixties, was a community leader and retired nurse who openly affirmed her identity and her barrio's as black. "*Ponce*," she often told me, "*es una ciudad clasista, elitista, y racista y San Antón es un barrio de gente pobre y de gente negra*" (Ponce is a classist, elitist, and racist city, and San Antón is a barrio of poor and black folk). Doña Judith's daughter, Maria Judith (the teacher I quoted about growing up in San Antón), also described herself as *negra* and disliked it when people called her *trigueña*. She knew people used *trigueño* as a euphemistic term for black and said she refused to be whitened that way.

However, such manifestations of black pride were not the norm during the time of my fieldwork. Instances when residents expressed an internalized sense of inferiority, claiming to be ugly, stupid, or less fortunate (often in the form of jokes) because of their blackness were not uncommon.[11] In contrast, residents frequently praised family members who had features such as light skin, light-colored eyes, or straight hair. I also heard young community residents mock neighbors they disliked by referring to them as members of "the African bunga-bunga tribe" to mean they were stupid, ugly, or aggressive. Similarly, I heard the phrase "African style" used in a joking sense by a young man to describe burned and overtly salty foods. Analogous self-deprecating dynamics of racial identity have been documented in other communities in Puerto Rico known for their "blackness" (see Hernández-Hiraldo 2006a; Lloréns 2008).

On the other hand, as evident in later chapters, residents also spoke of the power of ancestors, their mythical musical or culinary abilities, and a sense of solidarity, or they described a personal strength derived from having to confront difficulties or discrimination as positive qualities legitimized by their belonging to this barrio of emblematic blackness. However, to overrate the power of those moments would underestimate the power of collective forms of internalized oppression that reproduce systems of social inequality (Pyke 2010, 552) not just in San Antón, but across the Americas. Expecting residents of San Antón to proudly and consistently claim a black or Afro–Puerto Rican identity would assume such forms of internalized oppression are easily overcome. And as Maria Judith's interview evidenced, they aren't. The expectation of people upholding a black identity would also ignore the heavy weight of historical dynamics in Puerto Rico that for centuries rejected the self-embracement of blackness as a public strategy of self-identification or of political organizing in the Island (Rodríguez-Silva 2012; Guerra 1998). Moreover, it would deny the powerful hold that historically informed ideologies of *blanqueamiento* and government-sanctioned celebrations of mixture have on personal strategies of self-identification here or elsewhere in Puerto Rico. Because of the hold of such ideologies, San Antón is either pushed toward the margins of the modern nation as "traditional" and "unique," or placed at the bottom of the social hierarchy of urban living in Puerto Rico for being "violent and dangerous." Either way, the barrio was essentialized as black vis-à-vis the normalcy of other places considered "more mixed" and representative of contemporary Puerto Rico, like Constancia. With this context in mind, one can better assess residents' understandable irritation with outsiders' representation of the community as homogeneously black and "less mixed" than the rest of Puerto Rico.

The Historic Zone of Ponce

Both Urbanización Constancia and the barrio of San Antón formed part of an intricate urban grid in Ponce composed of thirty-one barrios, eighty-nine upper- and middle-class housing complexes, and twenty-four public-housing projects.[12] San Antón residents—whether employed in the service sector, unemployed, or retired—navigated this landscape daily by public transportation or car. Highways, government offices, and a variety of local and North American–owned businesses are part of the city scene. Options at the time of my fieldwork ranged from local *fondas* or *cafeterías* where one can have rice and beans for lunch, to megastores such as Builder's Square and Kmart. Well-known Puerto Rican public and private university campuses and museums also form part of Ponce's greater urban area.

At the heart of this urban mesh is the town's *plaza*, with its commercial and residential surroundings. Established in 1670, the general urban contours of this Historic Square are like those of other towns built under Spanish rule in the Americas. The main plaza is surrounded by public and private buildings that include the cathedral, the mayor's office, tourist shops, and fast-food restaurants. A noteworthy historic firehouse from the late nineteenth century, painted in bright red and

Figures 2a, 2b, 2c, 2d. Aristocratic residences of Ponce's Historic Zone. Photos by author.

black stripes, dominates the plaza and is often visited by tourists. One can also find a variety of local and U.S. businesses, banks, stores, and museums such as the Ponce History Museum. Many of the structures of the historic zone display elaborate detail in their neoclassical architecture, infusing the city with a "dignified" air of past prosperity. (See Figures 2a, 2b, 2c, and 2d.[13])

At the time of my fieldwork, tour guides left Ponce's central plaza regularly to take visitors on a free trolley ride along Ponce's most noteworthy sites. No trolleys, however, ever went to San Antón. References to the African constituents of Ponce were only marginally incorporated in touristic representations of the city, relegated to the realm of *carnaval*, music, dance, and rhythm. This quote from a tourist brochure is a telling example:

> Ponce, the Southern Pearl, has been historically denominated as the Aristocratic City [Ciudad Señorial] because of the beauty of its residential architecture, the neoclassical pride of the cathedral's towers, the magic of the lion's fountain, and the graceful seriousness of its public buildings. Ponce is a city with a European touch facing the warm waters of the Caribbean Sea under a tropical, shining blue sky. Ponce was the meeting place for the immigrants, namely British, French, Italian, German, Spaniard, who with a vision of [the] future created an community open to the rest of the world, delineating the destiny of the country. That heritage was enriched with the Africans' legacy. The music, the beliefs and personality of black [sic] add taste, color, and rhythm to the culture of Ponce. (Gobierno Municipal Autónomo de Ponce, 1995[14])

This characterization of Ponce's African heritage informed the folkloric (non-modern) script against which Ponce's government charted its "preservationist" agenda for the San Antón housing project. That notion, like other scripts documented throughout this book, also became intensely contested.

Statehood Housing / Commonwealth Housing

Everyone who talked about pre-1950s San Antón spoke of a vast area. In the years that followed, the construction of a river canal and three bordering highways, the establishment of Urbanización Constancia, and the rise of electrical energy facilities turned that vast sector into a smaller, subdivided community. Government agencies expropriated land from residents, forcing them to move elsewhere, severing their family and community support networks. Those who managed to stay lived in poor housing conditions and could not enjoy the benefits available to those who now occupied the new cement houses of the adjacent *urbanización*.

In the late 1970s and then again in 1984, residents from San Antón organized to deter this trend and demand better housing and living conditions from the government. Doña Judith Cabrera (the retired nurse who openly asserted her black identity) played a key role. She had been politically active in the ranks of the Popular Democratic Party (the commonwealth party) and thus knew about benefits of community organizing: "*Hay unas cosas que hay que bregarlas con el colectivo*" (Some things have to be dealt with by the collective), she said. This kind of militancy and keen social outlook helped her in leading the Comité Pro Conservación y Mejoramiento del Barrio de San Antón (Committee for the Conservation and Improvement of the Barrio of San Antón) along with other women from the barrio who were—as she put it—"*guerrilleras como yo*" (guerrilla fighters like me). Musicians and community leaders also joined in the struggle by launching the Fiestas of Bomba and Plena in 1978, which brought broader attention to the importance of the community's permanence in Ponce's landscape.

Doña Judith recalled those days with a mixture of rage and enthusiasm since, as a result of their initiative and public pressure, the then-mayor of Ponce, Joselín Tormos-Vega (a statehood supporter), made a political promise to construct new housing in San Antón. However, although a housing plan was designed, the promise was not carried out until much later. It took fifteen years and different political leadership for that promise to be honored. Doña Judith explained that the reason for the delay was ex-mayor Joselín Tormos-Vega's involvement in financial scandal and his later conviction for extortion. She recalls that she confronted him. With open eyes and pointing her finger directly at me, she performed the gestures she had used then, when she told him, "Joselín Tormos-Vega, I'm going to tell you something, you might leave us living like animals, here in San Antón, but I guarantee you that you're going to die in jail, for being a thief. I guarantee it *como que aquí"*—and she showed me the long palm of her open hand—*"no me crecen pelos* [like hairs don't grow here, on the palms of my hands]." A few months later, Tormos-Vega was arrested and jailed, and all plans for housing improvements in San Antón were halted.

Rehabilitation plans for San Antón resumed in the 1990s under the leadership of a different municipal administration and political party in Ponce: the Partido Popular, or commonwealth party. Ideological differences between this party and the previous pro-statehood administration need to be noted, because they influenced housing plans in San Antón. In distinguishing themselves from pro-statehooders, commonwealthers or *populares* often present themselves as the "upholders" of Puerto Rican culture and traditions. This defense of Island culture translates into discursive principles that reject elements of traditional nationalism such as a radical condemnation of U.S. imperialism and the claim for political independence but maintain and uphold ideals of "nationalist pride" through the cultural affirmation of those "things" (i.e., hospitality, music, folk art, food, language, ways of being, traditions) that supposedly distinguish Puerto Ricans from U.S. North Americans (Duany 2002; Dávila 1997).

Although the pro-statehood party also makes use of this friendly nationalism or colonial nationalism, their accent on Puerto Ricanness highlights concepts of unity, "progress," and "economic development" as goals that will be achieved through statehood. Accordingly, they often place the accent on the United States side of the United States/Puerto Rican formula of national affirmation. Consequently, commonwealth politicians often construe their difference with pro-statehooders by referring to a controversy between "those who affirm Puerto Rican culture and those who do not."

These ideological differences between statehooders and commonwealthers manifested themselves in the housing project of San Antón through two proposals. The original proposal, backed by statehood supporters in Ponce, emphasized the idea of "progress" and Puerto Rico's integration into the United States. This proposal supported the integration of the barrio into the surrounding middle-class neighborhoods and recommended that houses be built of cement.[15] In this proposal, houses also followed a linear arrangement, similar to the "modern" setup of *urbanizaciones* like Constancia. (See Figure 3.[16])

A second proposal, championed by the commonwealth party administration, conceived of a housing project of wooden houses arranged according to a pattern that resembles "traditional *patios*" of San Antón (see Figure 4). A *patio*, roughly defined, is a small plot of land owned and occupied by members of the same family in which different houses share an internal common area or areas. A representation of some of the *patios* in San Antón can be appreciated in Figure 4 and in Figures 5a, 5b, 5c.[17] Approximately 68 percent of families in San Antón were established in this arrangement at the time the housing project was proposed.[18] *Patios* varied

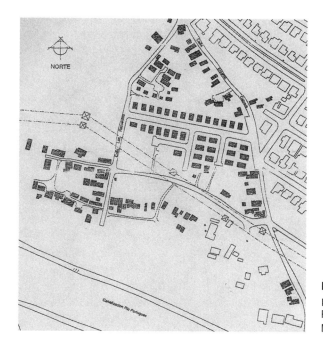

Figure 3. Linear housing proposal (1994). Source: Ponce Municipal Government, Mayor's Housing Office.

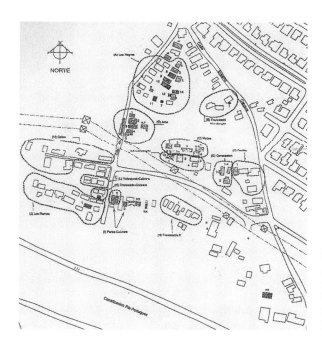

Figure 4. Sketch of family *patios* before the housing project was developed (1994). Source: Ponce Municipal Government, Mayor's Housing Office.

Figures 5a–5c. Views of family *patios* in San Antón before the housing project. Photos by author.

in shape and composition, the smallest made up of three persons and the biggest of approximately fifty-seven.[19] Generally, *patios* were referred to by the name of the family who occupied them (for example, the *patio* of the Franchesci or *patio* Arce).

The commonwealth housing proposal adopted this idea of the *patio* as an organizing principle for the spatial distribution of living units in the new development, providing a common green area in the center to be used by the extended family (see Figure 6).[20] Other elements of the commonwealth proposal (such as the architectural and lighting designs for the houses) were intended to give San Antón's housing project an air of "historicity."

Before the actual implementation of the housing project took place, these contrasting pro-statehood and commonwealth views on how to revitalize San Antón were the object of bureaucratic power disputes. Finally, the commonwealth administration won the battle, and their proposal received the preliminary green light from the *municipio*'s permit office to begin building forty-one units in the central area of the community.[21] The permit office stated that "the concept presented is in harmony with the planning objectives for recognizing the existing family structures, creating new blocks defined on the exterior by vehicular pathways and defining its milieu by internal pedestrian semi-public spaces destined to reorganize family life in 'patio' formation, thus respecting the lived culture of the barrio."[22]

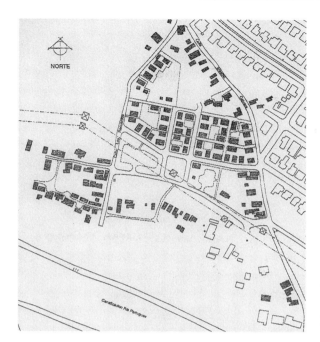

Figure 6. Commonwealth Government's Housing Proposal (1994). Source: Ponce Municipal Government, Mayor's Housing Office.

The plan was also approved for funding by the corresponding U.S. federal funding agencies (HUD and Section 108 LGA). This irony of funding *la puertorriqueñidad* with federal money, however, was only one of the many negotiations that took place in a process of "exalting San Antón's heritage."

The Housing Project: A Preservationist Proposal

When the final proposal for the housing project was approved in 1995, it received coverage in the national media (Puerto Rico) and the local media (Ponce) as an innovative step to preserve this famous barrio. Headlines covering the housing project spoke of Puerto Rican culture, *bomba* and *plena,* and the preservation of this barrio's "sacred roots" (Millán-Pabón 1995, 5). In an interview for a major newspaper, Ponce's mayor Rafael Cordero-Santiago said, "The facades of the houses will be from the last century. They will be structures of wood, with peaked roofs and wood columns in the porches with casement windows with lattices and carefully maintained details . . . The rehabilitation will respect the *patios* of [various families] . . . as well as some trees where people used to gather, and still gather, to sing the *bomba* and the *plena*. This is important due to the cultural influences it brings. This barrio has had great laborers, great artisans, and great athletes that have brought enormous prestige to our city (Millán-Pabón 1995, 5).[23]

From the government's point of view, the above-mentioned *patios* were both a captivating and a problematic feature of the community. They were captivating because they told a story about a past era and family values. *Patios* in San Antón typify settlement among the poor peasantry in the 1900s in Puerto Rico, a pattern also documented among the emancipated peasantry of the English Caribbean as "family land" (Besson 1984a). In the Hispanic Caribbean, a *patio* is legally defined as a *sucesión* (González Tejera 2001) or tenancy in common (Crump et al. 2004), where land is inherited from the original first generation and all family members are entitled to ownership of the land. Although much had changed in San Antón since the 1900s, *patios* in the 1990s were still a reference point for community members.

Patios had other positive qualities for the liberal architects and city planners in charge, who sought to keep family groups together as a first priority. Structurally, *patios* add an outdoor dimension to homes. They are designed to facilitate bonding, support, and socializing among family members and friends. Outdoor spaces located in between houses are often swept, cleaned, and kept regularly just as if they were another living room. Although some *patios* are accessible to pedestrians, these spaces are considered private. An outsider is not supposed to "walk right in." These spaces are also gendered, as it is often women who adorn and maintain them regularly.

For all these reasons, the explicit attempt to follow the model of San Antón *patios* was heralded in the press as an effort that would preserve the community's essence. However, *patios* were also problematic from the government's point of view for various reasons. First of all, the clustered arrangement of houses made access for fire trucks and ambulances troublesome and in some cases impossible. The nonlinear setup of houses also complicated the establishment of underground infrastructure for water pipes, electricity, and cable TV. A mere renovation of the houses might have solved problems with individual residences, but according to the government this strategy would have left intact the problems of access and infrastructure. Another setback to renovating houses as they were was the fact that not all residents owned the land on which their homes lay. This land-ownership factor prevented the government from making a permanent investment in housing facilities, since landowners could ask residents to leave at any time. Furthermore, there was the issue of titling. Legal stipulations in Puerto Rico do not require that residents who inherit family land have formal land titles in order to claim ownership.[24] But the issue of who was a rightful heir of the family plot was not always clear-cut or easy to interpret (for similar land-titling issues in Latin America, see Ward et al. 2011). To solve the issues associated with clustering, uneven land ownership, and what the government perceived as clouded land titles; the government planned to buy the land of three *sucesiones* from residents and parcel it into individually owned plots. They would then sell those plots and the new houses to

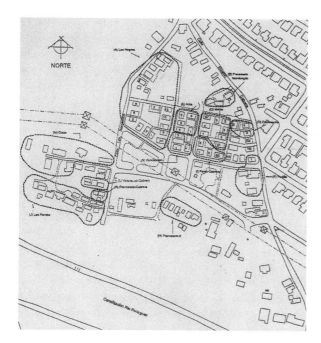

Figure 7. Sketch of planned *patio* reconfigurations (1994). Source: Ponce Municipal Government, Mayor's Housing Office.

previous residents and heads of households at a subsidized price.[25] Because residents would be placed next to their kin in the new arrangement, the government claimed they were respecting the *patios*. Yet the project did not maintain but rather re-created the *patio* format, under a different individual tenancy format that placed individually owned housing units of kin members who previously belonged to the *sucesión* next to the individually owned houses of kin members from the same family. In fact, the initial plan provided a tentative assignment of blocks for each family as in the proposal shown in Figure 7.[26] Hence, houses in the new development were not to be built on the land of the *sucesión*, but on single plots that would be individually owned by particular family members. New houses were planned with frontal access to the street and a back door facing a common green area in the center. This common area and the houses surrounding it in block formation were to be occupied by members of the same extended family.

The creator of this new design is an architect who moved to Puerto Rico from Europe in 1992. For him, the extended-family living arrangement of the *patio* was telling of San Antón's African heritage:

> I see it in terms of the barrio's urban organization: how the houses are organized, how the family has characteristics that are essentially more African than Latin [*sic*], and this is apart from any influences that it has received from outside. The African

culture is ... ah ... the Puerto Rican culture is clearly there also, but it's the [African] one that predominates and so ... it seems to me ... I see it as a foreigner, I guess. I came to this barrio about four years ago ... and it seems to me like something totally distinct within Puerto Rico ... and that's the way I keep trying to see it today ... We know that, in San Antón, people are not just individuals, but that they are family. There are *patios* that have twenty-two or twenty-three family members together, fifteen, sometimes ten, five. And so we are going to try as much as we can to not separate big family groups.

Because the plan sought to reproduce, at least formally, the principle of connectivity and communal interaction, plots were not fenced. In fact, the project contemplated a series of semipublic corridors that connected yards and streets. In their goal of keeping the families together and not further subdividing the barrio, the government also avoided the need to relocate residents elsewhere while the project was under construction.[27]

The implementation of this complex initiative required a tenacious approach on the part of young architects, planners, and administrative officials. This staff, described by a Smithsonian journalist as a "savvy meticulous and driven group" (Jolee 1994, 64), had to maneuver around various financial and political obstacles to get the project going. For example, constructing wooden houses required some out-of-the-ordinary procedures, because federal regulations require that construction in low-income housing in hurricane-prone areas be done in cement. Still, the director of the Housing and Communal Development Office explained in a July 1996 interview, "I managed to get some 'waivers,' and that's because they normally don't allow the investment of federal funds in wooden houses, but because of the barrio's typical nature, we succeeded in getting their approval for this project. The normal thing is for it to be done in cement, if you are going to invest federal funds, and here, well, they allowed it.... That has been the priority of the municipality's administration, to maintain the barrio just as it was in its origins."

Other aspects characterize this "historical" or traditional orientation, such as the protection of fifty trees in the community, the use of historical lampposts, and a housing design that resembled the smaller houses of the Historic Zone. Finally, the mayor mentioned tourism as a positive asset of the project: "We are almost in the last phase of the project that will start with the first forty houses that will be constructed here, in the barrio of San Antón, respecting the idiosyncrasy, the history, and the culture of San Antón. So that in the tourist maps, people can come from this side or from the other and see San Antón again."

However, despite the mayor's emphasis on tourism, at the time it was not clear when or if the stated plans for tourist visits would be implemented. According to a tourist official in Ponce whom I interviewed, there were no concrete proposals to bring tourists to San Antón. More than a decade after her statement, San Antón is still not included in the twenty-nine tourist sites marked in Ponce's official tourist map. (See Municipio de Ponce 2010a.) As Arlene Dávila (2004) notes, while current tourism depends on the uniqueness of places, those spaces must also be seen as safe, comfortable, and entertaining (62). The concomitant construction of San Antón as a place of "modern/urban blackness" and all the associated stereotypes of violence, hypersexuality, and backwardness addressed by Cuto Colón and Maria Judith in their interview also affected the rentability of its folkloric culture. In addition, the commodification of culture for tourism requires, as Philip Scher notes, "the regulation of human activity to shape it into recognizable, repeatable and saleable forms" (2011, 18). But beyond the music festivals, there has been no state intervention to actively promote or ensure the commodification of expressive forms in San Antón. Hence, even when Ponce was trying to exalt its cultural uniqueness and heritages, not all types of culture (even folkloric ones) were equally profitable or economically viable for tourism there. More than tourism, the project responded to residents' pleas for better housing, to the cultural nationalism invigorated by Ponce's regional economic development plan, and to the electoral politics of the time. In that context, the mayor's mention of tourism in his speech is better understood as an idiom of populist praise and inclusion of the community into Ponce's overall plans for tourism. It was a means to exalt San Antón's cultural significance, locally and through the press, in front of an *imagined* national and transnational visiting audience that would rarely make it to San Antón.

Residents' Responses

How did San Antón residents interpret the local commonwealth government's preservationist intent and rehabilitation plans? This question was not seriously taken into consideration by the local government until after they initiated the actual construction of the houses. Before that, personnel from the *municipio* interviewed residents and conducted a detailed study of the housing conditions, spatial distribution of familial settlements, and ecological resources such as trees. Yet no details were offered as to how the project was to be implemented.

In 1994, while arrangements to buy land from absentee land owners in San Antón were taking place, the director of the Housing Office stated in the local newspaper, "As soon as we have a confirmation that those land lots belong to the Municipality of Ponce, we shall initiate a series of orientation talks for residents" (Ortiz 1994a, 12).[28] Those orientations did not take place until the day before initiating construction of the housing project: March 14, 1996. Only then did the mayor address the residents of San Antón to explain details of the project:

Good evening, fellow *ponceños* of the famous barrio of San Antón . . . The sector of San Antón has deep historic and cultural roots in the City of Ponce and in Puerto Rico. It has been the birthplace of successful Puerto Rican athletes and artists. It also possesses some natural and social attributes that deserve to be preserved in order to perpetuate the continuous social contribution that this sector and its residents have made throughout the history of Puerto Rico. With the purpose of achieving this goal of social, historical, and cultural preservation, the Autonomous Municipality of Ponce has undertaken the task of creating a novel concept and sold it to the federal [U.S.] government so that it may help us with what we are commencing here today.

After describing the efforts of the local government with corresponding federal agencies to get the project going, the mayor proclaimed: "*¡Ahora sí que estas tierras van a ser de ustedes ahora sí!*" (Now is when these lands are really going to be yours, now!)

In these and other government statements, municipal authorities kept emphasizing that the project would allow residents to become rightful owners of their property by providing them titles that could be recorded in the Registro de la Propiedad Municipal (the Property Registry).[29] Yet under Puerto Rico's civil code, such recorded titles are not required to claim property ownership; not even a formal will is necessary.[30]

When the mayor opened the floor for questions, various residents challenged the assumptions of his last statement regarding land ownership. One woman, for example, asked:

RESIDENT: If I have a house with a *patio*, why should I have to pay for a new house?
MAYOR: Because the land isn't yours and the house is new . . .
  Before he could finish the sentence the woman yelled, upset:
RESIDENT: Yes it is; the land is ours, it's ours!
MAYOR: Well, we're going to credit it to the house's account. But we're thinking of all of San Antón, not just of a single person. We're thinking of how this barrio, in all its extent, is turned into something adequate and beautiful and a place that tourists may visit.

Other questions posed to the mayor evidenced the lack of information that the government had given to residents. What would happen to people who depend on welfare? How would they pay? How would the actual distribution of land and housing change in the new setup? What would happen to the *patio* members who don't want to sell their land? What would happen to the people who live in San Antón Arriba (the sector cut off by the highway)? What would happen to the businesses? How long would the project take?

As the mayor answered these and other questions, he emphasized that each case would be dealt with individually. Finally, he asked for cooperation from all the residents by appealing to their common origin in Ponce as a regional identity that could surpass all personal and political differences: "Let's start with the premise that we are all *ponceños* and we need each other ... Let it be clear that that's all I ask ... I don't want political interventions in this project. Everybody here can vote for whomever they please, that's the prerogative of each and every one of you; nobody has to ask you. And if anyone does ask, you call me and let me know immediately!"

Implementation and Contestation

A week after the mayor spoke, construction began and some residents were hired to work at the site. For the next couple of weeks, everything went well, but by April 1996 (six months before elections), discontent among residents was obvious. The foundations of twenty-four new houses had taken shape, and the scant space for each and for the space between houses was noticeable, as illustrated in Figures 8a and 8b.[31] "They say that this is an *arrabal* [slum]," commented Marta from the porch of her wooden house, "but what they're building there is just another one: a modern *arrabal*." Besides criticizing the new houses for their size and for the proximity between each unit, residents criticized their high cost and wood construction. "Why move from one wooden house into another wooden house?" said Elisa. "All governments deceive the poor," said Evelyn while I paid for a soda at her small store. "I might be stupid, but everybody knows when they are being deceived." "We have the right to protest, Isar," said María while I walked with her to the elementary

Figures 8a, 8b. Houses under construction. The base was in cement; the small structure showing over the base is the bathroom. Photos by author.

school. "The majority of the people are against that project. The social workers don't give any information. How am I going to throw away everything I have to live uncomfortably?!" Residents also complained about the uncertainty of not knowing what would happen to their property: Could they choose not to participate in the project? Would the government expropriate their land if they refused to sell? If they moved, next to whom would they live? These questions remained unanswered. Other factors, such as the lack of parking space for a car or for cultivating plants, figured in the long list of complaints.

In the process of voicing these complaints, the heterogeneity of San Antón became evident as residents proposed alternatives. Arcenia, for example, favored a linear setup similar to that in Constancia and more "modern" urban neighborhoods. Armando, like many other *patio* owners, thought the best solution was to leave houses where they were and give each household money to fix them as they pleased. This was not, however, a viable option for the government. To make home ownership viable for everyone, they needed to relocate housing units in a uniform arrangement and homogenize the status of land tenure. Guillo, owner of the convenience store, agreed with Armando, but to deal with the dilemma of those who were not landowners, he suggested the municipal government build new houses on an empty lot adjacent to his store. Cari, another resident, said the government should do what they had done before and give money to residents so they could move from San Antón and buy a house in an *urbanización* elsewhere.

Despite different opinions, the general consensus among residents was that this was not the housing project they had hoped for. Even old-timer baseball player David, someone I never heard complain, said, "Those houses are a scam!" And while he looked toward the construction site from his usual afternoon bench he added, "¡*Aquí se va a formar un revolú!*" (This is gonna cause an uproar!)

It was not long before a group of residents formed the Comité Pro Defensa del Barrio San Antón (Committee for San Antón's Defense) to voice community concerns about the project and negotiate terms of the project with government officials. The Comité was composed of an accountant, a businessman, two housewives, one young man who worked for the local commonwealth government, and nine locals, among them a woman who identified with the pro-independence nationalist movement. The president, Guillo, owned a convenience store and favored statehood. The vice president of the group, Jaime, was a commonwealth supporter. He lived in a cement house, and so did most of the members of his *patio*. Other members of the Comité lived in wooden houses. Some of them owned land in San Antón. Others did not but believed the new houses were too small. Most of them lived in San Antón, except Guillo, the president of the Comité, who formed part of a *sucesión* but lived in another neighborhood. According to him, the government was treating San Antón residents like animals: "What they want to do is build a fence and corner us like animals. *Vamos a formarla grande* [We're going to make a lot of noise], we're going to call the news, if necessary. We are not going to allow them to knock us down. We do not live in one of those republics where people and governors do as they please. We live in a democratic country."

Guillo's reference to those "republics" resonates with a commonsense notion about corruption in sovereign countries in the Caribbean or in Third World nations (i.e., "those republics") whose political leaders cannot be criticized publicly. As a supporter of statehood for Puerto Rico, Guillo believed that because Puerto Rico is part of the United States, Puerto Rican people have democratic protections that people in other independent countries don't have.

In the spirit of democracy and in exercise of the freedom of public speech available in the modern U.S. colony of Puerto Rico, Guillo and other members of the Comité wrote to the mayor, sent out flyers throughout the community, and convened at the basketball court to discuss the project. I was impressed by the large number of people who attended, young and old. On the court, members of the Comité officially opened the meeting. Quique proclaimed loudly:

> *Estamos en el medio del océano y necesitamos la militancia de ustedes* [We're in the middle of the ocean and we need your militancy]. They want us to unilaterally accept the project, in a dictatorial manner. We are not going to let them take away our properties. They want to fence us in as if this were an Indian reservation. Like the Americans did with the Indians.

After formally introducing the members of the Comité to the community, Jaime, the vice president, began the meeting with this prayer:

> *Padre, perdónanos por ser más imperfectos, quizás más oscurecidos. Padre pero ilumínanos, danos sabiduría y perdona nuestras imperfecciones...* [Father, forgive us for being more imperfect, maybe darker. But father, enlighten us, give us wisdom, and forgive us our imperfections...].

When Jaime ended his prayer, Lolita (the Comité artisan who identified with the nationalist pro-independence movement) proclaimed: "We are meeting to defend our rights, which belong to us by the law of God and men." She spoke of the government's false promises, and critical comments followed from the audience. One woman questioned the government's approach of asking only certain residents to sell their land and move into the new wooden structures, while other residents had previously received permission to build in cement. She finalized her critique of unequal treatment by saying, "*¿O tó' blancos, o tó' prietos, qué es lo que pasa?*" (Either we're all whites, or we're all blacks, what's going on here?). With this saying, she meant to underline that either all residents should have privileges (as whites would), or no one should have them (as blacks wouldn't). By targeting only certain areas and households within San Antón, the project thus exacerbated previously existing racial and class inequalities among residents.

Another woman raised her voice to say that the mayor had promised to preserve the *patios*, "but what we're seeing is something else." Jaime added: "History is not fabricated. History makes itself. You can't plan culture. And it can't be that you come and build different houses from the ones we have always had."

Jaime, like most of the members of his *patio*, owned a cement house and family land. For other residents, who did not own land or cement houses, the project represented an improvement to their current situation. Hence they emphasized that they were not against the project per se but against the manner in which the government had handled it. Thus the Comité announced that there was no going back on their protest. *"Vamos a tener que piquetear"* (We're going to have to go to the picket lines). "Are you all in favor?" they asked everyone present "Those in favor, stand up." Despite their different positions, housing situations, and preferred alternatives, almost everyone present stood up.

Before the meeting ended, Lolita announced that in the following days a TV and radio crew would come to the community to interview residents about the housing project. She said: "Those that know anything about Areyto (Taíno Indian festivity), they're going to form a small Areyto group . . . The people who know how to dance, play, and do anything related to roots, it is crucial that they be there. San Antón refuses to disappear!"

Within two weeks, the community was meeting in front of TV cameras and radio reporters to make their concerns about the housing project public. The president of the Comité explained their plea to one radio reporter in the following way: "We are owners of the land that we live on. They intend to expropriate the land and the homes, businesses won't work either. To then make us . . . because it's been done arbitrarily and unilaterally, to make us contract an unwanted debt . . . What's happening here is that due to a lack of information, uncertainty reigns."

Regarding the issue of historical preservation, the Comite's vice president told the reporter, "This is simple—in other words, you can't move history from its place. History is where things take place. History is born, you can't, for example, make one of the houses that are being built over there and give it to the Franceschi family and then bring the tourist and say, 'This is where Juan Franceschi [the famous athlete] was born.' Juan Fransceschi was born over here. In other words, you can't move history from its place."

After his intervention, the reporter asked about the communal design of the new *patios*. "But what *patios*?" said the vice president. "What *patios*? That's an Indian reservation. In other words, there is no *patio*, Penchi [nickname], there is no *patio*."

Of Racial Scripts and Nation

Scholars interested in the social construction of nations have argued that the collection and rescuing of traditions, whether real or invented, is a prevailing nation-building practice (Bendix 1997; Hobsbawn and Ranger 1983; Handler 1988). Virginia Domínguez (1986, 550) suggests that all traditions are in fact inventions motivated by the desire to find legitimacy through history. This is because history is often constructed as a narrative of truth (Price 1998; Trouillot 1995; Yelvington et al. 2002). Néstor García-Canclini has linked such validating processes to elite readings of folklore, arguing that one reason those in power show interest in "popular traditions" is to strengthen their legitimacy to rule (1989, 194). In places like Puerto Rico, where national culture may be perceived as threatened by U.S. influence, the showcasing of black folklore can bestow political authority on those who seek to administer the "colonial nation." In that sense, the new *patios* of San Antón reveal more about those who implemented them than about those who occupy them.

However, as mentioned in the introduction, more than folklore, what is also at stake here are the racial scripts of blackness employed to mark San Antón as "singular" and "exceptional." Various elements taken together form the scripts that made blackness palatable in this way. First of all, we have the mobilization of nostalgia and the concomitant erasure of social inequality from the narrative told about San Antón. The controversy over housing showed the inadequacy of an approach that romanticized the community without considering the social relationships of power that shaped it and—more importantly—without discussing its transformations with residents. This intent to salvage "the folkloric traditions" of San Antón in the name of Puerto Rican culture reproduces discourses of authenticity and romance found elsewhere, whenever objectified properties of a nation appear to exist naturally and independently of power relations that mold them and give them significance (Bendix 1997; Handler 1988; Handler and Gable 1997). For the people of San Antón, it was not choice, but rather, need or lack of resources that determined features the government considered typical in this community. Wooden houses, for example, may seem "quaint" to outsiders, but residents may or may not value them. In fact, residents who had sufficient means to fix their houses did so by building new ones in cement.

In addition, the housing project failed to recognize San Antón residents' everyday practices and desires as modern, casting them instead as bearers of unchanging traditions. Ponce's mayor, for example, declared in the newspaper that the rehabilitation of San Antón would preserve the trees where "people used to gather, and still gather, to sing the *bomba* and the *plena*[32] (Millán-Pabón, 1995, 5). However, I did not hear *bomba* and *plena* played or danced in San Antón on a regular basis. Instead, *salsa*, *merengue*, rap, and contemporary pop songs were popular, especially among the youth. Older folks also listened to *boleros* or *música de trío* (*trío* music). *Bomba* and *plena* were genres reserved for performances in which the "outside" community was the main audience (see Chapter 7). Yet after years of cultural and structural transformations, land expropriations, and construction works that surrounded, divided, and significantly reduced the community, the mayor kept emphasizing that the project would enable people and the tourists that never got there to "see San Antón again."

These efforts of rescuing the "traditional" against the backdrop of a modernizing agenda resonates with what Renato Rosaldo describes as "imperialist nostalgia"—a feeling of mourning that colonial agents in a society express for the very forms of life that imperialism has destroyed (1989, 107). He argues such feelings closely relate to secular notions of progress that use "putative static savage societies" as reference points for defining progress and civilized identity. Similarly, Ponce's government's longing to recover a traditional essence in San Antón worked alongside the burden of developing Ponce. However, in this case, the production of this nostalgic nationalism also operates in consonance with ideologies of *blanqueamiento* that represent blackness as a different and vanishing element of Puerto Rican culture. Hence, behind such yearnings to maintain the barrio and its wooden houses as they were lies a longing to recover a black essence whose loss is meaningful only within the context of dominant discourses of *blanqueamiento* that construct whiteness as a mark of modernity and blackness as a singular localized fading element in the "almost white" modern colony-nation.

Another script that complemented this nostalgia was the idea of the harmonious and congruous matriarchal family. Scholars have noted that the institution of family has been peculiarly subject to mystification and as such is often central to discourses of national and cultural identity, a variety of which have been at the forefront of public discussions in Puerto Rico for much of the past century (Scarano and Curtis White 2007, 117; Milanich 2007, 439). In a racial spinoff of this schema, the European designer and architect of the project described the family structure in San Antón as African. After reading my dissertation (Godreau 1999), he clarified that he did not think San Antón's *patios* were of African origins. His perceptions, he said, had more to do with family structure, particularly with the relationship between the *patio* and the extended family. In this posterior interpretation, it was not Africa but the idea of extended kin networks that sustained his reading of San Antón's uniqueness.

A related interpretation, documented in a newspaper article, is that kin networks were gendered, since women, many of whom were prominent community leaders, often headed households. Hence, one journalist described San Antón as "matriarchal" (Mirerza González 1995, S-4) and linked that leadership to the *bomba* and *plena* traditions, reinscribing once again the presence of racialized subjects in this particular place. Certainly, black women in San Antón have played key roles in community struggles as well as in the everyday maintenance of networks and institutions such as the *patio* and exchanges of goods, labor, and emotional support. Yet similar networks of extended kin, often headed by women, can be found throughout Puerto Rico and the Caribbean.[33] The same can be said of the tenure of the *sucesión*. Land ownership patterns like the *patios* of San Antón can be found throughout Puerto Rico in neighborhoods that would not be labeled "black." The racialization of the community of San Antón and its *patios* stands out because "blackness" contributes to the casting of these dynamics as "unique or exotic." The recurrent use of the local term *patio*, instead of the legal, more broadly used term *sucesión*, was one of such discursive mechanisms, since using *sucesión* would have easily connected this land tenancy to similar formats across the Island.

Ironically, residents rarely described their *patios* as "traditional" or "matriarchal," much less as African. *Patios* were in fact rarely mentioned as important objects for my study. Only community spokespeople with links to cultural organizations or the media pointed to them as an issue of interest for my anthropological research. However, as the controversy evidenced, the *sucesiones* were a form of tenancy that residents did value, although not necessarily for the same "exotic" reasons the government did.

In Puerto Rico, land ownership traditionally guaranteed citizenship and was a common indicator of status. Notions of honor, *dignidad*, and work ethics were also closely linked to access to land (Carrasquillo 2006). Yet the government's public policy emphasized the sentimental or socializing aspects of the *patio*, and not the patio as an economic asset. Rather than preserving the *sucesión* tenancy, they focused on "form," charting contiguous living spaces over land that was not owned by the extended family. What is more, the government interpreted this form of tenancy (the *sucesión*) as one that could not guarantee the implementation of "a uniform project that would maintain a planned and organized development" (Cordero-Santiago 1996a). In contrast, they indicated that the new individual titling format would allow residents to become "absolute owners of their property for a moderate monthly payment" of 40 to 75 dollars (Cordero-Santiago 1996a).

Some scholars have argued that this regularization of property titles for de facto owners can increase the exchange value of their property, allowing residents, for example, to use the property as collateral for credit or to ensure a better transfer of the heritance, especially to second and third generations (Ward et al. 2011). Others described similar trends as strategies of multicultural neoliberalism and government decentralization that end up exacerbating communities' marginalization (Hale 2005). But whether these new titles represented an advantage for residents or not, the fact is that the government introduced a different individual land-tenure practice, while simultaneously speaking of "respecting" the *patio* traditions and the barrio's character. In a letter addressed to the community, the mayor indicated that "building in a different way would change the spatial configuration, the history, and it would no longer be San Antón. This configuration was carefully evaluated and revised by the Historic Center Office"[34] (Cordero-Santiago 1996a). Hence, professionals and technocrats, not residents themselves, are entitled to decide how San Antón should really look like in order to "preserve its history."

However, comments voiced by residents speak to the fact that they did not recognize the government's reinvention of the *patio* as their own. Using the same rhetoric of tradition as the government did, leaders of the Comité argued that history was emergent and could not be moved by design. Some residents also feared that new communal areas that the government called *patios* could be used by drug users or dealers. The openness of pathways made them worry about security. Moreover, the open spaces and yards also presupposed agreeable and congruous relations among family members and different family groups, which do not necessarily correspond to the reality of all families in San Antón nor take into account their expressed desire for privacy. Thus, while the government approached San Antón with nostalgic temporal and spatial distance, they expected residents to live in seamless proximity.

Furthermore, residents could not understand why some spaces were "empty" and were not used to build a house instead. During one of the community meetings, one young man and his female neighbor said they were upset with the idea that such spaces could be used as *placitas* (small plazas) by tourists.

> YOUNG MAN: "So that tourists can come in the trolley, sit there and people dance *bomba* and *plena* for them . . . And I don't know what *bomba* and *plena* they're going to get . . . ¡Serán tiros lo que cojan! [What they might get is shot!]"
>
> MARÍA: "So a space that can be used for us is going to be given to them?"
>
> YOUNG MAN: "Imagine those gringos coming here to laugh at us. ¡Qué feos, que salvajes! [How ugly, what savages!]"

Keenly aware of the exotic gaze of others who associate blacks with ugliness and primitiveness, this young man's critique of the *patio-placitas* speaks to the objectification of the community as a place of racial difference. It also contrasts the romanticized, folklorized vision of the government vis-à-vis the modern predicaments of residents' urban condition as signaled by their need to protect themselves against crime or even imagine the possibility of a tourist "getting shot."

All these racial scripts deployed through the housing project reinforced the construction of San Antón as a unique or exceptional community. However, some residents were suspicious or outright offended by this external characterization of San Antón. For example, Victoria, a seventy-year-old member of one of the biggest *patios* in San Antón, said this to me when I asked her if she thought San Antón was special:

I don't know if San Antón is a special community. *Hasta ahí me trajo el río* [That's as much as I can say]. Because I don't know about other places. I know about this one. And what if I say that San Antón is special, and the other places that are special also, what happens to them?

In our interview she also commented:

> I'm bothered by what they said on TV, that we were a *barrio de gente negra* [barrio of blacks]. It may be true that we are *tristes de color* [have a sad color], but to say that we are a *barrio de gente negra*, that word! They could say we are a barrio of people who are *trigueños*, but not to be so rude. We're mixed with African people, but that's going too far. Because there's racism in the U.S., and there's racism in Puerto Rico also. But the type of racism that's coming now is too much. In the old days, people weren't in that thing that "whites this" or "blacks that." Now people say things like that, and they start saying things like "this is a community of *negros*." It is true that we are black, it is true that we are *tristes de color* [have a sad color], but you don't say that word like that.

During our interview, I brought attention to Victoria's description of black as a "sad color," stating that my father was *negro* and that I had never heard anyone use the term *triste de color* before. She said: "As a black woman I feel proud. Blacks are something to be proud of, but that does not mean that other people can behave with such despotism. We know what we are, and that's enough."

Her answer specifies black pride as a viable premise only if generated by someone who is part of the community. The housing project, however, essentialized San Antón's "difference" through national and racialized markers charted by outsiders, without contemplating achievements that residents associated with pride and dignity, such as the *sucesión* or cement houses. Government officials went to great pains, even countering the U.S. federal mandate for cement housing in hurricane zones, to maintain the barrio "just as it was in its origins." Yet, in the context of dominant discourses that devalue and emplace blackness, locating it at the margins of an imagined "mixed" nation, residents like Victoria did not want a housing project that marked the barrio as "black" or "different," especially if that signification involved the government forcing them into small wooden houses.

The Aftermath: Modern Solutions to a Folklorizing State Approach

After San Antón residents organized to make their concerns heard, Ponce's mayor assured them that participation in the project was voluntary and that no one would be forced to sell their *sucesión* or move from their home if they did not want to.

 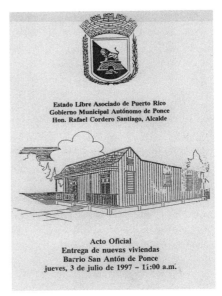

Figures 9a, 9b. Front and back cover of housing inauguration program. Source: Ponce Municipal Government, Mayor's Office.

Members of the Comité Pro-Defensa del Barrio San Antón agreed to these terms, and the president of the Comité participated in the inauguration ceremony.

On July 3, 1997, one year after the controversy, the first twenty-four houses of the project were completed. The program for the official inauguration act included a quote from Ponce's mayor that said: "It was not enough to admire San Antón for its *bomba* and *plena* legacy and for its sportsmen and artists; it was also necessary to meet its needs and share its aspirations. That is what we have done, and that is why we are here (Gobierno Municipal Autónomo de Ponce 1997). What had been language of traditions and sacred roots changed after the controversy to one that recognized needs and expectations for the future (see Figure 9).

Furthermore, once residents mobilized, government officials incorporated some of their demands into future plans for the community. As a result, only some *patios* were sold to the government, while others remained under the ownership of the *sucesión* and did not participate in the housing renovation model. In one case, most members of a *sucesión* moved into the housing project, but the government allowed one man, who refused to move, to stay in his old home. The project was thus not uniformly applied to the whole sector. Also, five new houses were constructed in spaces originally intended for communal use, altering, in some cases, the proposed family-bloc model.

The day after the ceremony, the people I talked with expressed satisfaction. "Now people are going to live decently," said an older resident. No one in the community at that time, however, spoke of the new block arrangement as *patios*. In fact, living arrangements did not replicate the master plan. Members of one family, for example, occupied houses on one block with members of other families scattered throughout. Only three communal areas remained, out of six that were originally envisioned. One of them remained empty. The other two were cultivated, beautified, and claimed by residents as part of "their property." Residents also lobbied to fence their property, and some separated their plots from neighbors and family members. Victoria's household, for instance, took advantage of fencing, but also of the open-yard model. She integrated her plot with her sister's and niece's plots by fencing the three properties off from those of other surrounding households. In this way, they created a communal space, shared by three households, equipped with chairs, swings for grandchildren, plantain trees, and domestic animals.

In a survey I conducted in 2002 among residents of the housing project, 60 percent reported being "very satisfied." Among the advantages listed were living comfortably, having better housing and infrastructure, having family members nearby, and being property owners (45 percent of those who moved to the project were not previous landowners). Ironically, those aspects causing the most dissatisfaction had to do with the reinvention of the *patio* and residences. For example, 73 percent of all residents interviewed said they disliked the fact that properties were unfenced; 65 percent said they disliked the fact that houses were made of wood; and 80 percent of those interviewed expressed dissatisfaction with the walkways that connected streets and properties. The reasons included unwanted noise and disturbance, fear of drug trafficking, and the desire to protect family members against police harassment.

These and other ongoing developments in the community revealed San Antón residents' desire for modernity as inscribed in the claim for privacy, comfort, security, and the clear demarcation of private property. Rather than endorse these desires uncritically, I have pointed out the limits of a patronizing state approach that did not consider them initially and the racial scripts contributing to San Antón's "exceptional" treatment. In the following sections, I explore how these and other racial scripts producing a "black exceptionality" have been legitimized, reproduced, and contested via the national discourses of benevolent slavery, Hispanicity, and race mixture.

PART I

Benevolent Slavery

Docile Slaves or Free People of Color?

CHAPTER 2

Slavery and the Politics of Erasure

On March 14, 1996, one day before construction was scheduled to begin in San Antón, the municipal government invited residents to the project's announcement ceremony. The meeting took place on San Antón's basketball court. Before the mayor spoke from the assembled wooden platform, a recently formed theater group from San Antón, Taller La Brisa ("Breeze Workshop"), performed a play for residents and government officials down below. The play challenged—albeit indirectly—the government's intervention in the community.

On one side of the stage (i.e., the basketball court), the theater group placed a representation of a new house, and on the other they placed a representation of a traditional San Antón structure. To represent the traditional structure, theater members used unevenly distributed pieces of wood roughly shaped into a box. One side of the structure read, "Colmado La Cócora" ("La Cócora Convenience Store"), and the other displayed the lettering "Colmado La Buena Fé" ("Good Faith Convenience Store"). Through the window one could see candles, a black doll, plants, and Santería altar offerings. Three *panderos* (*plena* percussion instruments) hung outside. A *quinqué* (oil/Argand lamp) added another "traditional" touch to "old San Antón." For the new San Antón, the theater group built a square, plain replica of a house, painted white (see Figures 10a and 10b).

The performance opened with Evelyn, a tall nineteen-year-old with amazing stage presence and voice projection, who walked slowly in front of the audience wearing an elegant, black flowered dress. Holding a microphone with one hand, she began her monologue:

Figures 10a and 10b. Scenic representation of a traditional *(left)* and a new *(right)* San Antón house. Photos by author.

Y hablando de casas, cosa muy a tono con la ocasión, El Taller la brisa se complace en presentarles a todos ustedes unas breves estampas de nuestro barrio. Pero primero, queremos que conozcan un poquito de nuestra historia.[1]

[And speaking of houses, something very much in tune for the occasion, Taller La Brisa is proud to present to you some short scenes of our barrio. But first, we want you to learn a bit about our history.]

Evelyn talked about the religious origins of the name *San Antón* and mentioned some of the haciendas that prevailed in the region during the earlier part of the nineteenth century:

As you all know, the ones who had to do the work were the slaves! ¡*Que mamey ah!* ... [Now, wasn't that dandy? ...] You must be asking yourselves, "How did we get here?" Well, years passed by, and mechanization was brought to the island and the haciendas, and logically, slaves didn't have to work anymore, it wasn't that necessary ... Hmm ... so just like that, Chaz [boom]! Slavery was abolished. Darn it! This wasn't good for slave owners! Now they had to set all those slaves free. Yes, free, like they were in Africa! Then an amendment was made, a government amendment that demanded that all hacienda owners house all those slaves, but listen ... free, free!! So the owners of haciendas Constancia and Estrella bought, listen, these lands. Yes, San Antón ... And they say they gave it to us!! Hmm! Listen ... they didn't give us anything! We earned it with our sweat, our blood, and our tears!!!

erasure" I mean a process of historical narration and representation that entails silence, trivialization, and above all, a simplification of the history of slavery in dominant registers of Puerto Rico's national culture.

A politics of erasure in historiography was common in the 1940s, 1950s, and 1960s, when scholars interpreted slavery as a benevolent and unimportant institution in Puerto Rico that facilitated racial integration, race mixture, and *blanqueamiento* at both the biological and cultural levels. Like other national discourses discussed in this book, this interpretation of slavery was and continues to be deployed to differentiate Puerto Rico from the United States. In contrast to Puerto Rico's so-called soft brand of slavery, upholders of this politics interpret U.S. slavery as a harsher system that created impermeable racial barriers and institutionalized racial segregation.

Benevolent Slavery—Catholic Slavery through the Lens of Puerto Rican Ideologues

Such comparisons were common in scholarship about Latin America and the Caribbean that turns to the history of slavery, the plantation economy, and colonialism to interpret the status of contemporary ethnic relations and racism in the Americas and the Caribbean (Giovannetti 2006). Frank Tannenbaum (1947), for example, drew systematic comparisons between Protestant "North European" (England) and Catholic "South European" (Spain and Portugal) slavery systems. Emphasizing ideological notions of "moral personality" or "religious ethos," he argued that the colonies of Catholic powers in the New World (Cuba, Puerto Rico, the Dominican Republic, and Brazil, for example) had more harmonious and milder race relations than the colonies of Protestant powers (such as the English-speaking Caribbean and the United States).[2] Some of his followers extrapolated his analysis to conclude that race relations were particularly severe in the United States and more democratic in Latin America. Comparisons between the United States and Latin America were drawn by ideologues who—in promoting national ideologies of race mixture and integration—belittled the problem of racism and the pertinence of "race" for understanding Latin American societies (Freyre 1977; Degler 1971).

In Puerto Rico, such interpretations of slavery and race relations had an impact on scholarship and in the formulation of national ideologies. Tomás Blanco, for example, contrasted what he believed to be a Puerto Rican racial democracy with the deeply segregated United States. In his book *El Prejuicio Racial en Puerto Rico* (1942), he accounted for the difference by backtracking to what he believed was Puerto Rico's "national source" (Spain) and finding an explanation in its supposedly benevolent Catholic tradition of slavery. Blanco argued that the Catholic tradition promoted the recognition of slaves as part of a community of Christian brotherhood, which made the Spaniards receptive to the mixing of races (1942, 116). The protestant inclination of the United States, however, encouraged *"un ambiente fanático y puritano donde se incubaban las represiones sexuales que habían de buscar aberrante canalización en el erotismo sádico de las masas linchadoras"* (a fanatical and puritan atmosphere where sexual repressions were incubated and went on to find deviant conduit in the sadistic eroticism of the lynching masses) (Blanco 1942, 110). According to Blanco, in Puerto Rico people had no such repressions toward mixing, because *"cada cual se casa o se 'apestilla' con quien su impulso genésico le dicte"* (each [person] marries or makes out with whomever their generative impulse dictates) (1942, 122).

Blanco was writing in the 1940s at a time of heightened discontent with U.S. colonial intervention in Puerto Rico. U.S. sugar corporations had displaced a local bourgeoisie sector of previous coffee and sugar *hacendados*, some of whom sought political independence from the United States (Díaz-Quiñones 1985, 22–24). By comparing Puerto Rico's so-called benevolent trajectory of slavery to the more brutal slavery regime and racial segregation laws that prevailed in the United States, Blanco sought not only to undermine the United States as a colonial power but also to legitimize the idea of self-government for the people of Puerto Rico.

An important discursive strategy in this effort was to evoke racial mixture as a mechanism that could bring gradual whitening of the population. Nationalism was linked to Europe, and this in turn linked the notions of Europe and of whiteness to projects of self-government on the Island (Rodríguez-Vázquez 2004). In this context, Blanco argued that "Puerto Rican people live within the general norms of Western culture. Although the mix of blacks and whites is significant, the African element has only exerted a very slight influence over the cultural traits" (Blanco 1942, 138).[3]

Blanco used the invocation of Spanish heritage to unify Puerto Ricans and to distinguish Puerto Ricans from the U.S. colonizing "Other." Hence, while he described the racial prejudice of the United States as "bestial," "collective insanity," or "authentic virus," he portrayed racial prejudice in Puerto Rico as *"una noñería"* (superficial), "child's play," "naive," "false," "more social than racial," and "foreign."[4]

For Blanco, this divergence was a question of degree, rather than of kind—a variance between two Western, predominantly white societies. According to him: "Island prejudices are prejudices common to the White race"[5] (138). The so-called superficial nature of racial prejudice in Puerto Rico (and its Catholic traditions) made Puerto Rico the more civilized of the two.

Other intellectuals, who published later, in the 1950s, 1960s, and 1970s, echoed Blanco's understanding of mild racism and benevolent slavery (Díaz-Soler 1981; Fernández Méndez 1976; Rogler 1946). Historian Díaz-Soler, for example, concluded that in Puerto Rico, "Slavery and liberty were relatively close to one another"[6] (Díaz-Soler 1981, 75). Like Blanco, Díaz-Soler alluded to the historical impact of Catholicism on the more humanitarian treatment of slaves and consistently represented Spain as a nation uninclined to slave trafficking. *"España no era una nación negrera"* (Spain was not a slave nation), he affirmed. "Trafficking blacks fell into the hands of foreigners committed to such despicable business"[7] (Díaz-Soler 1981, 373). Said foreigners were, of course, Protestant.

Proponents of the benevolent-slavery thesis also appealed to economic considerations to explain why slavery had not created racial divisions of social significance in the Island. In particular, they argued that Puerto Rico (unlike other Caribbean islands) never developed into a large-scale slave plantation society such as happened in the English and French Caribbean and that slavery was, in fact, an almost "accidental" aspect of Puerto Rican history.

These arguments voiced by historians during the 1940s, 1950s, and 1960s hark back to the late nineteenth century and early twentieth century and figure prominently in the narratives of *criollo* liberal elite, many of whom were from Ponce. Their reformist (not pro-independence) political projects aimed to achieve economic and political transformations that would grant more autonomy within the colonial regimes imposed first by Spain and later by the United States (Rodríguez-Silva 2012). At a time when imperial politicians from Spain and the United States equated blackness with unrest—in Haiti, the Dominican Republic, Jamaica, and Cuba—*criollo* liberals in Puerto Rico, including in Ponce, projected themselves as white representatives of a harmonious, whitened, and stable society in which the transition from slavery to abolition had been smooth and uneventful (Flores-Collazo and García-Muñiz 2009; Rodríguez-Silva 2012). Asserting the Island's whiteness amid the black, unstable Caribbean was thus a crucial strategy of liberal-democratic political regimes in Puerto Rico (Rodríguez-Silva 2012, 64; Santiago-Valles 1994, 2003), a posture that continued to shape intellectual and political life into the late twentieth and twenty-first centuries.

Of course, in order to work effectively, nationalist discourses cannot be crafted out of thin air, but must be anchored in some aspect of observable reality. Differences between Puerto Rico and sugar-producing colonies of England and France in the Caribbean were in fact significant. In Jamaica, slaves formed about 90 percent of the total population before the time of emancipation in 1838 (Turnbull 1840, 555), while in Puerto Rico the slave population never rose above 12 percent of the total (Figueroa 2005, 48; Mintz 1959). Upholders of benevolent slavery argued that the shortage of slave labor obliged masters in Puerto Rico to treat their slaves better (Díaz-Soler 1981, 374–75). This "well-treated" slave population was often described as docile (Díaz-Soler 1981), reinforcing the idea of passivity among blacks and harmonious racial mixture while minimizing historical antecedents that impelled confrontation between different racial sectors of Puerto Rican society.

Challengers

During and after the 1970s, such benevolent interpretations of slavery were challenged with varied emphasis. Scholars of Latin America and the Caribbean criticized comparisons between Catholic and Protestant forms of slavery for overgeneralizing, ignoring local particularities of servitude, and dismissing the variation in conditions of slavery over time (Mintz 1989; Williams 1944, 1957; Knight 1992; Hoetink 1967).[8] Related critiques regarding the overemphasis of isolated events, religious doctrines, and decrees instead of the powerful social economic and political contexts that shaped them were also launched by Puerto Rican intellectuals in the 1970s against Puerto Rican proponents of the benevolent or "happy slavery" thesis (García 1989, 49).[9] Scholars argued, for example, that while an initial languid economic period may have been favorable to interracial cohabitation, the plantation economy varied over time and was not always favorable to the blurring of racial boundaries. Coercive measures developed in the context of economic boom during the nineteenth century were felt and rejected by the enslaved population. The important work of the Centro de Estudios de la Realidad Puertorriqueña (Center for the Study of Puerto Rican Reality), known as CEREP, produced publications for broad audiences that sought to debunk the myth of benevolent slavery and slave docility, among them *La otra cara de la historia* (The Other Face of History, González and Quintero-Rivera 1970) and *El machete de Ogún* (Ogún's Machete, González and Vega 1990). Puerto Rican researchers have since written about slave rebellions (Baralt 1981), marronage (Nistal-Moret 1984), complaints lodged by slaves against their owners (Picó 1977; Cubano Iguina 2011), and slaves' efforts to attain their freedom before and after slavery (Figueroa 2005), as well as many other topics. Authors also wrote about how coercive measures developed against the enslaved not only affected the enslaved, but free blacks (Kinsbruner 1996) and maroon communities (Stark 2007; Chinea 2002). Others described how Haiti's revolution instilled fear of blacks in the planter's class and further limited legal rights of black people across the Americas, making evident the transnational and local currency of racism in the Hispanic Caribbean (Baralt 1981; Chinea 1996, 2005; Figueroa 2005; González Mendoza 2001).

Many of the scholars who questioned the benevolent-slavery thesis in the 1970s shared the ideal of political independence for Puerto Rico. Yet they did not support their orientation by aligning Puerto Rican society to Spain's traditions or by depicting harmonious integration in contrast to the United States. Rather, their work stressed how marginal sectors of society struggled to adapt and endure in conditions imposed by powerful local (Island) and global (U.S.) economic interests.

For example, in contention with the idea that Puerto Rico's population was primarily Hispanic in origin, José Luis González stressed the importance of the African and black population during the fifteenth, sixteenth, and seventeenth centuries. He argued that blacks and *mulatos* were the "first Puerto Ricans" because, unlike Spaniards, slaves could not easily leave the Island and had to adapt from the very beginning to the Island environment: "blacks and mulattos, historically speaking, constituted the cement of Puerto Rican nationality because they were the first to feel Puerto Rico as their true home and because they had no roots in or loyalty to Spain... or indeed anywhere else" (González 1993, 39).

González further maintained that, contrary to arguments that located racism only in the United States, black Puerto Ricans were quite familiar with racism on the Island. "The experience," he said, "of racism targeting Puerto Rican blacks came not from American, but from Puerto Rican society... those who have discriminated against blacks *in Puerto Rico* haven't been Americans, but white Puerto Ricans, many of whom moreover have always taken conspicuous pride in their foreign ancestry (Spanish, Catalan, Majorcan, etc.) (1993, 24).

Other publications, such as *Puerto Rico negro* by Sued-Badillo and López-Cantos (1986), continued the debate by emphasizing the importance of the black population on the Island, particularly during the seventeenth and eighteenth centuries.

Another tenet of the benevolent-slavery thesis, the characterization of the plantation as a color-blind institution, was also questioned and problematized.[10] Writers like Baralt (1981), Sagrera (1973), and Kinsbruner (1996) directly challenged historians' undermining of racial prejudice by writing about nineteenth-century coercive measures based on color (the infamous *Bando Negro* against the African race of 1848 is one example). In addition, Francisco Scarano argued that planters did make important racial distinctions as they depended on slaves, considering non-black free laborers a much less reliable source of labor. With slavery an essential part of the logic used to operate the sugar haciendas, fewer slaves did not equal better treatment. The enslaved population in Puerto Rico was subject to daily regimens and arduous routines similar to those found in other plantation societies in the Caribbean (Scarano 1984). Furthermore, *hacendados* believed slaves and the "African race" were predisposed to withstand the hard labor required in sugar haciendas (Scarano 1984, 31–32). Hence, race played a key role in workers' classification.

These and future works of historiography continued to challenge the benevolent-slavery thesis, recognizing the importance of slavery and the ideology of racism for sustaining a system of social, economic, gendered, and political relationships loaded with power struggles and class interests (Figueroa 2005; Giovannetti 2006; Findlay 1999; Picó 2007; Cubano Iguina 2006, 2011; Baerga 2009–10; Rodríguez-Silva 2012).

Contemporary Manifestations of the Politics of Erasure

Although scholars posed and continue to pose important challenges to the previously described politics of erasure in historical renditions of slavery, ideas about *blanqueamiento*, masters' benevolence, and slave docility are still prevalent in educational "scripts" disseminated in school textbooks, national monuments, and contemporary commemorations of the abolition of slavery (Lloréns and Carrasquillo 2008; Godreau et al. 2008, 2013).

For example, an examination of thirty-two newspaper articles published between 1995 and 2006 commemorating the Abolition of Slavery in Puerto Rico shows that few offered historical information about slavery and even fewer mentioned slave resistance.[11] The majority, nineteen out of the thirty-two (59 percent), discussed the issue of interpersonal racism.[12] Five of the articles covered cultural celebrations or music festivals that featured the rhythms of *bomba* and *plena*. Only eight addressed the history of slavery per se, and only three of those eight mentioned slave resistance.

In addition, historical renditions of slavery in the newspaper tend to ignore European responsibility in the slave trade while exaggerating European accountability for its abolition. Passive constructions such as *los esclavos que fueron traídos* ("the slaves that were brought") or *los esclavos que llegaron* ("the slaves who arrived") leave European powers and locally born white *criollos*[13] who benefitted from the slave economy unmentioned. On the other hand, authors or people interviewed by newspaper reporters attribute slavery's abolition not to the struggles led by the enslaved, but to the role played by white *criollos*, abolitionists, and international pressure exerted by England, the United States, and Catholic Spain (Arrieta Vilá 1998, 26). Furthermore, no information is provided about Puerto Rican *criollo* families who benefitted from the slave trade. The involvement of Spain (and the Catholic Church) in the trade is represented as almost accidental. As one author wrote, once slavery was abolished, "*2,000 amos felices pudieron extraer la espina que se clavó en el alma Cristiana*" (two thousand happy masters were able to extract the thorn that had been buried in their Christian soul) (Arrieta Vilá 2006, 27).

School discourses reproduce this understanding by silencing systemic racist principles behind the colonial enterprise, focusing instead on inhuman deeds of specific actors who strayed from Catholic guiding tenets of the Spanish tradition. Elementary school textbooks approved by the Department of Education for third grade in Puerto Rico (1992–2012), for example, state that:

> La esclavitud, como institución legal, estaba reglamentada por el gobierno. Las leyes tendían a garantizar un trato humanitario a los esclavos. Ofrecían seguridades respecto a su bienestar, salud y otros aspectos. Todo esto en teoría parecía razonable y hasta bonito, pero en la práctica la realidad era otra. Sólo algunos de los dueños de las haciendas eran comprensivos y humanitarios. En general, éstos eran crueles, sin sentido de caridad cristiana y dejaban el manejo de los esclavos en manos de mayorales inescrupulosos. (De León Monsalvo 2009, 113; Vizcarrondo 1992, 103)
>
> [Slavery was a legal institution that was regulated by the government and by laws that were likely to guarantee the humanitarian treatment of slaves and that looked

after their well-being, health, and other aspects. All of this sounds reasonable and even pretty, but in practice, the reality was different. Only some of the hacienda owners were understanding and humanitarian. In general, they were cruel, with no sense of Christian charity and left the management of slaves to unscrupulous overseers.]

In this way, the text justifies and legitimizes a "correct form of slavery," finding fault not in the institution of slavery itself, but in the cruel attitude of a handful of unruly individual slave owners who did not practice the Catholic and humanitarian principles recognized by the colonial government (Godreau et al. 2008).

Once this individuation of racial violence is established, textbook illustrations and historic monuments re-inscribe the "script" of slave docility and victimization by providing only images of slave suffering, in chains or being whipped. Taíno Indians, on the other hand, are shown in textbooks hunting, worshiping, playing sports, leading others, or defending themselves. (See Figures 11a and 11b.)

A similar process occurs with monuments. Hilda Lloréns and Rosa Carrasquillo (2008), for example, argue that in the town of Caguas there is a density of public art that renders blackness passive, foreign, and primitive. Similarly, in the town of Ponce, one finds that the only plaza and memorial dedicated to the abolition of slavery in Puerto Rico displays a freed slave, kneeling.

Figures 11a and 11b. Textbook images of Africans and Taíno Indians. Source: "Somos Puerto Rico: El País, La Patria." Editorial La Biblioteca, 2002: 138, 113.

The location of this statue in Ponce is not fortuitous, nor is the posture of the free kneeling black man. During the later decades of the nineteenth century, abolitionism as a political project—and later (after 1876) as a commemoration—was a central strategy for advancing the liberal reforms of *criollo* liberal elite in Ponce, whose political legitimacy hinged on the ideas of racial harmony, black docility, and Island gratitude to the motherland Spain (Flores Collazo and García-Muñiz 2009, 141). As a bastion of liberal reformist and autonomist political thought, Ponce sought to project itself (vis-à-vis Spanish and later vis-à-vis the United States) as a metropolitan modern city whose *criollo* elite were quite capable of leading the recently emancipated poor, black, and *mulato* workers, who were presented as docile and grateful for their emancipation.[14] The bronze statue was erected in 1956. Now Ponce's government-created tourist Web site proudly proclaims the monument as "the only monument of this type in the Antilles" (Municipio de Ponce 2010b), a statement echoed by Wikipedia (Wikipedia contributors 2013). Yet similar monuments commemorating emancipation can be found across the region. The passive posture of Ponce's *liberto* (ex-slave) in the plaza of *la abolición* (see Figure 12a) sharply contrasts with assertive images of resistance and agency found in other monuments of the region commemorating emancipation or resistance to slavery (see Figures 12b, c, d, e).

Figure 12a. Abolition Monument, Ponce, Puerto Rico. Photo by author.

Figure 12b. Bussa Emancipation Statue, Barbados. Photo by Keith B. of KBevPhoto.com.

Figure 12c. Mulâtresse Solitude Statue, Guadaloupe. Photo by Yarimar Bonilla.

Figure 12d. Zumbi Monument, Bahia, Brasil. Photo by Lucio Oliveira.

Figure 12e. Statue of the Unknown Maroon, Port au Prince, Haiti. Photo by Yarimar Bonilla.

Figure 13. Monument of the Plaza, Agüeybaná II "El Bravo" (Agueybana "The Brave") in Ponce. Photo by author.

The kneeling image of Ponce's *liberto* also contrasts with the proud posture of the Taíno illustrated in Figure 13 that appears in another monument in the sector of Playa in Ponce.[15]

Blanqueamiento and the Politics of Erasure

Contemporary politics of erasure not only uphold the script of a victimized/passive/docile slave subject, but also grant legitimacy to the ideology of *blanqueamiento* and to related scripts that render blackness an exception, a fading or "fugitive" element of the Puerto Rican nation (Lloréns and Carrasquillo 2008; Godreau 2002). Consider the following article, published during the time of my fieldwork in one of the leading newspapers of Puerto Rico, which began:

> Commemoration! Puerto Ricans will "bleach away" many of the physical traces of its African past by the year 2200, with the other Spanish-speaking Caribbeans following a few centuries later. "Puerto Ricans are *blanqueando* [whitening] faster than any other *mestizo* [hybrid] country," said Luis Díaz-Soler, a specialist on island slavery. In two centuries there will hardly be any blacks in Puerto Rico. (Bliss 1995, 30)

Writing to commemorate the abolition of slavery, the author continued to quote historian Luis Díaz-Soler:

Puerto Rico had the smoothest transition from slavery to emancipation of almost any American country," he said, crediting two factors for this situation: *a small population of blacks* during the nineteenth century, and the tolerance of white Spaniards towards intermarriage. (Bliss 1995, 30, my emphasis)

Such allegations regarding swift whitening as a result of small slave numbers are suspect. They ignore the impact of black immigrants from nearby Caribbean islands and mention racial mixture only as whitening. The fact that racial mixture simultaneously entails a darkening of the white sector is not contemplated, let alone celebrated, in this kind of interpretation of *mestizaje*.

These arguments also assume the so-called whitening of the population is an objective process, accelerated by increased immigration from European countries after 1815, under the legal provision of the Cédula de Gracias (1815). Yet, more than promote white immigration, the principal achievement of the Cédula was to provide citizenship to foreigners who had already established themselves on the Island (Marazzi 1974, 17). Hence, the census increase in the number of "whites" after 1815 does not necessarily mean that there were more "white" people on the Island, but that the previously undocumented—now registered as residents—were counted as such.[16] Moreover, as Harry Hoetink (1967) and others have argued, "white" identity was (and continues to be) claimed in liberal terms in the Hispanic Caribbean. According to Hoetink, people who belonged to the upper class and were identified as "colored" in nineteenth-century French or English colonies could be defined as white in the Spanish colonies.[17]

Besides the issue of "whites" and the elasticity conferred to "whiteness," the argument that African contributions to Puerto Rican society were less significant because Puerto Rico had few slaves is faulty. First of all, slave owners and state officials often underestimated the number of slaves they had. Planters did so to avoid tax payments. Furthermore, with the advent of the Industrial Revolution, the abolitionist movement, and the promotion of liberal ideologies that upheld free labor, England had been exerting international pressure on Spain and its colonies to restrict and abolish slavery. However, in an effort to satisfy the demand for slaves, planters, and traders in Puerto Rico, and especially in Cuba, Spain continued the trade by smuggling slaves. Thus—in the words of historian Francisco Scarano (1984)—in sugar-producing districts such as Ponce, "while slaves continued to pour in, official records indicated otherwise" (121).[18]

Last and most important, there was a substantial sector of people of African descent on the Island who were considered nonwhite but who were legally free during slavery. In fact, the number of free people of color in Puerto Rico always exceeded by far the number of slaves on the Island, and until the 1820s they constituted approximately 50 percent of the total free population (Mintz 1989, 87).[19] See Chart 1.

Chart 1: Puerto Rico's Racial Composition, 1775–1860.

	1775	1779	1790	1820	1830	1854	1860
Whites	48.5%	46.8%	46.3%	44.4%	50.1%	48.3%	51.5%
Free Colored	40.9%	42.3%	41.1%	46.2%	39.3%	42.2%	41.3%
Slaves	10.6%	10.9%	12.6%	9.4%	10.6%	9.5%	7.2%

Combined Sources: Jay Kinsbruner's *Not of Pure Blood*, 1996: 30, and Collections of the History Research Center at University of Puerto Rico at Río Piedras.

The prevalence of this population was partly due to the uneven nature of economic expansion of the sugar industry in Puerto Rico during the nineteenth century (Martínez-Vergne 1992). Because of drastic economic shifts, planters could not always retain their slaves. The institutional arrangements by which slaves could win their freedom also contributed to the growth of a substantial population of free people of color (Mintz 1989). In addition, from 1666 to the 1750s, the Spanish crown adopted an official policy of harboring slaves who escaped from colonies of competing European powers in order to disrupt their rivals' economic activities (Chinea 2002; Picó 1988).[20] As a result, the percentage of Puerto Rico's free people of color in the total population dwarfed those of Jamaica, Barbados, the United States, and, to a lesser degree, Cuba (see Table 1).

Scholars have traditionally either overlooked this "nonwhite" sector or argued that this was a mixed-race group contributing to the "blurring" of racial differences in Puerto Rico. Anthropologist Jorge Duany (1985), for example, stated that "the significance of the free colored sector is that it was the first to contradict the established social order, based on the separation between the European and African segments . . . This *mixed group* served to bind the social fabric together by forming a buffer zone between blacks and whites, masters and slaves" (22, my emphasis).

Presented this way, free people of color are cast as mixed, while slaves are represented as black. Simultaneously, blackness is reduced to slave and foreign (African)

Table 1: Freedmen as Percentage of Total Free Population in Selected Societies, 1773–1840

Society	1773–1775	1800–1802	1812–1820	1827–1840
Puerto Rico	54.1%	47.7%	50.9%	
Jamaica	19.4%	25.0%		
Barbados	2.8%	12.2%	15.7%	25.5%
Cuba	27.3%			25.4%

Source: Jay Kinsbruner *Not of Pure Blood*, 1996: 32

status, in disregard of free blacks who lived and were born on the Island during the slave period.

Similar uses of the word *negro* to mean "slave" are evident in nineteenth-century practices that distinguished between a large free population who called themselves *libertos, mulatos,* or *pardos,* and the less numerous slave population who were "racialized" as "black" by both whites and free people of color in the Hispanic Caribbean. Rodríguez-Silva notes that the category *liberto* was rarely accompanied by a racial adjective, unlike the widely used term *negro esclavo,* as if the term freed the person not only from slavery, but from race. *Negro,* by contrast, marked a certain purity of blackness, a direct link to slavery, and was also cast as foreign, to name West Indians or U.S. blacks (Rodríguez-Silva 2012, 5).

In the Dominican Republic, freedmen and women not only considered themselves different from the slaves whom they saw as the only blacks on the Island, but represented themselves as the *blancos de la tierra* (whites of the land) (Candelario 2007, 5; Moya Pons 1996). Having access to land or an autonomous mode of production differentiated this group, and this difference coded them racially (as honorary whites). Establishing such distance was particularly significant in the Caribbean at a time when next-door "black" neighbor Haiti had become the first black republic in the region, threatening the status quo of the planter's class across the Americas.

Long after slavery's abolition in the rest of the Caribbean, uses of the term *black* to mean slave continue to erase and simplify the multilayered positions of Africans and their descendants. Such uses were not common solely in the historiography of the 1940s, 1950s, and 1960s. Newspaper articles published during the time of my fieldwork, also, often interchanged the term *negro* for slave in their accounts of slavery. In contrast, free people of color (if mentioned) were racialized as *mulatos* (never as black).

School texts and discourses also use the word *negro* to mean slave or African interchangeably. The term *white,* however, is seldom used to label Spaniards (Godreau et al. 2008). Spaniards are described in ethnic terms (*los españoles*). A fourth-grade textbook, for example, states that "*En los inicios de la sociedad colonial en nuestra isla convivieron tres grupos raciales: los españoles, los indios y los esclavos africanos*" (At the initial stages of the colonial society, three racial groups coexisted in our Island: the Spaniards, the Indians and the African slaves") (Sánchez 2001, 114). In this way, slave status becomes part and parcel of an African "racial" identity. Similarly, contemporary popular sayings such as *me tienen trabajando como un negro* or *mi jefe es un negrero* (They've been working me like a black man; my boss is a black trafficker) reinscribe this equivalency among blackness, Africanness, slave status, and the past. Such politics of erasure and the correspondences they foster—blackness, enslavement, Africa, and the past—also bolster scripts that portray blackness as a fading, extreme, or exceptional element in Puerto Rico today.

Regions under Erasure: The Representative Highland versus the Alien Coast

The previously described scripts of blackness also have important spatial and regional dimensions. Politics of erasure regarding the history of slavery plays a key role in the construction of scripts that render certain municipalities and regions as more or less representative of Puerto Rican culture. For example, while the mountainous highland regions are often cast as racially mixed, whitened, and evocative of "Puerto Rican culture," the coast—where sugar plantations, slave-dependent regional economies, and black and mulatto communities developed more systematically—is considered "different" from the norm in both popular and scholarly renditions of the Puerto Rican landscape.

Scholars such as Kelvin Santiago-Valles (1994), Arlene Torres (1998), Luis A. Figueroa (2005), and Negrón-Portillo and Mayo-Santana (2007) have challenged this regional racialization. Kelvin Santiago has written that the post-1940 historiography "tended to imagine a 'white' peasant majority nostalgically representative of Puerto Rican national culture versus a handful of 'dark' coastal laborers who were *in* but not *of* the Island. On the contrary, important segments of this mountainous peasantry were of mixed African and Iberian heritage, harking back to the period between the sixteenth and late eighteenth centuries when runaway slaves (of both sexes) settled and intermingled with fugitive galley prisoners and former soldiers of various backgrounds and with remnants of the indigenous population" (Santiago-Valles 1994, 44–45, emphasis in original).

Launching a similar critique, Negrón-Portillo and Mayo-Santana (2007) point to the understudied role of slavery in the mountainous interior of the Island during the nineteenth century, stating that "[t]he vision of the interior as a world racially and culturally articulated by white peasants has historically circulated with enough force as to alter and demean the socioeconomic role played by the black and the slave, which was not insignificant" (17–18).[21] What's more, Scarano and Curtis (2007) point to a majority of black, *mulato*, and mixed-raced households in the early decades of the twentieth century (1910 and 1920) in areas around San Juan, but also in municipalities that are not coastal, such as San Germán, Yauco, and Cayey, which developed strong economies in sugar, coffee, cattle, and tobacco in the nineteenth century (133; for Cayey, see Picó 2007).

Still, the imagined contrast between a so-called representative "white" interior region (free of slavery and of blacks) and the less representative black coast persists. Important economic and historical dimensions could explain the endurance of this idea. In the highlands of Puerto Rico, a strong peasant sector survived on subsistence agriculture as early as the sixteenth century and continued to thrive up until the nineteenth century. The mountainous topography of the interior of the Island served as an effective barrier against sugar encroachment, allowing this peasantry to continue with a livelihood of subsistence agriculture. This reliance on subsistence farming supported a mixed-crop economy and made it difficult for the planter class to employ peasants in large-scale production of commercial crops during the eighteenth and nineteenth centuries. The production of coffee and tobacco that did develop in the interior relied primarily on the labor of landless free men, although some slaves were incorporated into the economy (Negrón-Portillo and Mayo-Santana 2007). In contrast, coastal districts such as Ponce, Mayagüez, and Guayama served as home of the most powerful *hacendado* bourgeoisie and accounted for more than half of Puerto Rico's sugar output (Scarano 1992, 14). These urbanized centers developed politically powerful élites, a disproportionate number of slaves, a strong class of black and *mulato* artisans, and marked levels of social, spatial, and racial differentiation (Scarano 1992; Quintero-Rivera 1987; Findlay 1999; Rodríguez-Silva 2012).

Quintero argues that, in contrast to these urban areas, the independent, self-sustaining economy that developed in the rural economic milieu has led scholars and common people alike to credit this rural landscape with the development of a national culture, independent from the Spanish metropolis. To illustrate this sense, he notes that while attending the funeral of Puerto Rico's political prisoner Andrés Figueroa-Cordero in the 1980s at his hometown in Aguada (a coastal town), he saw that people repeatedly spoke of this national hero as a *jíbaro de la montaña* (mountain peasant), even though Aguada had no mountains. According to Quintero, this rural nationalism is nurtured by the persistence of a long tradition of *marronage*[22] (i.e., camouflage, or living in retreat), which engendered a counterplantation culture in the rural areas. Under Spanish colonial control, this urban–rural dichotomy marked socially significant differences placing preferred autonomous forms of livelihood in the country (characterized by a counterplantation culture of smuggling, subsistence agriculture, and living in retreat) in opposition to state-controlled practices centralized in the urban context, particularly that of San Juan (Quintero-Rivera 1987).

Although more concerned with the rural–urban dichotomy than with the coastal–rural distinction I am emphasizing, Quintero points to important factors that explain why the rural has become emblematic of Puerto Rican national identity. His analysis nevertheless fails to take into account the allure of powerful scripts that have racialized the rural landscape as almost white in the formation of such national symbolism. In fact, Quintero's use of *marronage* (a term associated with blackness) to identify this rural sector is creative but misleading, as elites, intellectuals, and peasant dwellers alike conceptualized the mountains as a nonblack space.

In effect, eugenics and medical discourses prevalent among elite sectors of Puerto Rican society during the late nineteenth and early twentieth centuries appropriated the precepts of social Darwinism and geographic determinism to construct the interior highland as the site where white Spanish heritage would flourish, once *jíbaros* were given the adequate education and eugenic guidance

(Baerga 2009–10; Rodríguez-Silva 2012, 83–90). The cooler temperatures of the rural landscape were deemed more favorable to the white race according to ideas of the time that construed tropical heat as an unfit climate for civilization. The coast, by contrast, was understood to be less fit for the development of a true national identity. Members of the eugenic movement in Puerto Rico, like Valle Atiles, for example, understood that "*en la costa, la fiebre amarilla aflige al jíbaro blanco y respeta al negro*" (. . . on the coast, yellow fever afflicts the white *jíbaro* and respects the black) (Baerga 2009–10, 94). Like other intellectuals at the turn of the century, he believed that despite the fact that blacks were represented as more resilient in the context of the tropics and with respect to certain illnesses, they were predicted to disappear in the long run because of the supposed hereditary superiority of whites (Baerga 2009–10, 94). The prevailing notion was that, in time, with proper breeding, education, scientific reform, hygiene, and diet, the superior qualities of the white race would emerge in the Puerto Rican subject, the *jíbaro* rural dweller. In this way, the mountains became the cradle for the formation of Puerto Rican identity. Writing decades later, in the 1940s, Emilio Belaval would echo this sentiment by asserting that "*Al momento de la homogeneidad puertorriqueña hay que marchar hacia arriba, hacia la montaña, porque nuestro pueblo de la costa no tiene más que un blanco, argonauta, fracasado . . . y un negro en dilusión*" (At the moment of Puerto Rican homogeneity one should go up, toward the mountain, because our coastal town has only a white, argonaut, failed . . . and a black in dilution) (Belaval 1948, 31).

This discourse continued influencing scholarship decades later, with important variants that considered racial mixture as a positive rather than troublesome element. Historians privileged the insular highlands as internal frontiers that favored the development of a national culture through the synthesis of Amerindian, African, and Spanish traits. As a result, they argued, racial differences carried less social importance in Puerto Rico than elsewhere in the Caribbean. In the 1980s, Duany wrote:

> Puerto Rico escaped many of the internal caste divisions generated by the slave plantation system because the island continued to blur the social distinctions between black and white. By the late 1840s Puerto Rico was essentially a society of free men and women, forced to sell their labor and to till the land of others. (1985, 20–21)

According to Duany, peasant life "was highly syncretistic, although Hispanic traditions seemed to prevail in the end" (25). In contrast, he described coastal regions of Puerto Rico where sugar cultivation flourished as an exception:

> The plantation economy established its hegemony on the southern and northern coasts of Puerto Rico. This location was determined by the nature of the landscape and by the access to seaports from which sugar cane could be exported cheaply.

This explains why the coastal populations exhibit the most pronounced effects of industrialization upon the rural cultures (Steward 1956). Sugar cultivation made the towns and countryside of the lowlands markedly uniform in appearance and organization. *This sector of the Puerto Rican economy was similar to Cuba's plantation society.* (Duany 1985, 27, my emphasis)

In this way, the black- and *mulato*-populated coast is characterized as "different" or—as Duany states—a sector "similar to Cuba."[23]

The United States and the "Whiteness" of the Mountain Dweller: The *Jíbaro*

U.S. colonialism and the threat of Americanization not only provided fuel for the theories of benevolent slavery in the Island, but also informed development of such regional scripts regarding a mixed (whitened) Puerto Rican interior and an alien black coast. According to Lillian Guerra, the rural *jibarista* discursive claim to whiteness was elaborated by a Puerto Rican national elite in reaction to North American standards of "Otherness" that declared both popular sectors and the Puerto Rican elite themselves "less white" (and less capable of self-government) than North Americans. Colonial constructions of the Puerto Rican as an inferior nonwhite individual predated 1898, but its discursive deployment during the early twentieth century took place at a time when racial segregation was deeply entrenched in the United States and the North American presence in Puerto Rico was growing (Guerra 1998, 227).

In this context, U.S. politicians understood that their mission was to "educate the natives on self-government." When it came to explaining delays in the attainment of this goal, they often deployed race as the principal justification (Clark 1973, 220; Kennedy 1971). Social Darwinists like ex–speaker of the house Uncle Joe Cannon argued that Puerto Ricans would never be able to rule themselves because:

> when you talk about a people competent for self-government, certain things must be taken into consideration. One is the racial question. Another is the climatic conditions. . . . Why I undertake to say that if one of our people would go to Porto Rico . . . at the end of three or four generations, as the children would intermarry, with the enervating effect that come from the Tropics, they would not be as competent for self-government as their great-grandfathers were. Porto Rico is populated by a mixed race. About 30 per cent are pure African . . . (Clark 1973, 222–23)

In response to these and other colonial critiques of Puerto Rican inferiority, Puerto Rican elites crafted nationalist affirmations that were clearly anti-American but never antiwhite (Loveman and Muniz 2007). Borrowing from the conceptual apparatus of Oswald Spengler and his influential work *The Decline of the West* (1934), they argued that Puerto Rico's culture was the result of Spaniards adapting to the tropical environment. In the words of Emilio Belaval (1977): "From this white Spaniard, sunk in the tropics, disappointed about the land, thinking of the motherland, retracted in his hacienda, stems our common psyche and some of the bad habits that the unsuspecting find so hard to understand (41).[24]

Spengler's theory, one of the central postulates of imperialist thought, upheld that the unfavorable conditions of heat, rain, and humidity had thwarted the development of civilization in the tropics.[25] Yet, rather than use these ideas to legitimate colonial domination, elites argued that this light-skinned male individual with deep roots in the land was also deeply linked to his European past (A. González, 1992, 566). According to Guerra (1998), such *jibarista* "assertions of European lineage were a must in the context of colonial intervention because they put the elite, by virtue of their indisputable identification as white, on top" (226).

Poor Puerto Ricans living in rural sectors at the beginning of the twentieth century also reproduced this racial hierarchy in their discourse, but in more ambiguous and tenuous ways. In town centers of the rural interior, they sought the Catholic sacraments that made them "Hispanic" and tried to have whiter offspring in order to *mejorar la raza* (improve the race) (Quintero-Rivera 1987, 132). Correspondingly, interviews conducted by José Colombán Rosario and Cristina Carrión with rural *jíbaros* in the early 1930s reveal expressions of disgust, of suspicion, and of the desire to distance themselves from blacks (see Guerra 1998, 228).[26] Nevertheless, rural Puerto Ricans were either of mixed racial heritages themselves or shared membership in racially diverse communities. To mitigate such incongruities, Guerra argues that people defined "blackness" as something so categorically extreme and negative (and I would add distant) that it would seem unlikely that anyone in their community would be labeled as such, regardless of how dark they were (1998, 229). At the same time, denying the existence of racism and claiming that it was really class, not race, that mattered became an important strategy for popular-class communities to build horizontal lines of solidarity vis-à-vis incursions from without. In this way, Guerra documents how popular classes paradoxically rejected blackness and advocated the racial ideal of whiteness while denying the existence of racism among themselves (1998, 228).

The Unmarked Whiteness of the *Jíbaro* in Naranjito

Much has changed since the early twentieth century. Yet the rural *jíbaro* is still a racialized symbol used to characterize Puerto Rican identity and cultural practices that are premodern (sometimes also unrefined) and autochthonous to the Island. There are, for example, *jíbaro* musics, *jíbaro* foods, and *jíbaro* attitudes or ways of being.[27] There is also a famous *jíbaro* monument (built in 1976) beside the expressway that goes to the interior town of Cayey, which depicts a *jíbaro* man standing with his family (a woman, sitting down holding a small child) carved in white marble, with the mountains as background. The *jíbaro* and his *pava* (straw hat) also symbolize the commonwealth party (PPD party). Under the commonwealth program of industrialization, the *jíbaro*—often constructed as male—was to be educated, modernized, and acquainted with the new products of U.S. progress, while being the guardian of Puerto Rican patrimony.

After the 1970s, the socioeconomic order of progress and development established by Muñoz's party went into crisis, and the myth of the *jíbaro* also began to fall apart (A. González, 1992, 568).[28] Yet the premodern and patriotic significance conferred upon the *jíbaro* has not altogether disappeared. In the same way, also prevalent is the emblematic construction of the rural landscape as a cradle of national culture that is "white" or at least nonblack.

This became evident in a series of fifteen interviews I conducted in the interior rural town of Naranjito during the *Jíbaro* Festival in 1996. My interviews not only aimed to elicit information about the cultural and racial identity that people attributed to this national symbol, but also to draw out spatial (rural versus coastal) associations people might hold.[29] Most of the people I interviewed stated that a *jíbaro* was a person who cultivates the land and maintains Puerto Rican traditions. When I asked for a more specific answer, people usually defined such traditions in terms of foods or crops, such as eating rice and beans, growing *malanga* (taro), and eating *yautía con aceite y bacalao* (yautia with oil and codfish); listening to *el seis*, *el cuatro*, and *el Aguinaldo* (music genres);[30] and behavioral traits such as being humble, good-hearted, and simple. Answers were often phrased in quite patriotic terms that rejected U.S. influence over the Island. One man, for example, stated:

> *Jíbaro* is every person who loves his homeland and who wishes to live in the homeland, not sell out his homeland to any other, who would be satisfied with just eating bananas, who does not give up, but keeps positive, like the Indians, who maintain their way of being and maintain their culture . . .
>
> Woe to him who does not consume anything [local], and all that he eats is hamburgers and hotdogs. That's not a *jíbaro*. *Jíbaro* is the one who still eats rice and beans and pig's feet, that's a *jíbaro*.

Other, less patriotic responses located the *jíbaro* in the past:

- In this age there aren't many *jíbaros*, Yes, there are shy people, but jíbaros there aren't . . . there might be some outside the metropolitan area . . . because there always are some . . . You visit a lot of barrios of Bayamón, Comerío, and the rest of the island and there are *jíbaros* and very nice, they're very humanitarian and have a lot of heart.

- Well, the idea that I have of a *jíbaro* is of the man that existed in Puerto Rico let's say around the 1940s and the '50s, around there, those people who started, who lived off the land and had no contact with the industrialized life that we have today.
- The *jíbaro*, as such, no longer exists, there is a concept, an idea.

When I asked people who is not a *jíbaro*, a common answer was "a person who is born and raised in the city." Hence, a rural–urban dichotomy (more than a rural versus coastal dichotomy) prevailed in the interview responses. Overwhelmingly, the coast was either subsumed within the larger urban category or it was recast as rural and included as part of everything else that is not San Juan (i.e., la Isla).

When I directly asked people if they would consider a black cane worker from the coast a *jíbaro*, some people answered yes and left the racial issue untouched. There were, however, a few others who commented further when confronted with the idea of a black *jíbaro* from the coast. One young man from the city of San Juan responded:

> I would say yes, but . . . that's not the generalized idea. The idea of the *jíbaro* almost always tends to be more from the mountains, tends to be whiter, more mixed, more like Spaniards, European customs. Blacks, in that sense, no, but since I think it's a feeling, I even believe that a Cuban, who comes and lives here for thirty-five years, can easily be called a *jíbaro*, if he's lived that way. But when we think of a black man, I would think so—it depends on how he acts—but that is not the generalized idea, obviously. I believe that people think that a *jíbaro* is this individual kind of white, darkened by the sun, not black, darkened by the sun, that's what we think a *jíbaro* is, by the stereotype. Now, I think that if he feels or acts like a *jíbaro*, I know black men that are *jíbaros*, depending on the area you're in, obviously. My old man is from Yauco [a mountain town], and over there the majority of the people are white, but Guánica [a coastal town] is nearby and there were people who went up there and grew coffee, and they have those customs and they're black and *jíbaros* too, they have the same customs we have.

In this interview, as in the ones that follow, the *jíbaro* was determined by his mountain dwelling, a location that made a black subjectivity problematic.

An old woman from Naranjito stated:

> No . . . No . . . I don't think so. I mean, it depends, because Puerto Rico is all *jíbaro*, know what I mean? Because, there may be *jíbaros* who are Africans, you know that Puerto Rico has African ancestry, ah . . . Indian, but the *jíbaro* people from Puerto Rico are from Puerto Rico, you might say that those blacks from over there from the coast are African that they come from . . . ah . . . Haiti, and other things, but the *jíbaro* people from Puerto Rico are from Puerto Rico: *jíbaro*.

Another woman stated:

> No, blacks and the people who work on the coast, no, those are *jornaleros* (laborers). Because the concept is more like country, inland, but if... if you see that the guy that cuts the cane more or less represents the charisma of a *jíbaro*, yes. But it's not the *jíbaro* that you see with the cow, with the pigs, plowing with oxen, carrying a bunch of plantains....

And a woman from Fajardo (a coastal town) said:

> Actually, that's also going to depend... because, the image that I have of a *jíbaro* is not that type, because they were the first ones here. See? And who also worked the land, but maybe, since I'm from the coast, because I'm from Fajardo, maybe I visualize the *jíbaro* like the people that work in the center of the Island.

Commenting on the construction of the *jíbaro*, Isabelo Zenón has noted that "the most serious problem with regard to our research is not that the *Jíbaro* has been made to represent the maximum expression of Puerto Ricanness, but that the black man has been excluded from *jíbaro*-ness (Zenón-Cruz 1975, 2:232).[31] Surely these interviews confirm his statement. People who elaborated on the question I posed stated that a black person from the coast deviated from the prevalent type of a *jíbaro*. Furthermore, in at least two instances people described black people as foreigners, either because they were from Africa or Haiti or because they were not "the original ones" who settled here.

However, the majority of people interviewed never voiced such racial identities explicitly. Only one person talked without further probing about a white identity when answering my question about what is a *jíbaro*. Even when I asked for a physical description, people rarely defined the *jíbaro* in racial terms. Instead, they provided descriptions of clothing (boots, long pants folded at the bottom, a worn-out long-sleeved shirt, a straw hat, the machete). Those who interpreted my use of "physical" to mean "racial" stated that race did not matter: "Well physically, I would say we're all alike." Another said: "No, because we're all brothers, *el blanco, el negro, el colora'o* [the white man, the black man, and the red man], like I say, we're all children of God." Only when I specifically asked about the black *jíbaro* from the coast did I get more elaborate comments on the question of "race." The *jíbaro*'s whiteness was presupposed but mostly unspoken. What was clearly voiced by people was the rural highland aspect of this identity.

Hence, to understand the underlying precepts behind the unspoken racial image of this national symbol (and the racism Zenón rightly exposed), one must also look at the racialized construction of regions in the production of national identity. This includes not only racialization of the rural landscape as an authentic national space that is nonblack, but also the corresponding erasure of coastal communities from national registers.

The Marked Whiteness of *Jíbaros* in San Antón

While in Naranjito, the regional category of "interior highland" took precedence over race in my interviews about the *jíbaro*; in San Antón, the process was almost the opposite. Here I found that residents—especially older residents—use the term *jíbaro* as a racial one to mean "white," regardless of that individual's ties to the land or mountain dwelling. I even heard an older resident describe a woman who was born and raised in San Antón as a *jíbara* because her skin color was lighter than most residents.' Associations of whiteness with *jíbaros* also take on spatial significance in the barrio. Some people, for example, used the term "white San Antón" to describe an area cut off by the Las Américas avenue. Later I found out that this was an area where *jíbaros* had settled.

Such labels were also used in sports. According to one man who was born and raised in San Antón, when he and other kids of the eastern sector played baseball with those who lived across the avenue, they used the names "White San Antón" and "Black San Antón" to distinguish the teams. He said:

> Where we're standing, they used to call it "Black San Antón," and where I used to live, "White San Antón." But if you notice, I'm not white. I'm darker than the blacks from Black San Antón. And there was a rivalry in sports. When we organized teams, well, the area of Black San Antón organized a team and the area of White San Antón organized a team, and then over there, that's "Rebel San Antón." And Rebel San Antón were the players who didn't play with Black San Antón or White San Antón, they were the ones left over.

When I asked him whether these names corresponded to the color of the players, he laughed, making a mocking grin, and said:

> No, no . . . no that wasn't true, that wasn't true. What happened is that the area that I'm talking to you about, which was called White San Antón, which is the area where the Avenue of the Americas divides, let's say east and west . . . the people were lighter, then that's why they mostly called it White San Antón. But really, if we take a look, the proportion in terms of color was more or less the same.

Two older residents I interviewed laughed at the *white* label, commenting that the barrio had always been known as a community of black folk. They did mention, nevertheless, that the western section—the so-called White San Antón" (also referred to as *la Solaya*)—was in fact an area where lots of *jíbaros* (or white folks from the mountains) had settled in the old days. The important issue being underscored was, nevertheless, that people were lighter.

Thus, while the highland origin of *jíbaros* took precedence over racial criteria at the Festival of Naranjito, in San Antón, the racial description of "white" took precedence over the criterion of highland origins. In this context, the whiteness (or at least lightness) of the *jíbaro* was a marked category.

Blanqueamiento in Ponce

Just as the coast/highland strategy of *blanqueamiento* operates at a broader national level, local constructions of Ponce also locate blackness somewhere else (in San Antón, for example). In this process, Ponce often presents itself as urban (not as coastal) in relationship to other sites of the Puerto Rican landscape. Hence, while Ponce proudly affirms itself as "the most Puerto Rican city" and flaunts its cosmopolitan "aristocratic" past in tourist brochures and public documents, San Antón is construed as a "pre-modern folkloric colorful exception." This does not mean traditions associated with African heritage are necessarily rendered unrepresentative of the city's history (it would be impossible to do so in Ponce). Yet dominant representations that speak of the black folklore of certain communities often isolate them from other "privileged" fragments of the city's past in ways that render black sites like San Antón "less mixed," "less modern," and "more homogeneously black" than the rest of the aristocratic city.

Certain historical antecedents could justify the interpretation of black sites such as San Antón as separate and racially segregated barrios of Ponce. As a sugar-producing urban region, Ponce fostered a powerful class of merchants and *hacendados* whose businesses depended upon the institution of slavery. The economic growth generated by these favorable conditions also created hierarchical distinctions between the urban and the rural, between the rich *hacendados* and the poor agricultural workers, between the free and the slave, between those classified as white and those classified as black (Quintero-Rivera 1988, 46; Findlay 1999; Rodríguez-Silva 2012).

Historically, however, urban centers such as Ponce also provided a variety of occupational opportunities for free blacks and slaves in areas such as domestic work, construction, transportation, and the crafts. These sources of labor entailed constant interaction among those classified as "black" (usually slaves), those classified as *mulatos*, *pardos*, and *libertos* (usually free people of color), and those classified as "white." They also allowed slaves a greater degree of economic independence, distinguishing their experiences from those who worked only in the rural sector. In cities, a number of slaves were able to find additional sources of income and living conditions independent from the hacienda, placing them in a better position to buy their freedom. Raul Mayo and collaborators have emphasized that the physical immediacy provoked by the crowded conditions of dwellings and business establishments in cities also brought people of different racial and class backgrounds together, shortening social distances and creating "*espacios de convivencia y sociabilidad cotidiana*" (spaces of cohabitation and of everyday social living) (Mayo-Santana et al. 1997, 36). Cities such as Ponce thus provided the enslaved with a network of social relations and opportunities no doubt built upon a very racist foundation, but that allowed them some degree of autonomy, increasing their options for improving their socioeconomic situation in close interaction with other sectors of society.

Inhabitants of San Antón also participated in interactions that crossed class and racial boundaries. In fact, San Antón was predominantly populated by free blacks and a number of people classified as white during the slavery period (before 1873). Yet popular representations of the barrio's history fail to acknowledge this complex past, insisting on scripts of blackness that cast San Antón as a homogeneous community of ex-slaves. Links between such scripts and the previously discussed politics of erasure are further elucidated (and challenged) in the next chapter.

CHAPTER 3

Unfolkloric Slavery

Alternative Histories of San Antón

In 1995, a year before construction work began in San Antón, a national newspaper published the following account of the origins of the barrio:

> La comunidad de San Antón se organiza por grupos de esclavos que llegaron a Ponce de la mano de colonos extranjeros. Estos, atraídos por los incentivos de la Cédula de Gracia, promulgada en el 1815 por la Corona Española, llegaron a Ponce aportando en gran medida al desarrollo económico del poblado. Y con ellos también llegaron grandes comunidades de esclavos....
>
> Con la abolición de la esclavitud promulgada en el 1872 [sic], se dio una transición de labor esclava a una asalariada. La mayoría de los esclavos fueron desalojados [sic] de sus plantaciones, y pasaron a ocupar terrenos sin uso, ya bien cercanos a las plantaciones mismas, o a los poblados. Así San Antón creció hasta convertirse en uno de los mayores asentamientos de esclavos libertos de Ponce. Con la abolición de la esclavitud se registra una nueva comunidad de asalariados a finales del siglo XIX en oficios diestros y trabajos urbanos como carpinteros, tabaqueros, albañiles, tipógrafos, barberos, sastres, costureras, planchadoras y cocineras.[1] (González 1995, S-5)
>
> [The community of San Antón was organized by groups of slaves who came to Ponce *by the hand* of foreign settlers. These, attracted by the incentives of the Cédula de Gracias, issued in 1815 by the Spanish crown, arrived in Ponce contributing a great deal to the economic development of the settlement. And with them, large communities of slaves also arrived....

With the abolition of slavery, proclaimed in 1872 [sic], a transition from slave labor to wage labor took place. The majority of slaves, having been thrown out of the plantations, went to occupy unused lands close to the plantations or to settlements. This was the manner in which San Antón grew into one of the largest free slave settlements of Ponce. With the abolition of slavery, at the end of the nineteenth century, a new community of wage earners was registered in skilled trades and urban jobs such as carpenters, tobacco workers, masons, typographers, barbers, tailors, seamstresses, persons who ironed clothes, and cooks.] (González 1995, S-5, my emphasis)

Although the author recognizes the skilled labor of the men and women who lived in San Antón, this article reproduces the aforementioned politics of erasure in its representation of the enslaved as passive subjects who came to Ponce "by the hand" of European settlers. As discussed in the previous chapter, historians and others challenged this benevolent point of view after the 1970s, as evidenced during the Housing Ceremony when San Antón's residents and the theater group Taller La Brisa presented a defiant rendition of their community's history, proclaiming San Antón slaves made Ponce "with their sweat, blood, and tears."

However, despite important differences between these two historic renditions of the community, they share one thing in common: they locate San Antón's origins in post-abolition times. Whether the land was given, occupied, or "earned" through hard work, we are told that those who settled here were slaves who gained their freedom after the abolition of slavery in 1873. Intellectuals who value the preservation of San Antón's cultural patrimony also share this interpretation. For example, in her article "Identity, Power and Place at the Periphery" (1998) Wanda I. Mills, a progressive urban planner from Ponce, states: "Located in close proximity to the fields and three central sugar factories, the proletarian community arose from the marginal flood-plain lands, along the banks of the temperamental Portugues [sic] River. When the enslaved peoples received their freedom in 1873, the former masters passed on land rights to some residents, while others migrated to San Antón from nearby municipalities and distant Caribbean islands" (Mills-Bocachica 1998, 39).

However, we know from census documents that there was already a sizable population of free skilled laborers in San Antón *before* official emancipation in 1873. In fact, comparing San Antón's population figures for 1860 to the figures for other barrios, we see that San Antón had the second-largest concentration of free people of color in all of Ponce.[2] Those classified as whites formed the second-largest group in the sector and slaves the third (see Table 2).[3] Population figures in this sector did increase after the abolition of slavery. However, much more drastic increments in population are noted before the abolition of slavery, between 1841 and 1868, when the population of the sector almost doubled from 354 to 657.

Table 2: Nineteenth Century Census Data for San Antón

Year	Whites	Free People of Color **	Slaves	Total
1827	n.a.	n.a.	n.a.	105^
1838	28^	33^	66	348
1841	n.a	n.a	57	354
1850	143	189	n.a	332*
1860	187	190	163	540
	35%	35%	30%	
1868	212	258	187	657
	32%	39%	28%	
1869	195	277	188	660
	30%	42%	28%	
1871	222	299	153	674
	33%	44%	23%	
1897				824
1899				963
1910				1,163

Combined Sources: Historical Archives of the Autonomous Municipality of Ponce, Puerto Rico. Box #: S54–S548, S-599 and *Ponce y Sus Barrios* (Junta de Planificación de Puerto Rico, 1953: 3).
** Free non-whites or free people of color included here are those people listed as *pardos, negros libres, mulatos libres*, or *personas de color* in the census.
* San Antón and Bejuco Blanco appear listed together.
^ Head of Household listed only
n.a Data not available

Of course, colonial census data are not neutral and reproduce the inequalities that made them possible, before they entered the archive (Trouillot 1995). However, the point to make here is that in this case, the dominant discourses silence an available record. Despite the relative accessibility of these census documents, the key role played by free people of color during the slavery period in San Antón is not contemplated or mentioned in representations of the barrio's history—not even by those who seek to put forth an alternative rendition. Overwhelmingly, the barrio's origins are traced to post-abolition times. Lay versions of San Antón's origins also invalidate the impact of "white" peasants in the area, highlighting instead the presence of slaves. Why?

Scholars have argued that the past does not exist independently from the present (Trouillot 1995; Handler and Gable 1997). Stories people tell about the past are constructed in a context where powerful political and cultural forces operate to produce narratives and silences. Hence, it is important to examine not only "what happened," but also "that which is said to have happened" at a particular moment (Trouillot 1995, 2). Although San Antón's post-abolition origin story may not make sense against the historical record, much can be learned by asking why this version is the one that predominates and has social currency.

Post-emancipation origin stories about San Antón grant public salience and cultural legitimacy to the barrio as a site of Afro–Puerto Rican musical traditions such as the *bomba* and *plena*, which are linked to Africa and to the cultural knowledge that slaves brought with them. One account of the development of *bomba* in Ponce, for example, states that "The *bomba* constitutes one of the most deep-rooted musical genres in the area of Ponce. The diverse African rhythms brought by the first slaves settled into the atmosphere of the Antilles, and through the years turned into the *bomba*. On holidays, *slaves were permitted* to celebrate their festivities, which included the dance of *bomba*. *These dances had a great preponderance in the barrio of San Antón, a place where a large number of free slaves resided*" (Departamento de Educación 1992, 33, my emphasis).[4]

Such tracings of San Antón's genealogy to slaves facilitate public recognition of *bomba* as a cultural product of the community. Stressing the role that free people of color played in San Antón prior to the abolition of slavery would complicate facile connections between slavery and the development of the *bomba* and the *plena* in San Antón, so vital to the national folkloric script. Hence, in the dominant discourses, either slavery is completely erased from the narratives or it is simplified via scripts that efface the efforts of free people of color to survive and seek dignity within a system that tried to deny it to them.

Scholars have documented how associated silences are sustained in historical sites restored for tourism (Flores 2002; Handler and Gable 1997; Trouillot 1995; Handler 1988; Pinho 2010). Touristic investments that use national culture as a tool for neoliberal development in the Afro-Atlantic world often draw on sanitized versions of histories that bypass internal conflict and inequalities to entertain those who can afford to invest in the experience (Collins 2008; Pinho 2010; Scher 2011; Cuning and Rinaudo 2008; Roland 2006; Gotham 2007; Handler and Gable 1997; Pattullo 1996; Giovannetti 2006; Edmonds 2003). Post-abolition renditions of San Antón's past were not primarily motivated by tourism, since, as mentioned previously, there are no plans to take tourists there. Yet similar process of representation occurred here as government agencies, local intellectuals, cultural activists, and Ponce residents could imagine the community only in terms of such dominant scripts of Afro–Puerto Rican culture. Hence, the politics of erasure that sustains such scripts in San Antón and elsewhere does not necessarily need the economic draw of tourism to thrive against any counterevidence available. These scripts persist because they are "easy to think," because they rest on ideas about the past that are broadly disseminated, are well known, and are built on tacit agreements that, in turn, inform practices and activities (and housing initiatives) that make proponents look like good citizens who are proud of their African heritage. Articulating them, in the context of prevalent silences about slavery, may even seem like a dissident or counterestablishment stance. On the contrary, challenging the post-abolition narrative that equates blackness with slavery to highlight free people of color provokes the dissonance of evoking a past that is not well known, shared, or celebrated. Furthermore, as Trouillot points out, the unearthing of an alternative not only requires producing new facts, but also the extra labor of creating a new narrative and context in which the story can find significance—an alternative script, one may say. In the words of Trouillot (1995), "The unearthing of silences and the historian's subsequent emphasis on the retrospective significance of hitherto neglected events, requires not only extra labor at the archives—whether or not one uses primary sources—but also a project linked to an interpretation" (58). In the case of San Antón, the alternative interpretation would summon a colonial subjectivity (rather than a national one) that easily transcends the boundaries of San Antón, making the struggle for survival within a colonial/slavery regime wide-ranging and typical rather than localized and unique.

The erasure of free people of color and whites from renditions of San Antón's history is thus part and parcel of the previously discussed politics of erasure that equates blackness with slavery and casts it as an exceptional and geographically contained aspect of Puerto Rican history. In the context of such discourses, San Antón becomes a proxy, not only for blackness but for slavery. In this sense, the history of slavery is, to use Jacqueline Nassy Brown's phrase (2000, 363) enslaved itself, held in captivity within the boundaries of the community. Thus, while slavery is declared unimportant at a national level, in San Antón historical antecedents can *only* be about slavery. While notions of race mixture and *blanqueamiento* are emphasized for Puerto Rico, San Antón is essentialized as black and the region's links to slavery simplified. My criticism of such representations does not seek to extend notions of *blanqueamiento* or benevolent slavery to San Antón. Rather, I seek to question the script that claims it is *only* in San Antón where slavery mattered and that, when it mattered, its effects upon the community adopted such essentialized forms.

On this issue of historical production, Trouillot has noted that "the past ... is always a position" (1995, 15). What makes one story better than another is not empirical exactitude but the relationship between information and circumstances (political, moral, ethical) of the present. Authenticity, according to Trouillot, always resides in "the struggles of our present" in the "current practices that engage us as witnesses, actors and commentators—including practices of historical narration" (1995, 150–51). Thus my goal in this chapter is not so much to argue for or against any truth claims made about the institution of slavery or to argue that a story about free people of color should always be privileged over slavery in San Antón. One narrative does not have an inherently decontextualized value over another. Narratives about slavery can have the subversive potential of summoning and denouncing the prevalence of racial hierarchies produced by this history. As we saw in Chapter 2, Taller La Brisa used a narrative of slavery to question the government's position as "givers" of land in San Antón. The performance illustrates that while scripts are mediated by powerful actors, folklore practitioners might very well use them in unexpected contexts to challenge a dominant rhetoric.

Here I do not argue primarily for or against any truth claims made about the institution of slavery or its ties to San Antón. Confronting the historical record with dominant renditions of the past is important. Yet, more than historical *accuracy*, my concern is with historical *relevance*, since such post-emancipation renditions of the barrio's origins had little or no correspondence with many residents' own understandings of their community.

When I interviewed older residents about the barrio's history, there was no mention of the community being established after or before the abolition of slavery. Furthermore, when speaking about the community's history in general, people spoke of changes in the landscape as they described how properties were attained, sold, bought, and transformed into different spaces. In that sense, knowing about the community's history did not have to do with the practices of origins as much as it had to do with knowing the practices of change.

Furthermore, I found residents' stories about the barrio's past to be predominantly informed not by *bomba* and *plena* or slavery but by personal narratives that addressed issues of land tenure, kinship ties, and work in the cane industry. Therefore, and following Trouillot's understanding that "authenticity belongs to the present," the following sections draw on these locally meaningful thematic categories to reconstruct an alternative history of the community.

An Alternative History of San Antón

Residents' descriptions of San Antón's origins differ from the previously discussed post-abolition origin story that traces San Antón's beginnings to the benevolent gesture of *hacendados* who "gave away their land to their slaves." Rather, what is highlighted in residents' narratives is the fact that the land was already theirs. When I asked Anelo how San Antón originated, for example, she answered:

> I don't know about that. I know that since I can remember, almost everybody who lived here were the owners of their own land. Like now, that almost everybody has his or her land and their own home, that's what I remember. There where Don Ramón lives, that was my uncle's. He was my aunt's husband, my mother's sister, huge pieces of land. That man was the uncle of the Perezes' grandmother; his name was José Torres. On this side, that place on this side belonged to another family. This little piece here was sold to a lady whose last name is Torruella; my dad told me about that, they bought this here to build that cooperative. We lived there, because, since my father was the secretary, he was the bookkeeper, so we lived there. And look, here, that belonged to the Franseschi family, that land was theirs, until many years

later after they were going to build the [electrical] tower, because Fuentes Fluviales [the Power Authority] bought that from them and put them over there. This little piece here, where the basketball court's at, belonged to Don Rafael Saurí, who's the owner of Central Constancia. That's who my brother bought this house from. The rest over there were properties. Where the little store is over there, that belongs to the Rentas family, Malena's store. All of that, in that direction, belonged to her father.[5]

In this way, San Antón residents draw a map of their community that speaks of modes of reckoning "community" and belonging. Cardinal points in Anelo's map are marked by family names of landowners. Her story is also one of change and impermanence, as she describes how properties were sold, bought, and transformed into different spaces (the basketball court, the municipality's electrical facilities).

When I asked Don Gustavo how San Antón was established and what were its origins, he said:

> I'm going to tell you something. It has never been said here . . . it has never been said here, how San Antón was long ago. In those years . . . well, since what I know, you see. But since the time that I've lived here in San Antón, I've never heard talk of how everything was in San Antón. Nor who founded it . . . nothing like that . . .

Don Gustavo is a seventy-two-year-old man who describes himself as "indio." He was brought to San Antón as a small child by his father when he moved from Guayanilla to Ponce to work at the Hacienda Estrella. Unlike other people in San Antón, who live in family clusters, his was a one-man household and he did not own the land he occupied. He recalls that when he came to live in San Antón with his father, they lived in the barracks of the hacienda. He explained: "They weren't houses like these, they were barracks next to railroad tracks . . . the train and cane freight cars passed through there." When they moved from there, they rented a house in an area people used to call *el fanguito* (the muddy place). They lived there until the municipality expropriated the lands to channel the river. Then Don Gustavo moved once again, still renting but always within the boundaries of San Antón. In these and other stories that residents told me about the barrio's history, they emphasized the different transformations the community had undergone and how things were not the same now as they were before.

Like Don Gustavo, Arcenia offered me a story about change and spatial transformation. At age seventy-four and retired, Arcenia lived in a small house in the western section of San Antón (the section cut off by the avenue). She explained this was so "since they divided this—'cause San Antón is divided, my child, right now we're here, the channeling of the river and after that the expressway, the cyclone fence that they've made—*nosotros estamos como acorralados* [we're basically fenced in]. Arcenia could point to how San Antón had changed, but when it came to talk about how it began she said:

> ARCENIA: Can you believe that I don't know.
> ISAR: Or who were the first persons to establish themselves here in the beginning?
> ARCENIA: No, I don't know. I can't say. That would have to be told by a person ... well, if any of them still exist, who could tell you. And that should be over there in the archives. So if you don't find the information to that question you asked me, it's got to be there.

Archival References

According to Ponce's historical archives, San Antón makes its first appearance as a bureaucratic unit for census purposes in 1827, a time of heightened economic development for Ponce, particularly in the sugarcane industry. The geographical location of San Antón at that time is hard to determine, since it does not appear on any of the nineteenth-century maps available in Ponce's archives. Most nineteenth-century maps of Ponce limit themselves to the urban zone, the area most affected by government administration and impacted by its infrastructural public works. San Antón was somewhat marginal to this state-controlled space. Its residents' lives were more regulated by the local power structure of the haciendas than by state bureaucracy. In fact, San Antón does not even figure in a list of fifteen barrios prepared for the population census of 1827.[6] Similarly, the barrio's correspondence is scarce in comparison with correspondence sent by deputies of other barrios to the city council. Nineteenth-century letters from the city council addressed to the deputy mayor of San Antón remained, for the most part, unanswered.

This somewhat marginal relationship between the barrio and Ponce's state bureaucracy is also evident in the maps produced before the turn of the twentieth century, since San Antón is neither represented nor named in any of them. Exactly what the physical parameters of this region were is thus not a question that can be easily answered. Nevertheless, U.S. population census data indicate that the estimated area for this sector in 1899 was 1.15 square miles with a population of 963 people (Junta de Planificación de Puerto Rico 1953). We also know from Spanish census documents that prior to 1827, San Antón was called Bejuco Blanco. Fortunately, there is an 1818 map of Ponce that shows Bejuco Blanco, which gives an idea of San Antón's location in relationship to the town of Ponce (see Map 3).[7] Here San Antón and the former Bejuco Blanco were situated between the Portugués and the Bucaná rivers, a location that probably afforded extra labor for the irrigation of nearby sugarcane fields but that also increased the possibility of floods, making these lands ill-favored for living.

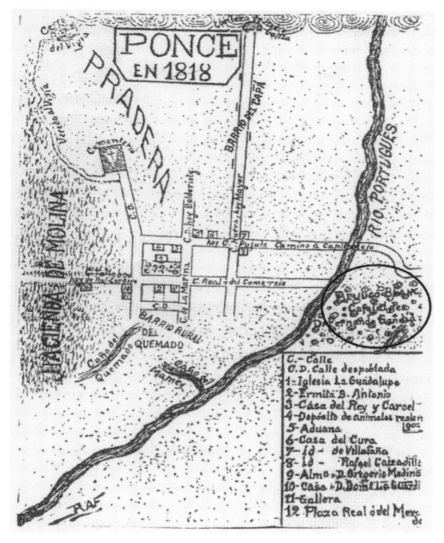

Map 3. Map of Ponce (1818). Area corresponding to Bejuco Blanco is circled. Source: Historical Archives of the Autonomous Municipality of Ponce, Puerto Rico.

A document from 1867 lists thirty wooden houses and fifty-one *ranchos* or *bohíos* (small house structures) in this sector. It is possible that, upon manumission, some of the ancestors of present-day residents of San Antón established themselves in these uncultivated lands adjacent to the sugarcane fields that belonged to Haciendas Estrella and Constancia, along the shore of the Portugués and Bucaná rivers. Since free people of color enjoyed a considerable degree of freedom compared to slaves, it is also possible that ancestors of present-day San Antón residents bought the land from *hacendados*. According to historian Jay Kinsbruner, free people of color had access to the courts and to the town councils, where they could, for instance, appear to request the purchase or rental of a piece of land owned by the town (Kinsbruner 1996, 44). They could own stores, acquire land, and inherit property without restrictions (Kinsbruner 1996, 25). In fact, free people of color constituted 33 percent of the land-owning class in Puerto Rico by the middle of the nineteenth century.

San Antón residents listed in nineteenth-century documents as free people of color (usually referred to as *pardos* in the census) worked as skilled laborers. Skilled jobs listed among the free people of color in this area during the earlier half of the nineteenth century are laundress, seamstress, *jornalero* (laborer), shoemaker, mason, carpenter, *fumasero* (tobacco-leaf worker), and *arrimado* (resident farmhand). The skilled nature of some of these jobs suggests that these free people of African descent played an important role not only in the development of nearby haciendas, but also beyond San Antón in the broader urban context of Ponce. The 1860 census registers additional job activities such as coach maker, merchant, tailor, domestic, and lathe operator.

A detailed investigation of the historical record may point to interesting pre- and post-emancipation landholding patterns among the free colored population of San Antón during the first half of the nineteenth century. Such research is beyond the scope of the present study. Nevertheless, Don Carlos offered some interesting information about the process of land attainment when he talked about his grandmother. He talked about how she saved money to buy land in San Antón, money that the wife of one of the owners of the Hacienda Estrella kept for her.

What was the name of your grandmother?" I asked.

"Lucrecia Roque," responded Carlos. "At that time Luisa Gastón offered her *un cuadro de terreno* [a piece of land] there [pointing to the lands that are now occupied by the Puerto Rico Electric Power Authority]. When she offered her that piece of land there where Fuentes Fluviales [the Power Authority] is, Doña Maria Subirá, the wife of Don Arciso Subirá, shareholders of Hacienda Estrella, had kept the money for her and told her, 'Petronila, here is your money, put me down as a witness,' and she put her down as a witness."

When I asked Don Carlos about his grandmother and what she looked like, he said,

> Well, *trigueña* . . . [black/brown] because according to my ancestors, the mother of my grandmother *pertenecía* [*belonged*] to a small hacienda that was somewhere around there, her name was Luisa Roque—my grandmother's mother. Then my mother was born in the Estrella. My grandmother's job was cleaning filters, because it wasn't

like in the Central, where there were *prensas* [presses]. Not then. In the old days, you had to do it with a brush. That was her job, and she put some money together to buy that land over there. Then, when Don Rafael Saurí [son of one of the owners of la Hacienda Estrella] married the American girl, Doña Isabel, who was Betsy, then Don Felix Saurí left her the house . . . but the office was downstairs. But they were upstairs. During that time my mother was born in the Estrella. That's where she [his grandmother] put together the money to buy that over there. Those deeds are in San Juan, when they expropriated that land." [My emphasis on the word *belonged*.]

It is interesting that many residents of San Antón trace ownership of houses to women, an issue that deserves further study.[8] In this case, Don Carlos spoke of a grandmother who was the daughter of a slave who saved money to buy the land. The reader might notice that Don Carlos's use of the word *belonged* (*pertenecía*) allowed him to talk about his great-grandmother in terms that alluded to her slave status but that did not label her explicitly as such. Similarly, his use of *trigueña* alluded to her mother's nonwhite status but did not label her as *negra* (black).

Doña Laura, another resident, also traced the ownership of the first family house to her grandmother, Francisca Roque. Doña Laura described her grandmother as a woman who was "*no* prieta *prieta, sino morena, o sea, más clara*" (not *black* black, but dark, you know, lighter). According to Doña Laura, she was married to Gerónimo Arce, a slave who appears on the census of 1873 as having been born in Africa in 1818. Neldi also traces the land to her grandmother in our interview: "My father was brought up in poverty. There, in that cleared piece of land, he lived there, because that land belonged to them . . . to my grandmother."

When I asked her if she knew how her grandmother obtained the land, Neldi responded, "Those people in the old days worked and they had their foremen and overseers, and if they didn't have money to pay them, they'd give them a small piece of land. But how they [her family] got that land, I don't know."

Historian Andrés Ramos Mattei further explains Neldi's statement about *hacendados* giving land in exchange for work. *Hacendados* benefitted from the labor of small landowners whose land had been absorbed by the hacienda by allowing them to stay in their former plots of land in exchange for their labor. *Hacendados* also provided housing to those whose work was crucial for the performance of daily activities in the hacienda (Ramos-Mattei 1982, 95).

This was a small price to pay, since the work of the *liberto* was highly valued. Before emancipation, *libertos* performed tasks related to the processing of sugar in the mills. The high temperatures and loud noise of the processing factories made these the most onerous tasks. From the point of view of *hacendados*, however, *libertos* were also the most knowledgeable labor force and the most familiar with daily routines of sugar production. That placed them at a high position in the hierarchy of labor. As stated in a report offered in 1875 by the British consul: "In fact in the process of sugar making, the more skilled *liberto* (freed slave) is generally employed within the boiling house while the free laborer does the rougher task of cutting and carrying the cane"[9] (Consul Pauli quoted in Ramos-Mattei 1982, 114, see also Rodríguez-Silva 2012, 111). As the sugarcane industry became more mechanized, the knowledge and skills of *libertos* became more indispensable, especially after the harvest, or *zafra*, when the workforce was reduced to its minimum.

Consequently, after the abolition of slavery in 1873, *hacendados* adopted various methods to try to keep *libertos* working for them. One strategy consisted of offering *libertos* small plots of land on the grounds of the hacienda.[10] *Libertos* could farm and grow animals for their family's subsistence in these plots. The opportunity to have a living unit and plot of land was an improvement over the communal and crowded barracks where they previously lived as slaves. The ownership of land, albeit small, also gave *libertos* some degree of autonomy. According to Ramos-Mattei, most *libertos* stayed on the haciendas and continued to work for their former owners after emancipation (Ramos-Mattei 1982, 106). But the new living arrangement also benefitted *hacendados*, since it guaranteed them a supply of skilled labor. Many *hacendados* also freed themselves from the obligation of providing meals for their workers, or protecting them in case of injury.

Settlement and living arrangements in San Antón were not only determined by land acquisition. During the nineteenth and early twentieth centuries, many landless *jíbaros* migrated from the mountains to do seasonal work in the coastal cane industry. Forced to work under the labor laws of *el régimen de la libreta* (1849–73), *jíbaros* migrated during the harvest months (from January to May or June), when there was sugarcane to cut, transport, and grind. In San Antón, these landless free men remained stationed in temporary living quarters located on the grounds of the hacienda. After the harvest, during *el tiempo muerto* (harvest downtime), many returned to their families and original towns, but others stayed in San Antón.

Settlement patterns among *libertos* probably changed between the beginning and the middle of the twentieth century. However, it seems that certain elements in the landscape prevailed many decades later. Two male residents in their late fifties and sixties, Guillo and David, told me that people in San Antón called the *jíbaro* quarters of Hacienda Estrella *la prángana* [penniless]. Guillo remembers because he was about twelve years old then. The *jíbaros* who stayed there slept on hammocks. Some brought their wives with them, and others came by themselves and stayed, they said. "*Ahí fue que la raza se fue aclarando*" (that is when the race started getting lighter), pointed out Guillo, "*porque esos jíbaros se quedaban con las negras de acá*" (because those *jíbaros* stayed with the black women from here). Guillo said that was the case of Joaquín, Elena's husband, *el cócoro* [nickname], who came from Adjuntas and afterward did not want to go back. "He said he was from San Antón; he came to cut cane with his uncles, one they called 'Juan el Coco' [Juan the Coconut]."

Social Dynamics of Cohabitation

How did the black *libertos* of San Antón see themselves in relation to the seasonally employed and less skilled "white" *jíbaros*? Some scholars have argued that this sharing of low-status economic positions by those labeled white and those labeled black served as a social equalizer between racially diverse groups. The crucial cleavage, it is often argued, was social class—not skin color (Duany 1985; Dungy 2005). Kathryn Dungy, for instance, argues that "While Puerto Rico was not a racial utopia, the co-existence of rural free people of color and poor whites of this pre-plantation era island helped to alleviate many of the tensions which persisted elsewhere in the Caribbean during the late eighteenth and early nineteenth centuries" (2005, 84).

Many of the jobs listed for *pardos* (free people of color) in San Antón in the 1860s were also shared by whites, although the overwhelming majority of whites (67 percent) are listed as *labradores* (farmhands). Certain job activities, such as *hacendado* and *agricultor* (farmer), appeared only next to the names of those listed as whites. Additional job activities listed for whites and rarely for *pardos* in San Antón were majordomo, industrial worker, and military sergeant. Overall, however, there is evidence of significant overlap between the job activities of those listed as "whites" and those listed as *pardos*. This trend in San Antón supports the observation made by other scholars that in nineteenth-century Puerto Rico there were many examples of "whites" occupying low-status positions in the economy. One census entry for 1850, for example, shows a "white" man listed as a *labrador* (farmhand), his wife as a laundress, and his three older daughters as servants.

Based on this information, one could conclude that *jíbaros* and *libertos* were thrown into highly egalitarian social relationships. Yet the situation seems to be more complicated. Although *libertos* and *jíbaros* occupied similar positions in the distribution of wealth and resources, their positions were not perceived as equal. In fact, it's very probable that the status difference between them influenced the local code of racial dynamics in ways that privileged *libertos*—and therefore blackness—in San Antón. Guillo and David, for example, told me that "*El negro no corta caña*" (The black man doesn't cut cane). "Why is that?" I asked. "I don't know why," was David's answer, "but that's how it was. Blacks did other kinds of work," such as filling up wagons, shoveling, working the machinery, he said. They used Don Carlos as an example. He drove the engines of the hacienda. They told me they used to call the biggest engine "La Petra" and that there was another one called "Macundú." "*Era raro que la gente de aquí picara caña*" (It was a rare thing that people from here cut cane), concluded Guillo.

Another factor that complicates the assertion that landless free blacks and whites were social equals is the powerful stigma of slavery. The fact that *libertos* occupied a higher ranking in the social hierarchy of labor certainly complicated but did not undermine the very powerful racial prejudices of the times. *Libertos* might have enjoyed a preferential position in San Antón and within the context of sugar production in general, but social relationships among the people of this community did not operate independent of the racial precepts of nineteenth-century Puerto Rican colonial society.

Jay Kinsbruner (1996) argues that during the nineteenth century, free people of color were a disadvantaged community whose political, social, and economic performance was diminished by racial prejudice. While it is true that this sector of the population enjoyed relatively broad latitude of participation in the economy, Puerto Rico was a racially restrictive society. As such, free people of color were presumed to be illegitimate children of obscure or "vile" birth who also carried the stigma of slavery. Lines of demarcation between whites and nonwhites were often established on census documents, town council proceedings, and notarial records. Furthermore, Spanish colonial legislation prohibited people of color from holding prominent positions in civil bureaucracy, in the church, and as officers of the regular army. Individuals of "dubious" racial status had to prove their *limpieza de sangre* (purity of blood) through formal documentation that would make them eligible for holding public office as whites. Marriage was another realm in which racial purity mattered, especially for the *criollo* bourgeoisie; parents could object to the proposed marriage of their sons or daughters on the grounds that their fiancé or their families were *mulatos*.

Such dynamics of race and class make themselves evident in Neldi's account of the relationship between her white grandfather and black grandmother. Her grandfather was one of those *jíbaros* who came to San Antón to cut cane during the *zafra* and stayed afterward. She recalls:

NELDI: He was short. He had blue eyes. *Jíbaro*. Like we say, *jíbaro*. He was so nice. My father used to say that our grandma worked in the cane fields, and that's where they fell in love.
ISAR: And what did your grandma look like?
NELDI: My grandma was *estilo africana* [African type], her name was Antonia Tricoche, and she was one of the tall ones . . . she had la *nariz grande* [a large nose], she did, but my grandpa was *perfila'o* [narrow nosed]. I think they had six children. He lived here, with her, but his family, since they were white and she was black, well, they didn't like it, our dad used to tell us. And he came to live over here and they never went back there.

The fact that *libertos* occupied a higher ranking in the social hierarchy of labor but a lower ranking in the racial order complicates any facile premise about their being equal to the so-called "white" *jíbaros*. It also complicates the facile prioritization of class over race, and the common assertion that when people share similar positions in the distribution of wealth and resources color matters little, a theory often voiced by historians prior to 1970.[11]

On the other hand, because racial categories are always highlighted by people's position in the economy, one cannot disregard the importance of class and status in promoting or discouraging alliances among those considered of the same "racial background." Important distinctions among nonwhites who were free were made in census documents and in everyday life between free "blacks" (usually referred to as *negros libres* in the census) and *mulatos* (sometimes also referred to as *pardos* or as *de color* in the census). Although color was an important symbol of social status, these distinctions were not implemented on the sole basis of phenotype but also had to do with people's socioeconomic position. Those classified as blacks were, for the most part, slaves or *libertos* who worked in agriculture. Those classified as *mulatos*, *de color*, or *pardos* (the use of categories varies depending on the census) were usually skilled artisans (masons, carpenters, smiths, and coopers) who worked in the city. Many also performed skilled jobs in the hacienda, constructing and repairing the buildings and machinery of the plantation. After each harvest, for example, a mechanic was hired to get the processing equipment ready for the next grinding.

These skilled laborers were nonwhite, but they were not considered black either. Martínez-Alier (1974) has noted that, in Cuba, it was a general aspiration among free people of color to become as light as possible and to get as far away from slavery as possible. Writing about the early nineteenth century in the Dominican Republic, Moya Pons noted that for many colored Dominicans, only the slaves (and Haitians) were black and could be treated as such (1996, 16).[12] In Puerto Rico, some free people of color (often classified as *pardos*) were two or three generations detached from slavery and were regarded as "respectable" members of their societies by the *criollo* elites. Ponce, in particular, had a large sector of black and brown urban artisans who participated actively among the ranks of liberal political parties and urban social life at the end of the nineteenth and beginning of the twentieth century. Urban artisans had mutual aid societies, publications, education circles, dances, and theatrical performances, and they were important political brokers in the city (Rodríguez-Silva 2012, 112; Findlay 1999; Hoffnung-Garskof 2011). These *pardo* patricians were of a very different social class than *libertos* and probably went to some efforts to distinguish themselves from them. The flight from slavery not only meant placing a high premium on whiteness, but also included establishing social distance from those who were closer to its stigma. The dynamics between *libertos* and skilled artisans in San Antón must have been influenced by these factors.

Another factor that influenced racial categorization among free people of color was land ownership. The census of 1838, for example, listed a total of thirty-three *pardo* families, most of whom had *arrimados* also listed as *pardos*. *Arrimados* were people who settled on someone else's plot of land in exchange for labor and/or a share of the crops harvested in the occupied land. Further research needs to be done in this area. Yet I would venture to say that, although categorized under the same racial label for census purposes, the landless status of these *pardos arrimados* translated into informal racial markers that distinguished them from the *pardos* who owned the land they occupied.

Work in the Cane Industry (Post-Emancipation)

Most of the information I obtained about San Antón through interviews was about post-emancipation times (not about free people of color during the slavery period). In particular, the work people did in the nearby hacienda as Estrella and Constancia figured prominently in residents' stories about their community. Don Carlos, for example (born in 1905), addressed my first question about San Antón's origins in the following way: "Well . . . let's start with Hacienda Estrella . . . Hacienda Estrella was of Don Félix Saurí and Suvirá." "And what were they like?" I asked. He answered, "Well, *bien blancos* [very white], Spaniards . . . very white." Don Carlos recalls that when he was a small boy, he worked for these men on Saturdays. They paid him a dollar to take care of the oxen that carried wagons full of cane.[13]

Ancestors of present-day residents of San Antón worked for the owners of these haciendas as *paleros* (shovelers), as *fonderos* (in charge of boilers), and as overseers. They also worked filling up wagons, cleaning irrigation canals, spreading fertilizer, and cutting sugarcane. The work was onerous and the pay insignificant. Neldi recalls of her father:

> He was a *palero*. *Paleros* are the ones who work in the cane when they plant it, they're making holes, cleaning up trenches, those are the *paleros*. And they planted right there. My father planted cane. Life was a little bit tight, but it was better than now . . . There's too much *bandidaje* [delinquency] now, there was none of that before, and if there was *eso estaba tapa'o* [it was hush-hush].
>
> In those days . . . if you cooked lunch, you couldn't make supper, 'cause there wasn't enough, one would go to sleep with a glass of water. You earned little: three dollars, five dollars, to take care of the house.

A retired needle worker, Neldi lives in a wooden house with her daughter Dora. Other houses in her *patio* are occupied by her daughter Hilda and her son Roberto. Another son also lives near this small compound. Neldi's family used to own a big *patio* (family land), but their land was expropriated by the government. In its place, the government built one of a series of electrical towers in the 1950s. These towers now cut the eastern section of the barrio in half. Following the electrical lines toward the northwest, across the avenue that borders this section of San Antón, one comes to another section of the barrio, where Arcenia Rosado (age seventy-six) lives. Like Neldi, Arcenia also worked embroidering. In our interview, Arcenia talked about her father's and mother's work:

> My father was a *hacienda* laborer. It was said that they would go in at six in the morning, be all day in a cane field, cutting weeds, digging trenches to earn a half dollar. I don't know if you've heard about that, 'cause people talk about it. From six in the morning to six in the evening to earn a half a dollar. That was an abuse, but like I told ya, food was cheap . . . I say we used to go hungry 'cause Mom earned her living washing on the stones in the river . . . there, in that river. She'd take her tub, she washed for the outside . . . She washed for fifty cents a dozen. Well, with what she earned—she washed for different people—well, she bought what she could for us to have. But listen, there were times that my mother didn't even have for making us coffee. And what would she do? I tell you now 'cause that happened years and years ago and I'm not ashamed of saying it . . . my mother boiled the dregs, the coffee dregs.

Residents' narratives about labor in San Antón spoke of toil and hardship. Neldi explained that her mother worked in the coffee industry.

> When they said they were going to open the warehouse, everybody, the women would go over there and they would put 'em to work, and they would work till the end of the coffee harvest . . . The need was so great that both had to work. My mom worked in La Playa. They brought the coffee from the country, and they would put it in a machine to clean and later in baskets . . . They'd fill 'em up for them and spill it to take out the rotten ones, stones, glass: all the bad stuff. Ten cents a basket. And if the coffee was bad, they'd come out with thirty cents a day, the ones who'd hurry. The ones who didn't, with twenty, if not with ten.

Many women of San Antón carried out domestic work in the houses or establishments of rich families (ironing, cleaning, or cooking). Anelo (born in 1919), for example, recalls, "Long before I was born, my mother took care of children. She took care of three girls of rich families, as they said. And later, she did not want to take care of them anymore, and later she ironed. She ironed for the owners of the Meliá Hotel. She worked there. Later she worked for the owner of the store—maybe you have heard of it—El Cometa."

These forms of employment were particularly important during the "dead season." The dead season, or the *invernazo*, as elders in San Antón call it, is that time when there is no cane to cut or grind. The mother of Don Eduardo (he was born in 1909) also did seasonal work in the coffee industry:

> My mother worked in the area of La Playa in Ponce, in a coffee-gathering factory. Those people cleared the coffee beans, since that coffee came full of soil. And those women would clean it and take the dust out and so on. They grew it in the

mountains, and they brought it down to the Playa. There were men who turned the carts over for the women. Those came in *convoyes* [carts/wagons] that were big. The men would turn those carts so that the women would not have to use any strength. Then the women came and they started fanning it (the coffee) with cardboard, and all the residue would stay there. My mother worked for some time in the coffee [industry], during the bad times. One could say they went there to kill time, because she didn't earn anything

Then the *zafra* [sugarcane harvest] would come, there was work during the *zafra*. Men would cut the cane, it's true that it was hard, but you earned money. There were some people who cut the seeds, others filled up the carts for the mill to grind. During the time of the Spaniards, there were oxen and with the Americans those oxen went to rest and the tractors came. They attached thirty freight cars to a train and only one man filled them up—imagine all that was being earned there! . . . There was the overseer of the sugar mill, the overseer of the shoveler, and the superintendent. The overseer ranked below the superintendent. The superintendent gave him some extra money during Christmastime.

Don Eduardo and most of the other elders I interviewed connected these forms of plantation labor to the Hacienda Constancia and the Hacienda Estrella. Some residents mentioned that they had ancestors who worked on haciendas other than Estrella or Constancia during the earlier part of the nineteenth century, but they could not recall their names. One source lists a Hacienda Miramar and another named Matilde in San Antón at the turn of the twentieth century (Vaiá 1980, 24).[14] The questions, however, of when these other, perhaps smaller, haciendas were established in San Antón, and how they supported their surrounding slave and free populations, were much harder for residents to answer. This is not only because this period is further situated in time, but also because national discourses have silenced public discussions about this historical period and its free black population.

Memory and Shame: The Evasive Topic of Slavery

Community leaders like Julia consider this devaluation and lack of knowledge about African ancestors unfortunate. She was, for instance, outraged by the fact that some young people in the community had gone so far as to deny that slavery had ever taken place in Puerto Rico:

> JULIA: You know there are people here that don't read about history. There were two or three that claimed that there had never been any slavery here. But of course, sure there was, because . . . when was slavery abolished, you tell me.
> ISAR: Between 1873 and 1876.

JULIA: Well then, there was, wasn't there? That has been written already because it happened in 1876, and we were in existence by then, meaning my ancestors existed.

ISAR: I have found lists that date to 1826.

JULIA: But of course, of course, but since there are people here, you know, who don't read history.

ISAR: Or aren't taught it either, Julia, because the system . . .

JULIA: But listen, my child, if I went to school and they didn't teach me this thing or the other and I live in a place that is said to have a history and that sort of thing, then I try to familiarize myself with the history, with my roots. But no . . . No way. You can't find a person around here that may say, "Let me read this book to find out where I come from." Then when somebody else writes that what was written down there is true, both what María Judith and what I said, well, listen it's a reality. So they said, that that thing about slavery, that slavery never happened here. You see? So then I say, well then, some say one thing, then tomorrow another, and in the long run nobody knows anything. Ask around, "When was slavery abolished?" to see if anybody is going to tell you. You can ask [she names three male community members], people like those you can ask, and they'll tell you, but the rest are not interested, and it's a shame, that's a shame . . . because there are people who live life just for the sake of it, they're not interested. I say, I want to go to the Museum of History and seek and fill myself with . . . to see if I find something even deeper, and I've never been able to go.

Julia and I went to the museum of Ponce's history a couple of weeks after this interview, but there was nothing there that contributed to her search for a deeper understanding of the community's history. Considering the politics of erasure prevalent in cultural nationalism, that search would have to begin in San Antón, from the particular interests and biases that are relevant to residents. For example, most of the residents I interviewed did not mention the subject of slavery directly but provided an archaeology of San Antón's beginnings via the subject of family names. At these moments, the topic of slavery sometimes surfaced in a very matter-of-fact manner. Doña Laura, for example, began to list the names of the first families to establish themselves in San Antón: "The Franceschis, surname Roque, surname Arce, who was one of the first to come here. Those people had . . . were . . . had *amos* (owners), were slaves . . . in those days they had the same surnames as their owners, hmm . . . then those were the first surnames to arrive in San Antón."

Through these family-centered narratives, residents provided an archaeology of the community that spoke of different power relationships between black settlers and *hacendados*. Anelo's narrative is another example. When I asked if she considered San Antón to be a typical Puerto Rican community, she framed her answer in terms of the surnames of the families of San Antón:

> Yes, I think so, because the majority of the people that have lived here have been Puerto Rican, from here, born here. . . . Although not always, because there were some . . . the Franceschis' grandfather's surname was Palmieri. That surname is not from here, it's not from Puerto Rico; I think it's Spanish. Because, you know, a lot of Spaniards came and had children with Puerto Rican girls, especially with the slaves. That's why a lot of them around here don't have their father's surname, they have their mother's surname. They were of Spaniards who came and had relations with Puerto Rican women. Then they went away and those children stayed without a last name, but with the surname of the mother, that is the case.

Besides providing information about family names and their ties to the institution of slavery, Anelo represented *hacendados* as irresponsible and foreign. She characterized them—or at least their last names—as *no de aquí* (not from here). She referred to slave women, on the other hand, as *puertorriqueñas*.

Foreign Settlers and San Antón

A few relevant facts about such foreign settlers and their role in the development of San Antón prior to the abolition of slavery (1873) can be extrapolated from secondary sources and from census documents. Census documents reveal that during the earlier part of the nineteenth century (1826), Hacienda Constancia was owned by two German merchant partners, Overman and Voigt, who migrated from St. Thomas and moved to Ponce between 1826 and 1830 (Scarano 1989; Pérez-Vega 1988). These foreign non-Spanish immigrants formed part of a select group of German, Danish, and English settlers who came to occupy the highest ranks of Ponce's bourgeoisie sector. Spaniards, French, and *criollo hacendados* were, on the other hand, better represented among the middle and lower strata of the *hacendado* class (Scarano 1989, 40). Availed by the provisions of the Cédula de Gracias, these immigrants purchased land with the specific purpose of establishing haciendas even before they settled in Ponce. As a general rule, they increased their capital through their involvement in the trading business. Overman, for instance, established a prosperous business in 1831 dedicated to the trading of sugar and slaves.[15]

Constancia was among the most prosperous of Ponce's haciendas during the early nineteenth century (Pérez-Vega 1988, 105). (Table 3 shows that Constancia had a total of seventy-three slaves, a figure that was surpassed by only three other haciendas.)

The other important hacienda in this area, Hacienda Estrella, was probably established later than Constancia. (Census figures of 1860 indicate that Estrella had

Table 3. Principal Haciendas of Ponce, Their Owners, and Their Slaves

Year of Arrival of Slaves	Name of Hacendado	Hacienda	Nationality	Place of origin	Number of Slaves
1811	G. Madina	Vayas	(Canary Islands) Spain	Barcelona y Venezuela	111
1783	Gutierrez del Arroyo	Quemado	(Puerto Rico) Spain	Venezuela	110
1818	Archbald	Citrona	(Nevis) UK	Nevis	83
1819 1820	Overman and Voigt	Constancia	Germany	St. Thomas	73
1803	Pedro Gautier	Pámpanos	(Córcega) France	Guadalupe St. Thomas	64
1816	P. Bettini	Rábanos	France	St. Thomas	52
1816	Duprel y			Venezuela	52
1819	Proust		France	St. Thomas	

Source: Pérez-Vega *El cielo y la tierra en sus manos* 1988:105

a total of 150 slaves who belonged to Juan Franceschi.) During the later years of the nineteenth century, the ownership of Hacienda Constancia and Hacienda Estrella passed to the hands of another partnership of *hacendados*, Saurí and Subirá. They continued to manage both haciendas into the twentieth century.[16] Although south-coast sugar declined after 1870, Central Constancia did not lose ground, because the sugar produced there (*azúcar moscabada*) was of excellent quality (Ramos-Mattei 1988, 56).

Most of the slaves who appear in nineteenth-century census documents are listed under the names of the owners of these haciendas. However, not all the slaves who lived in San Antón in the nineteenth century belonged to *hacendados*. There were also white *labradores* in San Antón who appear to have owned anywhere from one to sixteen slaves according to the census.[17] Still, most of the slave population was in the hands of a few *hacendados*. The census of 1868, for example, listed 212 whites, 258 free people of color, and 187 slaves, the great majority (167 total) of whom belonged to the *hacendado* Don Juan Franceschi. Some of the most prominent *hacendados* during the nineteenth century in San Antón were Don Juan Rondón (1838), Don Remigio Arce (1850), Valentín Tricoche, and Don Juan Franceschi (1868). As noted, San Antón residents are quite aware of this family genealogy, and it is often through these family names that they trace the barrio's origins. Such names are in turn closely related to people's identification with family *patios* in the community that bear these same last names (including *el patio de los Arce, el patio de los Franceschi*).

Heterogeneity and Land Ownership

According to residents of San Antón, once a person acquired a piece of land and built a house, family members continued to build other houses on the same plot. *Patios* could be occupied by members of an extended family, by close friends of the family, or by *arrimados*. The census of 1838, for instance, listed a total of twenty-eight *arrimados* in San Antón (eight "white," one "black," nineteen *pardos*). Their names are listed under the name of five "white" families and eleven *pardo* families. That information about *arrimados* leads me to conclude that, out of a total of thirty-one *pardo* families or families of free people of color, at least eleven families (33 percent of the total) owned their own plot of land and had *arrimados*.

This type of settlement arrangement has been documented in other parts of the Caribbean under the name of family land.[18] Charles Carnegie (1987) has noted that the discovery of this particular form of land tenure in the Caribbean was "tremendously exciting because it offered evidence of home-grown institutional forms among a displaced, uprooted and formerly enslaved population. It represented the creation within a couple of generations of their emancipation of a system permitting one generation to pass the baton of property rights smoothly on to the next and in a manner significantly different from the template offered by the society which had subjugated them" (83).

In fact, Jean Besson has interpreted the prevalence of family land as a form of resistance against the institution of slavery and the plantation regime (1984b, 4). In her analysis of this institution, Besson follows Mintz's approach to Caribbean peasantries and his understanding that

> Caribbean populations, whether slaves, indentured laborers, or contract laborers, have consistently struggled to define themselves either within culturally distinctive *communities* or as members of family *lines* . . . A key to this assertion is the significance of land for Caribbean rural folk—a significance that far exceeds any obvious economic considerations. The slaves sought desperately to express their individuality through the acquisition of material wealth . . . Torn from societies that had not yet entered into the capitalist world, and thrust into settings that were profoundly capitalistic in character on the one hand, yet rooted in the need for unfree labor on the other, the slaves saw liquid capital not only as a means to secure freedom, but also as a means to attach their paternity—and hence, their identity as persons—to something even the masters would have to respect. In these terms, the creation of peasantries was simultaneously an act of westernization and an act of resistance. (Mintz quoted in Besson 1984b, 4; Mintz's emphasis)

In Puerto Rico, the legal framework for this kind of land tenement is best understood as a *sucesión*, which is best translated as a "tenancy in common" (Crump et al. 2004).[19] Residents of San Antón described this form of settlement in *patios* and as a gradual process that took place over generations. However, they added that, since so many of the original families had moved or had been resettled by the government, the *patios* I saw now in San Antón were nothing like the original ones they remember from their childhood. These "original" *patios* were much bigger and more beautiful. "*Ya esto no es nada de lo que era antes*" (This is nothing like what it used to be before) was a commonly voiced opinion among these elders.

Patios are still, nevertheless, an important reference point for community residents. They are also an important institution that facilitates familial bonding, support, and socializing. Doña Victoria, for example, is a member of one of the biggest *patios* in San Antón, which is constituted by approximately fifty-seven people:[20]

> I remember that when I was about fifteen years old, there were about three houses on the *patio*. All of us were born and raised here. My mother had twelve children, assisted by *comadronas* [midwives]. The midwives were from right here: Doña Paulina, Doña Vicenta, and there was another one that was from up there. The main house has always been the big house, and after that one there was my mother's brother, and the other one was my mother's sister, whose name was Clara Tricoche. The good thing about living in a family *patio* is that if one gets sick, one sister watches over one, and this way we all take care of each other.

Gloria, who is a member of another *patio*, states, "I like to live like this better than living in an *urbanización* [residential complex] . . . Here you can . . . sometimes we celebrate parties, of sons, cousins, nephews, and . . . brothers and we'll stay there till after midnight, with live music or a disc jockey." Her mother adds, "And nobody's going to say 'Turn that off because it's too loud' or something." María adds: "You can do a party here till daybreak and nobody here complains. Everybody goes to sleep and without a bother; if you come great, if you don't want to come we accept you just the same, but we're not in the thing of . . . If you go to a residential complex and you put the music or the TV a little loud, they immediately call the police, attracting attention, there's animosity, there're fights . . ."

As recounted in earlier chapters, *patios* were considered an important institution in San Antón. However, if one were to draw a map of San Antón using the *patio* as its main organizing referent, one would realize that it would be a mistake to define *patios* as just "a piece of land that belongs to one family." It is not that simple. Questions such as who came first, who left, who sold what to whom, and what is considered factual "proof" of land ownership don't have easy answers. These issues can frustrate the most meticulous of researchers—not to mention government authorities, since property rights are not passed on as smoothly as Carnegie suggests in the quote on page 14. In fact, questions of who is supposed to own what and live where were not always settled issues among residents. In the interview segment that follows, Gloria offers her version of how such confusion begins to take place:

> Yes, because if they had a lot of land, they would say "Well, listen, *compay* [from *compadre*—the godfather of your child or the father of your godchild; a very close family friend], I'm going to build a house there," and there was that the person would stay living there for years and he would have kids, and then when all those people died, well, all those people thought they were inheritors of that, but no, it was that the owners had lent them a piece, and that's what's happening here. . . . Look, that house you see down there . . . that's where Carlito's father was born, and his brothers and everybody, the one that's fallen—that was the hurricane Federico that knocked down that house. Now, that *patio* belongs to the Arces . . . the *patio* belongs to the Arce-Tricoches, and so the ancestor told the other: "*Compay*, build your house there"; his name was Allende, and so he built that little house there, and all his sons were born there, the others died, and today, well look, everybody is *liga'o* [mixed up] there. But the mother of one of them, whose name is Evelyn Arce, has the deeds to the whole lot. . . . You know Rosín Roque? . . . Well, those are the owners of all of that there. Not these, these don't own anything there, they live there 'cause . . . but nobody there's an owner, nobody in those houses owns that. *Ahí hay un revulú* [There's a messy confusion there] because of that now . . . a *bochinche* [quarrel] because of that *patio* there.

Similar stories about family members who left one *patio* and moved to another, who sold their land and rented it to others, or who left their house in the care of another and then never came back to claim it continue to confirm the complexity and heterogeneity of San Antón.

Housing Erasure: A Conclusion

Unfortunately, that heterogeneity recognized by San Antón's residents became simplified and fixed, not only in the stories told about San Antón's origins and its *bomba* and *plena*, but also in the housing project, particularly through the model of land ownership applied there. As mentioned, houses in the new development were not built on the land of the *sucesión*, nor were they built with the idea of expansion in mind. The project promoted individual ownership of plots and houses, and building additional structures on these plots was, in fact, prohibited by the government (Cordero-Santiago 1996b). Hence, although architects and bureaucrats worked hard, even bent the rules a bit, so that this community and its families could prevail, at no point did they contemplate flexibility or expansion as valuable and pertinent characteristics for a housing project in San Antón.

When I asked the director of the Oficina de Ordenamiento Territorial (Municipal Planning Office) why they did not consult further with the community, he responded that there was little consensus among residents on the matter of how their community should be improved. Besides what he called *"poca visión común"* (very little common vision), he added that there was also *"poca fe en el verdadero propósito de una entidad gubernamental. No creen, no confían en el 'empowerment'"* (There is almost no faith in the true purpose of a government entity. They don't believe, they don't trust "empowerment"). He said his office had been more effective in solving the problems that came up with the projects than in getting people involved in the projects: *"Cuando metemos la pata* (When we mess it up), we find out fast and we resolve it. We're more perceptive of the community's problems . . . But when it's about them becoming the actors of one's initiatives, there are problems . . . I don't know if the problem is here or there."

Apart from the fact that one could hardly call "empowerment" a process that is based on the expectation that residents follow the government's *lead*, part of the problem lies in the government's expectation that the people of San Antón should speak as one. This requirement of uniformity and spontaneous consensus also resonates with a politics of cultural nationalism that has silenced and simplified the heterogeneous experiences of *negros, libertos, artesanos*, and *mulatos* during and after the slavery period. Furthermore, government interventions that call for the empowerment of residents to follow *their lead* underestimate what have been historically diverse pre- and post-emancipation practices of self-sustenance that take advantage of, but cannot solely depend on, the opportunities provided by powerful actors who can also take them away (whether it is the government or *hacendados*).

In this chapter I have drawn attention to such strategies of survival, family settlement, and cohabitation as a challenge to a politics of erasure that trivializes, silences, and simplifies the history of the slavery period and its aftermath. I have argued that this politics of erasure engaged the United States as a backstage but key interlocutor that buttresses related remarks about slavery's milder effects on the Island. In the next section, this racial dialogue with the United States (and the specific consequences it had for San Antón) becomes more evident as I explore different, though closely related, national discourses that upheld the white/Hispanic element as the most enduring, desirable, and dominant feature of Puerto Rican national identity.

PART II

Hispanicity

Shades of "Whiteness" between Empires

CHAPTER 4

Hispanophile Zones of Whiteness

Long before the municipal government intervened in San Antón to build the housing project in 1996, similar rehabilitation projects had been carried out in other working-class neighborhoods of Ponce. However, the site given the utmost priority in terms of government intervention was the urban center or Zona Histórica (Historic Zone), also known as the Historic Center. Here, visitors can find the traditional mayor's office and visit the Spanish-style plaza with a Catholic church. Tourists can take a ride in horse-drawn carriages along marble-bordered sidewalks adorned with historic "gas lamps." Ponce's association with this urban center of European influence in the architecture explains why the town is often referred to as the Ciudad Señorial (Aristocratic City).

Ponce's center did not always have this dignified look. As mentioned in the introduction, ex-governor Rafael Hernández Colón (RHC), a native of Ponce, played a key role in this aggressive restoration plan, making the rehabilitation of Ponce's Historic Zone a priority during his administration (1984–92[1]). However, while the government gave all its attention to the urban center, the housing needs of a number of poor, black, and *mulato* barrios such as San Antón remained unaddressed. Time went by, RHC lost the election in 1992, and support for all initiatives associated with the Ponce en Marcha project dwindled after a pro-statehood administration took over the central government from 1993 to 2000 (Ayoroa-Santaliz 2003).[2] In Ponce, initiatives continued, with scant support from the central pro-statehood administration, under the leadership of commonwealth mayor Rafael Cordero Santiago.

When the housing project of San Antón was finally implemented in 1996, newspaper headlines described it as an *"arduo camino de revitalización"* (arduous journey of revitalization) (Ortiz 1994b, 14).[3] Another declared that the housing project had been inaugurated *"tras años de planificación y espera"* (after years of planning and waiting) (Alfonso 1997, 11). Reporters provided details of long administrative procedures and delays in the acquisition of land necessary for the project's implementation. The tardy intervention, however, can also be explained by the Eurocentric priorities embedded in the restoration of Ponce's Historic Zone, which limited the type of funding that the local government could use to implement the housing project in San Antón. In effect, special funds available for restorations in the Historic Zone during the late 1980s privileged areas with Spanish influence in urban planning and architecture. The barrio of San Antón, which fell outside the boundaries of the officially designated Historic Zone of Ponce and lacked a significant sampling of architecture that could be associated with Spanish heritage, could not benefit from such funding.

* * *

Scripts of blackness documented in this book do not operate independently but are constructed in relationship to competing notions of whiteness, some of which draw heavily on Eurocentric discourses of Hispanophilia. Discourses of Hispanophilia anchor the origins of "the nation" in Spanish heritage, in the Catholic religion, and particularly in the use of the Spanish language. Europe and more specifically Spain operate here as important identity referents, since Hispanophile proponents consider Puerto Rico an offshoot of Spain and Puerto Rican culture a product of Spain's colonizing influence.

However, more than a discourse in favor of Spain, Hispanophilia was first and foremost a discourse that sought to differentiate Puerto Rico from the United States. I have discussed how, in the context of enduring colonial discourses that stressed the natives' incompetence for self-government, claims to Spanish heritage and European traditions validated Puerto Ricans as equally capable of self-government as any European nation. Claims to the cultural influence of Spain also provided an important unifying element between Puerto Rico and a community of independent Latin American nations. Africa was, on the other hand, understood as a backward influence that had to be contained, mitigated, or diluted through assimilation, mixture, and education. At a time when colonial powers associated blackness with unrest in Haiti, Cuba, and the Caribbean, *criollo* elites also had to prove they were best equipped to lead the black and *mulato* working class into a "civilized" national project, which required negotiating reforms for self-government with the colonizers. In this context, Hispanophilia arose out of the two-pronged desire of an aspiring *criollo* class to culturally differentiate Puerto

Rico from the United States, on the one hand, and "domesticate" the destabilizing signs of blackness, on the other.

In the process of confronting this double-headed monster, ideologues and political figures constructed the nation at two different, although highly interrelated, discursive levels: the realm of biology and the realm of culture. Within the first, they placed a premium on phenotypical whiteness and whitening. Previously discussed politics of erasure are particularly important for this biological realm, because they support *blanqueamiento* and the idea that benevolent slavery encouraged mixture and the gradual whitening of the population. As discussed, casting slaves as the only blacks of Puerto Rico was also part of this discursive strategy.

Yet notions of "race" were not articulated just in terms of biology but most prominently in terms of culture. By "culture," *criollo* intellectuals meant learned behaviors defined by proponents of Hispanophilia as customs, traditions, and "ways of being" that Puerto Ricans inherited from Spain. It is in this second but most prominent realm of "cultural whiteness" or "Spanish whiteness" that Hispanophilia offers a strategic line of political defense against U.S. encroachment. Proponents of Hispanophilia argue that (although Puerto Ricans are not white) the nation is *culturally* white. In the context of narratives that distinguish Puerto Rico from the United States, such "cultural whiteness" can be qualified as Spanish or "Hispanic whiteness" vis-à-vis "Anglo-Saxon whiteness." The latter appears in Hispanophile nationalist narratives of the 1930s as the mark of the greedy, materialistic, immature, and less civilized young and impulsive U.S. nation. In contrast, Hispanics, especially the *criollo* elite, presented themselves as heirs of a European cultural tradition that is older and more cultivated, cultured, and sophisticated.

Despite this distinction, *criollos*' own Darwinian theories and ideas about the superiority of the "white race" (which legitimized their leading role in Puerto Rican society) put them at odds with the threat that these "other whites" posed for their Hispanic race (Cubano Iguina 1997). Astrid Cubano documents how at the turn of the century, upon the advent of the U.S. occupation of Puerto Rico, some *criollos* perceived Spain as close to their "hearts" but at odds with their "minds" (Cubano Iguina 1997, 653). She quotes Ezequiel Martínez Quintero stating: "We, who in the midst of a great admiration for the high qualities of that race (Anglo-Saxon), *temblamos por las imitaciones irreflexivas* (shudder because of the thoughtless imitation) of their political-social ways in our country, also, sometimes get carried away by a vague idolatry towards the old England or towards the young United States" (Martínez Quintero in Cubano Iguina 1997, 644).[4]

Rosendo Matienzo Cintrón, an active voice in the movement for political autonomy, also feared that with the U.S. invasion, Puerto Ricans could disappear by natural selection if they did not hold on to the "*gérmenes de vida*" (seeds of life) of the Spanish motherland (Cubano Iguina 1997, 645). In spite of these anxieties (or maybe because of them), by the 1930s—faced with the economic challenges of the Great Depression and the authoritative policies of an evidently exploitative colonial U.S. regime—many members of the *criollo intelligencia* turned to Spain as a source of political legitimacy and civilizatory strength.

Of course, not all sectors of the Puerto Rican population shared the anti-Americanism that motivated such exaltations of Hispanic heritage. Spain also took on less honorable, shadier connotations in the narratives of those who critiqued Spain and the *criollo* elite for its disdain against black and working-class sectors of Puerto Rican society. Such anti-Hispanic animosity (or Hispanophobia) coexisted and coincided with U.S. dominant colonial notions of white supremacy that constructed Spain as an inferior and backward declining power in comparison to the emergent, modern, and democratic U.S. nation.

Chapters in this section examine the interpretations of whiteness (as Hispanic or Anglo) that coexisted with the Hispanophilias and Hispanophobias that nurtured political aspirations and hopes for a better future in the Island. This analysis is important because notions of "Hispanic whiteness" as cultural, normative, enduring, and civilized position "scripts" of blackness by contrast as exceptional, primitive, impulsive, and biological. In this chapter I focus on Hispanophilia, beginning with its emergence in the 1930s. I then trace the contradictory applications of "Hispanic whiteness" to the 1980s and 1990s, when the discourse resurfaced in political attempts to distinguish Puerto Rico from the United States, thereby informing policies that impacted developments in San Antón. In the following chapter I focus on the counternotion of Hispanophobia and its connection to the pro-statehood movement, since this counterdiscourse (and its political variant of statehood) also influenced the timing and debates surrounding the housing project in San Antón.

The Hispanophilia of the 1930s

The construction of Puerto Rico as an essentially Hispanic nation can be traced to the eighteenth century, but it wasn't until the 1930s that this discourse became firmly established among an educated Puerto Rican elite (Ferrao 1993). The 1930s were characterized by economic depression, political instability, discontent, and deep polarization of popular demands. The U.S. military had occupied the Island since 1898, but economic and social effects of the colonial regime made themselves particularly evident thirty years later. The Great Depression of 1929 impacted the Island in the form of high unemployment rates, low wages, and exploitative working conditions. At the same time, dispossessed *criollo hacendados* whose tobacco, sugar, and coffee industries had flourished under the Spanish regime viewed with resentment the political and economic stronghold of U.S.

sugar corporations. Others who had initially welcomed intervention from the North had reevaluated their political stance by the 1930s, as the colonial disposition of the new regime revealed its authoritative character and intensive Americanization campaign (Díaz-Quiñones 1985). The dream of turning Puerto Rico into a modern and democratic nation was slowly fading.

The economic uncertainty and political turmoil of these times encouraged and nurtured the question "Who are we?" among an intellectual elite that was predominantly light-skinned, urban, well educated, and privileged in relation to the rest of the population (Ferrao 1993). Black and *mulato* voices such as those of Ramos Antonini (1898–1963), Albizu-Campos (1891–1965), and José Celso Barbosa (1857–1921) were exceptions among the more numerous voices of intellectuals such as Blanco (1896–1975), Pedreira (1899–1939), Muñoz-Rivera (1859–1916), Vicente Géigel Polanco (1904–1979), Emilio S. Belaval (1903–1972), Luis Palés-Matos (1898–1959), and Jaime Benítez (1908–2001), who identified as heirs of a threatened culture, the origin of which they located in Spain (Díaz-Quiñones 1985; Ferrao 1993).

Discourses of Hispanicity produced by this core group of intellectuals of the 1930s were not, however, homogeneous. Their forging of a national identity was a polemical and highly debated endeavor. Emilio S. Belaval and Antonio J. Colorado, for instance, believed Puerto Ricans were *españoles hasta los huesos* (Spanish to the bone) or referred to "Spaniards who have lived in Puerto Rico for four centuries"[5] (Belaval 1977, 55; Colorado quoted in Ferrao 1993, 49). Intellectuals like Antonio S. Pedreira and Francisco del Valle Atiles, on the other hand, believed that only some Puerto Ricans could lay claim to a Hispanic heritage, blaming Puerto Rican backwardness on the negative qualities of African blood (Pedreira 1992; for del Valle Atiles, see Baerga 2009–10). Furthermore, while Pedreira's blatant racism considered racial mixture detrimental to the psychological makeup of the nation, others, like Salvador Brau and Tomás Blanco, chose to exalt hybridity. Blanco, for example, argued that hybridity fostered social harmony and facilitated the cultural assimilation of blacks into Hispanic culture (Blanco 1942; for Brau, see Rodríguez-Silva 2012, 76–83).

In contrast, issues of blackness and "racial hybridity" in the biological or phenotypic sense remained practically absent from the discourse of nationalist leader Pedro Albizu Campos, one of the most influential voices of the 1930s (Carrión 1993; Santiago-Valles 2007). For Albizu, Puerto Ricans were members of the Ibero-American race, a broad *cultural* community of Latin American nations and peoples (Rodríguez-Vázquez 2004). Inspired by Vasconselos's (1925) notion of the "cosmic race," he appealed to the idea of a spiritually and aesthetically superior mestizo who could resist the racism of the "tyrant yanqui brutes" who are used to "*levantar la división entre los hombres por la epidermis*" (raising divisions among men based on the epidermis) (Albizu Campos 1974, 194; see also Santiago-Valles 2007, 119). "In the United States," wrote Albizu, "there is no Christianity. That is why the *yanquis*, when a black man sits in a train seat that does not correspond [to his race], they simply hang him from the back and they drag him so that other blacks can look at him" (213).

Like most educated men of his generation, Albizu characterized Puerto Rico as a racially harmonious society, aided by a morally elevated sense of *hidalguía* and Catholic mores. But unlike his *criollo* counterparts, Albizu saw racial harmony as articulated "from bellow" (Santiago-Valles 2007). As Kelvin Santiago Valles (2007) argues, his notion of racial fusion and harmony was not based on the patrician bestowing of Hispanic culture onto the so-called inferior races, but was considered the positive force and intelligence that nonwhite constituents represented for the nation (122). Furthermore, unlike his counterparts,' Albizu's Hispanophilia was a discourse against U.S. imperialism and the exploitation imposed by its sugar corporations, and in favor of a Puerto Rican independence that could bring dignity to the people.

Pedreira's highly elitist political stance, and Blanco's liberal one, thus sharply differed from Albizu-Campos's revolutionary and anti-U.S. imperialist project. However, despite different emphases, these intellectuals of *la generación del treinta* were committed to the concept of "Hispanicity" (whether racial, cultural, or geographical). They all deployed the idea to counteract the political and economic colonial encroachment of the United States over Puerto Rico. For different reasons, they sought in Spain a unifying element to define national culture. This desire led them to overlook Spain's Moorish influence, "disregard" the impact of other black immigrants on Puerto Rico in the nineteenth century, and remain inattentive to the persistence of strong anti-Hispanic sentiments on the Island. While Spain remained a positive referent in their national narratives, Africa and the strong influence of African peoples on the Island were belittled and whitened, if not made practically invisible.

If Ponce's municipal government had strictly followed the precept of Hispanophilia according to this generation's ideological orientation, the community of San Antón would not have been considered worthy of preservation at all. However, in the ethnographic present, when Ponce's administration was negotiating its inclusion as a historic site in the 1990s, the effects of Hispanophilia were different. They manifested in the tardy implementation of San Antón's housing project through restoration policies that made urban areas with "Spanish influence" a higher priority, causing delays and making this predominantly black community ineligible for funding targeted at "historic sites." What were the ideological precepts that informed these urban policies and political agendas?

Reemergence of Hispanophilia in the 1980s and early 1990s

A somewhat similar but more contemporary spin-off of the 1930s notion of Hispanophilia arose in Puerto Rico between 1984 and 1992, through the figure and public-policy initiatives of the *ponceño* ex-governor Rafael Hernández-Colón (RHC). RHC made unprecedented efforts to promote commercial activities and cultural exchanges between Spain and Puerto Rico, and also between Puerto Rico and Latin America. RHC's Hispanophile-oriented discourse, however, differed substantially from discourses of the 1930s.

Contrary to the 1930s generation's outlook, RHC's national discourse did not outwardly reject U.S. control over the Island. As a commonwealth-party discourse, Hispanophilia was evoked to highlight Puerto Rico's cultural (not political) distinctiveness from the United States and to support specific initiatives that sought greater political autonomy for the Island. In the context of political-party politics, RHC's Hispanophile orientation also sought to undermine the opposing party's project of statehood for Puerto Rico and their corresponding orientation toward the United States. Specifically, the exaltation of Puerto Rico's affinity with Spain was used to challenge the statehood option on the grounds that, under statehood, Puerto Ricans would lose their cultural autonomy and Hispanic culture.

San Antón and the Rhetorical Ascription of RHC

In 1988, during one of his many visits to Spain, RHC made a speech at the central office of the Instituto de Cooperación Iberoamericana (Institute for Ibero-American Cooperation, also known by its Spanish initials as the ICI), in which he explained how Spain reproduced itself in America with a fidelity that is sometimes overwhelming.[6] Then, unaware of the subsequent political cost of his words, he declared:

> The truth is that the society that exists today in the Antilles has been to a great extent inherited through Spanish heritage. The natives were practically erased from the census, and the Africans that followed were assimilated almost completely by the dominating culture. So in no way can we, the Puerto Ricans, vindicate that *adscripción retórica* [rhetorical ascription] to a remote American Indian past or to Africanism, even if they are a valuable component of our national identity. Whichever may be the color of our skin, the sign of our culture—language, religion, perceptions, and idiosyncrasy—is Spanish.[7] (Hernández Colón 1988b, 2–3, my emphasis)

These statements provoked quite a controversy in Puerto Rico that was articulated in the local media. Although *adscripción retórica* (rhetorical ascription) was a rather obscure phrase, critics highlighted its meaning as a spurious mention that minimized indigenous and African cultural heritages' contributions to Puerto Rican culture (Maldonado-Denis 1988, 54). Most people centered their critiques on RHC's denial of blackness and the racism behind his remarks. Leaders of opposing political parties promptly took advantage of the remarks, accusing the governor of being arrogant, racist, and irreverent regarding valuable contributions that blacks have made to Puerto Rican culture. One pro-statehood leader (Romero Barceló) threatened to organize a rally of black people in front of the governor's house (Pérez 1988, 54).

In the midst of that controversy, San Antón emerged as a symbol of what was being ignored when Antonio Martorell, a renowned plastic artist, criticized the governor on TV during San Antón's eleventh Fiesta of Bomba and Plena. Martorell stated that if RHC had gone to San Antón's Fiesta of Bomba and Plena, he would have noticed that the Puerto Rican reality was very different from the way he represented it in Spain (Martorell 1988, 67). The governor answered Martorell's statement in a newspaper article titled "Spain, San Antón, and Our National Being," arguing that he never meant to deny such a valuable component of our nation (Hernández-Colón 1988a, 53). His aim, he said, was to celebrate the harmonious synthesis of the races in Puerto Rico vis-à-vis that of other countries that have not been able to overcome racial differences. He stated:

> While in some Caribbean islands or countries like Guyana, black culture and its population predominated, in Puerto Rico . . . that rich heritage was assimilated, just as the indigenous was, by Hispanic culture, creating our own national culture that cannot be classified as Taína, African, or Spanish, but rather as the harmonious synthesis of all three, which is Puerto Rican. This is why in the barrio of San Antón, in my city of Ponce, Toño Martorell heard a music with black rhythms, sung in Spanish, in which the musical instruments reflect our ethnic heritage. They weren't playing African music; they were playing Puerto Rican music.[8] (Hernández-Colón 1988a, 53)

In line with previously discussed discourses of benevolent slavery, RHC distinguished Puerto Rico from the Caribbean—particularly the English Caribbean—arguing that Puerto Rico had been harmoniously Hispanicized (i.e., whitened). Martorell refuted RHC's notion of a "harmonious synthesis" by highlighting domination, rape, and violence as prominent signs of the Spanish colonial enterprise. "It has been to the rhythm of whips," wrote Martorell (1988), "that the dominating culture has tried to suppress the different elements, and failing in its effort, and due to the vitality and chameleon survival capability of African cultures, this dominating culture is forced to add, with the necessary cosmetic modifications, what it has not been able to subtract (67).[9]

Furthermore, Martorell argued that when the Guayacanes of San Antón sing in Spanish, it is not evidence of harmonious integration but rather the product of resistance, camouflage, and the everyday struggles that people of African descent have waged against a racist colonial legacy.

Many people echoed Martorell's comments, but a number of other voices joined the dialogue in the press to defend the governor. For instance, Tite Curet-Alonso (1926–2003), a famous black composer, stated: "As far as I know, this man has never expressed himself against my race, or *nuestra gloriosa africanía* [our glorious Africanisms]. Blacks, whites, mulattos, Indian-featured, or *jabaos* [high yellows], toward all he has had the same hand and attitude. Concerning blacks, he got to know them well in his teenage years, in Ponce, his native town. . . . And he must have heard the *panderetas* of the Barrio San Antón, owner of that *negritud* [blackness] that is part of Ponce's culture"[10] (Curet-Alonso 1988, 42).

Other writers, such as Castro Pereda (1954–2000), believed critics of the governor were overreacting, since he only meant to praise Spaniards in his speech. He argued that "If the audience had been Mexican or African surely the tone and content would have varied, at least in its emphasis"[11] (Castro-Pereda 1988, 67).

In a somewhat different and much more Hispanophile note, writer Salvador Tió (1911–1989) defended and further elaborated RHC's statements, declaring that Puerto Rican culture was "white":

> I have never said that Puerto Rico is white. I have said that Puerto Rican culture is white. And the value of a black in our society is measured by his or her capacity to distinguish his or herself in any of the manifestations of that culture. . . . The fundamental contribution of the Taíno element or the Negro element in our formation is not an *adscripción retórica* [a rhetorical ascription] but an *adscripción biológica* [a biological ascription]. There is no way of exactly measuring it, but it suffices to take a wide look, to notice that the ratio of white blood is much greater than the ratio of American Indian or black blood. *But the blood is there, it's an important part of our genetic composition, but not of our culture*. We are a Western culture. And its language, which is the maximum expression of a culture, is the Spanish language.[12] (Tió 1988, 46; my emphasis)

Salvador Tió (a poet, essayist, journalist, and ardent supporter of cultural development in Puerto Rico) actively participated in and sometimes presided over, prestigious institutions such as the University of Puerto Rico Press, the Ateneo Puertorriqueño (Puerto Rican Athenaeum), the Puerto Rican Academy of Spanish Language, and the Institute of Puerto Rican Culture. His words are a classic example of how Hispanophile claims to whiteness operate in the realm of culture. Tió interprets such "cultural whiteness" as a more encompassing and important marker of national identity than "biological whiteness" when he states that blackness is "part of our genetic composition but not of our culture." A similar disclaimer was voiced by RHC in Madrid when he said that "whichever may be the *color of our skin*, the sign of our culture . . . is Spanish"[13] (Hernández-Colón 1988b, 2–3; my emphasis). Such Hispanophile interpretations assume that while "black genes" or "black blood" cannot be completely eradicated, black people can be "domesticated" or assimilated into Western/white traditions inherited from Spain. In this sort of "rescue of race by culture" (Michaels 1992, 658), African influences are relegated to the "less important" and superfluous realm of blood, and the contributions of black people are recast as contributions to a Hispanic culture.

Transnational Hispanic Culture

This rescue of race by culture as the medium for achieving "Hispanic whiteness" was not an original idea of Tió's, nor of RHC, nor is it unique to Puerto Rico. Spanish American intellectuals developed similar projects of national identity in the 1930s in response to U.S. dominance in hemispheric affairs and the drastic changes brought about by modernization. Hispanophile claims to cultural whiteness were developed in the process of forging a national project in Latin America by elites who borrowed from elements of European nationalist discourses and adapted them to their specific contexts. For example, since the last decades of the nineteenth century, intellectuals in Brazil, Mexico, and Argentina produced their own "soft" brand of eugenic science, arguing about the positive qualities of race mixture as "constructive miscegenation" (Stepan 1991). According to Nancy Leys Stepan (1991), this Latin American brand of the eugenics movement did not so harshly condemn racial hybridity but rather focused on promoting hygiene and improving the quality of reproduction as ways of bettering the racial and hereditary traits of a nation (including the whitening of the population).

Later, the notion of "culture" as popularized in the work of Oswald Spengler (1934) became central to emergent nationalisms in Latin America, and Puerto Rico was no exception. According to Aníbal González (1992), intellectuals of *la generación del treinta*—like their Latin American counterparts—approached "national culture" as a form of moral and rational consciousness. To them "culture" (i.e., Hispanic culture) was "the product of a conscious intellectual endeavor rather than of spontaneous or natural generation" (564–65). It was not the responsibility of the popular masses, but of intellectuals. This conceptualization of "culture," as Hispanic and elite, not only differentiated Puerto Rico from the United States, but also differentiated Puerto Rican intellectuals from those internal "others" they considered unfit to lead the nation's future (Rodríguez-Vázquez 2004).

Besides supporting this paternalistic notion of culture, national intellectuals were also in dialogue with Latin American thinkers who emphasized spiritual and moral dimensions in their definition of "culture" over material considerations associated with progress and the utilitarian spirit of the United States. José Enrique

Rodó's *Ariel* (1962[1900]), for example, maintained that the materialistic and individualistic tendencies of advanced societies like the United States threaten the development of a nation's spiritual/moral human dimension and the maintenance of national culture. Correspondingly, many Puerto Rican intellectuals of this generation represented the United States as a utilitarian, materialistic, and dehumanized society where discrimination and fragmentation prevailed.

Out of this twofold nationalist endeavor of criticizing U.S. modernism on the one hand and crafting the content of Puerto Rican difference on the other, the concept of "culture" emerged as a key companion to notions of whiteness. According to Aníbal González (1992), "the American takeover's most dramatic and immediate effect on Puerto Rican intellectual life was the immense importance the island's intelligentsia suddenly gave to the very concept of culture ... The Puerto Rican patricians also realized that culture was in fact one of the few areas of island life over which they still had some power" (564).

Palés's Challenge: Black-Centered National Narratives

The centrality that the Island's liberal elite gave to Spain in the construction of what was considered "Puerto Rican culture" did not go unchallenged. During early years of the decade, writers like Luis Palés Matos (1899–1959) intervened to launch an alternative black- and African-influenced construction of Puerto Rican identity that caused quite a stir among members of the Puerto Rican *intelligencia*. Palés was part of a broader literary movement that began in Puerto Rico, Cuba, and the Dominican Republic at the beginning of the twentieth century with writers such as Zacarías Tallet (1893–1989), Ramón Guirao (1908–1949), Emilio Ballagás (1908–1954), Manuel de Cabral (1907–1999), and Nicolás Guillén (1902–1989) (Badiane 2010, 99). These writers sought to valorize blackness and rethink national identity in terms of its Antillean context and its cultural links with Africa. Palés's poems, in particular, exalted the black component of Puerto Rico's national being as a powerful rhythmic, almost magical or spiritual, element that gave the Island membership in the syncretic regional and cultural community of the Hispanic Caribbean or of Las Antillas.[14] Palés believed that this regional and cultural membership characterizes Puerto Rican people—not as white, not as black, but as a new mix of culturally acclimated *mulato* people whose reality is distinct from that of the Hispanic world. In a 1938 interview Palés said, "I don't believe in black poetry, white poetry, or any color of poetry. Poetry is an art that is extracted from pain, anguish, and emotion. I have tried to incorporate the theme of blackness, forgotten and underestimated, as a serious part of art. Its rhythmic values, above all, weigh too much in the culture of the Antilles, to evade its significance"[15] (in Font-Saldaña 1998, 10).

Palés's Afro-Antillean verses provoked reactions as varied as outrage, praise, mockery, and fear among the reading public in the 1930s (Roy-Féquière 1996, 83). For example, de Diego-Padró (1973) questioned whether there was, in fact, any place in Puerto Rico for a so-called Caribbean art form detached from European influence. Following a Spenglerian logic, he maintained that when two cultures meet, the superior one absorbs the inferior through a natural selection process. Blacks' "inferior," "rudimentary," and "primitive" culture had therefore been completely assimilated into Hispanic/Western culture. In the context of this argument, color matters little, for it is in "culture" that the Western element of our national being prevails. In a statement that predated Salvador Tió's and RHC's assertions about the Hispanic whiteness of their *adscripción retórica*, de Diego Padró declared: "The majority of the existing population of the Antilles, *in spite of the diversity of color and origin*, is of an eminently European psychological structure and culture"[16] (1973, 59; my emphasis)."

The "Panic" of Hispanic in the 1990s

The panic that Palés Matos caused among his peers of the 1930s generation demonstrates that despite the apparent unimportance granted to biological "whiteness" vis-à-vis "cultural whiteness," Hispanophile nationalist narratives often cast racial blackness as a disturbance or destabilizing component that must be subdued. This panic also prevailed during the period of RHC's Hispanophile politics. Just like the writings of *la generación del treinta*, responses in defense of RHC's Hispanophilia were often characterized by a certain anxiety, not only over the question of nation building, but also over the question of race, and specifically blackness. This anxiety—or panic—partly explains ex-governor RHC's need to add a disclaimer about the African and indigenous components of Puerto Rican culture in his speech in Madrid. Like RHC, many enthusiasts of Hispanophilia are not content to celebrate the "Spanish legacy" but must also belittle or "tame" the impact of "non-European blood" on the Puerto Rican nation.

Another characteristic of this anxious response is the common disclaimer that racism is practically nonexistent in Puerto Rico, as opposed to other places (namely the United States). This nervous defense of racial harmony is furthered accompanied by warnings against the dangers of giving public salience to issues of racial hierarchies. Bringing up racism, it is argued, fosters division among Puerto Rican people. According to this logic, to name racial differences is to *create* differences. For example, famous black composer Curet-Alonso (1926–2003) concluded that "Trying to stress the issue of racism is precisely that, to seek racial disintegration and put whites and blacks in conflict, which would be our return to social backwardness"[17] (1988, 42).

Writer Guillermo Moscoso (1988) echoed his sentiment, stating that "It would be regrettable and lamentable if in light of the governor's probably confusing statement in Spain a move develops (and there seems to be evidence of it already) to plant the seed of racism (both ways) in our society, which would bring forth in the hearts of Puerto Ricans animosities, resentments and jealousies. This will only serve to divide our already politicized society and pull it away from the fair degree of social harmony and unity it has enjoyed throughout the years" (16).

Finally, writer and journalist Castro-Pereda (1954–2000) argued that "To encourage racial resentment and even a conflict of *castas* [castes] in a mixed-race society like ours is irresponsible and dangerous. *Es un caballito de batalla fácil de montar, pero difícil de controlar* [It's a horse that is easy to mount but hard to ride]"[18] (1988, 67).

Yet, if racism is practically nonexistent, why should bringing up the issue be so dangerous? Why panic? This contradiction of fearing a problem at the same time that one declares it nonexistent was particularly evident in the narratives of those who engaged in debate about the *adscripción retórica* (rhetorical ascription).

The debate and panic further exemplify a broader commonwealth-party strategy of creating alarm over the fear of national disintegration and using its antidote, Hispanophilia, against its political rival: the pro-statehood party. To confront this other "threat" of statehood, RHC launched initiatives that deployed Spain as a bastion of cultural distinctiveness during his administration. For example, the "Spanish First" legislation (drafted one year before elections) sought to make Spanish the official language in the Island, where both Spanish and English were recognized. To commemorate the passing of the bill, the commonwealth party organized a luxurious black-tie ceremony that opened with music by Mozart, followed by *décimas* (a Spanish literary and oral form) sung by light-skinned *jíbaros* (Negrón-Muntaner 1997). As Negrón-Muntaner points out, the stress on European and Hispanic roots not only glossed over the black heritage of Puerto Ricans, but also ignored the cultural contributions of those U.S.–born and U.S.–raised Puerto Ricans who do not speak the Spanish of the Real Academia Española (Royal Spanish Academy).

Other high-profile Hispanophile events, such as the celebration of the 500-year anniversary of the so-called Discovery of the Americas, also sought to undermine the statehood project. The 500-year anniversary included an International Grand Regatta, local art exhibitions, concerts, the remodeling and construction of historic plazas, and Puerto Rico's participation in Seville's international Expo Pavilion in Spain. When asked if the celebration of the 500 years contained a political message for the United States, RHC's response was that "the message to the United States was certainly a political one, but it was not a threat, it was about brotherhood."[19] With this friendly posture toward the old (Spain) and current (U.S.) colonial powers, the Hispanophile policies of the RHC administration not only ignored the dehumanizing and exploitative effects of colonialism, but also upheld "Hispanic whiteness" as the normative identity marker of the culture that needed protection against the threat posed by the pro–statehood party agenda.

Hispanophilia in Zoning and the Project of San Antón

These Hispanophile policies had specific consequences for the restoration of Ponce's Historic Zone and later developments in San Antón. In fact, some of the funds used for the restoration and revitalization of Ponce's Historic Zone came from allocations granted by Spain on the occasion of the commemoration of the 500-year anniversary of "the discovery" of America. Spain funded research that had considerable impact on the city aimed at establishing guidelines for historic revitalization. The study was directly sponsored by the Spanish government, as part of a series of artistic and humanistic initiatives they developed in cooperation with Latin American countries to commemorate the 500-year anniversary of "the encounter."

In 1988, influenced by RHC, Spain selected Ponce as one of the preferred sites for historic renovation. RHC's previous contacts with Spanish institutions, his Hispanophile orientation in politics, and his deep concerns for his native city of Ponce combined to make "the Aristocratic City" a top priority for receiving Spanish funds.[20] Once approved in 1988, the contract signed between Puerto Rico and Spain reiterated that the purpose of the collaboration was: "To promote the retrieving of *our common cultural roots*... and due to the characteristics of San Juan, Puerto Rico/Ponce, with an important historical and artistic center, currently subject to a dangerous process of substitution and deterioration, that said city should be the object of a protectionist study that will permit its conservation and maintenance"[21] (Convenio entre España y Puerto Rico 1988; my emphasis).

During their stay in Ponce, Spaniards provided technical and professional training to the Puerto Rican architects, urban planners, and technical personnel involved in the restoration and rehabilitation of the city's Historic Zone. The operational arm of this initiative in Spain was the Institute of Ibero-American Cooperation (ICI),[22] located in Madrid. This was the same institute where RHC gave his speech and comment about "rhetorical ascription." In Puerto Rico, the operational arm was the Institute of Puerto Rican Culture, as represented by its branch in Ponce. Mariana Díaz[23] was the director of that office at the time. She explained the role of the ICI in Ponce: "The ICI initially provided technical and professional help. The agreement entails sending or bringing a complete team of urban center restoration professionals and technicians to train Puerto Rican professionals in the techniques and methodology. But the agreement requires that, in exchange for

Spain's collaboration, [Puerto Rico's] government commit to developing a restoration program for the urban center and also developing legislation or regulations for the maintenance, conservation, and repopulating of the centers."[24]

The ICI's intervention in Ponce was greatly needed. According to Díaz, Ponce "*era tierra de nadie*" (was a no-man's land), and many even referred to its Historic Zone as "La Zona Histérica" (the Hysteric Zone), in reference to a continuing population exodus that began in the 1950s. In view of the abandonment of dwellings and local businesses, the revitalization project sought to spur the social and economic life of the urban center of the Historic Zone.

Díaz described the ICI's methodological approach toward the rehabilitation of historic sites as a holistic one that analyzed structures in the context of their social milieu. The approach entailed a gradual differentiation of the urban center (where most business and government buildings from the colonial era stand) from the traditionally designated Historic Zone, which encompasses residential areas. Administrators applied the concept of homogeneous clusters, areas, not necessarily within the zone, that had characteristics and patterns that merited consideration. The municipal government and the ICI recruited young architects who would be receptive to the new trends in architecture. The goal of the collaborative effort was to establish criteria that would define what to preserve, how, and why. This meant that architects and urban planners had to open a record for each structure and lot, describe its characteristics, provide a photograph of the house or building, describe constituent materials, and provide all other relevant information about the structure. The methodology also provided an opportunity to redefine the boundaries of what would henceforth be considered the Historic Zone of Ponce.

The Housing Project: Bureaucrats Negotiate Exclusions

Between 1988 and 1992, the perimeter of the Historic Zone was extended to include poor communities such as Mariani, Bélgica, and parts of Clausells and Cantera (Santana 2004).[25] Díaz's account explains in detail the ICI's methodology and some of the constraints faced by architects in the process of redesignating the Historic Zone of Ponce:

> Since the most important factor for the revitalization research was that it should have the greatest amount of information possible . . . well then, of course, where do you stop, where do you leave off the study of the city's development is . . . [*Díaz sighs, indicating difficulty*]. Going beyond the city's center they start noticing that, as the city evolved, as it separated from the center you would find architectural characteristics that were very interesting with probably some traces of the center, that incorporated others that were original, therefore creating new styles. And since

they were architects, they would say, "Ah, and how am I going to leave this!" And when we realized it, there was—in addition to the center, which was large enough already—a whole series of scattered kernels that had their own economic and social history, their own architectural style, their own way of life. So then I'll mention . . . the original Alhambra, San Antón, Bélgica, Morel Campos.

This was the chance to redesignate the zone, meaning change its limits . . . The problem was, "What are we going to include? What is going to be called Ponce's Historic Zone?" Especially since what was going to be called the Historic Zone . . . required regulations and norms. In addition to that, it required—and this was part of the agreement with the ICI—that the government commit to assigning all the funds directly, all the possible funds for restoring all the areas.

In this way, the Spanish advisors and their Puerto Rican associates traced new boundaries for the Historic Zone, renaming it and expanding it according to a methodology that impressed Díaz in its detail and integrated approach.

However, the team also operated within a logic that prioritized the urban center as the focus of interest. According to that logic, San Antón was too far away and thus remained peripheral to the team's spatial order.

DÍAZ: When I arrived, the zone had basically been chartered.
ISAR: Had San Antón been included, or not?
DÍAZ: No, San Antón was one of the ones that had not been included.
ISAR: Okay, but other sites that had been left out in the original plan were included?
DÍAZ: Yes, the closest ones.

This criterion of proximity to the urban center is not accidental. San Antón's "faraway" location vis-à-vis the urban center speaks to the power-laden relationships and racial differences that existed between the urban *criollo* bourgeoisie and the *mulato* and black cane workers who lived in the rural working-class barrios of the nineteenth century. Historians have documented how *criollos* availed themselves of the idioms of morality, health, hygiene, labor, and sexuality to control the black and brown working-class poor who lived in the fringes of cities like Ponce (Findlay 1999; Rodríguez-Silva 2012; Santiago-Valles 1994). Anti-vagrancy laws enacted between 1817 and 1862 restricted access to land and criminalized the black and *mulato* population as vagrant. In Ponce, these so-called vagrants were identified with black and poor neighborhoods such as La Cantera, Bélgica, and San Antón, which were commonly represented in public discourse and newspapers managed by *criollo* elites as "dark dangerous places, where ignorant, unruly people danced the *bomba* to African rhythms, believed in witchcraft, and where funerals resembled Haitian voodoo customs with cries and vulgar songs" (Findlay 1999, 80). In their attempt to contain the growing laboring poor and fend off migration from these areas to the city's center, *criollo* elites devised various measures. For example, an Island-wide decree issued in 1893 established that in order to prevent further damage from fires, cities should be divided into three zones. Structures in the zone surrounding the main plaza (zone 1) had to be built in rubble masonry; structures in the areas surrounding zone 1 (zone 2) were to use stone, and structures in the outer fringes of the city (zone 3) were to be built with wood (Rodríguez-Silva 2012, 102). Those who could not abide by the code had to leave the zone. Thus, as Rodríguez-Silva states, "The physical reorganization of cities, in effect, translated into a new regime dividing physical spaces along racial and class lines, with the heart of the city becoming the reserved domain of the upper-class whites" (2012, 102). In effect, the research team's decision to construct San Antón houses in wood reproduced the nineteenth-century spatial logic or racial segregation that they were trying to challenge in the first place as they attempted to mark San Antón a Historic Zone of Ponce.

Besides the Eurocentric bias of a methodology that privileged the city's central plaza, important governmental and funding restrictions influenced the decision to leave San Antón and other working-class barrios out of the Historic Zone. According to Díaz and other government personnel I interviewed, funds for rehabilitation were limited. The line had to be drawn somewhere. "*Yo me imagino que ahí fue la decisión difícil*" (I imagine that this was the moment of the difficult decision), states Díaz in defense of the Puerto Rican architects and urban planners who formed part of the research team. There was, according to her, a genuine interest on the part of these *muchachos* (guys) in applying the same guidelines of historic preservation to areas that had been left out. San Antón, with its *patios*, distinctive familial compounds, and history of *bomba* and *plena*, surfaced in their minds as a site of special interest. "I remember," said Díaz, "when things were pretty far along in Ponce . . . the guys were always thinking about the city and the thing was, well . . . in the same way they wept about not having money for Morel Campos, they wept about not having money, for example, for San Antón."

Consequently, government officials interested in preserving the traditions of the barrio of San Antón had to look for alternative resources through federal funding agencies. Rehabilitation efforts were further complicated by the fact that some of these federal agencies imposed regulations contrary to the municipal government's intent of historical preservation. As Díaz recalls:

> The problem is that if you look for money without . . . having an idea of what a Historical Zone is, there's nobody who can keep an eye to make sure that things aren't done like this [*she makes a sweeping gesture with her arms*] and lay down four cement houses. What worried some of the architects about some of the people of the community was . . . we're going to look for the money but we're not going to disband the community. The preoccupation about the community was not to disband it, and my experience with the task force . . . was that they did not at all want [to disband the

community]. That was also a Spanish policy . . . meaning we're going to remodel, it's not a thing of knocking down the houses, no, that's not it, they're built of wood, so we'll build them of wood also, they're that small, so that's how small they will be . . . [although] we may improve them a little bit.

The opportunity to fund the housing project in San Antón came later through federal HUD funds. However, normal procedure under HUD was to demolish existing houses and build new ones. Nevertheless, the team succeeded in getting the support they needed for the preservation research by adopting creative bureaucratic strategies. Díaz described the fine line they walked with HUD:

I mean, I'm definitely not going to say anywhere that this is definitively a Historical Zone, nor am I going to say that it isn't. I'm going to say that it has historical value and see if it goes through, okay? And it did go through initially. That's where I was telling you that *nos la jugamos frías* [we danced with the devil].

Accounts such as these demonstrate interest on the part of government officials in the revitalization of San Antón and in the preservation of the community. Residents' militancy over the years also contributed to raising awareness about the barrio's deteriorating structures and the will of residents to endure in their community. In addition, prior public controversies over the *adscripción retórica* in 1988—the fact that RHC (the governor from Ponce) was accused of being racist and that San Antón was evoked as the emblem of what RHC was ignoring—must have also prompted official interest in marking San Antón as "historical" and worthy of preservation.

However, beyond personal intentions, architects and public officials involved in the project confronted institutionalized limitations mediated by the Hispanophile climate and Eurocentric priorities that structured the research endeavor from the beginning. Those priorities required new tactics in order to mark San Antón as a historical site even when it fell outside the boundaries of the Historic Zone. The process also required negotiations in terms of design, for in order to mark the barrio as "historical," architects could not veer far from those aesthetic scripts that people (including residents of San Antón) identified with the "official" Historic Zone of Ponce. As Ponce's mayor explained to residents during a visit to the community in July 1995: "We have tried, close to 80 percent, to have this project look like San Antón, more or less, used to be. The only thing that will be different is that instead of having narrow alleys, it will have its streets and its lampposts, just as if it were, as it is: a Historic Zone of Ponce."

In this way, the historic lampposts marked the barrio not just as a traditional community, but as a legitimate part of the "Aristocratic City." They presented themselves as frontier signs of affirmation and distinction between areas the state designates as historic, traditional, and part of the cultural patrimony, and areas it designates as modern, global, and interchangeable, such as the mall, the *caceríos* (public housing projects), or the neighboring *urbanización* Constancia.

In terms of the housing design, structures in the new development corresponded to what Carol Joplin in her study of Puerto Rican houses designates the "Pueblerino (vernacular)." This style incorporates elements of the Criollo Pueblerino style that predominated in houses owned by *criollo* hacienda owners (Joplin 1988, 32). She states that these houses "adapted and incorporated various specific, mostly European architectural elements, such as hip roofs and wrought-iron balustrades, which were selected for their appropriateness to the Puerto Rican situation and their resonance with the historical background of their owners" (29).

Joplin describes the owners of the hacienda residences exhibiting the model Criollo Pueblerino style as immigrants from Corsica, Mallorca, the Canary Islands, Galicia, Asturias, and Andalusia. With the gradual development of a middle class in Puerto Rico, simpler, owner-built wooden houses began to incorporate these elements into a new style that Joplin describes as Pueblerino (vernacular). She states that most of the existing examples of that style "are now also painted in bright colors, particularly light green and aqua, and have been further ornamented with various decorations patently North American in inspiration" (1988, 34). Examples of this vernacular style can be appreciated in the also renovated working-class barrios of the urban center, located at the margins of what is now part of Ponce's extended Historic Zone (see Figure 14). The housing project in San Antón used the same basic models (see Figure 15), replacing the heterogeneity of previous structures with uniformity in design. Like the working-class houses located at the frontier of the Historic Zone, the *criollo* houses of San Antón were also painted in pastel yellow, aqua, pink, and light purple in the new project.

Figure 14. *Pueblerino* (vernacular) style of houses in the margins of the Historic Zone of Ponce. Photo by author.

Figure 15. Houses in San Antón near completion (1996). Photo by author.

Residents did not associate all these architectural developments with the "traditions" of the community. Street lighting, for example, is a relatively recent commodity there. In fact, many elders I interviewed talked about how they used to light their way with "*hachos*" (ignited wood) when they came home from work. However, most of the residents I spoke to appreciated the historic lampposts in their streets. One girl told me her mother wanted to live in one of the houses that had the lamppost in front of it but that she got another one instead.

In terms of house design, some residents said the new houses resembled some old houses of the community. Not all housing formats, however, were represented, as houses in the barrio exhibited a variety of architectural styles, and many had add-on structures that altered original plans.[26] Regarding the color of the paint, when I asked a resident what colors people preferred in the old days, he said, "None, people did not have money to paint their houses."

The comment brings to light the problem of applying the same conservationist methodology in San Antón that architects had applied to the Historic Zone without questioning the different social and class relations of power that informed the "traditions' in each case. By using the historic lampposts, the Pueblerino (vernacular)–style houses, and the pastel colors, architects and government officials exacerbated the Eurocentric bias they were trying to challenge when they turned their "preservationist gaze" toward the barrio. On the other hand, had they done otherwise, that is, had they restored the actual housing structures and diverse housing designs (in all their heterogeneity and flexible form), people would not have recognized the housing project as "Historical" (with a capital H). To the extent that "History" is defined and identified visually and spatially in terms that privilege the urban center, they could not veer too far from the architectural script of the Pueblerino (vernacular).

On the other hand, the bureaucratic maneuvering to mark San Antón as a site worthy of historical recognition demonstrates that Hispanophile politics of exclusion neither operate evenly nor have all-encompassing effects. San Antón's traditions—the *bomba* and *plena*, the achievements of residents in sports and arts, their histories as free people of color or freed slaves who had earned their land—did not figure in the cultural repertoire of Hispanophilia, nor in the aesthetic repertoire of what is considered Spanish heritage. Yet public officials felt they had to negotiate and make room for San Antón (albeit marginally and superficially), or room would not be made for them as representatives of the people. In this way, the unresolved problem and anxiety over the question of black inclusion/exclusion always troubles Hispanophilia as an ideal constantly challenged in its Caribbean applications.

The Irony of Ponce as a "Hispanic Site"

Another contradiction that surfaced in the application of Hispanophilia to urban-renewal initiatives in Ponce relates to the weak rationale that justified the invention of the Spanish government in the city of Ponce as a site of "common cultural roots" with Spain. As discussed previously, the reconstruction of Ponce's urban center was facilitated by the allocation of Spanish funds destined to commemorate the 500th year of the "encounter" between Spain and Latin America. The initiative formed part of a broader effort to sponsor research studies in historic sites of the Americas that had been shaped deeply by Spain's colonial presence. However, the characterization of Ponce as a site of "Spanish influence" is neither common nor self-evident. Other cities in Puerto Rico demonstrate Spanish influence more distinctly in terms of architecture and spatial arrangement. San Juan, with its El Morro fortress and the military might of its governmental brick buildings, is the most obvious.

However, unlike San Juan, which was the bastion of Spanish military control, Ponce belonged to a *criollo* elite that saw itself differently positioned—both economically and politically—in relation to Spanish authorities. Álvarez-Curbelo and Enrique Vivoni (1998) point out that "contrary to what one might expect, Ponce did not become a peninsularized city. As in the case of other cities in the Caribbean—Santiago in Cuba, Santiago de los Caballeros in the Dominican Republic—Ponce grew into maturity as a Creole city, with a distinctive urban culture in many ways the opposite of San Juan's" (210).

Travel difficulties between Ponce and San Juan contributed to their divergences and independent economic development, particularly in the nineteenth century. Other, more significant factors, such as the large number of non-Spanish immigrants who established themselves in Ponce, also explain the particular character of the city. For example, the influence of English settlers accounts for the establishment in Ponce of the first Protestant Church (1874) ever built in Spanish colonies (Santiago de Curet 1985, 11). Ponce also had a school dedicated to the teaching of foreign languages, particularly English and French (Santiago de Curet 1985, 12). And it is no coincidence that the river that crosses the city is called the Portugués in honor of one of the first settlers of the area. In fact, in a late nineteenth-century report, R. H. Davis stated that "Ponce itself held more foreign flags than we have ever seen. Judging from their number one would have thought that the population was composed entirely of English, Germans, French, Swiss and members of the Red Cross Society" (quoted in Santiago de Curet 1985, 9).

Factors that fostered this foreign European migration to the city of Ponce varied, but traffic in contraband with nearby non-Spanish colonies played a major role.[27] The dynamic and enterprising ventures of these settlers and their culture of contraband often conflicted with colonial regulations and Spanish authorities' intentions of maintaining a monopoly over Island commercial affairs. As this *criollo* class prospered economically, their political ambitions for self-governance grew. That aim required political legitimacy and the formulation of a project that would address the concerns of all citizens. Consequently, they developed a political rhetoric that construed social conflicts in terms of an oppositional relationship between Puerto Ricans and Spaniards (Quintero-Rivera 1988). Many black and *mulato* artisans from Ponce's urban center joined this political cause (Hoffnung-Garskof 2011). Their participation not only gave legitimacy to the movement, but also advanced their own struggle to gain acceptance as dignified citizens of Ponce's urban society (Quintero-Rivera 1988). Other sectors of the rural population were also integrated into the liberal project. The national arm of this cause was the Autonomist Party, and its geographical bastion was, of course, Ponce.

It was within this context of national affirmation, at the end of the nineteenth century, that Luis Muñoz-Rivera, the most important leader of the liberal-autonomous movement, referred to Ponce as "the most Puerto Rican city of all Puerto Rico"[28] (Quintero-Rivera 1988). In contrast to the official, Catholic, and conservative San Juan, Ponce thus rose as an alternative urban center consisting of prosperous Island-born *criollo* citizens of European descent conjuring up an alternative political project at the end of the nineteenth century.

Ponce Es Ponce: Aristocratic Nostalgia

Much of the political and commercial autonomy gained in Ponce was lost at the turn of the century when the United States established its centralized colonial administration. Yet, although Ponce lost its aura as the *Ciudad Señorial* (Aristocratic City), *ponceños* still take pride in its "aristocratic and cosmopolitan past," as evidenced in the common saying *Ponce es Ponce* (Ponce is Ponce), voiced by members of the upper and working classes alike. Populist and commonwealth mayor Rafael (Churumba) Cordero later gave the saying a more modern twist: *"Ponce es Ponce y lo demás es parking"* (Ponce is Ponce, and the rest is parking) (Emmanuelli Jiménez 2010; González Olán 2009), revealing a strong sense of distinction with respect to San Juan's urban sprawl.

For Don Ismael, this sense of regional pride was also an important asset and source of community support when he immigrated to New York in the 1960s. Born and raised in one of Ponce's working-class barrios (Machuelo) and having served in the U.S. Army in 1953, this light-skinned man migrated with his wife to New York City, where he worked in factories. There he and other *ponceños* founded Casa Ponceña, Inc.[29] He recalls how, when Casa Ponceña was established, many Puerto Ricans in New York believed

> [that] the people of Ponce thought they were superior, that they were proud and arrogant, but these people don't understand the past, that this was part of its tradition, its culture ever since Ponce started to evolve. It's something that the pioneers who founded Ponce established, due to the quality of life and the quality of people that settled in Ponce. They were a different type of people, of a very high social level. Due to this, they created a way of life different from all the other Puerto Rican townships . . . [The New York Puerto Rican] does not understand that Ponce was one of the towns where all those aristocrats, all those people from the upper social level, found, in Ponce, the ideal place, because of its tranquility, its nature, and its coasts. They immediately understood that it was the place to settle and that it adapted well to the way of life they were accustomed to in Europe.

This nostalgia and regional pride that people like Don Ismael feel for Ponce has earned *ponceños* a reputation for being arrogant, elitists, or regionalists, especially among *san juaneros*.

Friction between Ponce and San Juan went beyond sayings, personal reputations, or historical conditions during the time of my fieldwork. They took on legal and political manifestations, as well, when Ponce's commonwealth local leadership sued the pro-statehood central government for withholding funds for public works that had been appropriated as part of the development plan of Ponce en Marcha. Municipal leaders accused the new pro-statehood central leadership of discriminating against Ponce's pro-commonwealth administration for political reasons, since the money had been approved by the previous administration headed by political rival RHC.

Slogans used in this twentieth-century battle between San Juan and Ponce bore a striking similarity to the rhetoric used in the power struggles between cities in the nineteenth century. In a statement that seemed to echo nineteenth-century

Autonomists' sentiments against a central government that hindered progress, Ponce's mayor declared in one of his 1996 reelection campaign brochures that "In spite of all the attempts of the central government to trample on those rights, trying to stop and undermine infrastructure projects for our city's development as a whole, the people emerge with the will to resist"[30] (Partido Popular Democrático de Ponce 1996a).

In another flyer, the mayor declared: "And, with the nostalgia produced by the memories of an illustrious and aristocratic history, with the dynamic strength that boosts us into a vanguard of progress and makes us a model for our neighborhood towns and cities . . . our strong and vigorous will to resist was born"[31] (Partido Popular Democrático de Ponce 1996b).

This "will to resist" also became the motto of a group of residents named Ponceños de Verdad (True Ponceños), who periodically organized activities to promote the development and completion of public works that corresponded to the Ponce en Marcha plan but that had been deferred or halted by the pro-statehood central government. I participated in one of their demonstrations as they organized to protest against the inaction of the pro-statehood administration. When I got there, participants dressed in yellow T-shirts exhibiting the words "Ponceños de Verdad" were preparing to march across the Historic Zone. A bus carrying big speakers headed the crowd. As it moved forward, a group of young *batuteras* (baton twirlers) began their routine. People gathered behind the bus while a man voiced slogans through the speakers: "*Ponceño, ¡reclama lo tuyo!*" (*Ponceño*, claim what is yours!). As the march started he declared: "*¡Esto es una marcha señorial con señorío . . . No es una fiesta patronal, ni un festival playero, esta marcha es un reclamo al gobierno Central!*" (This is an aristocratic march, in an aristocratic manner. This is not a patron saint's festival, nor is it a beach party, this march is a demand to the central government!).

Middle-aged men and women identified by their T-shirts as Ponceños de Verdad formed the bulk of the march. Many appeared to be middle-class, light-skinned residents of Ponce. Although the movement did not align itself with any particular political party, the majority of participants were known to be supporters of the commonwealth party. In the midst of the marching crowd, I noticed the familiar face of a black man and realized he was Pucho, Julia's brother. Unlike Julia, who lived in San Antón, Pucho lived in a middle-class *urbanización* that was somewhat removed from the barrio. According to Julia, Pucho married only white women. His fifth wife (a plump, light-skinned woman with bleached blond hair) accompanied him that day at the march. After we greeted each other briefly, Pucho turned to speak to a couple of women who had been teasing him about his white hair. While we marched, I heard him say to them jokingly: "*Si en San Antón tú ves negros viejos de 100 y pico de años que no tienen ni una sola cana y tú te preguntarás ¿cómo es eso posible? Pues . . . porque no usan la mente*" (In San Antón you can see old black men who don't have a single white hair and you ask yourself, how is that possible? Well, that's because they have never used their brains). The joke implied that the reason he had so much white hair was that he—unlike the people of San Antón—did use his brain.

Pucho's effort to distinguish himself from the poor—and, according to him, "stupid"—black folk of San Antón struck me, considering Julia was his sister and lived in San Antón. Like other participants in the march, he was wearing the bright yellow T-shirt that identified him as one of the Ponceños de Verdad. But maybe the T-shirt whose bright yellow color gleamed against his very dark skin was not enough to establish "sameness." Could his comment be an attempt to assert his identity as a Ponceño de Verdad among that predominantly light-skinned crowd of middle-class folk and in the midst of all the aristocratic display of city pride taking place during the march?

Judging from the Eurocentric tone of the march, the answer seems to be yes. Race- and class-infused signs of aristocratic pride were everywhere. Banners used by participants displayed famous quotations upholding the special status of Ponce as a city both representative of Puerto Rico and different because of its distinguished history. Various banners read:

> *Ponce es baluarte irreductible de puertorriqueñidad.*—Rafael Pont-Flores
> [Ponce is the unyielding stronghold of Puerto Ricanness.]

> *Ponce ya no repite la historia, la mejora*
> [Ponce does not repeat history, it improves on it.]

> *Ponce era para el resto de la Isla lo que Cataluña era para España, algo aparte y singular. No es que los ponceños nos creamos diferentes a los demás ciudadanos de la isla, sino que verdaderamente actuamos y nos sentimos diferentes.*—Mariano Vidal Armstrong
> [Ponce was to the rest of the Island what Catalonia was to Spain, something separate and unique. It's not that people from Ponce believe we are different from the rest of the citizens of the Island, but that we truly act and feel different.]

The refined language of these banners, the use of historical quotations, their reference to the past, and the analogy to Catalan separatist sentiments charged the atmosphere of that march with particular class and racial meanings activated by the nostalgia for a white *criollo* nineteenth-century society. That kind of nostalgia upholds Eurocentric definitions of the nation that distances blackness to the margins and grants social currency to Pucho's debasing joke about San Antón. On the other hand, it is also a nostalgia that challenges Hispanophile renderings of Ponce as a site that shares "common cultural roots with Spain."

In this way, fieldwork dynamics during my stay in Ponce revealed at least three different kinds of whiteness that were historically (and politically) mobilized vis-à-vis blackness in the process of defining Puerto Rican "culture." One notion was mobilized in the Hispanophile narratives of RHC and his commonwealth supporters, who upheld Puerto Rican cultural nationalism (as Hispanic whiteness) vis-à-vis statehooders. Another kind operated at the local level of Ponce (as cosmopolitan-European whiteness) vis-à-vis the "less aristocratic" San Juan. Finally, a third emerged in the context of pro-statehood/pro-U.S. narratives that upheld ideas of progress and modernity (as Anglo-Saxon, democratic whiteness) vis-à-vis the specter of Spanish colonialism. Chapter 5 focuses on this last flavor, by taking a closer look at Hispanophobia and some of the corresponding political discourses and agendas that also became entangled in the housing renovation project in San Antón.

CHAPTER 5

His-Panic / My Panic

Hispanophobia and the Reviled Whiteness of Spain

As we have seen, exaltations of Spain in Puerto Rican national discourses in the 1930s were and continued to be class- and race-loaded responses to the colonial presence of the United States on the Island. Yet not all sectors of the Puerto Rican population shared the anti-Americanism that motivated such exaltations. In this chapter, I pay particular attention to the raced and classed positions informing political projects that considered the United States as a political ally. In this exploration, I also address the continuities of such discourses with the ethnographic present, and particularly from the perspective of those who favored statehood in San Antón.

Juan Luis "Cuto" Colón, for example, was a pro-statehood district representative and resident of San Antón. He did not agree with the commonwealth proposal of building "traditional housing" and supported, instead, the linear setup of cement houses. According to Cuto, San Antón should be a community *"de cara al 2,000"* (facing the year 2000).[1] Wearing a T-shirt that displays a U.S. flag, an eagle, and the letters USA, Cuto expressed his wish to see San Antón look just like the surrounding urban neighborhoods of Ponce. "We want to be part of Ponce, not a community isolated from Ponce . . . That is, if we are in the middle of two *urbanizaciones* and three important avenues, why not be on a par with the progress of that?" According to him, discourses about San Antón's cultural traditions had been used to stall progress in the community and promote racial stereotypes:

> San Antón is more than a simple *pandereta*, gourd, or *maraca*. I mean, every time San Antón is talked about, they say: *"Ah, sí, los negritos aquellos que tocaban bomba y plena."*

["Oh, yeah, those little black people that played *bomba* and *plena*."] Hey, but what about . . . ? Is that San Antón?! Is that San Antón?! There are nurses here, there are engineers here, there are realtors here, there are housewives here. What's the matter?! There are carpenters here, there are plumbers here, there are physicians here now, there are educators, I mean San Antón is more than that. This is the error; it's the stereotype, San Antón is THIS. And I think . . . it gets me mad, I'll tell you the truth . . . I get enraged that people still think like that, and permit that kind of thinking to continue . . .

In our interview, he described the commonwealth party's showcase of San Antón's traditions as something that benefitted only Ponce's upper class:

I said that that project pleased Ponce's bureaucrats, the aristocrats of Ponce who wanted to live in their good cement houses [such] that when hurricanes arrive, they would put hurricane wind shields and stay there [in their homes]. And, nevertheless, the people of San Antón, *cuando digan huracán* [when a hurricane comes] they are going to have to run for their lives . . . Hence, I say that they could have done something better: aligned it with its sidewalks, with its yard, in other words, that each person can say from here to here is *my* property, I mean, the right to have. There, nobody has anything because all the yards are intertwined.

In his view, the project not only exacerbated class hierarchies by denying San Antón residents the opportunity to live in safer cement houses. The "traditional" design of the patio imposed by the commonwealth government, with its connecting corridors and communal areas, also denied residents the privilege of fully participating in a U.S. capitalist market that values private property and the need to fence it, a privilege that Ponce's upper class fully benefitted from.[2]

Socialists and Republicans

The class and racially loaded propositions contained in Cuto's critique of Ponce's aristocracy and defense of progress and modernity in alliance with the United States have important historical precedents. During the earlier decades of the twentieth century, black and *mulato* working-class people endorsed the democratic principles and liberal traditions they associated with the United States and organized in favor of statehood. Contrary to the educated Hispanophile elite of the 1930s, who tended to romanticize a supposed prosperity under Spanish rule, these sectors assumed a clearly anti-Spanish stance.

After four centuries of domination by Spain, peasants and particularly black members of the lower classes seized the opportunity of the recent arrival of U.S. troops in 1898 to express their disdain for Spanish landowners and merchants who had benefitted from what had been a racist, repressive, and exploitative economic system. That disdain found expression in riots, shootouts, and acts of arson committed against haciendas and other properties of Spaniards, particularly at the turn of the century (Negrón-Portillo 1997; Santiago-Valles 1994). *Criollo* proprietors were targeted, as well.[3] Even after the American military campaign ended in August 1898, assaults continued and U.S. soldiers found themselves in the very odd position of having to protect the few Spaniards who were left. As historian Fernando Picó (1997) states, "In this way, curiously, those who came to 'liberate' Puerto Ricans from Spaniards had as their first task, the protection of Spaniards"[4] (627). Mariano Negrón-Portillo (1997) tells us that in Ponce, a black leader of the urban marginal sectors named Antonio *"el negro"* Guilbe "used to walk the streets along with followers who foul-mouthed members of the elite. Astonished, the proprietors watched as this black man paraded gun in hand, with the U.S. flag wrapped around his shoulders" (43).

Blacks who welcomed the invaders in 1898, like *el negro* Guilbe, anticipated social transformations in accordance with the perceived liberal postulates of the U.S. democratic tradition. With the advent of the United States, that action found political expression in the Socialist Party, which allied itself with labor unions, and the Socialist Workers Party in the United States. Because many members of the party were black/dark *mulatos*, critics called them *la negrada socialista* (black socialists) (Rodríguez-Silva 2012, 160). In urban areas particularly, workers, artisans, and peasants joined to form strong social movements and unions as members of the working class and made alliances with U.S. labor organizations.

Memories of Spanish colonialism and its obsessive concern with racial lineage as a means of control also influenced how the United States was perceived by black and *mulato* politicians who joined the Republican (pro-statehood) Party. It is no coincidence that the founder and main leader of the Republican Party was a black physician of working-class origins, named José Celso Barbosa (1857–1921). Spanish authorities had denied Barbosa professional and political appointments because of his color. When Puerto Rico passed from Spanish to U.S. hands, Barbosa played a key supporting role that later earned him the patronage of U.S. colonial authorities (Jiménez-Román 1996). Barbosa's ideals of annexation might seem contradictory at a time when segregation and lynching were common in the U.S. South, but Barbosa's experience in the United States was forged in Michigan, where a relatively tolerant racial climate prevailed. There he obtained a medical degree in 1880 at the University of Michigan at Ann Arbor, where he enjoyed an active intellectual and social life before returning to Puerto Rico (Jiménez-Román 1996, 16).

Barbosa argued that, under statehood, the laws of Puerto Rico would be made by Puerto Ricans, and this would prevent racial prejudice and other "foreign practices" from taking root on the Island (Jiménez-Román 1996, 20). Puerto Ricans would be, in that sense, mere "spectators" of the U.S. racial situation. He also maintained that racism in Puerto Rico was a minor problem of personal rather than institutional dimensions that could be avoided if the black man recognized "his place" in society: "Since there is no *color problem* in political life or in public life, and since the colored element has never attempted to cross or erase the social line, the *color problem* does not exist in Puerto Rico"[5] (Barbosa 1937, 31–32; emphasis in original).

Barbosa's professional experience did not confirm this alleged separation of public and private life, for he never assumed formal leadership of the Republican Party or of the Republican Newspaper *El Tiempo*, which he founded, exerting instead a behind-the-scenes leadership throughout his entire career (Jiménez-Román 1996, 17). In a context where there were few institutional outlets for confronting racism, not attempting "to cross or erase the social line" was not just a liberal's sociological assessment of "the color element." It may have also been a life strategy to steer clear of humiliating situations where his own color could become a more public issue.

But more than a personal tactic, voicing a racialized sense of self or denouncing racism was something that politicians like Barbosa handled cautiously because of the complex and multifaceted political consequences. On the one hand, the Republican Party sought to gain the electoral support of the predominantly black and expanding labor movement. Barbosa, for example, was very aware of the close relationship between race and class and sometimes used this to his political advantage, accusing the rival Union Party of being racist for not attending to workers' needs for economic uplift and equity (Rodríguez-Silva 2012, 155). On the other hand, the Republican Party and the working-class movement strongly differed in their class and political orientations (liberalism versus socialism). Blackness and associated popular expressions of poor working-class folk were considered backward by the party's *criollo* leadership, who also limited participation of black male intelligentsia in party decisions (Santiago-Valles 1994; Rodríguez-Silva 2012, 177). Furthermore, as Rodríguez-Silva (2012) notes, a politicized black identity was associated with unrest and the anticolonial movements that had taken place in Haiti and in the rest of the Caribbean, including Cuba, with its 1912 race war and massacre of the black members of the Partido Independiente de Color (188). In that context, an explicit racialized discourse stood at odds with U.S. colonial representatives, with whom annexationists like Barbosa, as well as socialists and labor union leaders, were trying to negotiate better wages, employment opportunities, legal protection, and U.S. citizenship. Explicit debates about racism were also inconvenient for political elites, who wanted to project themselves to the United States as illustrious men in charge of a multiracial society free of racial conflict. Making claims to racial harmony proved their capacity to negotiate the colonial relationship with the racially segregated United States. Undermining racial conflict was also important for maintaining key political alliances among white *criollos*, artisans, and the working class (Rodríguez-Silva 2012). Hence, despite major ideological and class differences, politicians, intellectuals, and labor organizers sought to deracialize their politics (Rodríguez-Silva 2012). Overwhelmingly, they suppressed the assertion of a black identity, judging the marking of such difference a divisive act of racism itself.

Hispanophobia, Statehood, and San Antón

Much has changed in the pro-statehood movement since the first decades of the twentieth century. The emphasis that the earlier pro-statehooders placed on the democratic ideals and institutions of the United States changed to much more conservative postures in the 1940s and 1950s, when an elite that benefitted from the sugar industry and the economic encroachment of U.S. corporations gained control of the movement, in alliance with an emergent middle class (Meléndez 1993). After the 1950s, the pro-statehood party sought to broaden its support by appealing to the poor, reframing statehood as a short-term goal that would guarantee equality and emphasizing the benefits of U.S. federal transfers (Meléndez 1993; Romero Barceló 1974).[6]

Despite these important transformations, class and racially loaded positions entrenched in the early twentieth century between those who favored annexation to the United States and those who sought more autonomy were still present during my fieldwork in the 1990s. Like his republican counterparts from the turn of century, pro-statehooders like Cuto were not interested in promoting a politics of racial identity that would call attention to the barrio's racialized citizenry, considering such a politics of difference to be racist itself. Furthermore, a focus on San Antón's racialized working-class contributions to a Puerto Rican national "difference" vis-à-vis the United States would undermine the political ideal of statehood and its related goal of economic uplift.

When addressing other factors that could undermine the statehood project for Puerto Rico—such as the issue of U.S. racism—Cuto Colón argued that Puerto Rico would not be affected under statehood. His reasoning, nevertheless, was quite different from that of Barbosa, who argued that Puerto Rico did not have a "race problem" at the turn of the century. Quite the contrary; he said:

> The problem is that here in Puerto Rico there are some serious racial problems. Here, even, in Ponce, there is a club where a black person cannot become a member and they arrange it so. And in San Juan, the same thing happens and you know it. That is, here in Puerto Rico there is a lot more racism . . . There are even schools here where they put up a lot of obstacles to [prevent] a black child from getting in.

When I asked him how he would define such racism, he responded:

> Racism is the complex that a person might have of not daring to socialize with another, who they see as so superior or inferior that they don't dare to cross beyond that mentality. But let me tell you, and I guarantee it, in Puerto Rico and in Ponce there is just as much or more racism than what there might be in the U.S.

"What is the difference?" I asked

> The racism from over there is more sincere. If they don't want you, they don't want you, "that's it" [*stated in English*]. But the one from here is underhanded, and that is the one that bothers you most.

For Cuto this kind of underhanded racism was also prevalent in the housing project. When I asked him about the possibility, mentioned by Ponce's mayor, of bringing tourists to the community, he said:

> Remember that all of this has to do with the aristocracy of Ponce, where we go back to the same thing. I've heard people say, "I have to go to San Anton to eat this, I have to go to San Antón because there they do this" . . . instead of saying, "Look, I have to go to San Antón because I have friends there, and I have to go see them." I mean, they weave together one thing with the other. And what is my fear? To be honest, it is that these white people could take this to come here and sell their product. Because that is what they will do, because remember that the tourism industry is the one that moves the most money around the world.
>
> What they want is to show, what? Their project [*Cuto answered his own question and continued as if addressing the mayor*]. And why don't you bring [the tourists] now? [*He continued in a daring tone.*] Bring them now! Bring them down here! And we will take them inside the community so that they can see the serious infrastructure problems in San Antón. Bring them now! Why don't you bring them now? [*he continued asking his imaginary interlocutor. And then concluded*] Ah, no! He is going to take them to see *his* project, because he is not going to expose them to San Antón; he is going to expose his project, and that is the problem with this.

As mentioned previously, formal plans for bringing tourists to San Antón never materialized. Yet Cuto's comments bring to light the contradictions inherent in a housing project that in seeking to celebrate "traditional blackness," from his point of view, also celebrated "traditional poverty" and denied San Antón residents access to modernity. His expressed concern about the representation of stereotypical images of blackness also speaks to how such class and racially informed concepts of culture can become a commodity for the white tourist and for the rival commonwealth party, as well.

As a statehood representative, Cuto (like his political counterparts from the early twentieth century) recognized race and class as mutually constitutive categories with rich political potential. Political undertones in Cuto's narrative constructed the rival commonwealth party in charge of the housing project as elitists, indirectly marking the pro-statehood party he represented as the one that could ensure progress and economic advancement for poor black people under the U.S. flag. However, this principle of progress, upheld by annexationists since the beginning of the twentieth century, does not question the link between U.S. capitalism and structural inequality, turning a blind eye to the constitutive relationship between U.S. racism and the incorporation of Puerto Ricans into a colonialism/capitalism matrix. Furthermore, once this expressed conflation of blackness with poverty is established, it is difficult to see how economic uplift would not entail a moving away from cultural expressions that are racialized as black. Pro-statehood accusations of political contenders of being racist (whether in the early or late twentieth century) did not translate to supporting strategies that called for racial solidarity, the politicization of a black identity, or its positive reformulation. In this sense, pro-statehooders' rejection of the emphasis on racialized black cultural expressions could be understood as a promotion of whitening that is achieved by moving up the social-class ladder laid by U.S. capitalism.

Cuto Colón's critical posture toward the housing project and its emphasis on "traditions" was not shared by everyone in San Antón. María Judith Banchs, for example, felt the project launched by the commonwealth administration was valuable because it respected the composition of the families and maintained the barrio's essence, something previous developments had not considered. The reader might remember her compelling statement (Chapter 1) about growing up in the barrio, where she said she began to learn who she was. Unlike Cuto, who criticized the overemphasis of the cultural products associated with black culture in San Antón, María Judith felt that by emphasizing the barrio's cultural contributions one could help raise people's self-esteem and instill pride in their African heritage.

Although she no longer lived in San Antón, her strong sense of commitment to the community led her to represent the barrio in the Juntas de Comunidad organized by Ponce's municipal government in the early 1990s to ensure community participation in city developments. As a theater teacher, she also collaborated with San Antón's Fiestas de Bomba and Plena by organizing *comparsas* (a chorused musical parade with costume) with her students in the community. María Judith saw herself as following in her mother's footsteps since she had previously led community initiatives to demand better housing infrastructure for San Antón. She recalls her surprise in the 1990s when she learned, as a representative of the Juntas, that the municipal government planned to build houses in a linear setup, commenting on the lack of correspondence between that linear model and the barrio's *patio* traditions: "The project wasn't designed right because it didn't respect, in any way, the ways of the people that live here. I mean, it didn't respect the barrio's configuration, which is based on the *patios*. That's when I went into an orientating and advising phase, where I wanted them [government personnel of urban planning] to interest themselves in coming to the barrio to investigate: the barrio's shape; the number of families, why we're in this situation. Why, despite the overcrowding, people persist in staying in the same place; the sense of belonging that the people have."

Hence, she had personally accompanied government planners house by house to help gather information on household compositions, housing structures, family income, trees, and other natural assets of importance to the community.

One day, while the construction was in progress, and before conflicting positions accelerated into the public debate that ensued later, María Judith and I visited one of the family plots that was soon to be intervened. The visit was not an ordinary one, for we arrived with two U.S. anthropologists who were in Puerto Rico for a conference and who had come to visit my field site (two women and the male partner of one of them[7]). Upon my request, María Judith had kindly guided us to where the first houses were being constructed. When we entered the family *patio*, María Judith introduced the three North American professors to Victoria (the matriarch of the family), a statehood supporter and longtime friend of her family. As we walked toward the back area of the *patio*, a male member of the family approached us to voice his criticisms against the commonwealth housing project. Cari, a tall black woman of approximately forty-five years of age, also questioned the government, stating they should have moved residents to *urbanizaciones*.

In what I perceived to be a rather tense conversation, María Judith told Cari that that was not the idea behind the project. The purpose was to keep the families of the community together. If residents moved to *urbanizaciones*, the community would disappear. She argued her point further by stating that:

> Nadie me puede decir a mí que yo soy una negra bruta porque yo me siento orgullosa de lo que yo soy. Pero aunque la gente se vaya a otro sitio a vivir siempre van a decir que son de San Antón y no los van a aceptar. Por eso es mejor mantenerse donde están las raíces de uno y con orgullo de ser lo que uno es.
>
> [Nobody's going to tell me I'm a stupid black woman, because I'm proud of what I am. But even if people leave to live in some other place, they're always going to say that they're from San Antón, and they're not going to be accepted. That's why it's better to stay where one's roots are, and be proud of who you are.]

Cari disagreed but did not confront María Judith directly. Some members of the *patio* also remained silently skeptical during her intervention.[8] Others members echoed her positive remarks about her black identity, saying they also were proud of being *de éste color* (of this color). However, rather than accepting the premise that they will not be accepted elsewhere, Cari challenged the racist thinking of those who felt superior to black people, stating:

Pero es que: ¿quién en Puerto Rico es blanco? En Puerto Rico nadie es blanco. Porque aquí los únicos puertorriqueños verdaderos eran los Taínos y después llegaron todos los demás—alemanes y europeos y trajeron a los africanos—y ahí se les "chavó" la raza.

[But, who's white in Puerto Rico? In Puerto Rico nobody's white. Because the only true Puerto Ricans were the Taínos, and later the others arrived—Germans and Europeans and they brought the Africans—and that's when their race got messed up].

I commented: *"Bueno, se mejoró"* (Well, it got better[9]), and she said: *"Bueno, pero que tú sabes lo que yo te digo. Es que aquí todo el mundo tiene algo de negro."* (Yeah, but you know what I'm saying. It's that everybody here has some black in 'em.)

Cari worked in the public health service sector and explained (while I translated for the visiting anthropologists) that she was the only one "of this color" in her workplace and that everyone accepts her. They call her *la rubia* (the blond one), she said, laughing. "The important thing is to get along with everybody, *mira la nieta de esa mujer tan prieta*" (Look at the granddaughter of that woman who's so black), and she pointed to an elderly family member and to her fair-skinned granddaughter. *"¡Mira pa'llá! ¡Café con leche!"* (Look at that! Coffee and milk!) Then she turned to one of the anthropologists, an Afro-American woman, and said jokingly that now she and her husband (a "white" man) had to do the same: *"Ahora ustedes tienen que juntarse para mezclarse y hacer lo mismo. Café con leche. Nosotros somos café con leche."* (…now you have to get together to get mixed and do the same. Coffee and milk. We're coffee and milk.)

The conversation had just as much to do with housing as it had to do with race and the U.S. interlocutors present that day. The remarks Cari voiced before them about "coffee and milk" were meant to diminish the importance of racial hierarchies based on whiteness for Puerto Rico, where process of mixture had tainted it or, as she said, "messed it up." She also seemed to favor the tactic of "getting along with everybody" even if (or maybe especially if) they were not of her same color, rejecting the strategy of racial and residential solidarity proposed by María Judith. Just as liberal statehood leader José Barbosa positioned himself vis-à-vis the United States in the early twentieth century, Cari was not invested in a living arrangement or in a politics of self that drew attention to the barrio's blackness. Striving for a society where race could be insignificant, she opted to minimize the issue, presenting Puerto Rico's *"café con leche"* motto to the U.S. visitors (especially to the African American woman and white male partner) as a model to follow.

However, later, during one of the community meetings held to protest against the housing project, Cari questioned the unequal treatment of the government, who had allowed some residents to build cement houses but not others, stating, "*o todos blancos o todos prietos*" (either we're all white or all black). At this other moment, she used racial language of black versus whites (not of mixture) to denounce the government's unfair treatment. Positions regarding the idea of mixture thus varied, depending on the situation at hand.

Despite these variations, there were important discursive commonalities in the rhetoric of pro-statehood residents like Cuto and Cari, who opposed the housing project. They both critiqued Ponce's elite (and their racism) by stressing the principles of class equality, their right to progress, and their desire to live in a modern neighborhood or *urbanización* as the means to achieve it. This does not imply that political affiliation predisposed residents toward assuming a particular position vis-à-vis housing. As mentioned previously, residents' opinions about the housing project had more to do with their economic status (i.e., as renters or owners) and with the condition of their houses than with their political affiliation. Hence, not all statehooders opposed the "traditional" commonwealth housing model, and not all commonwealth residents favored it. In fact, the vice president of the Comité Pro-Defensa del Barrio San Antón—a commonwealth supporter—called the project an "Indian reservation." Rather, what I wish to emphasize here are some relevant tendencies and continuities between pro-statehood discourses of the early 1900s and the discourse of statehood residents who opposed the housing model proposed by the commonwealth party. Namely, we see a common emphasis on "progress" and equity over cultural nationalism, the resistance to draw attention to racialized identities, the awareness that class and race are mutually constitutive and rich in political potential, and the related accusation of racism launched toward those who prevent the economic uplift of the poor.

San Antón is not the only place where one can find such continuities. During the 1980s and later in 2000 and 2002, a similar debate that mobilized the notion of progress as availed by the ideal of U.S. statehood emerged in the northern town of Loíza, also known for its blackness. There, spokesmen of the pro-statehood party critiqued environmentalists and residents associations that opposed the construction of private hotels and other (mostly high-cost) housing developments in the area of Piñones. Residents and leaders of the statehood party (such as the town's mayor) argued that such opposition was founded on the "racist" thinking of people who wanted to hold back progress for *loizeños* and deprive them of economic opportunities available to people in other municipalities (Hernández-Hiraldo 2006b, 75). On the contrary, other *loizeños* and residents associations argued that high-cost housing and the tourist interests of private companies had been prioritized over housing and facilities for the poor and threatened their ecological resources and traditional means of survival (Hernández-Hiraldo 2006b, 75). Posters prepared for public protests proclaimed they wanted "development with conservation." But for others, this defense of "traditions" and the language of conservation meant the perpetuation of poverty. Some complained that it was easier for Loíza to receive money for cultural purposes than for basic services such as a medical building (Hernández-Hiraldo 2006b, 75).

Bienvenido de Jesús Correa, for example, presided over the organization Emancipación (Emancipation), which supported private developments in Loíza. According to him, politicians who opposed the development of Loíza were "leaders of perverse mentality who have indoctrinated blacks from Piñones to accept poverty and inequality as a good thing and who pretend to expand that vision to all blacks from Loíza." He critiqued an environmental report that called for the preservation of the area's culture, local settlements, and "architectural symbolism" as expressed in the *bohíos* and *kioskos* (rudimentary structures made of palm leaves, wood, and aluminum), arguing that towns populated by white folks were never subject to such restrictions (De Jesús Correa 2002, 12–13).

Bienvenido de Jesús was not known as a pro-statehood advocate, evidencing that such critical positions are not always clearly established along party lines. Nevertheless, his statements strongly resonate with a discernible political pattern in pro-statehood rhetoric that capitalizes on the relationship between blackness and poverty and supports the notion of development in alliance with U.S. interests while labeling the opposition racist. Samiri Hernández (2006b) argues that such party tactics are also closely linked to contemporary neoliberal politics and to the increased public attention that issues of race and racism gained in the 1990s. Commenting on the pro-statehood rhetoric of Loíza's mayor, she states that "The mayor, sitting under a large photograph of Governor Pedro Roselló, indicated that Loíza could not continue to be victimized and had to move forward, with the support of the PNP. The increase in the private sector economic influence due to the PNP government's privatization efforts since the early nineties and a surge in the popularity of issues pertaining to racism caused the Loíza government to play the race card to obtain state funding and, according to many, conceal its corruption (Hernández-Hiraldo 2006b, 75).

San Antón's controversy differed substantially from Loíza's because the development under discussion in San Antón was a residential initiative supported by public funds, not a tourist development with private sector-interests. Yet in both cases, pro-statehood representatives upheld a discourse of progress, modernity, and equal treatment and rejected agendas that appealed to national culture and the desire to preserve the traditions of a black community. In Loíza's case, the defense of "traditions" was labeled racist. In San Antón, Cuto Colón said they favored Ponce's bureaucrats and aristocrats.

Spain and the People of San Antón

In the previously discussed controversies, charges made by pro-statehood supporters against the racism of national elites and their concept of "traditional blackness" did not point directly to Spanish ancestry. The "white" identity that people alluded to in their narratives about racism or elitism remained unqualified. However, at other points during my fieldwork, people qualified such whiteness, making explicit connections between "Spanish heritage" and a particularly racist attitude. This occurred regardless of people's political affiliation vis-à-vis the United States and had more to do with people's self-positioning in a racial hierarchy that placed "Hispanic whiteness" on top.

San Antón residents, for example, expressed disdain for Spaniards in various ways in formal and informal conversations, regardless of their political affiliation. Carlos Vélez Franceschi, the folklorist and leader of the well-known local musical group Los Guallacanes de San Antón, once said: *"De los españoles hay gente que dicen que son la Madre Patria, pero España no fue una madre sino una madrastra"* (There are some who say that Spain is our motherland, but Spain was not a mother but a stepmother). On a similar note, Marta, a large black woman in her forties, once told me, *"Los americanos fueron los que nos liberaron de los españoles porque esos dicen que eran unos hijos de la gran puta. Y por eso es que aquí hay tanta mezcla, porque los españoles fueron los que trajeron a los africanos"* (The Americans were the ones who liberated us from the Spaniards, because people say those [Spaniards] were sons of bitches. And that is why there is so much mixture here because the Spaniards were the ones who brought the Africans).

Other pejorative comments about Spaniards came up in discussions of the U.S. occupation of Puerto Rico, such as in this statement from Anelo:

> When the Spaniards were here, my dad was real young, that was before 1900. My dad used to tell me that when the Spaniards were in charge; they had some sort of anarchy, because their laws were very strict... The day the Americans came she [my mother] was out in the fields gathering grass for the animals, and she says that when the first cannon was fired, that was the signal that the Americans had arrived. She says that when they announced that there was going to be an invasion, a lot of women started screaming and having *ataques* [becoming hysterical] because they believed that it was an invasion with war and everything. My dad used to like to see those things, my mom used to say that he was *averigua'o* [nosy]... My dad got dressed immediately and he went to the docks where the Americans were. And the Spaniards, my girl, started to run after making such a show and acting so brave! Mom used to say that when they were running away, some of them would go up to the *vigía* [lookout post], and they stopped at the houses asking for water, they would drink the water, and didn't hand back the cups, they just threw them down and went

on running. The Americans built something like *pertrechos* [camps] and put up tents, my dad worked there. Those who worked there cooked, and my mom says that dad used to sneak out and bring home all sorts of things. He would bring chocolate; he brought all sorts of things. They stayed there till the Americans had settled in other places, then the Spaniards had to leave. They say that when the Americans arrived they said, "*Puerto Rico mucho bueno,*" yes, because they found a lot of riches, my dad used to say that, not because somebody told him, but because he lived it.

Anelo's vivid report represents Spaniards as cowards, irresponsible imperialists who quickly fled once the U.S. military landed in Puerto Rico in 1898. Her interpretation sharply contrasts with Hispanophile renditions that link Spain with honor, dignity, and benevolent Catholic mores. From Anelo's account, we also learn that, far from expressing any loyalty to the "old motherland," her father quickly began to work for the U.S. army after its arrival in Ponce, finding in that alliance a new means to help his family.

In another instance, Doña Laura (born 1925) recalls a story her father used to tell her:

They say that the Spaniards were real mean [*in a low voice*], real mean. They used to talk about it, the things they did. And when they left, they left a store with hats with nails and corsets with nails too, so that when the women put them on they'd die. Yeah . . . everybody used to say that. And the store was, they called it the *Pisá* store, it belonged to Spaniards. Hmmm . . . Yeah . . . and little hats with those things so that when they put them on babies they would sink in . . . they were really . . . you know. The *Pisá* store doesn't exist anymore, but it belonged to Spaniards, that's where they had those things.

These stories do not portray Spaniards as a civilizing source of national identity but rather as a barbaric people engaged in gruesome practices. I found comments against Spaniards particularly harsh when people talked about them in the context of the arrival of North Americans.

However, opinions about Spaniards were less negative in narratives of older residents who were more specifically grounded in San Antón and who personalized stories through telling about their own families. For example, when I interviewed Don Carlos, a community elder, he described the relationships between white Spaniards' *hacendados* and their workers as one of respect and of reciprocity. According to him, the rich people of the haciendas helped the aged poor and saw to it that they had a proper burial. "Before, all those rich people, well, helped." Throughout our interview, Don Carlos talked about the lives of these *hacendados*, their family quarrels, the houses they lived in, their family names, and their associates. He talked about them with great respect, dedicating much of the interview to this subject without much prompting on my part. At one point, his son Roberto interrupted to encourage him to talk about the people of San Antón. "It's to tell him," he explained, "because otherwise he's going to keep on talking only about those people." Roberto then addressed his father:

> Listen, Dad, what she wants . . . well, what you talked about, that's all right, [but] what she wants is for you to talk about the history of San Antón. You know, about the people from here, about the folks who started it, like in the times of Don Pablo Roque, Doña Petra Manomé, you know. She wants to know about the barrio; you've already talked about the owners of the Central and the hacienda and all of that. She wants to know about here, about San Antón, how it started, the sugarcane patches, where they were and that stuff.

When I turned off the tape recorder, Roberto repeated his request to his father in a more racially explicit manner. He reminded him once again to talk about "*los prietos de acá. Esos Sauri y eso eran los blancos*" (The blacks from here, those Saurí [owners of the hacienda] and those people, they were the white ones). As I put the tape recorder away, Roberto explained to me, "Now in San Antón you see white people, but before, all the people who lived in the barrio were like this, this color [touching his dark-skinned arm], there weren't any whites here." From the point of view of Roberto, white *hacendados* were not part of San Antón. From the point of view of his eighty-seven-year-old father, the history of San Antón was also the history of those who owned the haciendas. Issues of community membership are therefore perceived differently according to how criteria of race and class are read by people of different generations.

Similar generational differences became evident when I asked Mía, the mother of Doña Judith (age ninety-four), if people complained about racism when she was a young woman. She said: "*No, todo el mundo se llevaba bien, todo el mundo . . . Los negritos con los blanquitos . . . todo el mundo compartía lo más bien, no había nunca . . .*" (No, everybody got along fine, everybody . . . the blacks with the whites, everybody used to share, there was never any . . .). Before Mía could finish her sentence, Doña Judith turned toward me and said:

> Isar, Isar, they had to get along fine, because there was way too much hunger and, in order to survive, people had to help each other, see? You would eat lunch here, eat dinner in another house, they would come in the morning because they didn't have any coffee or anything, you know, through need, people had to be united, because there wasn't anything . . . And if that other one worked with a family [meaning rich families], she would come at night carrying baskets of food and things from the white people's house . . . because things were really hard.

Doña Judith's intervention was meant to place her mother's rendering of harmonious race relations within the context of economic hardship. Like Roberto, who prompted his father to change the actors of his narrative, she intervened in order to give a more specific rendering that would speak to the effects of racial and class hierarchies in the community. Both of these interventions reflect important generational differences concerning how racial issues are perceived or at least voiced by San Antón community members. Both also challenge ideas that have traditionally supported "white" or Hispanic privilege: the ethnocentric view of San Antón's history in one case and the notion of racial democracy in the other.

Beyond San Antón: Hispanic Whiteness as Racist Whiteness

Critiques of racism and privilege associated with a Spanish heritage extend beyond San Antón and impinge on family and community narratives across the Island. As the following two interviews illustrate—one from the capital of San Juan, the other from the rural town of San Sebastián—people elsewhere also reference Spanish heritage as indicative of a racist kind of whiteness. Nanette, for example, a graduate student from San Juan who openly describes herself as black, offered the following story about her grandmother and grand-aunts:

> My grandmother married a white man. My grandmother is of descent... I mean, her mother was Spanish. And she married a white man because her father and mother told her that it had to be like that, and they chose her husband and the whole thing. That man died and my grandmother married a black man, she has this *chorrete de hijos* [whole lot of children], they are nine. All came out black, basically, that is because there may be three with white skin but they are *jabaos, jabaos, jabaos* [high yellow]. And so, thank God that my great-grandmother died, because she would have died of shock [*jokingly*]: of the bad impression.

Out of this union came Nanette's mother, who, according to Nanette, had the fairest complexion of all her siblings. This made her the preferred niece among her aunts. This fair-skinned niece, however, also married a black man, much to the dismay of Nanette's great-aunts. Mocking their Spanish accent, Nanette described them as her *tíazz abuelas ezzzpañolas* (Spanish great-auntsssss). She recalls meeting them for the first time when she was about twelve years old, when her *Titi* Iris—an aunt from her father's side—took her for a visit. She explained:

> Now, of course, as I was saying about my famous *tías abuelas ezzzpañolas* [Spanish great-aunts; she says this imitating a Castillian accent], I am the eldest daughter of their niece, Angelina. And so, "We've got to meet the girl" [she is imitating her great aunts in a high-pitched tone of voice] and they would say, "*¡Por favor, tráiganme a la nena que yo quiero ver a la nena de Piruzzza!*" [Please bring me the girl, I want to see Pirutha's daughter!" she says, imitating the Castillian accent again, mockingly stressing the Spanish "z" so it sounds like Pirutha.] So my aunts take me... It was the first time I saw them... I'm almost sure it was when I was twelve years old.

Nanette described this first encounter with her "white" great aunt as hypocritically cordial:

> At least when we came in [the house], I remember her [doing] [*imitating a gesture of kissing*]: "Oh, Iris, how are you," and *muá, muá* [*sound of kisses*], those false kisses, on the cheek, *blah, blah, blah*. And when she saw me . . . well, it was a thing, ah, something very strange, well, it was like: "Oh my God, it's Piruza's daughter, my beloved niece's daughter! . . . but she's black [*in a low tone*]. [*Nanette laughs.*] Oh how horrible!" . . .
>
> And so that visit was very particular, because at all times she avoided touching me. If anything, she only touched my clothes . . . Then Aunt Iris played with my hair, and the lady then, if she touched me, it was on my clothes. And that kind of detail, I've always been very observant in that aspect. But it's that she didn't touch me, period. I've always . . . since I was brought up with a lot of love, I've always been very *tocona*, [a person who likes to show affection through touch] see? So then in a moment when she's going to bring me something else, I tell her, "Listen, no, please, I don't want any, thank you." And I grab her and I say, "Thank you, but it's that I'm really full!" [*stressing the phrase*]. And she . . . what she kept looking at were . . . the hands on her arm, *my* hands on her arm. And she didn't do anything to take them off, or anything of that sort, and that's when I felt like, "This woman, what did she want to see me for?! Because what I'm feeling is a wall between her and me! What I'm feeling is *un frío demasiado espectacular*" [an extreme spectacular chill]! When we left that place I said, "Aunt Iris, what did that lady want to see me for?" She says to me, "Listen, Nanette, to see you, to see how you came out, that's all she wanted; to see if you, if you had come out black, or if you had come out white. If you had come out like Piruza or if you had come out like your dad." That was the main reason why she wanted to see me.

Nanette's account points to the subtleties and kinesthetic dynamics of physical proximity, touch, and looks that inform how racism operates in interpersonal and family encounters. In her interview, she mockingly stressed her aunt's Spanish ancestry to further emphasize and position her aunt's racial suspicions, anxieties, and hypocritical racist attitude toward her own (Nanette's) black body.

Elisa is a light-skinned, middle-aged, poor woman from the interior of the Island who differs from Nanette in age, educational background, and upbringing, yet her narrative grants similar connotations to her family's Spanish ascendency in her personal experiences with racism. Elisa was born and raised in the rural town of San Sebastián. I met her during the town's La Novilla festival while she organized a *comparsa* (costumed group) of children painted in blackface.[10] As soon as I told her my research addressed racism, she commented:

> Oh my child, that's everywhere, plus, with my boys . . . [then in a low voice] right here, right here [*pointing to the neighbors*] I've had a lot of problems with my boys,

in this same neighborhood. Since [*in a very low voice*] they are the only black kids around here. That man's daughter even took me to court, because my boy played with her daughter—a really pretty little blond girl. Then they . . . their daughter . . . got to hating me 'cause my boy played with her daughter.

Elisa's story of family discrimination is intimately linked to her experience of living in a town located in the mountains, where blackness is understood as foreign. Her description of her sons as the "only black kids around here" has a regional significance, because the town of San Sebastián—is considered to be a place predominantly populated by "white" folk. In this context, Elisa and her family faced discrimination from her neighbors, and also from her family.

> **ELISA:** . . . since my family is . . . you know, they are *de tez blanca* [fair-skinned] and the only one that married a black man was me, and they kind of reject me. At the beginning of my marriage they rejected me, a lot.
> **ISAR:** Your mother and . . . ?
> **ELISA:** My mother, my brothers, my family. So the discrimination was huge.
> **ISAR:** And they said it was because of that, just like that?
> **ELISA:** They said it was because I was the only one of my house that . . . I had married black man.
> **ISAR:** Like that, they said it like that?
> **ELISA:** They told me upfront. I felt bad, I didn't visit my house. Because of that I had many problems. But God brought me to this level, so . . .
> **ISAR:** Have they changed, or are they still the same?
> **ELISA:** Yes, after some time he [meaning her husband] won them over. And I used to say, "So mom—you know . . ." My mom is of race . . . what is it called . . . ? I mean . . . Spanish. You know, my family is Spanish, because my ancestors were Spanish. My grandmother was Spanish, my grandfather was Spanish. You understand? On my mom's side and all my mom's family is of *alcurnia* [lineage] . . . And so therefore that's why I never . . . And I have a niece who is still racist. And I always, as a prank, always for the Three Kings' Day celebration, I buy her daughter a *negrita* [*she laughs*], a black doll. And I taught them . . . And well now they are crazy about my children, because my children have turned out to be very good, still to this day.

Elisa later explained that both families opposed her marriage, "my family because he was black and his family because I was white." To counteract their racism, Elisa employed shocking strategies, such as marrying her husband in secret—but also playful ones, such as buying black dolls for the daughter of her racist niece.

Elisa and Nanette come from different class and racial backgrounds, yet both of their narratives challenge Hispanophilia in at least three important aspects. First, Spain figures as a negative referent in their stories, as both of them connected racist attitudes to their family's Spanish ascendancy. The phrase *raza española* (Spanish race) in Elisa's narrative, for example, described her family's whiteness but also revealed their racism. In Nanette's story about her *tiazz ezzpañolazzz*, Spain also figures as the referent of a particular kind of "whiteness" that is exclusive, hypocritical, and fearful of blackness. Second, their narratives introduce all sorts of people who challenge Hispanophile yearnings for *blanqueamiento*. In one case, it's a grandmother and mother who defy their family's orientation toward whiteness. In the second interview, Elisa indicates that her husband's family opposed his marriage with a white woman. Thus one learns that there are black people in Puerto Rico who do not adopt *blanqueamiento* as a social value. Furthermore, far from benevolent, the Spanish ascendency of family members is presented in their stories as triggering anxiety over degrading their family's pedigree with black husbands, grandchildren, nephews, or grandsons.

These stories make clear that, even when Hispanophile ideas of the Puerto Rican "nation" continue to circulate, the basic exclusive premises of this ideology do not go unchallenged. Regardless of how these two women define *lo puertorriqueño*, their personal trajectory and strategies locate them in a Puerto Rico that is anything but harmonious in attitudes toward ideas of *blanqueaminto* or Hispanic ancestry.

Spain from the Perspective of the New Colonizers: American Hispanophobia

Thus far I have outlined similarities between people who considered Spanish ancestry an indicator of racist attitudes in the 1990s and the anti-Hispanic sentiment of black and *mulato* working-class people who hoped to benefit from the democratic institutions of the United States at the turn of the century. Yet the Hispanophobia of the black and *mulatto* working class was not the only brand in circulation during the early decades of the twentieth century. The United States also adopted a colonizing discourse that pointed to the evils of Spanish influence and the inferiority of Spanish blood in order to justify their colonial intervention in Puerto Rico and the Hispanic Caribbean.

Colonial authorities who upheld this colonizing discourse vehemently argued that the incompetence of Puerto Ricans to rule themselves was primarily caused by the cultural and biological influence of Spain. That negative political legacy, according to the newly arrived representatives of the United States, made it necessary for the Island to undergo a period of tutelage and adaptation to U.S. rule that would enable them to become modern. In this context, Spain stood for backwardness, underdevelopment, and all that had to be uprooted from the Puerto Rican psyche in order to bring progress to the new territory. The following excerpt, written by a colonial official nine years after the U.S. military takeover of the Island, exemplifies the position well:

The Porto Ricans being chiefly of Spanish descent or having been closely associated with Spaniards, have many of the general characteristics of the Latin race. They are impulsive, excitable, talkative, demonstrative . . . The Porto Ricans are extremely fond of the spectacular . . . As a people, they are pleasure loving, light-hearted, without care, and without any adequate idea of responsibility. [T]hey have not yet learned the dignity of labor. Their ideas, probably derived from the Spaniards, led them to disdain the appearance of work. (Fowles 1906, 46, 47, 51, 52)

Forty years later, U.S.-appointed governor R. G. Tugwell also warned his fellow citizens about the backward implications of the Hispanic influence on Puerto Ricans. Tugwell describes the notion of *dignidad* (dignity), for instance, as a sense of pride verging on obsession and which leads frequently to the substitution of fancy for fact, preventing public acknowledgment of inferiority and leading toward mediocrity. This trait, according to Tugwell (1972), can also be attributed to the hot, overmastering Spanish blood that still runs in the veins of Puerto Rican people (311).

This view of Spanish influence prevailed not only in literary and political venues, but also in artistic forms produced in the early decades of the twentieth century. Cartoons that appeared in magazines and daily newspapers, for example, depicted Spain as a backward and comical country, as shown in Figure 16.

Figure 16. 1898 U.S. Caricature of Spain. Source: *La Gráfica Política del 98* (Junta de Extremadura Consejería de Cultura y Patrimonio,1998: 81).Originally published in *El Diablo*. Venezuela,1898.

Lanny Thompson's (2007) excellent analysis of the photographs and texts of the widely circulated multivolume book *Our Islands and Their People* (1904), published at the turn of the century to describe the newly acquired U.S. possessions, also demonstrates the U.S. disdain for Spain and its influence on the newly acquired territories (Puerto Rico and the Philippines). Photographs included in the book portray images of poverty, decay, and "barbaric customs" to demonstrate the detrimental effects of Spanish colonialism on the Puerto Rican people. Others characterize Spaniards as "white," wealthy, and domineering landowners who exploited the Puerto Rican people.

Thompson explains that, while Spaniards are depicted as greedy landowners, Puerto Ricans are presented in the text of *Our Islands and Their People* as members of the subaltern classes who—despite the negative influence of Spaniards—had great potential for being Americanized. Photographs used in the book helped to mold that strict dichotomy between an exploitative white Spanish class and the Puerto Rican people, by making invisible the *criollo* bourgeoisie (men in particular). When and if recognized, the U.S. represented the dominant class with pictures of Spanish women. They appeared elegant and refined but unfit to govern themselves, suggesting the need for the masculine presence of Anglo-Saxon U.S. functionaries (Thompson 2007, 57). In this way, photographs and text symbolically eradicate the presence of a male Puerto Rican governing class of Spanish ascendency, avoiding any discussion about the political and economic displacement of this "native" sector as a consequence of U.S. colonization.

Racial Innocence: The Cousin of Racial Democracy

Equally convenient to the colonizing mission was the U.S. representation of Puerto Ricans as naive people who paid no attention to racial differences. In *Our Islands and Their People*, photographs depicting a very mixed population are followed by a text that states: "In Porto Rico . . . there are no social distinctions on account of color. The people do not know what the color line means. . . . These conditions within themselves show the absence of all prejudice on account of color. But the African race is declining, and will eventually either disappear or be amalgamated with the white race. Whether this will produce a higher or a lower type of humanity is a question for the sociologists to settle" (José de Olivares, quoted in Thompson 2007, 69).

Such representations of Puerto Ricans as innocent and unaware of racial differences supported the U.S. colonizing discourse. Lack of knowledge about racial distinction was understood as a sign of naivité, which from the point of view of American colonizers further evidenced the native's lack of understanding of social hierarchies, governance, and power. The claim that Puerto Ricans did not recognize internal differences among themselves also made U.S. colonial intervention appear undisruptive of a previous order, exempting the United States from the accusation that they were displacing a privileged sector.

At the same time, stressing the natives' so-called unawareness of racial differences favors predictions about the gradual whitening of the population via race mixture. Despite prevalent ideas in the United States that defined mixture as degeneration, propensity to mixture was sometimes also understood (and negotiated) as a positive characteristic of the colonized. It suggested that the population was culturally homogenous and prone to whitening, thereby increasing the possibility of cultural and economic assimilation of Puerto Ricans to U.S. interests and institutions. Colonial discourses about the mixed race of the colonized thus served two purposes. On the one hand, they explained why the natives (lacking the vitality of a purer Anglo-Saxon race) were unfit for self-government in their present state (Kennedy 1971). On the other hand, an emphasis on race mixture also served to portray Puerto Rico as a promising land whose population could eventually whiten, learn, and turn the colonizing mission into a successful one.

Ginetta Candelario has documented the use of similar discursive tactics in the Dominican Republic in the nineteenth and early twentieth centuries (2007). Responding to the threat that neighboring Haiti posed as the first black republic in the Americas, U.S. officials, capitalist entrepreneurs, and travel writers represented Haiti as dangerous, black, and African. Meanwhile, they narrated the Dominican Republic as safe, Hispanic mixed, and (almost) white relative to Haiti. In this context, U.S. expansionist interests in the Dominican Republic were gauged based on (among other complex interests) assessments of the racial composition of the population and particularly on the country's potential to minimize, dilute, or displace its blackness (Candelario 2007, 45). As some historians argued, "the more ardently expansionist the reporter, the lighter the racial portrayal of the Dominican people" (Martínez-Fernández quoted in Candelario 2007, 49).

This emphasis on whitening was not a discourse deployed equally in all U.S. territories across the Caribbean. As Thompson (2010) points out, island territories that came under U.S. military and political dominion after 1898 (Cuba, Guam, Hawaii, the Philippines, and Puerto Rico) were represented in quite different terms in colonial documents and photographic records. While the Philippines were predominantly represented as the least civilized territory, with racially different "exotic" tribes, Hawaii was represented as the most civilized and advanced. Cuba and Puerto Rico fell somewhere in between this civilization ranking, but Puerto Rico was depicted as more mixed and less prone to "Africanization" than Cuba, given the latter's considerable black population and black religious organizations (Thompson 2010, 91–94). Puerto Ricans were also generally regarded as "more settled" and less conscious of the color line than Cubans (Kennedy 1971, 307–8). Cartoons of the time represented Puerto Rico as a lighter, less

Figure 17. 1898 U.S. Caricature of Puerto Rico and Cuba. Source: *La Gráfica Política del 98* (Junta de Extremadura Consejería de Cultura y Patrimonio, 1998: 81. Originally published in *Chicago Inter Ocean*, 1905).

problematic "child" than Cuba, who had gained political independence under the leadership of important black generals such as Antonio Maceo, as Figure 17 illustrates. In Cuba, the Partido Independiente de Color (Independent Colored Party) had also waged a war in 1912 against the marginalization of blacks and segregationist policies imposed with U.S. support after independence. In that context, the United States portrayed Cuba as a black-faced and ill-mannered child in need of a stern fatherly figure (i.e., the United States) who would guide Cubans into political adulthood (Pérez 2008).

In contrast to Cuba, personified as a child needing only tutelage, the United States planned on cultural assimilation for Puerto Rico, anticipating they would Americanize the population by means of public education, including instruction in English (Thompson 2010, 158). The prospect of whitening was an important aspect of this agenda. Representations that stressed race mixture and the whitening of the population were also prevalent in colonial accounts of Cuba, but in Puerto Rico they took particular salience as the United States justified the future promise of its investment and Americanization campaign. As Thompson (2010) points out: "The whiteness of the population and its possible further whitening was a metaphor for the potential cultural and economic improvements that the United States would oversee. In general, Puerto Ricans were described as a mixed race—white, mulatto, black—of peasant and working-class origin. Furthermore, the term *mixed race* implied that there were no clearly defined racial or ethnic groups" (105).

U.S. colonizing discourses also established a subtle but important distinction between being "Spanish" and being "white." U.S. officials represented Latin (and African) ancestry as backward influences but heralded the phenotypically white characteristics of certain sectors of the Island population as positive indicators for the promise of the U.S. civilizing mission and the effectiveness of U.S. rule.

The best-documented instances of this paradox are the numerous pictures of white well-educated men and women urbanites published in the U.S. Census reports of 1898 for Cuba and Puerto Rico. The photographs, published alongside tables and figures, showed local census enumerators and supervisors employed by the U.S. War Department under the supervision of the Secretary of War. Virginia Domínguez (2007) and Thompson (2010, 58–60) have written about these photographs of white elites as instances in which the colonial logic of "otherizing" was suspended in favor of a type of representation that sought to establish similarities between the colonizer and the colonized (Domínguez 2007; Thompson 2010, 58). Gervacio García has also argued that the elites who allied themselves with U.S. authorities shared core values with colonial officials and were not "others" in this regard (García 2000). Furthermore, I would argue that the racial representation of light-skinned local men and women who worked as census supervisors and enumerators served to grant legitimacy to the census and validate its accuracy. Thus, rather than being an apparent contradiction of colonial practice, visual and textual publications of white Puerto Ricans granted credibility, reliability, and respectability to the bureaucratic endeavors of the colonial enterprise. In this context, the men and women photographed were not posing as Puerto Rican *criollo* elites of Spanish lineage but as white local allies of the U.S. colonizing mission.

Commenting on the circulation of colonial narratives that also upheld whiteness and granted an almost-white status to the population in the Dominican Republic, Candelario argues that such representations were not an imposition on a local racial imaginary. In the Dominican Republic, such U.S. narratives supported and echoed the anti-Haitianism of emerging *criollo* elites. In this sense, colonial and travel narratives of the United States worked in tandem and alongside an elite national project of casting the Dominican Republic as an Indo-Hispanic (not black) nation. Similarly, one could argue that in Puerto Rico, U.S. colonial officials, their allies, and even *criollo* national leaders who opposed U.S. colonial intervention all upheld discourses of whitening. Hence, regardless of the opinion granted to Spain's legacy, the promise of whitening (whether it be through the emergence of Hispanic or Anglo influences) remained a positive aspiration in both colonial and anticolonial narratives. Similarly, the idea that Puerto Ricans did not recognize or grant importance to "race," as disseminated in travelogues, colonial documents, and elite publications, was part and parcel of colonial and anticolonial views about the possibilities of whitening the Island population and the feasibility of its governance (be it under colonialism, statehood, autonomist, or politically independent regimes).

However, from the point of view of the Puerto Rican *criollo* bourgeoisie, establishing racial distinctions (and distance from the racialized poor and black masses they sought to lead) was just as important as it was to U.S. colonizers. This was irrespective of whether these elite sought statehood or more autonomy from the United States. Claims to whiteness gave local elites social and political leverage, not necessarily vis-à-vis the United States, but internally at the local level of social hierarchies. However, for those *criollos* who became subordinated allies of the United States, and whose political and economic decisions depended on a U.S. monopoly over commercial affairs, Spain was a problematic symbol that had to be reconciled with the modern customs, traditions, and values (efficiency, comfort, and speed) that symbolized U.S. hegemony in a new era. In this process, questions about traditions and the search for cultural roots came to the fore, informing not only practices of self-representation in writing, but also styles, fashions, and designs.

Negotiating Modernity and Hispanic Whiteness through Architecture

One of the ways in which the *criollo* bourgeoisie who benefitted from the U.S. occupation reconciled their claims to Hispanic whiteness with their desire to form part of modern U.S. trends was through the architectural design of their houses. Mansions, castles, and cultural institutions built during the first decades of the twentieth century reconciled tradition with modernity, materializing the aspirations and desires of the newly rich *criollo* elite in the context of "modern" times. Defiance of the neoclassical style, for example, was part of a process through which the *criollo* elite claimed greater autonomy from Spain and expressed their desire to be linked to modern tastes and fashions associated with the United States (Vivoni-Farage and Álvarez-Curbelo 1998, 21). Ironically, this defiance of "old country values" found inspiration in a particular style known as "Spanish revival."

"Spanish revival" became particularly popular during the 1930s. Impressive residences built during this decade responded to the search for cultural identity among wealthy Puerto Rican sugar lords and business magnates. Not only did these residences communicate social and financial prosperity, but they became a way to reinterpret their owners' link to a Hispanic past in the face of modern times. In this quest for identity, Hispanophile houses and buildings thus made a double assertion. On the one hand, they served as the symbol of a lineage that reflected a dignified Spanish heritage. On the other hand, they affirmed that the owners were attuned to the styles preferred by the powerful and famous in other modern latitudes (Vivoni-Farage and Álvarez-Curbelo 1998, 48).

One of these latitudes was Hollywood. Ever since the 1920s, Spain—former enemy of the United States—had captured the imagination of movie producers. By the 1930s, Hispanophile mansions had become very popular in films and in U.S. architecture magazines. Furthermore, Spanish style evoked a legendary exotic existence that went well with the United States' conquest and civilizing campaign of the time. That campaign began during the first years of the twentieth century in Puerto Rico, with a vast construction plan that employed the "California Mission" style. Government architects considered this eclectic Mediterranean style that combined Moorish and Renaissance elements "appropriate" for "frontier" sites such as Florida and southern California. For them this so-called Spanish architecture also suited the idiosyncrasy and "new frontier" of Puerto Rico, serving as a bridge between the values of yesterday and those of tomorrow (Vivoni-Farage and Álvarez-Curbelo 1998, 24).

A classic example of this type of architecture in Ponce is the Castillo Serrallés (see Figure 18). Built in the 1930s, the castle was the Serrallés family's home during the boom of the sugar and rum industry. The building is located at the foothill of the central mountain range, on the south side of El Vigía Hill, overlooking the city of Ponce and its Caribbean sea coast. Even though it stands at a considerable distance from the official Historic Zone, it is one of Ponce's main tourist attractions. The residence, now turned into a museum, features temporary exhibits and a permanent exhibit about the sugar and rum industries. The museum offers local and U.S. visitors a tour through various rooms, bedrooms, vestibules, and terraces of the house, where elegant furniture, decorative china, lamps, and works of art are displayed. In the tour I took, the guide emphasized the architectural features of the mansion and talked about the European origins of certain pieces of furniture and their cost. Making a joke that also reconciled Puerto Rico's insertion into the modern "American" economy, she said, "*Todo es original de la época excepto el papel de baño que es Charmin*" (Everything is original from the epoch, except the toilet paper, which is Charmin). Pointing to various portraits of the Serrallés family, the tour guide noted that the first Serrallés generation was of Spanish descent and that their grandchildren traveled periodically to Spain and to Miami. As we moved away from the formal dining room, she showed the group a family photograph and mentioned the names of the descendants of two former first ladies of Puerto Rico.

Figure 18. The Serrallés Castle, Ponce. Photo by author.

Needless to say, none of these images showed black or *mulato* faces. In fact, spaces such as the kitchen, where black and *mulato* servants labored, received little or no attention at all during the tour. I was informed that the servant living quarters had been transformed into offices and into a museum store. Probably not considered worthy of preservation, these rooms were put to more contemporary uses by museum administrators, thereby producing a historical narrative that effaced the cohabitation practices of the Serrallés family and black working-class service personnel in the household. In a tour I took later in 2007, I was particularly startled to see a tall, pale white mannequin dressed in a black dress, white apron, and heels next to the dining room table.

Just as San Antón's housing project did not contemplate the white peasant cane cutters who lived in the area as part of the origin story of this community (see Chapter 4), the Serrallés Castle Museum did not incorporate black workers and servants or their living quarters in their showcase of this privileged household. Such racially segregated representations of history run counter to a society that prides itself on mixture and harmonious race relations. Yet they make sense in the context of practices of representation that reproduce racial hierarchies and Eurocentricity in the telling of history while showcasing race mixture as an emblematic aspect of the Puerto Rican nation.

In this chapter and the previous one, I explored how people at the turn of the twentieth century and during the time of my fieldwork deployed Hispanophilia or Hispanophobia to challenge or bolster those racial hierarchies vis-à-vis the colonial specter of contending colonial powers (the United States or Spain). Different interpretations of whiteness (as Hispanic, Anglo, or European) prevailed in the class- and race-informed Hispanophilias and Hispanophobias that nurtured people's personal and collective pursuits of respectability, autonomy, sophistication, honor, social justice, progress, or modernity. In these competing and apparently self-contradictory narratives, Hispanic heritage could be interpreted as sophisticated, backward, cultured, racist, or barbaric. But despite these differences, to the extent that white privilege and the restraint of the black working class are inextricably entangled with the pursuit of political hegemony, colonialist, anticolonialist, and liberal reformists alike coincided in evoking myths of racial harmony and the prospect of whitening when it came to justify their fate to lead and the feasibility of their politics. Notions of whiteness and honor embedded in the discourses that guided such political pursuits, albeit shifting and disputed, helped co-construct blackness as primitive, dishonorable, backward, and fading. In the chapters that follow, I explore how such formulations became incorporated but also refashioned in later discourses and "scripts" that exalted the virtues of race mixture and its African component.

PART III

Race Mixture

In the Blood or in the Making?

CHAPTER 6

Flowing through My Veins

Populism and the Hierarchies of Race Mixture

Dominant discourses articulated during the housing controversy couched the barrio's Afro–Puerto Rican legacy as representing a race that had blended with two others. As Ponce's mayor declared during the inauguration of the housing project:

> Ponce tiene unos símbolos que significan mucho para Ponce, pero no solo para Ponce, para Puerto Rico, inclusive para el mundo. Porque en esta tierra donde yo estoy parado hoy, aquí los africanos aportaron lo que tenían a nuestra raza. Y nuestra raza no es otra cosa que la mezcla del africano, el español y el indio Taíno y de ahí sale la raza puertorriqueña... Nosotros teníamos que de alguna manera reciprocar lo que San Antón ha significado para la historia de nuestro país y de nuestra ciudad.[1]
>
> [Ponce has some symbols that mean a lot to Ponce, but not only to Ponce, to Puerto Rico, even to the world. Because on this ground where I am standing today, here the Africans contributed what they had to our race. And our race is nothing else than the mixture of the African, the Spaniard, and the Taíno Indian and from that comes the Puerto Rican race... We had to reciprocate in some way what San Antón has meant to the history of our country and of our city.]

Such celebratory references to African heritage and race mixture were not common in the 1930s. The biological definition of Puerto Ricans as a mixture of three races—the Taíno, the Spanish, and the African—had been circulating since the nineteenth century in both *criollo* and U.S. writings about Puerto Rico, but before the 1950s, this was not institutionally constructed as an object of national pride.

In fact, as presented in Chapter 4, blackness was something relegated to the realm of biology and treated as an influence that could be "ameliorated" through the whitening power of culture. Intellectuals of the 1930s acknowledged that Puerto Ricans were a mixed-race people, but this notion of mixture was not celebrated as a foundational principle of *cultural* distinctiveness.

It was after the 1950s that the ideology of race mixture was taken up as a populist State discourse and implemented through the Institute of Puerto Rican Culture. Race mixture became, in fact, a central part of the state's cultural program of development and modernization for Puerto Rico. How did this shift come about? What events marked the valorization of this racial syncretism and of the attributes assigned to the black element of the mixture?

The Politics of Inclusion: Populism and Its Racial Dynamics

In the 1950s and 1960s, Puerto Rico underwent a process of rapid industrialization set in motion by U.S. policies, institutions, and private investments that marked the end of an agriculture-based economy. The economic structure was transformed, infrastructure boomed, social programs pumped cash into family budgets, thousands of Puerto Rican men became U.S. veterans, and tourists began to arrive. In addition, large numbers of Puerto Rican families were lured to the United States by federal programs to fill particular employment niches, creating the present situation that finds almost five million Puerto Ricans living in the States (U.S. Census Bureau 2011; CB Staff 2013). As part of this process, Puerto Rico was transformed into a heavily assisted, welfare-based economy. These shifts also brought about an expansion of the urban middle class and the incorporation of the working class into a new trend of mass consumption of U.S. goods (Álvarez Curbelo and Rodríguez Castro 1993).

Antecedents to these events are intimately linked to the United States, which had just come out of the Great Depression and World War II. Franklin D. Roosevelt's New Deal set certain liberal standards that benefitted the populist project led by the commonwealth party and gave prominence to its rhetoric of consensus and social equalization (Rodríguez-Castro 1993). That rhetoric declared that the political status of the Island vis-à-vis the United States was not the most important issue, and that what mattered most was improving the socioeconomic situation of Puerto Ricans. As one man said to me in regard to the leader of this endeavor, Luis Muñoz Marín: "*Muñoz sabía que este pueblo es bien nacionalista... pero él decía que con la barriga vacía no se puede hacer mucho*" (Muñoz knew that this country is very nationalist... but he used to say that you can't do much with an empty belly).

With the slogan "Pan, Tierra y Libertad" (Bread, Land, and Liberty), Luis Muñoz Marín and the newly created Popular Democratic Party (or the commonwealth party) won the elections in 1940 by an overwhelming majority. Their program for social justice included health, education, labor, and land reforms to be implemented through an interventionist state policy. During the 1950s, the commonwealth government encouraged the development of private U.S. industries manufacturing products on the Island for export, discouraging large-scale agricultural production. Large investments of U.S. capital benefitted from a series of tax exemptions and government-subsidized programs, not to mention lower salaries paid to Puerto Ricans on the Island. Massive numbers of Puerto Ricans who had been agricultural workers on the Island were displaced to work in factories in the United States. This series of measures came to be known as Operation Bootstrap.

In accordance with these developments, the commonwealth party promoted a new democratic image of Puerto Rico shaped by a series of laws and stipulations redefining the Island's relationship with the United States under the rubric of Estado Libre Asociado (Free Associated State). The times coincided with a United Nations decolonization campaign that committed nations with colonies to pave the way for autonomous governments in their territories. Pressured by the United Nations on the one hand and the Puerto Rican people on the other, the U.S. Congress allowed Puerto Ricans to draft their own constitution and elect their own government officials. With the constitution in effect by 1952, more autonomy was granted to the Island on local affairs, although the U.S. Congress reserved the right to determine which federal laws would apply to Puerto Rico (Picó 1988; Rivera-Ramos 2001).

Racial Democracy for Development

Both the United States and Puerto Rico's commonwealth government employed a significant number of social scientists to evaluate the development programs implemented (Duany 1987; Lauria-Pericelli 1989). As a result, during the 1940s and 1950s, Puerto Rico became one of the most intensively studied societies in the world (Duany 2010; Briggs 2002; Lauria-Pericelli 1989; Ramírez 1978). As U.S. academics, policy makers, researchers, and journalists flocked to Puerto Rico to assess the rapid process of industrialization, they also recorded varying observations on the question of race. Upon comparing Island racial dynamics to the Jim Crow laws of the United States, many concluded that racial discrimination was not an issue of social significance. In scholarly publications, class, not race, was understood as the key factor that accounted for unequal opportunities in Puerto Rican society (Williams 1944; Garver and Fincher 1945, 21; Tumin and Feldman 1961). The argument also served to uphold the commonwealth development program for the Island. As sociologists Tumin and Feldman (1961) concluded, "Assuming that skin color remains as irrelevant as it was at the time of this study, it can be predicted that Puerto Rico can move toward its desired social goals without concern for the kind of trouble and conflict which the Mainland society has experienced in its attempts to assure equal opportunities and jobs. . . . the absence of color bars and disabilities on the Island must certainly be counted as a positive asset" (246).

Anthropology remained somewhat marginal and sometimes critical to the literature that wholeheartedly endorsed the commonwealth government's development agenda (Lauria-Pericelli 1989; Duany 2005; Ramírez 1978). Nevertheless, U.S. ethnographies overwhelmingly described racism as an interpersonal or surface phenomenon. For example, Morris Siegel (1953), who did the first extensive ethnographic study in Puerto Rico in the town of Lajas, concluded that "Puerto Rico is an outstanding example—perhaps the outstanding example—of a society in which people of different physical traits have proved their ability to live in harmony, to work side by side without undue friction, to intermarry; in short, to avoid to the greatest extent the poison of racism so destructive to the societies of other countries" (167). Ironically, Siegel documented numerous instances of racial discrimination but did so under the analytic mantle of "discriminatory attitudes." Similarly, the Columbia Group in charge of the well-known comprehensive anthropological study *The People of Puerto Rico* (1956), in which Sidney Mintz and Eric Wolf participated, addressed racial hierarchies at the level of interpersonal dynamics and attitudes and not as systemic phenomena. As Mintz (1978) pointed out later, the broader ideological level that systematically undermines the African component remained unexplored in this study.

Puerto Rican scholars who focused their research on "race relations" also emphasized the interpersonal or psychological manifestations of racism (Sereno 1947; Rogler 1944).[2] Many attributed the problem of discrimination to the influence of the United States (Rodríguez Cruz 1965, 379; Sereno 1947). Even African American intellectuals, who saw in Island Puerto Ricans a group with similar second-class citizenship, described racism as a surface phenomenon that had been imported by those from the mainland in their imperial endeavors (see Alamo-Pastrana 2012, 215–16).[3]

Sociologist Eduardo Seda Bonilla began to challenge these views in the 1960s by addressing racism as a systemic problem for Puerto Rico (1961, 1968). He strongly critiqued the U.S. assumption that racial thinking did not exist in the Island or in Latin America, arguing that racial stratification was a key aspect of social structure in these societies (Seda-Bonilla 1968). His critique of the "imperialist blind-spot" of U.S. researchers on race, however, overlooked the link between racism and the construction of a national identity. It was not until the 1970s that Isabelo Zenón Cruz conducted a systematic analysis on this topic with his groundbreaking two-volume work *Narciso Descubre Su Trasero* (1975). Zenón's more than seven-hundred-page study analyzed historical documents, poems, literature, jokes, religion, song lyrics, political speeches, everyday language, and expressions of popular culture to document the systematic marginalization of the black subject from dominant constructions of the "Puerto Rican." Before his study (during the 1940s, 1950s, and 1960s), local and U.S. researchers argued that racism in Puerto Rico was more a problem of "prejudice," "race relations," or "racial attitudes" than a problem of structural or institutional significance. And even after Zenón's intervention, this trend continued. Members of the local intelligentsia minimized or failed to acknowledge the link between racism and the construction of a national identity.[4] As a 1976 reviewer of Zenón's book concluded,[5] "In general [in Puerto Rico], there is no conscious expression of discrimination. (Zenón may give examples that contradict this but not enough to make a general rule.) Social relations between black and white people are smooth and natural" (Fernández 1976, 104).

Racial Democracy, Populism, and Luis Muñoz Marín

U.S. researchers who favored the development agenda in Puerto Rico taking place during the 1940s and 1950s saw in the so-called absence of a racial problem the plausibility of success for the U.S. economic enterprise. This was also true for the commonwealth government. Yet racial mixture and the rhetoric of harmonious synthesis was more than an attractive selling point for North American investment. For the commonwealth party, the myth of racial democracy also evidenced and endorsed the preparedness of islanders to assume greater control over the Island's development process.

Luis Muñoz Marín—the first Puerto Rican elected governor and probably the most renowned Puerto Rican political figure of the twentieth century—promulgated this new era of industrialization and "democratic" development based on a color-blind rhetoric of progress. Like other populist figures in Latin America, such as Cárdenas in Mexico, Perón in Argentina, and Vargas in Brazil, Muñoz led the country toward modernization, development, and social democracy by deploying unifying symbols that could effectively mobilize heterogeneous sectors of the population toward political consensus (Álvarez-Curbelo 1993,16). To this end, Muñoz often used the metaphor of *la gran familia puertorriqueña* (the great Puerto Rican family) to describe Puerto Rican society in his speeches and writings. An important quality of this "great Puerto Rican family" was racial harmony and racial mixture. *La gran familia* also appealed to poor and "black" people, since Puerto Rican families can have members of different "racial" types. Darker-complexioned offspring are often valued less, but *la gran familia* did not contemplate inner conflict.

Muñoz's notion of a racially harmonious great family did not operate by itself but was closely linked to a complex culturist discourse that separated the affirmation of "Puerto Rican culture" from the struggle for political sovereignty and "liberty" vis-à-vis the United States (Álvarez-Curbelo 1993). In contrast to *la generación del treinta* (the 1930s generation), the "Puerto Rican culture" of Muñoz's populist project would no longer be about those Eurocentric values and Hispanic referents that differentiated Puerto Ricans from the barbaric "North Americans." Muñoz knew that Spanish referents were an important identity marker for an educated elite but remained a distant referent for the majority of the Puerto Rican *mulato* and black population. Instead, "culture" in Muñoz's populist discourse became the container of past "traditions" (as expressed in music, religion, and folk art) and values (such as hospitality, modesty, and decency) that all Puerto Ricans supposedly shared. Culture also became the product of the three ancestral (or racial) groups described as coequal in the constitution of Puerto Rican culture.

The rescuing of this democratic past was assumed to be an innocent endeavor that would automatically reveal unifying practices and identity referents for all sectors of society, no matter how differently positioned in the social hierarchy (Flores-Collazo 1998). Albeit innocent, this process of national definition was not understood by Muñoz as natural or free-flowing. According to him, if Puerto Ricans did not assume deliberate command over the cultural process, "*se puede malograr la personalidad puertorriqueña en inextricables burundangas sin mucho pie ni cabeza*" (the Puerto Rican personality could deteriorate into an inextricable hogwash without much head or tail)[6] (Muñoz Marín 1985, 99). It is therefore no coincidence that after 1945, the government established a number of public institutions dedicated to historical investigation and the disciplining of cultural knowledge (Gil 1994; Flores-Collazo 1998; Harvey 1988). Cultural legislation was a fundamental part of this agenda. As María Elena Rodríguez (1993) Castro notes: "If the 1940s was characterized by an intense social and economic legislation, the following decades saw a significant increase in cultural legislation. Various reasons justified this interest: the cultural strengthening of the Commonwealth, especially in regard to international representation, support for the tourist industry's development, and the preservation of values and institutions. The first two respond, above all, to imperatives of change, the second to stability: central paradigms of the modernizing project"[7] (102–3).

It was in this context of intensive cultural legislation that the Institute of Puerto Rican Culture was created in 1955. Its mission, as stated in law, was to "preserve, be custodian of and enrich the cultural values of Puerto Rico so that there may be a greater knowledge of the historical and cultural heritage of our people and to have this knowledge accessible to the public through its divulgence" (Law 89 of June 21, 1955, of L.P.R.; quote taken from Harvey 1998, 42). In consonance with that mission, the Institute of Puerto Rican Culture (ICP) promoted the restoration of Spanish military structures, churches, and private buildings in old San Juan and Ponce. It encouraged the preservation and diffusion of folk art, music, plastic arts, literary production, theater, dance, and folklore studies through fairs, contests, and the granting of scholarships. In addition, museums were built, conferences and exhibits organized, local artists promoted, and cultural centers opened throughout the Island, replicating the institute's mission at the local level (see Dávila 1997).

The Institute of Puerto Rican Culture and Its Racial Policy

Once the ICP was created, the board of directors elected as its first executive director the archeologist Don Ricardo Alegría. In an interview, Don Ricardo Alegría described the contributions of the ICP: "The work of the Institute of Puerto Rican Culture is monumental. Up until the '50s the only heritage spoken of was our Spanish heritage; nobody spoke of Native Indian or African heritage. And it is precisely the Institute that breaks away from that and creates the vision of a national integrated culture [mestiza]"[8] (in Nuñez-Miranda 1988, 14).

That new, integrated vision of the foundational racial triad is expressed in the official emblem of the ICP, conceived by Ricardo Alegría and designed by renowned Puerto Rican artist Lorenzo Homar (see Figure 19).[9] The emblem depicts a Taíno, a Spaniard, and an African male, equipped with the tools that symbolize their respective contributions to Puerto Rican culture: the book of Spanish grammar and a sword, in the case of the Spaniard; a crop of maize and a religious ceramic object for the Taíno; and a drum and a machete held by the African.

In this way, the Institute of Puerto Rican Culture developed the racial interpretation of *la gran familia puertorriqueña*, providing the identity tools and common historical roots deemed necessary for guiding Puerto Ricans to a better, modern, and industrialized future. This institutionalization of a conflict-free homogenous notion of national identity served the hegemonic aspirations of all the parties involved (Flores-Collazo 1998, 199) but was particularly beneficial for the commonwealth party, because it helped legitimize Puerto Rican nationality while "channeling any separatist goals into art and cultural programs rather than into political action" (Dávila 1997, 38).

Figure 19. Institute of Puerto Rican Culture Emblem. The author thanks the Institute of Puerto Rican Culture for providing the emblem's image.

In terms of "culture," the discourse of mixture assumes that each group contributed distinctive traits of importance to a homogeneous Puerto Rican culture. In terms of "race," the triad recognizes differences, but only as heritage symbols of a past diluted and replaced by a new mixed present where race and color are not an issue. Distinct racial identities such as "white," "black," or "Indian" are primarily recognized as historical identities of the past, while race mixture is hegemonically understood as the mark of the present. Accordingly, contemporary affirmation of distinct racial identities is declared irrelevant. As Miriam Jimenez and others have pointed out, a basic tenet of the race mixture or mestizo construct is the disappearance of its parts (Jiménez-Román 2001, 108). Thus, rather than interpreting Africans, Spaniards, or Taínos as "living ancestors " (Segal 1994), the discourse of the ICP constructs them as distant signifiers who have left a "biological and cultural trace" in all Puerto Ricans, regardless of their skin color or phenotypic features. One illustration of this appears in San German's mural depicted in Figure 20.[10] The mural shows a representation of each ancestral root, stating below, "Three Races: One Culture: The Puerto Rican." The three racial identities (located in the past via the use of symbols such as Spanish caravels and slave chains) are subsumed into one contemporary, homogenous culture.

Puerto Rico's relationship with the United States bolsters this understanding of distinct racial identities being irrelevant for the modern Puerto Rican mixed nation. As Miriam Jiménez points out, the "literal and figurative 'disappearance' of the *indio* and *negro* provides the necessary space in which to accommodate the 'red' and 'black' racial construct of the politically and economically dominant United States" (Jiménez-Román 2001, 108). She argues that, for Puerto Ricans, the direct

Figure 20. San German's Mural: "Three Races, One Culture: the Puerto Rican." Photo by author.

colonial relationship with the United States facilitates and encourages the displacement and outward projection of these racial constructions as being pertinent only to the United States. In this way, the United States becomes the place where "real" Indians and black people *still* reside. Puerto Rico's discourse of race mixture facilitates this understanding and the displacement of racial identities such as black, white, or Indian to other sites imagined as "less mixed": Africa, the Dominican Republic, the English and French Caribbean, and, especially, the United States.

Discourses of racial harmony and racial democracy run a par with such official displacements of racial identities and with concomitant understandings of race mixture as the process that cancels their pertinence. This is no coincidence, for it is in the context of antiracist struggles and antiracist organizing and social movements that racial constructs and identities become relevant and acquire contemporary public and social currency (Omi and Winant 1986). Yet, following the populist rhetoric of development under the Estado Libre Asociado, the corresponding ICP definition of culture does not contemplate racial strife. As Arlene Dávila (1997) points out: "Most of the people I interviewed within the context of the ICP groups denied that there is racism on the island. In fact, the 'lack of racism' has served as an important element for the construction of the 'moral' Puerto Rican in the nationalist ideology, in which only 'immoral' Americans are branded as racists" (83).

This posture on racial harmony translates into a particular interpretation of how the cultural practices associated with each founding racial group (Africans, Indians, and Spaniards) manifest themselves in the present. For example, Davila's (1997) work illustrates that in music, the *cuatro* (double-five string guitar), the *güiro* (gourd scraper), and the drums represent Spanish, Indian, and African influences respectively. In folk art, the wooden saints epitomize Hispanic traditions, the hammock is representative of the Taíno, and the *vejigante*[11] stands for the African root. Musical genres such as *jíbaro* music are overwhelmingly associated with the Hispanic tradition, while *bomba* and *plena* are linked to Africa. According to the ICP, all Puerto Ricans, regardless of color, can lay claims to these manifestations of Puerto Rican culture, which are presented as equally valuable.

However, as critics of Puerto Rican cultural nationalism have pointed out (Zenón 1975; Dávila 1997; Duany 2002; Torres 2006; Lloréns and Carrasquillo 2008; Géliga-Vargas et al. 2007–8; Jiménez-Román 2001), these cultural practices are not showcased equally. As the agency involved in constructing the official view of what constitutes Puerto Rican culture, the ICP serves as a "power grid" of national values. Racial hierarchies embedded in this "grid" are reproduced via a selective process whereby cultural practices of the racial triad are indirectly deemed more important or more representative of Puerto Rican culture than others. In the making of that selection, the ICP often romanticizes the idea of the exterminated Taíno Indian, places Europe and whiteness at the center, and leaves Africa for last.

The hierarchy is evident in the conceptualization of the ICP emblem itself (which locates Spain at the center). It is also patent in the following official description provided by the ICP regarding the cultural contributions attributed to each "race" in the triad:

> The emblem represents the three cultures and races that gave rise to the culture and the people of Puerto Rico.
> The contribution of the aboriginal element is represented by the *cacique* holding a *cemí*, a stone carving that is representative of Taíno art. The figure is surrounded by autochthonous vegetation: manioc, corn, and tobacco.
> The contribution made by the Spanish element is represented by the *knight* in sixteenth-century attire holding Nebrija's book *Spanish Grammar* on a background of the three ships, or *carabelas*, of the Discovery, with the Cross, the symbol of Christianity.
> The African contribution is represented by the *black man* holding a drum and a *machete*, or short sword. Next to him there is a mask and plantain foliage. The drum and the mask are symbols of the African heritage in Puerto Rican folklore. The *machete* refers to the enormous contribution made by workers to the growth of our agriculture, while the plantain foliage evokes vegetation imported from Africa.[12] *(Instituto de Cultura Puertorriqueña 2011; my emphasis)*

As Géliga and colleagues (2007–8) note, "this ranking operation grants 'chief' status to the Taíno, attributing artistic value to their cultural production; bestows nobility onto the Spaniard, regarding the conquest and colonization as a gallant quest and civilizing mission; and reduces the African to a 'hard-working' black common man, casting his primitive possessions as vestiges of a remote past that today find expression in Puerto Rican folklore" (117).

The effects of this hierarchy of national values can also be appreciated in the cultural activities the ICP dedicates to each "root." For example, the institute has sponsored more than ten permanent exhibits about the indigenous Taíno legacy and supported various archeological excavations and festivals throughout the Island, granting utmost importance to this pre-Columbian and no longer tangible heritage. Contributions associated with African roots have not, however, received similar attention. Writing in 1999, Duany noted that "compared to over a dozen museums showcasing Spanish and indigenous traditions, not a single one focuses on the African Element." The one museum that opened in 1999 is presently closed.

The Tardy Inclusion of *Bomba* and *Plena*

After the 1970s, the ICP turned to folklore as its central focus of activity. Peasant music, folk dances, and folk arts became the backbone of its programming (Dávila

1997, 64). And, for the first time, *bomba* and *plena* groups also started to be more broadly and officially recognized. The entry of these genres into the ICP's repertoire of national culture was not a swift or easy process. A member of a contemporary *bomba* and *plena* group interviewed by Dávila recalls how the ICP would recruit them only when it needed to show something "African." It was not until the 1970s that the ICP approached them. "They called us and told us that we should be affiliated, and since we were already famous, it was very easy to become affiliated with the ICP. No audition or anything. They knew us from TV" (informant quoted in Dávila 1997, 67–68).

Carlos "Cao" Vélez Franceschi, one of the founding members of the *plena* group Los Guayacanes de San Antón, recalls a similar experience when they became affiliated with the ICP in 1978. He said that "many groups around here have to do auditions. We didn't have to go through that *cedazo* [screening] ... we have the luxury of saying that we didn't have to be evaluated by the Institute of Puerto Rican Culture." Cao described the years prior to their affiliation as difficult, however. "[W]e had to work a lot, you had to move around, you had to offer the group to institutions so the group could have an active workshop ... even for free, let's say it like it was, there were occasions when I had to offer the group for free so people could get to know it."

Once affiliated, their group gained further exposure as a folkloric group throughout the Island and abroad. In Washington, D.C., they performed at the Organization of American States (OAS) during the celebration of "Hispanic week," and they also visited New York, representing Puerto Rico's traditions at a festival of African influence in the Caribbean. Sponsorship by the ICP, thus broadened Los Guayacanes' opportunities, granting the musical group and the community of San Antón itself international status as representatives of Puerto Rican culture and of Afro–Puerto Rican traditions.

Dávila interprets the recognition of *bomba* and *plena* groups by the ICP in the 1970s and its institutional shift in cultural politics as an outcome of the fact that the economic reforms developed by the commonwealth party were in crisis and the economy had stagnated. Muñoz's party had lost its stronghold, and the commonwealth hegemonic aspirations were curtailed by the rise of the pro-statehood party (Dávila 1997, 65). These developments resulted in a heightened preoccupation among intellectuals and the Puerto Rican political left over the encroachment of U.S. culture and imported cultural products (Dávila 1997, 66). That rising concern over "Americanization," in turn, led to the sponsorship of certain Puerto Rican autochthonous cultural practices that had been previously overlooked by the ICP, such as *bomba* and *plena*.

The recognition also came in response to public pressure from people who already valued the achievements of black and *mulato* musicians. During our interview, Cao made a point of recognizing the accomplishments of *bomba* and *plena* musicians who came before him and who made *bomba* and *plena* publicly known. Performers like Canario, Cortijo, los Cepeda, and los Ayala took *bomba* and *plena* "out of the street corner" and into the ballroom, the radio, and the TV for the benefit of a broader national audience. Cao further noted that Pedro Clemente, who initiated the *Festivales* of *bomba* and *plena* in Puerto Rico, advanced this struggle to attain a broader national audience in the 1970s. *Bomba* and *plena* festivals, in turn, encouraged the formation of folkloric groups across the Island.

During the 1970s and 1980s, cultural activities, musicians, and composers associated with *bomba* and *plena* continued to struggle (and still do) to gain recognition and respect in the mainstream media. By the 1990s, their efforts, combined with rising cultural nationalism, enabled recognition of the Afro–Puerto Rican rhythms as traditional Puerto Rican music. The genre of *plena*, in particular, acquired increasing popularity during the time of my fieldwork. Politicians used it in their campaign jingles, multinational corporations played it to sell Advil, and pop stars who used to sing ballads recorded *plenas*.[13]

Commenting on the reemergence of *bomba* and *plena*, Cao noted:

> We recognize all the workers of this genre, of *bomba* and *plena*, because it's a struggle that we have to wage so that it may survive, so that it isn't exterminated, so that it may live on, and this has taken many years of work . . . But there are some persons that have taken advantage of some things . . . There are a lot of opportunists in this business. Now everybody wants to be a *plena* player, because they see that it's being accepted by the public . . . What we did when there weren't any followers, recuperating that public, *ellos quieren montarse en esa guagua y coger pon* [they want to get on the bus and hitch a ride]. See?

Body and Rhythm as Foundations of Puerto Rican Blackness

The inclusion of *bomba* and *plena* into the ICP official program and their reemergence in the 1990s transformed but did not eliminate racial hierarchies embedded in the formulation and showcasing of Afro–Puerto Rican culture. *Bomba* and *plena* are still marginalized from mainstream venues and media (especially *bomba*), although Puerto Rican youth in the Island and in the Diaspora continue to play, create, and revitalize these genres in nonmainstream venues (Rivera 2007; Alamo-Pastrana 2009). Raquel Rivera (2007), for example, documented New York Puerto Ricans' renowned interest in *bomba* in the late 1990s and the early years of the twenty-first century (229). In Puerto Rico, Alamo-Pastrana (2009) has also documented the reemergence of *bomba* in the early twenty-first century among youth who see in its performance a venue for challenging racism, dominant notions of masculinity, and colonialism. However, despite these developments, the ICP and local media continue to couch *bomba* and *plena* as genres "in danger of extinction" and in dire need of preservation. Their value is often weighted in terms of how long these genres have been sustained or maintained over generations, and seldom in terms of the innovation of performers, their critique of current social issues, or dialogue with musicians of other Afro-Diasporic communities.

Furthermore, the ICP inclusion of the *bomba* and *plena* as *the* symbol "par excellence" of Afro–Puerto Rican contributions reproduces institutionalized understandings of African heritage, reducing African legacy to the realm of music, dance, and kinesthetic sensibilities. Such views about Puerto Rico's African heritage also impinge on San Antón. For example, in an article titled "*La plena, la bomba y el barrio de San Antón*," Socorro Girón (1979) describes San Antón's residents and states that if there is something that characterizes the black race, it is its sense of rhythm: "No other race is equal. No dancer has a better sense of rhythm than a black man. The corporeal movements of a black dancer or black baseball player are much more rhythmical than those of a white. If in Puerto Rico we were to pull the blacks out from the world of sports and music, Puerto Rico wouldn't be Puerto Rico. The black race is a third of the Puerto Rican culture. Our country owes plenty to that blessed race"[14] (13).

Such scripts (and the racial hierarchies they engender) are buttressed by the notion that African-derived sensibilities or essences reside and are passed down through the veins and the blood that runs through them. The following explanation, for example, was provided in a documentary about how the *plena* developed in San Antón: "The *bomba* and *plena* was born in Ponce's barrio *La Joya del Castillo*. Within this origin, some foreigners participated as well . . . but it developed more in San Antón because that was the area where they [slaves] were, there was an hacienda called Estrella, and there many [. . . *pauses*] slaves then [. . .] the descendent families of those slaves, *the African rhythm was naturally in their blood*, and that led San Antón to be, as they say, the capital of *la plena*"[15] (Festival de Bomba y Plena, Ponce, PR, 2011; my emphasis).

Such associations between rhythm and blood do not take place with *bomba* and *plena* only. Overwhelmingly, attributes such as *sandunguería*, food habits, spirituality, and other cultural manifestations recognized as African-derived are presented by institutions and cultural activists alike as ancestral qualities emanating from "deep within" and residing in the veins, roots, or inner nature of Puerto Ricans. Metaphors of blood, veins, and roots are not as common when referring to cultural manifestations of a Spanish or Taíno heritage. In contrast, manifestations of African heritage are by and large understood as "hidden traces," deeply rooted in the body, which may surface "naturally" at particular moments or "enter one's body" at others. Their transport from the blood to the veins to the epidermis to those manifest cultural practices deemed African is assumed to be a natural, free-flowing process requiring no preparation, thought, or cultivation. In other words, the assumption is that all Puerto Ricans *inherited* some African physical traits and so-called bodily aptitudes (rhythm, coordination, kinesthetic cadence, and strength) through the "natural" mixing process but did not *learn* anything from them. To build on Geliga's (2007) critique of the ICP's emblem and official description, whereas the icon of the Spaniard and the Indian are granted the social role of *caballero* (knight) and *cacique* (chief) respectively, what accounts for Africa in the emblem is the black body of *el negro*.

Negroide Aesthetics

This overestimation of the body and underestimation of intellectual, economic, or cultural contributions resonates with previously discussed Hispanophile interpretations produced by *la generación del treinta* that recognized only Africa's trace in the blood or in the physical attributes of black Puerto Ricans. Then again, they also resonate with the counter-Hispanohile project of Afro-Antillean national affirmation developed by Luis Palés Matos (1898–1959) and others during the same decade (see Chapter 5). A look at one of the most famous poems of Palés Matos (1974) can illustrate why his work is at the center of popular definitions that associate blackness with physical and kinesthetic qualities said to "run through our veins."

MAJESTAD NEGRA

Por la encendida calle antillana
Va Tembandumba de la Quimbamba
—Rumba, macumba, candombe,
  bámbula—
Entre dos filas de negras caras.
Ante ella un congo—gongo y maraca—

Rítma una conga bomba que bamba.

Culipandeando la Reina avanza,
Y de su inmensa grupa resbalan
Meneos cachondos que el congo cuaja
En ríos de azúcar y de melaza.
Prieto trapiche de sensual zafra,
El caderamen, masa con masa,
Exprime ritmos, suda que sangra,
Y la molienda culmina en danza.

BLACK MAJESTY[16]

Through the flaming street of the Antilles
Goes Tembandumba of the Quimbamba
—*Rumba, macumba, candombe,
  bámbula*—
Between two aisles of faces, black.
Before her, a Congo—gongo and
  maracas—
A conga rhythm-rhymes *bomba* and
  bamba.

Ass swaying, the Queen goes forward,
And from her immense backside slide
Erotic swings that the Congo turns into
Rivers of sugar and molasses.
Black mill of sensuous harvest
The immense hips, mass against mass
Squeezing rhythms, blood and sweat
And the grinding ends in dance.

Por la encendida calle antillana	Through the flaming street of the Antilles
Va Tembandumba de la Quimbamba.	Goes Tembandumba of the Quimbamba
Flor de Tortola, rosa de Uganda,	Flower of Tortola, rose of Uganda,
Por ti crepitan bombas y bámbulas;	For you, *bombas* and *bámbulas* crackle;
Por ti en calendas desenfrenadas	For you in uncontrolled fires does the
Quema la Antilla su sangre ñáñiga.	Antilles burn its blood, *Ñáñiga*.
Haití te ofrece sus calabazas;	Pumpkins are offered by Haiti;
Fogosos rones te da Jamaica;	Steaming rums are brought from Jamaica;
Cuba te dice: ¡dale mulata!	Cuba says: "Do it, mulatta!"
Y Puerto Rico: ¡melao, melamba	And Puerto Rico: "Lick me, molasses!"
Sús mis cocolos de negras caras!	Oh, my black faced blacks!
Tronad, tambores; vibrad, maracas.	Thunder, drums; vibrate, *maracas*.
Por la encendida calle antillana	Through the flaming street of the Antilles
—Rumba, macumba, candombe, bámbula—	—*Rumba, macumba, candombe, bámbula*—
Va Tembandumba de la Quimbamba.	Goes Tembandumba of the Quimbamba.

Besides celebrating black beauty and sensuality, Palés's poetry is full of allusions to body movements and body actions (sweating, bleeding, sliding) that blend with images of heat, passion, and cadence. Palés combined these images with onomatopoeic and rhythmic plays on word sounds such as *Tuntún, toco-tó*, and *ñam-ñam*, which he would also rhyme with Afro–Puerto Rican words such as *mondongo* and *candombe*, and with names of Afro-Caribbean places or deities like Ogún and Changó.

Palés's work and the poems of others who wrote in the *negroide* vein during the 1930s and 1940s, such as Fortunato Vizcarrondo (1895–1977), were not widely read or performed until the 1950s. It took two decades, and the thrust of a populist project that sought consensus, for this kind of black-centered aesthetic to be valued. Before that, intellectuals of the *generación del treinta* overwhelmingly considered these to be vulgar and subordinate themes that had no place in literature (Giusti Cordero 1996, 60; Badiane 2010, 23).

Interestingly, however, part of the criticism launched against this kind of poetry in the 1930s later turned into a motive for its fascination. The preface of the second edition of Vizcarrondo's book of poems *Dinga y Mandinga* (1976) illustrates critics' descriptions of this kind of poetry as a physical and almost metabolic creation: "In this class of poetry nothing is found that speaks to the mind or the heart in its whispers, but there is much in its *cadencia desarticulada* (awkward cadence) that, upon being felt by a good part of the mestizo population of those countries, accelerates the circulation of their blood, transmits activity to their nervous system and puts their muscles in movement" (Martinez Acosta quoted in Giusti Cordero 1996, 60).

According to Juan Giusti, the fact that Acosta wrote this for the preface of Vizcarrondo's book of poems is a sign of the general disdain that writers felt toward such poetry in the 1930s and 1940s. Yet, even decades after, and in the context of celebratory renditions of *negroide* aesthetics, the aforementioned appeal for *lo negroide* as a mindless force that runs through our veins still prevails in contemporary representations and celebrations of this kind of cultural production.

During the time of my fieldwork, Palés's work and other *negroide* poems were widely performed and are still showcased in government-sponsored festivals, community activities, school contests, and recitals. Usually, artists declaim his poems with Afro-Caribbean music or drums playing in the background, using swaying body and rhythmic movements as they speak.

Given San Antón's association with Afro–Puerto Rican cultural expressions, it is no surprise that the barrio inspired a poem in this venue. In the poem "Sarabanda," author David Santiago (1995) describes the atmosphere of the Sarabanda Club, which stands at the entrance of San Antón (73):

SARABANDA	SARABANDA[17]
Tum Tum . . . Sarabanda	Tum Tum . . . Sarabanda
Tum Tum . . . Voca é miedo	Tum Tum . . . Mouth 'voking fear
Tum Tum . . . Sarabanda	Tum Tum . . . Sarabanda
Tum Tum . . . Caballero	Tum Tum . . . Cavalier
Con su son repica	With his rhythm beats
Efraín Matos el tabernero	Efraín Matos the tavern keeper
Tum Tum . . .	Tum Tum . . .
Sarabanda pa'mis oídos	Sarabanda for my ears
luz negri-roja que quema el pandero	Behind old sacks
saltan las sombras locas	Crazy shadows quiver
tras los sacos viejos	By black-red light the *pandero*'s[18] seared
Después	**Then**
caderas negras/enormes nalgas	Black hips/immense butts
tufo a sudor	Stench of sweat
mezcladero de ron pitorro y ajenjo	Shaker of moonshine rum and absinthe
se estiran los esqueletos	Skeletons stretch
resuenan en la Cumbamba	They echo in the *Cumbamba*
rumbero canta a la noche	The rumba man sings to the night
duele el aire en Sarabanda.	The air hurts in Sarabanda
Tum Tum . . . Sarabanda	Tum Tum . . . Sarabanda
Tum Tum . . . Voca é miedo	Tum Tum . . . Mouth 'voking fear
Tum Tum . . . Sarabanda	Tum Tum . . . Sarabanda
Tum Tum . . . Caballero	Tum Tum . . . Cavalier
San Antón antiguo/ Canta	The San Antón of olden years
y baila para los negros	Sings and dances for blacks.

Like other *negroide* poems, David Santiago's "Sarabanda" places an emphasis on the "primitive" and the "body" by including references to stench, sweat, and large buttocks.

The prominence of these images is also reproduced in their performance. During a recital of his poems at the La Perla Theater in Ponce, David Santiago took center stage. Behind him, a group of black men—some of them residents of San Antón—played the drums, wearing no shirt or shoes. While they played, Santiago (a light-skinned *mulato*) stood in front of them, fully dressed in clothes of white color and black shoes, reciting his poems. In that context, the "rustic" and primitive look of the half-naked and barefoot bodies of black musicians served as props that stood out against Santiago's fully dressed performance and declamation of his poems.

Aware of the racial hierarchies embedded in this kind of imagery, scholars have criticized *negroide* or *negrista* poems and aesthetics for constructing black people in Puerto Rico as "the Other" and confining Afro–Puerto Rican culture to a narrow social geography of "fixed" and primitive traits (Zenón 1975; Giusti Cordero 1996; López 1986; Santos-Febres 1995; Roy-Féquière 2004; Branche 1999).[19] Giusti describes such traits as follows:

> sensuality (*sandunguería, sabrosura*), indeed a heightened experience and deployment of all the senses, directly corresponding to a deemphasis on the rational, and an appeal to the "primitive"; festiveness (*bachata*) to the point of self-conscious primitiveness; sensual and fluid body movements; upbeat music and rhythm, especially on hand drums; enchantment with the coastal landscape; idealization of the traditional, rustic lifestyle of the *negros de la costa*. (Giusti Cordero 1996, 59; his emphasis)

Critiques of *negroide* poetry have also condemned its gendered representations, arguing that its focus on large black hips and buttocks hypersexualizes black women's bodies in a caricaturesque way that renders them erotically primitive and less than human (Jackson 1976; RoseGreen-Williams 1993). In effect, if signifiers of "*negroide* culture" point to deep urges that emerge from within, these are dynamically channeled through the black woman's body. As the repository par excellence of black folklore, the black woman's alleged corporeal exuberance is often transformed into magical, erotic, or prohibited dimensions in *negroide* aesthetics.

Some authors argue that such exotic and erotic representations do not necessarily dehumanize the black female. They maintain that, instead, the emphasis on her body can be interpreted as a beauty-related form of cultural resistance that challenges the place traditionally assigned to white women as the symbols of beauty par excellence (Badiane 2010, 116). The argument that the celebration of black erotics implies a rejection of the desexualized European notion of angelic beauty and puritanical discourse on sexuality has also been advanced. Other authors maintain that representation of bodily aesthetics that place hips, buttocks, and breasts in bold relief derive from Africa and, in some poems, reflect a Yoruba bodily aesthetic that challenges Eurocentric ideals of beauty (Arnedo 1997).

However, the problem is that *negroide* representations are not just detached artistic or poetic renditions constituting cultural resistance. Their effects seep insidiously into people's daily lives, informing actions and limiting real-life opportunities on the basis of prejudice, which reads certain bodies as more sexually accessible than others, more primitive than others, and more prone to transgression than others. Writer Mayra Santos-Febres, for example, relates how signifiers of exuberance about the black woman's body informed her own parents' fears and their obsession for disciplining her body from the time she was a child, to make sure that she would not become one of "those black women" (Santos-Febres 1995). The black woman's body is always perceived as excessive, Santos-Febres states: "Too much flesh, too much space surrounded by her bodily fluids, occupied by her hips, that never ending enticing bottom forever trembling, escaping the full gaze of the beholder. None of that lineal, subtle beauty of the Caucasian nymph, the European woman child. Elongated necks, almost imperceptible curves of a body that prolongs its carnal presence to the regions of the spirit, always escaping, a flesh out of this world" (20).

Contrary to white women, Santos-Febres argues, black women can never aspire to this transcendental existence. Instead, "The black woman's body has to remain reachable—more so, accessible; there to be touched, tasted, savored, consumed" (20). Hence, as Magali Roy-Féquière (2004) puts it, "The point is not that the black anatomy so vilified by white supremacy is openly and frankly celebrated. The celebration is not without cost to the black body, seen—yet again—in its function as producer of profit and pleasure for the viewer who desires it" (242).

Black men are not exempt from this kind of hypersexualized representation; however, their stereotypes are constructed along different lines. Puerto Rican anthropologist Ramón López (1986) comments that *poesía negra* constantly reproduces "an image of black men as horny, machista, drunken, carefree, happy and infantile. The *poesía negra* [black poetry] that goes on stage nowadays fails to present rebellion, solidarity, the condemnation of exploitation or discrimination, or any of the other issues of daily life."[20]

Critic Jermome Branche agrees, arguing that by ignoring the sociopolitical realities of blacks, the predominantly white *criollo* elite who championed *negrismo* did not really challenge the colonial legacies of racism or provide an "inner perspective" of blackness (Branche 1999, 494).

Fieldwork Critiques of *Negroide* Aesthetics

During my fieldwork in the 1990s, a number of artists leveled these and other critiques against *negroide* aesthetics, calling attention to the fact that such forms of representation not only create racist stereotypes, but limit life chances and professional opportunities. Puerto Rican black poet Juan de Matta García, for example, strongly criticized *negroide* poetry in a lecture he gave in 1995 at the Catholic University of Ponce. Dressed in African garb, de Matta asked the predominantly light-skinned audience:

> What has the *poesía negroide* [Negroid poetry] done with the black Puerto Rican and the Puerto Rican *tarcualito*?[21] Instead of creating consciousness of pride in Africanity, it has made him feel ashamed of it. After listening to this conference, you are all going to feel extremely proud of that *which runs through your veins* and belongs to Africa, because that is where civilization was born. That is where the first man and the first woman emerged. (My emphasis)[22]

de Matta pointed specifically to the figure of Luis Palés Matos when he stated that

> As a writer, Don Luis Palés Matos deserves my respect, *me quito el sombrero ante él* [I tip my hat to him]. But I believe that his intention of communicating to the light-skinned Puerto Rican that Africa ran through his veins was distorted, it was used to make a clown out of the black man in front of the white Puerto Rican.

In the following poem, "Tarcualitos," de Matta launches this criticism against Palés Matos (de Matta 1991, 3–4):[23]

TARCUALITOS	TARCUALITOS[24]
Poesía negroide me pides,	*Negroide* poetry, you ask
poesía negrista te doy,	*Negrista* poetry I'm giving
puede no gane un concurso	Might not win a competition
pero a callarme no voy.	But to silence I'm not willing.
Ya se ha escrito bastante	Enough has been written
de esa chabacanería	of that vulgarity
y luego un negro payaso	and then a black clown
la repite día tras día,	enacts it repeatedly
haciendo burla del negro	ridiculing the black man
de las cadencias del son.	and the cadences of swing.
¡Ay, monigote! fue un blanco	Oh, puppet! it was a white man
el que escribió tu canción.	who wrote the song you sing.
O quizás ha sido un negro,	Or was it probably a black man
pero un negro blanqueado	But a black, bleached white
que no sabe lo que hace	Who knows not what he does
siendo payaso del blanco	Being the clown of the white.
Mira la forma en que habla	Listen to the way he talks
su lenguaje rebuscado.	his unusual form of speech
Yo soy negro y en Piñones	I'm a black man from Piñones

con mi raza ando mezclado,	Among my race is my seat
y hablando así a ningún negro	And I swear, I have never heard
te juro nunca he escuchado.	in that form a black man speak.
Remenea el torso, negro,	Move that torso, black man
cumple tu rol de payaso,	Fulfill your clownish role
deja que el blanco se ría	Let the white man laugh
de tu actitud de macaco!	at the monkey that you show.
Sigue repitiendo negro	Keep on repeating, black man
los despectivos clichés;	Those pejorative clichés:
pelo pasa, pelo malo,	kinky hair, bad hair,
negro jabao, bruto es!	high yellow nigger, dumb fool.
¡Sigue nadando en la caca	Keep on swimming in the shit
en que te metió Palés!.	that Palés got you into!

During his lecture, de Matta distinguished between *negroide* poetry and *negrista* poetry. The former ridicules the black man, using a vocabulary and imagery that is vulgar. The "oide" ending in the term *negroide* infuses the *negro* with a sense of artificiality and inferiority, an effect similar to the difference between being human and being "humanoid" (Giusti Cordero 1996, 58). *Poesía negrista*, on the other hand, is the kind of poetry that carries a positive message for black people. It is a poetry that addresses issues of racism, praises the beauty of black features, and speaks to the spiritual strength and resistance of black people against oppression.

In San Juan, other artists launched important critiques pertaining to the racist constraints that *negroide* aesthetics impose on their creative potential. For example, in the multimedia performance called *"You don't look like,"* actor Javier Cardona (1998) called attention to the predicament he and other black actors face when pressured to conform to racist expectations of producers who believe black actors are only good for playing the black maid, the thief, the witchdoctor, the drug addict, or the pervert in media and theater. Cardona stated: "If we take a look at the official culture, the characters available for us, black actors and actresses, are conceived within the scope of Caribbean folklore: dancers of *bomba* and *plena*, rumba and salsa, slaves or freed slaves, and *vejigantes* . . . Unfortunately, when a black is called to interpret a character in one of these commercial productions, he or she is usually not there by mere chance. The person is there because he or she has the 'typical characteristics' that are being stereotyped."[25]

Using a mirror as an important part of his theatrical props, Cardona directly engaged the audience in the co-construction of his black body, asking, "Do I look black enough for you now?"[26]

A similar critique of racial typecasting was launched during my fieldwork by a group of eight black artists through the exhibition *Paréntesis: Ocho artistas negros contemporáneos* (Parenthesis: Eight Contemporary Black Artists). According to the director of the exhibition, Edwin Velázquez, the concept of *Ocho artistas negros* emerged shortly after he attended an exhibition called *La Tercera Raíz: Presencia Africana en Puerto Rico* (The Third Root: The African Presence in Puerto Rico). "From that experience," said Velázquez, "I concluded that the works exhibited by black artists also corresponded to a stereotype that only considers us capable of painting *vejigantes* and typical imagery . . . From that moment on, I started to identify a number of black artists who, like me, were creating works of a universal context, and for reasons unknown to us, but that have nothing to do with the quality of our work, are not in galleries"[27] (quoted in Alegre-Barríos 1996, 72).

Ironically, *La Tercera Raíz*, the exhibit that the *Ocho artistas negros* were critically responding to, was showcased in 1992 to challenge institutional and government-sponsored discourses that promoted a romanticized notion of Hispanicity and made African heritage invisible, particularly during the 500-year anniversary of the so-called Discovery of the Americas (see Chapter 4). Yet, in challenging that invisibility, the 1992 exhibit made visible an imagery that, according to Velázquez, reproduced stereotypes limiting the artistic opportunities available for black artists. In contrast, the exhibition *Paréntesis* sought to grant legitimacy to their more "universal" or "abstract" forms of artistic production.

Supporters of the exhibit applauded the artists' initiative to reflect on the long-denied social problem of racism in Puerto Rico. On the other hand, it was this issue of discrimination—not the artwork itself—that caught the attention of the Puerto Rican media (out of five articles written, only two spoke about the quality of the work exhibited). Overwhelmingly, the exhibit was described in social rather than in artistic terms, with the affirmation of the artists' black identity taking center stage.

Critics of the exhibit argued that its subtitle—*Ocho artistas negros contemporáneos*—was divisive and irrelevant in Puerto Rico. Plastic artist Toño Torres Martinó (1996), for example, stated that the exhibition, "instead of reflecting a national reality, tends to promote situations of conflict that are identified more with the society of the United States"[28] (95). Plastic artist Daniel Lind responded to Martino's assertions:

> In our country, we are constantly reminded of our *negritud* [blackness] . . . yet to publicly say what we are is not acceptable. In our daily exchange with people of lighter skin, we have to put up with *chistesitos corrosivos* [corrosive jokes], veiled contempt, and disguised exclusions, coded in such subtle ways that [they] can only be deciphered by those who constantly struggle against this type of racism . . . Discrimination due to the color of skin is much more complicated than what people want to present. It is not the type of racism practiced by German Nazis, nor does it have the cruel aspects of some sectors of the United States. Unfortunately, ours is one that is

practiced among brothers: *racismo de clasificación tonal* [racism of tonal classification], rooted in the ignorance of not truly knowing who we are.[29] (Lind-Ramos 1996, 148)

In crafting an alternative discussion about who "we are," the exhibit *Paréntesis,* Javier Cardona's performance *You don't look like,* and de Matta's poem "Tarcualitos" all challenged the ICP, the Department of Education, and other powerful institutions that often operate under the assumption that the mere showcasing of "black themes" in textbooks, exhibits, or music performances is an indicator of racial inclusivity and harmony. This notion is presupposed in the race-mixture rhetoric that dissolves the marginalized identity of the "black" subject as irrelevant while showcasing scripted "black themes." Thus, had these artists chosen to present "black themes" in their artwork (without calling themselves *negros*), perhaps no controversy would have ensued. Yet these various artists provoked just that—the insertion of a pause, the seizure of a moment to stop and think about the need to transcend racism inherent in the construction and consumption of "black themes," and the concomitant censorship imposed on the voicing of a discriminated black identity. Their interventions demonstrated that such typecasting effects can limit opportunities for some while amusing others. They also questioned the notion of blackness as a taken-for-granted, predetermined truth by forcing the public to think about it not only in celebratory or inclusionary terms, but as an identity forged in the context of social marginality, racism, and limited opportunities.

The fact that these critiques were presented in the language of poetry, theater, or plastic arts is no coincidence, for it is in such artistic mediums that contributions of African heritage are often recognized. However, in explaining their creations, participants addressed the question of racial identity as a problem and their art as a result of conscientious work, not as a given or product that spontaneously flows from the veins of their black bodies. Cardona, for example, opened the floor for discussion after his performance, at which time he explained how he came to terms with his "black" identity (an identity that he had not previously given much thought to). He also explained how he developed the piece and how he transformed it over time, evidencing his creative process. Similarly, in an interview, participants of *Paréntesis* stated that the public presentation of their identities as "black" was strategically deliberated and discussed, first among the artists and then for the media, as not all felt comfortable showcasing their work under this label. In de Matta's case, even though he appealed to the African heritage that "flows through the veins" of his predominantly light-skinned audience at the university, he made it clear that his delivery was the result of careful examination, study, and reflection.

Besides revealing some of the concrete effects that *negroide* aesthetics have in artistic careers, critiques launched by these artists demonstrate that a "black identity" or "African heritage" does not always carry an essentialist meaning for people who describe themselves in racialized ways. Dominant and state-sponsored showcases of Afro–Puerto Rican culture, on the contrary, seldom invite such reflection; the blackness of participants is often taken for granted, and its cultural manifestations are assumed to be unproblematic spontaneous manifestations of ancestral forces that emanate from their body and veins.

Negroide San Antón for TV

Negroide signifiers and related ideas about their "spontaneous flow" became evident in December 1995 when a TV crew arrived in San Antón to film a Christmas music special for the private local station, Canal 2.[30] The Christmas special featured the musical group Plena Libre and the renowned Puerto Rican singer Danny Rivera. The filming crew arrived unannounced at the barrio. Almost immediately, I received a call from Doña Judith at home.

> **DOÑA JUDITH**: Come down here a second.
> **ISAR**: Why? What happened?
> **DOÑA JUDITH**: Come down, come down.
> **ISAR**: Does it have to be now?
> **DOÑA JUDITH**: Yes, *mi amor*.
> **ISAR**: Okay, I'll be there in a second.

I hung up the phone and got myself ready. When I got there, I saw cars parked in front of the entrance and a couple of big vans carrying elaborate filming equipment, lights, microphones, and other things. Doña Judith told me later that she called me because she thought "the invasion" was a police operative and she was nervous. As it turns out, her daughter María Judith knew one of the crew members and she offered to help him with the setup. I sat in a corner and began to take notes on the TV production.

Technicians and performing artists began to set up at the entrance to San Antón. According to the director, they had chosen San Antón because it was considered the birthplace of the *bomba* and *plena* dance genres. As the filming proceeded, community residents gathered around the performers, and the director invited some of them to participate. The first to join in were children, who were asked to promenade from side to side. One of them was given a *vejigante* mask, which only impeded the boy's attempts at coordination. The director then asked two local male residents to pose in front of the Sarabanda Club. Others participated by playing the congas at the entrance to the brightly colored pub. Silvia, a woman approximately fifty years of age, broke into a dance. Her neighbors told her to get off the street that served as stage, but the singer and star of the show, Danny Rivera, yelled out, "*No, no la saquen. Yo voy a bailar con ella al final*" (No, don't take her away. I'm going to dance with her at the end) Then he sat down next to her in the *placita*'s bench to take a break. Women residents, young and old, took advantage of the moment to ask him for autographs and to talk.

> ¡Adios Danny!, a middle-aged woman said., *Yo creía que tú eras prieto pero tú te vez de lo más... ah...* [Oh, Danny! I thought you were black, but you look... quite... ah ...] "¡No, no!" said Danny Rivera, *"yo soy prieto, ¿qué te pasa a ti?"* [I am black. What's wrong with you?] *"Lo que pasa es que no cojo sol, mi amor"* [The thing is, I don't catch any sun, my love], and, as he said this, he took her hand and kissed it. *"¡Que Dios te bendiga esa voz, mi amor!"* [May God bless that voice, my love] said the woman, and she continued on her way.

As filming continued, a group of women praised Danny for being "so down to earth" ... "a humble guy." A member of the crew later approached them to ask if he could film a group of them praying with a rosary. Julia said she would not do it because she was not from that religion (Catholic). Another woman who agreed to do it jokingly said, *"¡Ay que bueno, por fin salí en cinta!"* (This is a Spanish pun meaning "Oh how great, at last I'll be on film/be pregnant!") They joked with each other about the fact that she didn't know how to use the *rosario*. *"¿Cómo es que se usa esta cosa?"* (How do you use this thing?)

I asked one of the men on the film crew if they had requested permission to film in the community. He responded that the police had been informed, but not the local residents. In this way, they would avoid attracting too much of a crowd, "and it would come out better, you know, more natural," he told me. Julia, a community resident from a longstanding family of San Antón, criticized such unannounced visits to the community. She complained about the photographers, researchers, and reporters, who, in their zeal to document the birthplace of the *plena*, neglected to provide sufficient time for residents to get prepared and even dress appropriately. These curious outsiders, on the other hand, *"siempre llegan con su ropa fina y bien arreglados"* (always arrive turned out in the finest clothes and perfectly made up), Julia remarked.

Julia's critique calls attention to the role of improvisation and the power dynamics of staging Afro–Puerto Rican culture. According to Patricia Fox (2006), improvisation has been a key foundational aspect that permeates the everyday lives of African descendants in Latin America. She argues that in the face of adversity, limitations, and uprootedness, Afro-Latin Americans always have had to improvise with food, clothing, music, jobs, family arrangements, and even time. This is not only to get by, but also because by gaining a vantage point on a situation or making a sly commentary, people can disrupt the dominant code. In fact, she argues, the skill to improvise and related abilities such as play, joking, and rhyming contests are values celebrated and esteemed by people of African descent for the same reason.[31]

However, in this particular situation the need for improvisation did not arise from socioeconomic constraints or from local codes of conduct, but was rather imposed by the unannounced visit of the filming crew, who wanted things to be "more natural." This expectation of a "natural flow," I argue, does not operate independently of national formulations that locate the origin of African-cultural expression in the Puerto Rican mixed biology. In the dominant scheme, improvisation is not a challenge to the established order but is rather *the* dominant expectation for how African-derived contributions manifest themselves.

During the shooting, Danny Rivera's wife (an attractive *mulata* professional model) moved with great zeal to the beat of the music, shaking her shoulders and her behind. Upon seeing her, a white female member of the filming crew commented, "*¡Como dicen por ahí, se le sale a uno lo de negro pa'fuera!*" (As they say, that blackness will always come out, ya can't hide the nigger in ya.) "*¡Así mismito es!*" (That's right), she answered. As she crossed the street with her seductive movements, a group of young women from the barrio watched her suspiciously, with hands-on-hips challenging attitudes and postures.

This common saying, "the blackness will always come out," is used by people of all physical types in the Island to indicate loss of control over belligerent impulses, aggressive impetus, or, in this case, rhythmic urges that one has not been able to restrain. Its everyday application in the context of arguments in which people warn the other that "their blackness might come out" illustrates how the black ingredient in the mixture can be considered a vital essence but also an aggressive or dangerous force that cannot always be contained or tamed. Other more positive but related ways of referring to the black component in the Puerto Rican mixture—as something that one *lleva por dentro* (has inside), that one *lleva en la sangre* (has in the blood), or that *corre por las venas* (runs through the veins)—reinforce the notion that black cultural expressions are deep-rooted, spontaneous expressions that require no disciplined intellectual endeavor or formal preparation for their authentic materialization.

As Silvia waited for her turn to dance with Danny Rivera, I thought about her stained shorts and mussed-up hair, which, of course, she hadn't the time to style. I suggested to María Judith that perhaps she might lend Silvia one of the dresses she kept in the community for the *comparsas* (chorus parade) of the *bomba* and *plena* festivals. María Judith quickly brought out a billowing skirt and a small, bright orange turban. Thus outfitted, Silvia now looked like one of the typical black mammies appearing on the *Tanairí* soap opera series, or the Mama Inés of the televised ads for Café Yaucono, or the granny of *¿Y tu abuela dónde está?* (And your granny, where is she?). After suggesting she dress up in these clothes, I realized she looked so typecast that she no longer bore any resemblance to herself. When seeing her, a local girl chuckled to her neighbors, "*Mira ahí está Silvia, leyendo el futuro*" (Look, there's Silvia, just waiting to read your palm.)

As an outside observer of the TV production, it occurred to me that few of these images bear any relation to the daily activities I had observed in this community. In the TV scheme, male residents were made over to form a rum-laced backdrop of carefree revelry. However, I never saw men frequenting the Sarabanda Club at such an early hour in the day. People also do not dance in the main street leading into San Antón, which is generally bustling with the traffic of daily shopping trips, family visits, or transporting of children to and from school. Furthermore, few middle-aged women would use such anachronistic headgear. If she had more time, Silvia would probably have visited a beauty salon to have her hair straightened (Godreau 2002). Nevertheless, once again the "blackness" of San Antón is made to seem exotic and esoteric so that it can be "authentic" and "national."

Alongside this backdrop, the TV production showcased two sophisticated professional dancers whose thin, Lycra-coated bodies, carefully rehearsed routines, and makeup contrasted with the simple steps and rudimentary attire of the local residents who were caught on film. These added elements created a televised version of San Antón that was rustic, unrefined, and "natural." The contrast between primitive and sophisticated also allowed the singer Danny Rivera and the Plena Libre performers to shine with a brilliant aura of casual neutrality.

I am not arguing that these elements were designed or planned in advance. In fact, the inclusion of elements from San Antón occurred rather haphazardly and spontaneously in some cases—as with Silvia—and they were certainly not foreseen by the film crew. Nonetheless, these typologies are so deeply rooted in the scripted concept of blackness that they almost take on a life of their own. The men playing drums outside the bar, the children dressed as *vejigantes*, the impromptu dancer, all facilitate an immediate reading of what viewers, including those whose everyday lives challenge such typecasting of blackness, understand as "black Puerto Rican culture."

Hence, that day, the *negroide* rather effortlessly eclipsed the quotidian without effort and with the cooperation of some residents. María Judith, for example, distributed the dresses and turbans she had on hand, which had been previously created for the *bomba* and *plena* festivals. Finally, I also participated when, in attempting to prevent Silvia from appearing like some drunkard or lunatic, I initiated a process that wound up reproducing the stereotype of a black mammy or psychic palm reader. And so, almost automatically, an act of representation eventually culminated in the same folkloric model that everyone knows and celebrates.

However, beyond my representation of residents' apparent compliance in this particular event, the production of black folklore in San Antón is not a passive endeavor that is externally motivated, always thrown upon community members, or tolerated without debate. In the next chapter, I explore how community members themselves interpreted and responded to such constructions in ways that also challenged and complicated the limits of *negroide* aesthetics and concomitant expectations about its "natural flow through the blood."

CHAPTER 7

Irresolute Blackness

Struggles and Maneuvers
over the Representation of Community

San Antón residents did not live their lives according to the cultural precepts of *negroide* aesthetics. They did not dress in "traditional garb," nor did they spend their free afternoons singing or composing *plenas* under the trees. However, many residents I met shared a strong sense of themselves as members of a community that deserved recognition for its important contributions to the city of Ponce and Puerto Rico. At least ten community members I met actively participated in coordinating activities that honored, showcased, or meant to strengthen this sense of community. Many had created formal organizations to this end: the Comité Pro-Defensa y Mejoras del Barrio de San Antón (Committee for the Defense and Improvement of San Antón) in the 1980s; San Antón en Acción (San Antón in Action); Casa Negra Inc. (Black House Inc.); and the recent Comité Pro-Defensa del Barrio San Antón (Committee for San Antón's Defense), not to mention the various other organizations related to *bomba* and *plena* events and festivals.

Dynamics of representation of "community," however, varied a great deal depending on whether such public events were organized for residents or for a broader national audience. In local gatherings I attended, such as Christmas dinners, Mother's Day celebrations, and Father's Day celebrations, the singularity of "community" was defined by kinship, shared enjoyment, and a sense of solidarity often expressed through signs and symbols associated with mass consumption, not black folklore. Although these activities were organized by residents in public spaces of San Antón (some with sponsorship from the government), they were in areas located at a considerable distance from the main street, making them inconspicuous to an outside audience.

For example, to celebrate Mother's Day, community organizers set up a table decorated with white and pink balloons and flower arrangements that lay over a shiny white mantel in the basketball court (no folkloric referents here). In front of the table, four mothers who were chosen to receive tribute for their longevity sat in a row of chairs. After the designated MC called forth the *madres de San Antón* (mothers of San Antón), each of them received a bouquet of white and red carnations. A little girl recited the poem "Nana a la madrecita del alma mía" (Lullaby to the dear mother of my soul), whose religious and rather sentimental tone could not place it further from *negroide* poetry. Then, eleven girls from San Antón (dressed in coordinated black and white tight sport outfits and tennis shoes) performed on the basketball court, providing an elaborate rap-dance routine they had been rehearsing for days. The MC concluded, "*¡Verdaderamente se la han comido!*"[1] (That was really great!) and he continued narrating the event over the microphone.

The community also celebrated Father's Day. This festivity did not have the same "staged" setup as the Mother's Day celebration, and fewer residents—approximately twenty—attended, but it was equally important in terms of constituting a sense of community for participants. Guillo, the manager of the local convenience store and president of the Comité Pro-Defensa del Barrio San Antón, had decorated his place elaborately for the occasion, with lights that hung from some of the surrounding trees. There was also a round multicolor disco light hanging over a wooden stand placed in front of his store. Next to the light, bordering the street, lay a group of metal chairs, some of which were occupied by residents. Few people danced, but two little girls who had not participated in the previous Mother's Day dance routine were now performing the dance informally next to the tall speakers. Amenities for that night also consisted of a music group Guillo hired to play *música del ayer* (oldies), beer, refreshments, and appetizers. After the musical group left, residents continued to listen to salsa, rap, and merengue over the speaker set. At one point, I overheard Lucy teasing one of the family members from her patio, saying, "*¡Mira a ver, que si quieres me pongo una tanga y te lo bailo!*" (Watch out, because if you want, I'll put on a thong and dance it for you!). Lucy is a very large black woman. She spoke forcefully and with a challenging attitude that recast the highly sexualized stereotypical image of the voluptuous black woman with comical overtones, at once self-satirical and facetiously threatening.

Local events such as these were mostly organized around religious activities, family oriented or preestablished holidays. In contrast, public events targeted to an outside audience centered on Afro–Puerto Rican or Afro-Antillean music (sometimes also sports) and predominantly *bomba* and *plena*. At the time of my field research and shortly thereafter, more than ten staged cultural events of this sort occurred in the community. These included the First National Day of *bomba* and *plena*, featuring the presentation of a video and the performance of the Afro-Mexican group Iyá; the *Fiestas* of *bomba* and *plena* (one in July 1995, the other in November 1996); the colorful Comparsas organized by Maria Judith for the *fiestas de bomba y plena*; a photographic exhibition featuring images of San Antón at the Sarabanda Club; the festival of La Quenepa; a concert celebrating the anniversary of the folkloric group Bomplené; and two big concerts with Island-wide promotion, featuring the famous Cuban groups Los Papines and Los Muñequitos de Matanzas.

The organization and management of these events took place through a series of concerted efforts between cultural leaders of San Antón and government offices that could include *la alcaldía* (the mayor's office), the local branch of the ICP, the Office of Art and Culture, the Office of Tourism, and private sponsors. Leaders in charge of these folkloric activities were not the same ones who controlled the previously discussed celebrations I attended. Leaders of local communal activities were activists among the ranks of the commonwealth or pro-statehood party who could tap into the resources of particular district representatives to support their local initiatives. Others were owners of local bars or convenience stores. Most of them lived in the community and were not considered artists. Folkloric leaders, on the other hand, had recognized talents in music, theater, or painting and maintained contact with government officials in charge of Ponce's cultural patrimony as well as with promotion agencies, media personalities, and artistic figures interested in showcasing San Antón's traditions. Although all were members of established family *patios* and maintained close ties with the community, not all of the folklorists lived there at the time of my fieldwork.

Different views about what made San Antón distinctive also distinguished these two sets of leaderships. Osvaldo, for example, a young community leader who held a clerical job for the popular commonwealth party in the municipality, criticized the overemphasis on folklore to the detriment of other ways of defining culture:

> Culture may also be collecting some trash and setting fire to it, which is something that's always been done here. But, for them, culture means dancing, masks and *comparsa* [dancing in costume]. But anything I do is culture. If I take out a hammock and lie down there, out in front, that's also culture.

For him, the traditions of San Antón were exemplified foremost in the social interaction that prevailed among residents:

> Sincerely speaking, San Antón is very unique. We have some customs . . . we can fight among ourselves, [but] don't let nobody come over to fight with us, nobody from the outside. Because we become one person.

> I can get mad at my neighbor and my neighbor with me, over differences, which there have been . . . But if during the night I say "Ugh" [*expressing pain*], he's the first one to arrive, the first one to arrive is your neighbor . . . Something that has always been done here, and is still a custom, is that you cook and you dish up a plate for your neighbor, and the neighbor dishes up a plate of what he's done. That has always been our custom, that custom has always been kept.
>
> I've had the opportunity to organize Christmas celebrations, which you've been at, and you've seen how people unite, the sharing that goes on is the greatest, many communities don't have it. We're talking that nowadays, in urbanized areas, residential complexes, you live twenty years in a house and you don't know your neighbors. That's the reality being lived in today's world . . .

Folklorists like "Cao" Vélez Franceschi also praised such demonstrations of solidarity among community members, but he did not take them at face value. To him, the question of how and what cultural practices people used to express this sense of community and solidarity mattered. In his view, listening and dancing to rap music, for example (which the reader might remember was used to animate the local Mother's Day celebration), was not conducive to ensuring continuity and strengthening the community:

> It grieves me to see youth so involved with these foreign things, they don't know what they're doing, they don't know what they're talking about, or what they're dancing. In fact, some of the themes are pornographic, *de chabacanería* [vulgar]. I mean, these themes in no way contribute or educate. And it is a pity that this foreign genre has seeped in so much here, because you hear it in the radio, discos, and wherever you go. These genres do not contribute to our identity. I believe that on the contrary, they create more confusion among our youths, of who they are, and where they're going, because a youngster who's listening to rap music is a youngster who doesn't know what *bomba* is, what *plena* is . . . that feels nothing for what is his.

Such differences in leadership and vision between community as folkloric or as contemporary and familial were not always clearly drawn. Members of the same family could participate in different capacities or assume both roles at different moments. However, there were times when community representatives felt a need to establish their respective operative arenas and set the record straight about who controls what in the representation process, especially when it came to showcasing black folklore. Next, I narrate one of these incidents when community leaders tried to delimit who could speak on behalf of the community's folkloric patrimony. My goal is to illustrate that, far from being "in the blood" or neutral and carefree or an externally motivated process, the marking and celebration of San Antón as place of black folklore is driven by the community itself in a way that requires a great deal of work and the assertive leadership of community members from within. By highlighting that "work" and related controversies, I seek to challenge conceptions of Afro–Puerto Rican culture as a "natural essence" that flows from people's veins.

* * *

The controversy took place over a cultural competition celebrated in the northern town of Loíza in honor of San Antón. Loíza is a town located in the northern part of the Island that—like the much smaller community of San Antón—is well known for its predominantly black population and Afro–Puerto Rican traditions (Hernández-Hiraldo 2006a). The activity called Octava Competencia Nacional Afroantillana (Eighth Afro-Antillean National Competition) formed part of the events scheduled for Loíza's famous Carnival of Santiago Apostol, which has become an emblematic tradition of *loizeño* identity and its African traditions.[2] Sponsors of the Octava Competencia Nacional Afroantillana were the municipal government of Loíza and Puerto Rico's Tourism Company (in coordination with independent organizers). The competition included a short ceremony to pay tribute to the barrio's contributions to Puerto Rico's culture. The Office of Tourism in Ponce was in charge of coordinating this with the people of San Antón. They provided certain amenities, such as free transportation from Ponce to Loíza, which took about two and a half hours each way by bus. They were also in charge of contacting San Antón's residents prior to the activity and collaborating in planning their participation in the honoring ceremony. The coordination was not seamless, however, and problems arose because it was not clear who would constitute the appropriate community leadership. Ponce's municipal government had to decide who should participate, and the process of identifying San Antón representatives became conflicted.

Mercedes's Account

Mercedes, the director of the theater group Taller La Brisa (see Chapter 2) and a recent resident of San Antón, was among the first to find out about the activity. Despite her recent initiatives involving San Antón youth in theater, Mercedes had not been born or raised in the community and did not have status as a folkloric leader. Although she was a resident, she was a recent newcomer and was not generally considered a community member.

Mercedes said she found out about the activity by chance when she went to the mayor's office and someone there gave her a flyer announcing the activity. She then talked to Osvaldo (one of the local community leaders and an active member of the commonwealth party) about the possibility of taking a group of residents to Loíza the day of the competition. She continued encouraging neighbors of the barrio to participate in the competition, especially Yayi, a young boy who was well known in the community for dancing *bomba* and *plena*.

A few days prior to the event, three folkloric leaders, Tito, Doña Judith, and Rafa, questioned Mercedes's involvement in the activity. Not knowing about their argument, I asked Mercedes a few days before the event about the time and place of the activity. She answered furiously:

> *¡Ay mira, yo ya ni sé!* [Hey, listen, I don't know anymore!] Go ask Tito, Rafa, and those people, because I don't know what's going to happen over there. Tito came over here with Judith to ask me why I hadn't said anything, that if I thought that I was the owner of culture, *que si yo me había "guillao" eso...* [that I had kept that to myself...]

Mercedes continued to explain that this was not so, that

> they always do that type of competition in towns. I simply went to the mayor's office one day and they gave me this flyer. Now I don't know what's going to happen over there! What will probably happen is what happens when people take a trip to another country, they all unite... maybe when the buses leave from here... over there the people will get together and be happy...

Tito's Account

Two weeks after the event, I talked to Tito about the activity, and he said, "*¡Ay chica, si eso fue un revulú!*" (Gee, girl, that was a mess!). He said a woman from the mayor's office gave the invitations to Osvaldo, and he and Mercedes *montaron el Kiosco* (made up the show). According to Tito, Osvaldo and Mercedes already had a group of people set up to represent the barrio. He found out about the invitation a week before the activity when he received a call from Loíza to confirm the event. As soon as he found out, he went to see Doña Judith and talked to Rafa (a musician resident of the community), and they all went to Osvaldo's house to tell him, "*Eso no podía ser así*" (That couldn't be like that).

Tito criticized Mercedes for wanting to appear as a leader of the community and for thinking she was the owner of folklore: "*Mercedes no tiene su ombligo allí* (Mercedes doesn't have her umbilical stump there[3]). How is she, who just moved in the other day, going to want to go above the things that have been established? Listen... even me, who's from there, I've got to have a lot of respect for the things of my barrio, and I've been dealing with folklore for twenty years!"

Mercedes was perceived as lacking this sense of respect for *el orden establecido de las cosas* (the established order of things). As for Osvaldo, Tito described him as someone who was into politics and not working with folklore: "What he does is make small little parties in the barrio, a booze-drinking sort of thing, but that's not real folklore." Tito also criticized the people in the municipal government for not contacting him beforehand. Apparently, they had prepared a whole plan for the event at Loíza without consulting the community. They even nominated David Santiago (author of the *negroide* poem "Sarabanda," discussed in the previous chapter) to represent the barrio. "How can David represent us, if he's not from there? *¡Eso es una falta de respeto!*" (That's a lack of respect!). Hence, he and Judith planned to have a meeting with the mayor to make it very clear that certain people in the community had to be consulted first. They also picked a group of people who could better represent the barrio and sent explicit instructions to the organizers of the event about who would be able to speak that day.

Doña Judith's Account

Doña Judith shared Tito's perspective. When she found out that the *alcadía* had sent the invitations to Osvaldo and Mercedes, she and Tito went to each of their houses to set things straight. Standing in her kitchen, she explained to me that these were people who "*quieren ganar indulgencias con escapulario ajeno*" (want to get to heaven with other people's prayers). As far as the role that the municipal government had played in this incident, she said:

> *Ese relajito que tiene el municipio con el barrio tiene que parar* [the little game that the municipality has with the barrio has to stop]. *Los "culturetos" esos* [Those "culture-critters"]: the ones from Tourism, the ones from Arts and Culture, and the ones from the Institute, all those people that believe they're the owners of Ponce's culture, they have to learn to respect this barrio. This is a poor people's barrio, and it's one of the oldest barrios in Ponce, and this barrio must be respected. Because *los culturetos esos* [those culture-critters] think they can give out invitations and make activities without consulting some people first, and it's not like that.

Doña Judith had written a letter to the mayor asking him for a meeting to discuss these issues. She signed the letter as the speaker of the Comité Pro-Defensa y Mejoras del Barrio de San Antón, the same organization she had directed in the late 1970s to demand better housing conditions. In the letter, below her signature, lay the seal of the association depicting a group of black men surrounded by wooden houses and palm trees.

In the end, Tito and Doña Judith's leadership prevailed. The names of those community representatives they authorized were read aloud, along with a description of their respective cultural contributions: (1) a musician and folklorist, (2) a civic leader in the restoration of the barrio, (3) a composer and writer, (3) a *bomba* dancer, (4) an ex–baseball player, and (5) a musician and owner of the club where *bomba*, *plena*, and other Afro-Antillean rhythms are played. Osvaldo, Mercedes, and the rest of San Antón's residents attended and participated in the event but were not called upon to speak on behalf of the community. Still, Tito mentioned them when he addressed the public, saying, "With me here today are persons who, in one way or another, collaborated in the development of this barrio of Ponce, San Antón.

Also here is a delegation that I want you to applaud yourself [*applause*], headed by Osvaldo Colón and the Office of Tourism, with whom we have coordinated this activity. So, for us, it is a pleasure to have this activity dedicated to us...."

Everyone applauded. A few hours into the event, I saw Mercedes standing by herself at the back of the public arena. As I approached her to ask about her impressions of the activity she said that "at the end everybody got together.... Yayi received lots of applause. It's the same thing that happens when people leave their country, at the end everybody gets together."

These and other power struggles over representation evidence that, far from being a taken-for-granted category, the black folklore of San Antón is not something that spontaneously flows from the bodies of its residents. To the extent that such blackness also becomes "cultural capital"—particularly in the context of an election year—community leaders must be wary of how San Antón's name is used and of what constitutes cultural representation. For those who have invested in the barrio's recognition over the years and have taken risks to ensure its continuity, the context surely warrants their say over this process. For example, Doña Judith knew that without her leadership, the activism of other community members and musicians like Cao Vélez who put San Antón's name on the map in the 1970s and 1980s, there would be no ceremony at the Octava Competancia Afroantillana in the first place. Her comments about people who "*quieren ganar indulgencias con escapulario ajeno*" (want to get to heaven with other people's prayers) and the "*culturetos* who have to learn to respect this barrio" speak to this understanding of San Antón's folklore, not as an end in itself, but rather as a recognition earned through their struggle for self-respect and for the concrete spatial existence of San Antón in Ponce's urban landscape. In the words of folklorist Cao Vélez:

> You know that in San Antón we have a series of movements, so that San Antón does not disappear, and one of the movements that we have is the restoration of the barrio. See? All these movements, folkloric and sport-related, have to make the people in government understand that San Antón is very concerned about what it has and that it doesn't want to disappear. And this is one thing that I want the mayors, the governor, and legislators to understand—that even though San Antón has been reduced in size, it has not been reduced ideologically. We have a greater strength than before. I mean, we are very clear in what we want, and we are working toward that. I mean, we are never going to let them do with San Antón what we don't want to be done. I mean, they are always going to find our resistance and our struggle against all those movements, let's say that are unfavorable, that want to remove San Antón, that want to eliminate San Antón.

Uses of folklore in the context of community struggles for self-preservation and community recognition are not unique to San Antón and have been documented extensively elsewhere in Latin America. Goldstein (1998), for example, explores how the folklorization of selected Andean cultural practices by the Bolivian government not only reflects the state appropriation of indigenous traditions, but at the same time creates spaces that indigenous people can take advantage of to ask for better services (e.g., roads, schools, health services). In this way, they are able to counteract their marginal status within the nation by claiming to be the "true" custodians of the national cultural patrimony. Similarly, in Puerto Rico, the showcase of black folklore has been used to promote the town of northern Loíza as the "capital of tradition." According to Hernández-Hiraldo, marketing African heritage in Loíza became a strategy in the 1970s for the development of tourism and the creation of jobs in the context of institutional neglect and also a means of survival for Loíza residents who earned their livelihood in the informal economy by selling goods and products associated with such traditions (Hernández-Hiraldo 2006b, 74–75).

Beyond Puerto Rico, the display of Afro-Latino folklore become not only an important motive for tourism, but has also (especially in the 1990s) been a crucial aspect of political mobilization in Latin America, particularly in the context of the black antiracist movement. Efforts to gain collective rights, including communal land rights, for black communities have been supported by claims regarding the maintenance and preservation of Afro-Latino cultural practices and cultural patrimony. In Brazil, for example, the state granted communal land titles to descendants of ex-slaves who had occupied *quilombo* lands (maroon settlements) for generations. The government's criteria for granting *quilombo* land titles varies and can be more or less flexible over a given time. Cultural criteria such as the ability of the group to recall stories about a slave's past, the preservation of cultural practices tied to the common use of land, cultural markers that point to African survivals, and the ethnic distinctiveness of the group as descendants of *quilombo* communities are often taken into consideration for land recognition (Cultural Survival Inc. 2002; French 2009). Jan Hoffman French, for example, describes how residents from a rural community in northeast Brazil effectively managed to tap into state resources available to gain land titles and needed infrastructure in their community (including running water, electricity, paved roads, and schools). They did so by organizing as descendants of ex-slaves and adapting their politics of self-representation to the racial and historical expectations of legal requirements, antiracist activities, and *quilombo* supporters (French 2006). The case is not an isolated one. For many rural black communities, this strategy of identifying as black descendants of slaves proved to be more effective than previous struggles they had waged as peasants or rural workers in favor of an agrarian reform which had been nearly paralyzed for years (Cultural Survival Inc. 2002).

Yet here (as in the case of San Antón), the question of who was able to claim entitlement once recognition and communal land were granted was contentious.

French describes feuds between fractions and families who supported *quilombos* and the *contras*: who were opposed to pursuing land recognition on the basis of claiming slave ancestry and labeling themselves black. This *contra* group (about a third) favored other channels (such as gaining the favor of local politicians) to improve conditions in their community (French 2006, 344–45). Once land entitlements were granted on the basis of *quilombo* status (and thanks to the political mobilization of those who favored the *quilombo* strategy), the *contras* who had opposed the movement were not allowed to work on the land by the group who had fought for *quilombo* recognition, even though they were considered black and descendants of fugitive slaves by the government. Only those residents who supported the struggle for self-recognition as *quilombos* were allowed to become members of the association that could hold the title for the *quilombo* land, increasing tension between factions in the community (French 2006, 344).

In the particular event at Loíza, the stakes were not as high as they were for Mocambo residents in Brazil. Yet in San Antón, as in Mocambo, the issue of commitment to the struggle for community recognition and the political self-identification that it required (i.e., either as black descendants of ex-slaves or as representatives of Afro–Puerto Rican folklore) took precedence over any racial categorization or cultural expectation assigned *a priori* to the community or its residents. Factions and struggles within the community are thus a testament to the fact that the racialized construction of practices known as "black culture" (despite its projection as natural and free-flowing expression) is the product of people struggling, debating, and negotiating with powerful structures to improve their lives.

In San Antón, the marketing of black folklore for a national audience gives recognition and facilitates work opportunities for performers, artists, and residents who sell *empanadillas yaniclé*, *bacalaitos*, and *domplines* (typical dishes and fritters) to visitors during these activities. Those who benefit from those opportunities also need to maintain control over the representation process to ensure its continuity. That responsibility, in turn, needs to be managed in ways that serve to guarantee the community's symbolism as icon of Afro–Puerto Rican traditions, not only in the face of U.S. cultural influence, but also in terms of the community's presence in Ponce's urban landscape itself.

In this regard, folkloric leaders of San Antón were careful not to turn the community into just "one more typical black site" of Puerto Rico or subsume it into a homogenized whole of *negroide* symbols, ultimately indistinguishable from other "black" places in Ponce. Doña Judith was especially critical of *los culturetos esos* from the government—who flaunt their condescending interest for San Antón without paying attention to the particularities of the community and respecting the leaders of its struggles. Other cultural leaders would emphasize how the *bomba* that developed in San Antón and in Ponce was played and danced differently from the *bomba* of Santurce or Mayagüez. They pointed to the particular attires and skits, the different ways of holding and mounting *barriles* (drums), and the specific names given to instruments. In terms of foods, residents spoke of *yaniclé con jueyes*, *domplines*, and other recipes especially developed in San Antón. Spiritual and religious attachment to the land and to the rituals that marked those belonging to a particular place in the barrio, such as burying the umbilical cord of babies in the family plot when they were born, were also important community referents.

These specific manifestations of community traditions had a better chance of being validated and publicized as part of the Puerto Rican culture to the extent that they operate within the limits and scripts that are hegemonically constructed and celebrated in Puerto Rico as "black" (i.e., music and dance, sports, food, and spirituality). Hence, cultural practices that extend beyond such scripts, such as individual and collective acts of solidarity and resistance, performing skilled jobs in the cane industry, buying one's freedom, or acquiring land for descendants, were not represented at the Octava Competencia Afroantillana or any other cultural event that showcased San Antón traditions (even though they were key achievements for ensuring San Antón continuity). No prominent counternarratives were available to sustain alternative categories for honorable mention. Although there were "honorable mothers," "descendents of skilled artisans," "cane workers," "fighters for social justice," and "*patio* owners" among the ranks of San Antón residents who attended the Octava Competencia Afroantillana, they were not specifically honored as such in Loíza.

When the MC called for the director of the activity and the personnel of Tourism from Ponce to begin with the formal honoring acts, they presented chosen representatives with a plaque that read as follows:

> En reconocimiento al Barrio San Antón de Ponce, por ser cuna de plena, cuna de gente humilde y de *sangre caliente en las venas*, lo cual ha permitido transmitir y sembrar la semilla en Puerto Rico de lo que es la plena. Por ser comunidad orgullosa de sus bailes, tambores y esencia; sabiendo preservar, comentar y divulgar su folclor y valores culturales, y por ser cuna de grandes deportistas . . . Dedicado a la gente humilde del Bo. San Antón de Ponce, la 8va Competencia Nacional Afroantillana. Dado en Loíza Puerto Rico hoy 28 de julio por parte del Honorable Alcalde y el Sr. Eddie Manso Fuentes, Presidente del Comité organizador 8va Competencia Nacional Afroantillana. Felicidades! [sound of *panderos*; my emphasis]
>
> [To acknowledge the barrio of San Antón as the birthplace of the *plena*, birthplace of humble people and of *hot blood in their veins*, which has permitted them to transmit and plant the seed of *plena* in Puerto Rico, for being a community proud of its dances, drums, and essence, knowing how to preserve, comment [on], and promote its folklore and cultural values, and for being the birthplace of great athletes . . . We dedicate this 8th National Afro-Antillean Competition to all the

humble people of San Antón of Ponce. Awarded in Loíza, Puerto Rico, today, July 28, on behalf of the Honorable Mayor Carrasquillo, and Mr. Eddie Manso Fuentes, president of the organizing committee of the 8th National Afro-Antillean Competition. Congratulations! (*sound of* panderos; my emphasis)]

Housing Essences

The notion that Afro–Puerto Rican culture flows spontaneously through the "hot blood" of San Antón residents (with no work or investment necessary for its manifestation) also made an impression in the housing project. In fact, the government operated under the assumption that, once they provided adequate housing, the traditions of the community would spontaneously emerge and prevail in the face of development. The Rehabilitation Master Plan states, for example, that "As a consequence of this transformation, there would be a modification in the spatial and morphological vision, from the point of view of formal observation. The social character and functioning of the *barrio*, however, are strengthened and consolidated by means of this mutation. In order to preserve the *essence* of San Antón's characteristic and unique culture within an organized framework, the inhabitants are given the necessary weapons with which to defend themselves against the dehumanizing effects of urban invasion."[4]

Since the municipal government understood that San Antón's "essence" would be preserved and even strengthened through this spatial modification, the housing project was not developed with a plan to invest in promoting or developing these traditions. The government did not, for example, sponsor workshops that would guarantee the maintenance of the *bomba* and *plena* in the *barrio* during or after the construction of the housing project. Nor did the municipal government contemplate construction of a museum that could showcase San Antón's traditions. And, although residents had previously asked the municipal government for a "cultural center," this was not a priority of the housing project.

Nevertheless, once it became evident that this was not the housing project they had hoped for, residents and members of the Comité Pro-Defensa del Barrio San Antón practiced other less showcased cultural practices and continuities, namely the ability to organize collectively in the face of adversity. The leaders of this struggle were not the same leaders who assumed an active role at the *8va Competencia Afroantillana*. That folkloric leadership (which had been very active in the late 1970s) assumed a somewhat marginal position during this housing controversy in the 1990s. Still, there were important similarities between these two leaderships. In both cases, they criticized the government for not consulting with the community first and for treating them disrespectfully. Also, in both cases, community members actively organized to set the record straight and assume control over the representation process. Furthermore, in both cases, their resistance had to operate within the discursive limits of what counts as Afro–Puerto Rican among people they sought to influence.

However, in the case of the San Antón housing project, the stakes and terms of contention were unique. This was not just an issue about who or what would represent San Antón in a cultural festival. In this case, answers that the government provided to the question of "What is San Antón?" (and what are the key referents for its continuity) had a bearing on how residents would live: the kinds of houses they would have, their spatial relationship to each other, and the ownership and distribution of land.

National scripts available for blackness regarding such issues, however, were limited, especially when it came to issues of land tenement and use. In the dominant scheme of cultural nationalism, it is the extinct indigenous Taíno, or the "almost-white" *jíbaro*—not the black African—who is endowed with the role of being the overseer, caretaker, and cultivator of the motherland. In particular, the no longer tangible but mythical Taíno is considered to be the ancestral keeper of all the natural resources of Puerto Rico, a role that finds international support in the global prominence of "the Indian" as a symbol of the pristine wilderness and guardian of nature (Haslip-Viera 2001). In contrast, there are almost no referents that point to the attachment and knowledge of the land in the dominant repertoire for Puerto Rican blackness. Granted, the preparation of certain foods, in the form of fritters such as *bacalaitos* and *alcapurrias*, is associated with traditions of black coastal dwellers. And certain crops such as plantains are recognized as coming from Africa. However, their successful cultivation based on wisdom associated with the land is not associated with Afro–Puerto Rican traditions, even though self-sustenance and the acquisition of land were key elements of resiliency for a large sector of free people of color in Puerto Rico and elsewhere in the Caribbean (see Giusti-Cordero 1994).

Such voids in the national repertoire for blackness also influenced the government's idealization of the housing project and conceptualization of the *patio* as something based on familial proximity and not on communal land tenement or farming. Overwhelmingly, *patios* were portrayed as traditional because they were sites of entertainment and family bonding; not because they were sites of production where animals or crops were grown or because their tenement was indicative of collective achievements. In fact, the project favored individual land ownership, and its guidelines prohibited keeping live animals like chickens, ducks, or goats in the internal yards.

El Indio Antón

The government and its agents were not the only ones bound by the nationalist scripts that privilege the mythical Taíno or the *jíbaro* as the "authentic" dweller of the Puerto Rican cultural landscape. National scripts for what is Taíno and what is black also influenced San Antón residents' strategies of self-presentation during the housing controversy.

When radio reporters reached San Antón to ask about the government's plan to rehabilitate the family *patio*, the vice president of the Comité Pro-Defensa del Barrio San Antón responded: *"Pero, ¿qué patios? ¿Qué patio? Eso es una reservación india. O sea, no hay patio, Penchi* (nickname), *no hay patio.* (But what *patios*? What *patios*? That's an Indian reservation. In other words, there is no *patio*, Penchi, there is no *patio*.)

This likeness of San Antón to an Indian reservation was brought up at various points during the controversy. The analogy served to bring to light the fact that the project required that some residents sell their land to the government and move to another individual plot that was not their original *patio*, as if land were easily interchangeable and without taking into consideration its history. The comparison with an Indian reservation in U.S. territory was also used to illustrate that the decision had been unfair and arbitrary.

In the context of denouncing such changes, other Indian metaphors came in to play. For example, residents and the press referred to the original *patios* as *bateyes*, a common term used to refer to indigenous Taíno settlements. The charge was that the government had not preserved them adequately. Moreover, in planning preparations for their appearance before the press, one of the leaders of the Comité called out to those residents who knew how to dance to organize *un grupito de areyto*, which is a Taíno ceremonial dance. I don't think they really meant for residents to dance this indigenous dance (and such a dance never took place), but the fact that this leader chose to refer to typical dances of the community as *areyto* is significant.

Jaime (the vice president of the Comité and a member of a well-known and prestigious *patio* in San Antón) also appealed to Indian things in a letter he wrote to Ponce's mayor under the alias of the Indio Antón (the Indian Antón). The letter was never mailed, but he distributed it among his family members and neighbors and shared it with me after the controversy subsided. The letterhead of Jaime's communication read as follows:

> *Carta al hombre blanco en el Municipio Ponceño*
> *De: El Indio Antón.*
> *Dirección: Praderas y Patios, Barrio San Antón*
> [Letter to the white man in the municipality of Ponce.
> From: The Indio Antón.
> Address: Fields and *patios* of barrio San Antón]

Jaime's letter begins by posing the following question to the mayor:

> ¿Cómo se puede comprar o vender el cielo, o el calor de la tierra? Esa idea me parece extraña, si no poseemos el frescor del día, el brillo del agua. ¿Cómo es posible mostrarlo? Cada pedazo de esta tierra es sagrada para mi barrio, cada rama brillante

de los árboles, la penumbra, la densa vegetación, cada claro y el suspiro de los insectos, son sagrados en la memoria y experiencia de mi barrio y de mis antepasados.

[How can you buy or sell the sky or the warmth of the land? This idea is foreign to me, since we do not possess the freshness of each day or the brilliance of the waters. How can I explain this? Each piece of land is sacred to the people of my barrio; each shining tree branch, the penumbra, the dense vegetation, each clearing, and the whispers of the insects are sacred in the memory and experience of my barrio's people and of my ancestors. . . .]

If the text sounds familiar to the reader, it is because it is inspired by the frequently reproduced letter that Native American Chief Seattle is said to have written to President Franklin Pierce in 1854 when Pierce proposed to buy a vast piece of Native American Suquamish and Duwamish territory in what is now the state of Washington. Over the last forty years, Chief Seattle has become a sort of environmental hero, and this speech has appeared in pamphlets and on Web sites all across Europe and the Americas.

Taking his cue from this international movement and the dozens of Indian nations that have sought official recognition of native lands from the federal government, Jaime adapted Chief Seattle's speech by adding references particular to San Antón and Puerto Rico in his letter. His adaptation spoke of the continuity of kin, the spirit of ancestors and their connection to the land, the *guaraguao* [which is an indigenous falcon of Puerto Rico], and all the birds, horses, and dogs of the barrio. He also included images associated with black folklore, stating that

> . . . nosotros . . . le enseñaremos a nuestros niños, que cada reflejo en el agua de nuestros ríos, cada retumbe o sonar de los tambores de los GUAYACANES, para entonar una bomba o una plena, hablan de los acontecimientos de la vida de mi barrio. Sabemos que el hombre blanco no comprende nuestras costumbres. Una porcion de esta tierra para el, tiene el mismo significado que cualquier otra cosa.

> [. . . we will teach our children that each reflection in the waters of our rivers, each echo and sound from the drums of the Guayacanes to play a *bomba* or a *plena*, speak of the events of the life of my barrio. We know the white man does not understand our ways. A portion of this land has the same meaning for him as anything else.]

In this way, Jaime drew from the Native American experience of land expropriation to garner support for residents' claims about land and their resistance to selling it. Likewise, his rendition of the "*Indio Antón*" served to underscore the sentimental and symbolic significance that the land had for some residents (a cultural repertoire not available for black Puerto Ricans). As the letter read:

> Por lo tanto, cuando el gran jefe manda a decir, que desea comprar nuestras tierras. No sabe que está pidiendo mucho de nosotros. El gran jefe dice, que nos preservará

un lugar donde podamos vivir satisfechos, que se convertirá en nuestro padre y nosotros en sus hijos. Por lo tanto, nosotros vamos a considerar su oferta de comprar nuestras tierras. Más eso no será fácil.

[Therefore, when the great chief sends word that he wants to buy our lands, he doesn't know that he is asking too much from us. The great chief says that he will preserve a place where we may live content, that he will become our father and we his children. We will hence consider his offer to buy our lands. But it won't be easy.]

Jaime was the member of a renowned family *patio* who refused to sell communal family land. Yet, as I have discussed, residents displayed a heterogeneity of positions regarding the future of their community, and some were in fact eager to sell and claim ownership over a new individual plot and house. This partly explains why the letter could not state that they were completely opposed to the project, but rather that they would consider the mayor's (alias great chief's) offer. Hence my analysis of Jaime's creative adaptation of the Indio Antón does not mean to romanticize "communal land" or propose it as a more representative criterion for blackness. Jaime's letter is better understood as one among a variety of positions that coexisted during the housing controversy. Nevertheless, the Comité chose to emphasize the family *patio* during the controversy. Why?

Members of the Comité Pro-Defensa del Barrio San Antón could not underestimate the discursive impact of the mayor's emphasis on the *patios* as an important aspect of the community's historic traditions and of his government's "preservationist" housing model. They had to walk a fine line between their desires for modernity and the public presentation of San Antón as a traditional community that deserved attention and just treatment. In this context, making reference to San Antón's traditional *patios* from within the community was an important strategy, not only because it referenced previous struggles and achievements that allowed the community to endure, but also because it construed residents as bearers of San Antón's traditions, granting them a status of inclusion, albeit marginally, in the nation's cultural patrimony. It also positioned the community at a strategic advantage when voicing critiques against the government's intent of cultural preservation because—as tradition bearers—residents, when interviewed on TV and radio, could legitimately state that the implementation of the housing project was not done correctly. Hence, although the preservation of the *patios* was only one among a number of other (even discrepant) concerns with the housing project, this issue—and the supporting metaphor of the Indian Reservation—took center stage in residents' representations of the controversy before the media and the outside community.

It was with this "outside community" in mind that Jaime adapted Chief Seattle's speech, in order to garner support for the residents' plight. Of course, one could argue that the letter is also an example of how blackness is erased via Indianization. Scholars have underscored how, in the context of persistent racism and the idealization of the Taíno, people and institutions in Puerto Rico often recast "black things" as Indian in an effort to legitimize their cultural practices as authentic (see chapters by Dávila, Duany, and Jiménez in Haslip-Viera 2001). Duany (2001), for example, argues that previously mentioned cultural politics of the ICP and the *indigenista* discourse of local intellectuals contributed to erasing the ethnic and cultural presence of blacks in Puerto Rico. He uses the phrase "making Indians out of blacks" to reference the symbolic displacement of the African by Taíno culture in scholarly analyses and public representations of Puerto Rican national identity (57). Commenting on the preferential treatment cultural institutions give to the Taíno versus the African, anthropologist Arlene Dávila (1997) also notes that, as a result, African contributions to Puerto Rican culture are often "Taínoized." "Traits that are not identifiably Spanish are attributed to the Taíno rather than as African, with the result that everything and everyone can trace a mythical descent to the Taíno" (71). Puerto Ricans may also explain their dark skin as due to Taíno ancestry or use the term *indio* to describe someone with dark skin and straight hair (Jiménez-Román 2001; Godreau 2008b).[5]

Fascination with the Taíno extends beyond the Island to the Puerto Rican Diaspora, where New York–based Puerto Ricans (many of them with visibly black features) founded Taíno "tribes," "councils," and "associations" in the 1980s and early 1990s. Some of them not only aim to revive what they believe is the Taíno religion, lifestyle, and language, but also participate at events organized by indigenous groups, cultural institutions, and U.S. agencies charged with defending indigenous rights.[6] Despite their critique of U.S. and Spanish colonialism, critics have described their politics as accomodationist, ahistorical, and supportive of a racist paradigm that bypasses Puerto Rico's African heritage and deters collaboration with African Americans and other Afro-Diasporic groups (see chapters by Haslip-Viera and Jiménez-Román in Haslip-Viera 2001).

Puerto Ricans are not the only ones who engage in such identity politics or appropriation of Indian things. The indianization of blackness has been, for example, amply documented in the Dominican Republic, where the recasting of Dominicans as *Indios* and Haitians as *Negros* became a key element of president Trujillo's official state discourse and political strategy to garner local and international (especially U.S.) support against Haiti during his dictatorship (1930–61; see Candelario 2007). The privileged romantic view of indigenous culture at the expense of Afro-descendant populations has also been documented in the Caribbean and Central America (Moore 1999; Helms 1977; Anderson 2009). In fact, appropriations of the indigenous for general commercial projects and environmental movements are quite common across the globe. Denise Low has argued that such consumption of the indigenous often entails a "cannibalization" of random images of "noble savages" collapsed and consumed without paying attention to specificity of place, time, or context, producing nostalgic images of nature (and antimaterialism) that sell (Low 1995, 410–12). The process also entails a disregard for authorship and exactitude, as people feel free to appropriate Native American symbols and manipulate them as they see fit.

Chief Seattle's speech—the text that Jaime adapted—seems to be the product of such a process of cannibalization (but not just by Jaime). According to various historians, the document was never written by Chief Seattle and is actually the creation of a white man named Smith, who claims to have taken notes of Seattle's speech and published his own translation thirty-three years later—a version whose anachronisms and inconsistencies are more attributable to Smith than to Chief Seattle (Kaiser 1987). Low (1995) points out that Smith's translation of Chief Seattle's speech retained references specific to the Washington State coastal landscape and the political events that transpired during the Suquamish and Duwamish treaty negotiations in 1854 (414). But later, more commercial versions of the speech (such as the one adapted by Jaime) ignored these matters altogether and introduced new content, omitting the nineteenth-century political context, adding sentimental descriptions of nature, and introducing landscape imagery that could fit a pan-Indian stereotype of tribes like the Sioux or Navajo (Low 1995, 414).

Considering all such manipulations of Chief Seattle's speech, who would blame Jaime for impersonating an Indian in his letter to the mayor? While it is true that blackness is often erased via its Indianization, in this case, Indian symbols and imagery also became a strategy to authenticate black people's claims to a national landscape that excludes them. Certainly, one must take into consideration what other scholars have noted—that undifferentiated representations of Indians such as Chief Seattle's cannibalized speech "relegate Indians to the long-ago and thus makes them magically disappear from public consciousness and conscience" (Dorris 1992). However, here, the Indio Antón became part and parcel of efforts to make San Antón visible in light of a national consciousness that makes black people invisible unless they dance the *bomba* and *plena*. Ironically, in this way, the people of San Antón usurped a government strategy used to erase blackness to critique the government's typecast interpretation of blackness.

Furthermore, the fact that people in San Antón used the Indian metaphors does not mean that people in San Antón identify as contemporary Indians or Taínos. In the words of Miriam Jiménez Román (2001), "For the vast majority of Puerto Ricans, of whatever political persuasion, the Taíno is a quaint historical figure, having little to do with contemporary life. Puerto Ricans are understood to be 'part Taíno'—as they are *part* Spanish and *part* African—but generally speaking, to call oneself a Taíno (or a Spaniard or an African) in Puerto Rico is the subject of ridicule, albeit for a variety of reasons. Within a racial hierarchy primarily based on phenotype, rather than ancestry, one may *look* Indian but '*looking* Taíno is never equated with *being* Taíno'" (113).

In fact, 2000 census results for San Antón reveal that not even 1 percent of residents identified as Indian or as Taíno (U.S. Census Bureau 2000d). Therefore, more than a personal identity display, evoking Indian things (on TV, in radio appearances, and by letter) functioned as a rhetorical strategy that allowed San Antón residents to authenticate their pleas and speak out about their attachment to the land in compelling terms, bypassing dominant expectations of "black folklore" that do not contemplate or recognize such attachments in their scripts.

The Folklorization versus the Ethnicization of Blackness

The aforementioned local move of adopting "indigenous models" to support claims to land in San Antón resonates with similar strategies launched by Afro-Latino populations in Latin America to frame their demands for collective rights based on indigenous legislation and models.[7] Latin American countries such as Brazil and Colombia have recognized communal land titles to descendants of runaway slaves who had occupied *quilombo* land for generations. These and other claims to resources were facilitated by multicultural citizenship reforms and legal precedents established for indigenous communities that declared themselves to be culturally autonomous from the rest of the nation. Such reforms were developed in many Latin American countries after decades of authoritarian rule, in an effort to restore democratic legitimacy and send a message about the state's recognition of the multicultural nature of the nation (French 2009; Hooker 2005; Paschel 2010).

Scholars have noted that not all black communities were able to seize upon the benefits of these changes in constitutional and legal frameworks regarding multiculturalism. Black communities that managed to frame their claims to land under the rubric of ethnic distinctiveness (as rural black communities with a particular culture and maroon or rural riverine heritage) have been better positioned to attain recognition of land rights from the state than those that don't (Hooker 2005; Paschel 2010; French 2009). The trend is telling of how claims based on indigeneity are more successful and appealing to national elites than claims based on blackness. For example, multicultural reforms that establish collective rights (in the form of land reform, multicultural education, and recognition of cultural autonomy) have been more broadly and swiftly approved for indigenous groups in at least fifteen different Latin American countries, including Argentina, Chile, Bolivia, Costa Rica, Guatemala, Mexico, Panamá, Paraguay, Peru, and Venezuela (Hooker 2005). Afro-Latino groups have been less successful in winning collective rights, although rural communities' descendants of ex-slaves have been able to gain (some) land rights as distinctive collective entities in Colombia, Brazil, Honduras, Ecuador, and Nicaragua (Hooker 2005).

Hooker and Anderson explain that the reason indigenous groups have been more successful than Afro-Latinos in gaining such rights is because their assignment has been overwhelmingly sustained on the premise of ethnic distinctiveness, which is an attribute that *indios* and blacks do not share equally (Hooker 2005; Anderson 2009). Following Peter Wade's analysis regarding the construction of indigenous and black subjectivities under different "structures of alterity," Hooker and Anderson argue that while *indios* are considered to have an ethnicity, Afro-Latino difference is overwhelmingly construed as racial (Wade 1997). In general, blacks are not seen as having traditional or ancestral cultures in the same way that Indians are. Furthermore, in the case of indigenous groups, claims to communal land are facilitated by the popular conception that their ancestral culture is "naturally" attached to the land. As Hooker (2005) states, "the notion that a "special" spiritual and nonmaterial relationship to the land is necessary in order to justify communal land rights places black communities at a disadvantage when claiming such rights, since they are generally [and often incorrectly] not thought of as having such relationships to the territory" (304). Discourses of *mestizaje* and racial mixture support this construction by maintaining that the majority of blacks assimilated and blended harmoniously into the broader national culture.

In the context of these transformations and the need to challenge official state (and popular) discourses that invisibilize blackness, Afro-Latinos have adopted strategies based on what scholars have called the "ethnicization of blackness" (Restrepo 2004) or the "right to difference" (Paschel 2010). According to Restrepo, ethnicization entails a specific construction of "blackness" (or "indigenousness") as a different kind of subjectivity that is forged according to interwoven notions of nature, territory, community, tradition, and identity. It also involves "a type of production and relation with the past, a way of imagining community based on origins and historically shared experiences, as well as a relocation of subjectivities and identities" (704). Powerful actors including academics, black activists, church officials, and NGOs mediate this assemblage of memories and identities and play a key role in the ethnicization process (Restrepo 2004, 708; Paschel 2010). Scholars have pointed out that such claims for the "right to difference" among Afro-Latinos appeal more to ethnicity and to discourses that distinguish Afro-descendant groups from mainstream national culture, than to discourses that emphasize racial discrimination, racial inequality, and the need for integration or equal rights (Hooker 2005; Paschel 2010). As Tianna Paschel (2010) notes for Colombia, "multicultural policies typically rely on the premise that ethnic groups, defined in terms of identity and culture, are the appropriate political subjects for specific types of rights" (764).

Hence, when Afro-descendants have won the same collective rights as indigenous populations (i.e., the Miskito and Garifuna in Honduras and Nicaragua), it is because they are seen as having an indigenous-like status, a distinct language and culture whose origin predates colonization or that developed (somewhat) independently from colonizing structures and processes of *mestizaje* (Hooker 2005; Anderson 2009). Winning collective rights from the government is therefore not necessarily akin to the state's recognition of the need to address racism and reverse long-standing institutional exclusions because of racism. In this regard, Hooker (2005) correctly argues that a potential negative consequence for Afro-descendants groups that focus their political mobilization on ethnic identities is that by privileging cultural recognition, questions of racial discrimination become demoted as a basis for political mobilization (307–10). As she states, "the emphasis on cultural difference as opposed to racial discrimination might allow states to ignore the continued existence of racism once cultural diversity is recognized, without necessarily addressing the special and economic aspects of racial injustice" (308). Commenting on Colombia's Law of Black Communities, Paschel (2010) further notes that the legal definition of said communities as rural, geographically bound, and ethnically distinct ignores the particular lived realities and issues facing the majority of the Afro-Colombian population living in urban centers (764).

There are significant differences between San Antón residents' uses of Indian symbols in Puerto Rico and the aforementioned deployment of an indigenous ethnic model by Afro-descendants' communities in Latin America. Of course, there is the issue of scope. San Antón's militancy is a case-specific demonstration of a small community of approximately three hundred residents vis-à-vis the government, not a mass manifestation linked to international and national political movements such as the black movement in Colombia, Brazil, Honduras, and other Latin American countries. Also, there is the issue of context. In Puerto Rico there is no comparable black movement. Also, there are no viable indigenous communities or groups claiming collective rights, multicultural reforms, and constitutional amendments.[8] Hence, there is no local constitutional or legal model of ethnic territoriality or "ethnicization" that Puerto Rican black communities can follow. The closest, most well-known model is the U.S. "Indian reservation." Yet Puerto Ricans do not associate the model of reservations positively with multiculturalism or democracy, but with U.S. violence and colonization.

Moreover, in contrast to Afro-Latinos who have fought for collective rights in Brazil, Colombia, Ecuador, and Nicaragua, the mobilization of San Antón residents in the housing dispute was not promulgated on the basis of an ethnic black identity. Residents who were most vocal during the controversy did not define themselves as slave descendants or appeal to cultural markers that would distinguish them from the broader national culture. Quite the contrary. Claims voiced by the Comité Pro-Defensa del Barrio San Antón stressed the principle of equal treatment as citizens who had contributed to Ponce (they did not organize or ask for distinctive treatment as Afro-descendants or blacks). In fact, most residents did not publicly uphold a black identity at all. As said previously, public affirmations of a black identity were rare during the housing controversy.[9] Furthermore, unlike black movements in Latin America, the Comité Pro-Defensa del Barrio San Antón did not explicitly address the issue of racism as a factor influencing their housing predicament. Neither were antiracist activists nor other powerful actors (church officials, academics, lawyers, folklorist, NGOs) involved in the community or collaborations to promote a black political subjectivity among residents (see French 2009; Restrepo 2004).

However, despite these important differences between events in San Antón, Puerto Rico, and movements led by Afro-descendant communities in Latin America, there are also telling similarities. In both cases, ideas about "culture" are deemed more legitimate and accepted more readily than ideas about "racial inequality" when posing community grievances. This is regardless of whether the "culture" being referred to is the Puerto Rican culture, with its folkloric Afro–Puerto Rican components, or the autochthonous black ethnic culture that is distinct from the Latin American mestizo nation. Despite the differences, in both cases, antiracism was at best a difficult, if not a nonviable, strategy for addressing social inequalities, while "culture" became the language that makes communities visible and their plight viable to national elites and governments.

Analyzing similar uses of "culture" in identity politics espoused by Island and Diasporic Puerto Ricans, Miriam Jiménez states:

> While race, like class, is perceived as an unpalatable notion, an ugly and potentially divisive issue that threatens Puerto Rican unity, culture is presented as a valid and honorable expression of group solidarity, untainted, morally justified and nonpolitical. Puerto Rican culture, built on the foundation of the New World's three "races" is simultaneously presumed to be empty of race or, at the very least, capable of transcending its significance. In practical terms, however, Black people are understood to have (the problematic) "race," while Indians—like Whites—have "culture" and spirituality. In the current climate of "color blindness" it is culture that remains an acceptable line of demarcation and defense. (Jiménez-Román 2001, 118)

Hence, just as multicultural regimes have facilitated greater politicization of culture (and ethnicity) than of race in Latin America and in the United States, discourses about race mixture in Puerto Rico (reinforced by the specter of a U.S. "Other") facilitated the greater politicization of "Puerto Rican culture" over "race" and promoted the construction of racism as a foreign (U.S.) phenomenon. Whether the subject is the ethnicization of blackness (in the case of South and Central Latin

America) or the folklorization of blackness (in the U.S. colony of Puerto Rico), both processes privileged notions of culture that fail to recognize racism as a key element of what counts as blackness in the first place. Both processes (ethnicization and folklorization) also contribute to the scripts that confine blackness to particular characteristics, ways of being, or sensibilities that fall outside modernity and are excluded from urban or contemporary scenarios of the nation. As Restrepo (2004) states in regard to the ethnicization of blackness in Colombia, "Who is or is not a member of the black community, and what black ethnicity means, have been rigidly defined through the pronouncement of laws and decrees" (707). Similarly, one can say that who or what constitutes Puerto Rican culture, and how blackness fits into its formulation of mixture, has been rigidly defined by cultural policies and discourses developed in response to Puerto Rico's colonial relationship to the United States.

Still, people do not just accept or reproduce the national scripts wholeheartedly but often work around them. In fact, the use of indigenous metaphors in the case of San Antón not only served to authenticate residents' claims of belonging to their barrio, but enabled them to bypass the tacit censorship on the question of racism. The metaphor of the "Indian reservation" and the Indio Antón's figurative address to the "white man from the mayor's house" allowed members of the Comité to criticize the mayor and his administration for acting just like the U.S. Anglos had acted against Native Americans. Ironically, Ponce's mayor (Churumba) did not have the phenotypic features that could earn him an unequivocal identity as "white" (even in the Puerto Rican context). Members of Ponce's elite could easily describe him as *mulato*. Yet when a San Antón resident (under the masquerade of the Indio Antón) refers to the mayor as the *hombre blanco* of the municipality of Ponce and when Comité members speak of the "Indian Reservation," they are also making a statement about the pertinence of race (and racism) for understanding the housing conflict at hand. Of course, in doing so, they bypass a collective black subjectivity. But to do otherwise (i.e., claiming to be the black victims of antiblack racism) would require a particular political construction of blackness aided by a movement and by technologies of racialization, similar to the ethnicization that Restrepo (2004) documents in Colombia, but not readily available in Puerto Rico. In the absence of a political movement or context that lends support, those who make such claims will most likely be called unpatriotic, ungrateful, or *acomplejados* (those with an inferiority complex), thereby losing general public appeal for their demands.

Furthermore, repertoires of cultural nationalism (and supporting theories of benevolent slavery) have sanctioned indigenous defiance by presenting the Indian (not the African) as the true representative of resistance to Western dominance. In this context of conflict, evoking indigeneity thus not only serves to validate claims to the barrio's ecological patrimony, but is also a way to legitimize resistance against the privileged "white" sectors (the *blanquitos*) who want to tamper with it. The no-longer-tangible but recognized Taíno (not the African) is the sanctioned protector of the national patrimony against North American racism and encroachment (see chapters by Dávila and Jiménez-Román in Haslip-Viera 2001). In confronting a populist administration that claimed to be upholding Puerto Rican traditions against North American influence, San Antón residents thus adopted a discursive strategy that allowed them to denounce racism without assuming a subjectivity (i.e., black) that dominant discourses have declared irrelevant for the contemporary Puerto Rican mixed nation.

To sum up, the ability to confront powerful actors and structures is always circumscribed by the options available, and those options are in turn constrained by the ideological baggage that prevails and by the kinds of subjectivities available at a particular place and moment in time. Certainly, the scripts of blackness as construed within national discourses of race mixture frame and limit how residents of San Antón can represent themselves and make their demands visible. Yet I have examined two aspects that warrant consideration in the process of assessing such effects. First, even when working within the limits of racial scripts, the result is not a carefree development that spontaneously emerges from within the community without conflict or strife. Rather, it is a negotiated process that reveals political stakes and interests that support such scripts. And second, when the scripts of blackness do not necessarily fit the problem at hand, people grab on to other scripts available (the indigenous ethnic paradigm, for example), making the ongoing construction of racial subjectivity even more evident.

Of course, the options at hand are not infinite. As I explained, the concept of "culture" (be it "Puerto Rican," "Afro-Latino," or even "Taíno")—and not antiracism—has become the acceptable language for struggling against colonial and racial oppression. Furthermore, Puerto Rico's relationship to the United States makes such culturalist discourses and strategies more attractive, viable, and palatable to the public than others. Yet, to the extent that the relationship of Puerto Rico to the United States is itself ambiguous and fraught with contradictions, discourses of Hispanophilia, benevolent slavery, and race mixture are subject to contestation in the production of irresolute identity effects. My aim has been to show that people oftentimes find ways through the cracks of such inconsistencies to get their point across and leverage their demands, sometimes in favor of and sometimes against the grain of academic, nationalist, or otherwise essentialist expectations about blackness and its scripts.

Conclusion

> Black consciousness does not simply entail respect for our way of
> dancing. Our appropriation of culture has to lead us each time to claim
> more ownership of our human, social and economic resources,
> so that we can improve them and change the position in which our
> communities have been historically located.
>
> —Dorina Hernández

In July 2010, three years after I conducted fieldwork in San Antón, a law was passed declaring the community an area of historic and cultural interest.[1] The law made no mention of constructing additional "historic housing" there. Rather, it called on the Institute of Puerto Rican Culture and the municipal government to join in the identification of the barrio as the "cradle of the *plena*," authorizing the establishment of a fund for its "historic development."[2] The four-page exposition constituting a rationale for the law described *plena* as a nationally recognized patrimony of Ponce, quoting various "experts" on the matter. One stated that the *plena* "lacks, as all folkloric music, polished and stylish qualities. It is rudimentary and intimate, quotidian and raw."[3] Another indicated the genre came about when a group "gave themselves with pleasure to the new dance, . . . [and] became so excited that somebody, possessed by a strange frenzy, shouted in his unconsciousness: *Plena!*"[4] With respect to the reference to the "genre's cradle," the law described San Antón as "a barrio that refuses to disappear and be absorbed by the *urbanizaciones*,"[5] adding that "San Antón is the picturesque barrio of Ponce that could very well be the Loíza [a town] of Santurce [a barrio] or, so as to not cross the people of Ponce, we could say that Loíza in Santurce is the San Antón of Ponce [*sic*]."[6]

Today, one can find a public sign that reads "Bo. San Antón, Cuna de la Bomba y la Plena" (Barrio [abbreviated] of San Antón: The Cradle of the Bomba and Plena) along main road #2 with an arrow pointing to the right. As one turns and follows the road toward San Antón, one sees a metal sculpture (displaying two male musicians with *panderos* accompanied by a female dancer) raised by the *municipio* in honor of *la plena*. The sculpture located in the small plaza at the entrance of the community was inaugurated in November 2012, following the passing of the law in 2010.

It is doubtful that the monument will benefit San Antón. Political merit may accrue to the *municipio*, and remuneration and recognition will go to the artist (who is not from San Antón). Nevertheless, in some ways *bomba* and *plena* have ensured the barrio's continuity in Ponce's landscape. According to San Antón musician and folklorist Carlos "Cao" Vélez Fransceschi, the *bomba* and *plena* festivals prevented the community's disappearance. In his words: "In 1977 and '78 they wanted to eliminate San Antón, they wanted to construct multilevel buildings, eliminate all the history and events . . . They had already splintered the barrio, because there was no protest movement. [Then] in 1978 we created the movement, and with the same Fiestas of Bomba and Plena we aimed to preserve San Antón, and this we accomplished"[7] (Carlos "Cao" Vélez in Primera Hora 2008).

Indeed, in the late 1970s, just as in the late 1990s, the celebration of Afro–Puerto Rican folklore in San Antón strengthened the political and communal protests against the government's plans to expropriate land there. However, the public-policy and development rhetoric prevailing in the 1970s varied substantially from that of the 1990s. While residents used folklore in the 1970s to counteract a policy focused on "development and modernization" that threatened to relocate residents, in the 1990s residents confronted a state discourse that focused on "culture" and the preservation of the community's historic patrimony.

This emphasis of the 1990s made the housing project a difficult target to criticize, at least from a liberal or "leftist" perspective. Compared to previous government policies that dismantled communities and moved people from slums into transitional *caseríos* (Dinzey-Flores 2007), San Antón's project was a significant improvement. It took into consideration residents' need to rely on family and friendship networks for survival by not forcing an exodus during the renovations or after their completion. The housing project also provided some members of this long-standing community with better infrastructure and gave property titles to residents who did not have them previously. It also represented a challenge to trends that established the whitened middle-class, nuclear-family housing model of the *urbanización* as the norm by following a more community-centered logic that sought to facilitate the support of neighbors and family.

Moreover, the housing project tried to challenge traditional Eurocentric approaches in urban planning that efface black communities from the canon of history and historic zones. As it is, San Antón's houses, with their "historical" color and traditional facades, are visually attractive and stand in the landscape as evidence

Figures 21a and 21b. Views of the housing project in 2013. Photos by author.

of an institutional effort recognizing a black community as part of a *municipio*'s historic patrimony (see Figures 21a and 21b). The fact that this unique initiative unfolded in Ponce, the cradle par excellence of a *criollo* elite, was and continues to be significant. In this way, the community activism of the 1970s mentioned by Cao Vélez combined with the liberal outlook of architects and planners in the 1990s to produce a development strategy that broke with previous relocation models of displacement. This partly explains why certain community leaders, folklorists, and cultural activists supported the initiative and remained at the margins when controversy ensued at the time of my fieldwork.

As a young researcher in the 1990s, my critical stance toward this project was (and still is) made uncomfortable and uneasy by such factors. However, the protests waged by San Antón residents at the time also evidenced that innovations and appropriations of "culture," no matter how well intended, run into trouble when designed from above and from outside. This is partly because, in the process of recognizing and celebrating marginalized communities and their cultural products, states and national elites (even cultural producers themselves) often flatten out or conceal the power dynamics that shaped the sites and community practices in the first place. To the extent that these efforts and their silences become entangled in national discourses and scripts that inform state practices, such sanctioned celebrations can also exacerbate racial inequalities. In this way, the same law that celebrates San Antón as the cradle of the *plena* describes *plena* as the "unpolished" product of unconscious excitement, likening the community of three hundred persons to a municipality (Loíza) of more than thirty thousand inhabitants and stating that Loíza is a sector of Santurce. However, Loíza is a town (not a sector of Santurce), and Santurce is actually a district of the municipality of San Juan.[8] The fact that the erroneous comparison and the derogatory characterization of *plena* go unquestioned, becoming part of a law, illustrates that the scripted emplacement of blackness often confounds, simplifies, and diminishes how African heritage is conceived at the national level.

Scripts of Blackness

My goal with this book has been to look critically and historically at these processes of representation and their effects.[9] To this end, rather than document local manifestations of African heritage in Ponce or Puerto Rico, I explore different vantage points on what counted as African heritage in the first place and how San Antón became marked as an emblematic site of said heritage at a particular moment in time. Overall, the book is thus intended as a case study of how communities or regions become known and celebrated as "black" in American contexts where race mixture and whitening (*blanqueamiento*) are valued as normative and how people deal with that process.

To understand the powerful discourses that structure such dynamics, I proposed the idea of "scripts" as a useful theoretical framework for conceptualizing the institutionalized and sanctioned stories told about the "positive" attributes that particular racial heritages add to Puerto Rican culture. In particular, I defined scripts of blackness as dominant frameworks that set standards, expectations, and spatial templates for what gets to be publicly recognized and celebrated as black *and* Puerto Rican. Preceding chapters present racial scripts and the supporting national discourses separately to illustrate their emergence in specific historical and socioeconomic circumstances. However, when considered as a whole, these scripts scaffold an overall national story that goes something like this:

> Once upon a time, there was an island inhabited by valiant and nature-loving indigenous Taínos. They defended their motherland bravely from the Spanish colonizers but were eventually decimated by war, disease, and exploitation. To create a substitute labor force, Spaniards introduced African slaves. Over time, the three races (Indian, Spaniard, and African) blended, because the Spaniards, being Catholic, practiced a benign form of slavery and were more prone to mixing than the Protestant and utilitarian Anglo-Saxons. Hispanic culture predominated because Puerto Rico (unlike the English and French Caribbean) was not a plantation colony, and there were very few slaves (i.e., blacks) on the Island. Slaves settled in coastal towns, but the majority of the inland population was Hispanic (or European in Ponce). This is why Puerto Ricans have whitened over time. And even if not all Puerto Ricans are white, their culture is Hispanic, since Puerto Ricans (unlike people in the United States) harmoniously blended all racial heritages into one culture. Still, Puerto Ricans carry the African influence in their blood, as evidenced by their love for music, their sociable and happy spirit, and their body rhythm, spontaneity, and *sandugueria* (spirited flavor). These cultural attributes (which all Puerto Ricans share) can still be appreciated in a relatively pure form as they surface naturally in a few exceptional coastal communities that have preserved this influence against the modernizing forces of Americanization.

Conclusion • 231

This national story (albeit oversimplified and caricatured here) is supported by a number of key discursive processes and scripts that may be pertinent to other sites and regions racialized as black across Afro-Latin America. First is the systematic use of "black" as an unspoken yet ever-present category that people attach to spaces and communities via metaphors and symbols that racialize particular communities and bodies as exceptional and exotic, while constructing the rest of the nation as nonblack. In Chapter 1, for example, I show how the commonwealth government in Ponce deploys the idea of the *patio* (with its matrifocality, facilitation of family togetherness, enablement of *bomba* and *plena* performance, associations with the past, and "unchanging" nature) to mark San Antón as distinct from other Puerto Rican communities.

Second, discourses of benevolent slavery bolster the racialization of such communities (and related meanings) as exceptional by creating sites of "condensed slavery," where the historical effects of bondage are exaggerated and simplified by a politics of erasure. These forms of representation minimize the impacts of slavery at the national level, equate blackness with slave status, and recast the numerous free people of color as a mixed (not-black) group. Such politics of erasure entails a concomitant simplification of the history of racialized coastal communities like San Antón that homogenize the community's ancestral population as just slave and "black." I argue that these politics simultaneously render the rest of the Island (and the interior highlands in particular) as more representative of the mixed (whitened) nation, where slavery is cast as accidental.

Third, I maintain that discourses of Hispanicity support such scripts of the celebrated "exceptional" black community by placing a high premium on the concept of culture—and Hispanic culture in particular—as the key, defining element that differentiates national Puerto Rican whiteness from foreign U.S. Anglo-Saxon whiteness. I show how *criollo* elites and U.S. colonizing discourses support notions of Hispanic whiteness, although distinctly. Still, whether anti-American or friendly toward the United States, colonials and *criollo* nationals alike strategically deploy notions of Hispanicity as cultural markers of whiteness that promote *blanqueamiento*. As we saw, the notion of Hispanic whiteness in the ethnographic present informed architectural scripts, urban-planning expectations, and spatial templates deployed to mark San Antón as a historic site in Ponce's landscape.

Fourth, I argue that constructions of Hispanic whiteness as culturally normative confine the significance of Africa to biological qualities associated with the body—specifically blood or the dark color of the skin. Such ideas about the body as the locus of "African heritage" found continuity in the institutionalization of formulations of race mixture that construct the black ingredient of that mix as a self-evident, mindless, kinesthetic essence that runs through the veins of all national subjects and surfaces naturally. In this context, rhythmic, sexual, and sport-related abilities are conceived as carefree natural developments that emerge without conflict, work, or discipline. They also become de facto proxies for the implicit racialization of certain places and communities as black *and* national, leaving other attributes unavailable. In the last chapter, for example, I document the effects of racial scripts about the indigenous Taíno that ascribe to this ethnicity productive knowledge and attachment to the land, leaving these attributes "out of stock" for communities and residents racialized as black.

My exploration of how the community of San Anton was celebrated as a site of Afro–Puerto Rican traditions in the late 1990s aims to illustrate that these scripts and corresponding national discourses are much more than mere ideological constructs. They had concrete effects because they framed the production of community developments (in terms of housing models, living arrangements, and the kinds of cultural activities that were sponsored there), limiting what residents and nonresidents could say or know about the community in relationship to Puerto Rican history, culture, or contemporary circumstances.

At the same time, the effects and ideological hold of such scripts are not completely hegemonic. They are challenged and contradicted in everyday practice, through artistic performances, in academic works, in people's narratives about their past, and through the activities of political organizations. Chapters in each of the three preceding sections thus present challenges to the nation-building discourses and scripts supported by them. In presenting such alternatives, I also hope to show that challenges are complex and can simultaneously question one national script while reproducing or accommodating another.

Nation and the Politics of Blackness

This focus on the "scripts of blackness" and the national discourses that support them puts this work in dialogue with scholarship that has challenged national ideologies of *mestizaje* and *blanqueamineto* as homogenous constructions of nations that invisibilize black people and Afro-Diasporic cultural expressions. Scholars of Latin America, for example, have documented and theorized black people's struggles to gain empowerment as citizens, resist assimilation, and attain rights over resources based on strategies that call for state recognition of their cultural distinctiveness (Hale 2002; French 2009; Hooker 2005; Anderson 2009; Paschel 2010). Because such affirmations of racial difference often run counter to ideologies of *mestizaje*, which tend to erase blackness and homogenize people as mestizos, some scholars have described these manifestations in Latin America (including Puerto Rico) as antinationalist. For example, Whitten and Torres (1998) theorize the emergence of black populations in the Americas as "ethnic-blocs" that derive their powers "from a collective, inner sense of a oneness of a people, in contradistinction to nationalist racialist hegemony" (Whitten and Torres 1998, 8). They define black culture as "that which is worthy of reverential homage by black people *within* their communities, regions and nation states" (my emphasis), further arguing that these processes are "especially evident" in Puerto Rico, where *mestizaje* and *blanqueamiento* are challenged by black ethnic blocs (4, 14). According to the authors:

> The 1898 invasion of Puerto Rico by U.S. troops and the events thereafter give impetus there to the nationalist ideology of *mestizaje* and especially to the dimension of *blanqueamiento*. This ideology was further reinforced by the view that the paternalist social order of the plantation contributed to the social integration of racial aggregates (Quintero-Rivera 1987). More than a hundred years later these ideological and literary interpretations of Puerto Rico's past and ethnic heritage are being challenged by black urban and rural Puerto Ricans who have, since the formation of maroon groupings on the island, maintained their autonomy. It is clear that Puerto Rico, while not a nation-state, is nonetheless characterized by a nationalist ideology of *mestizaje*, on the one hand, and the formation of black ethnic blocs on the other. (Whitten and Torres 1998, 14)

Contrary to this interpretation, in this book I do not theorize people or communities who are racialized as black in Puerto Rico as ethnic groups or blocs. I hope preceding chapters demonstrate that, although people in San Antón did share a strong sense of belonging and solidarity among community members, this sense was not expressed in opposition to a national identity; neither was it based on a collective or common understanding of black culture or Afro–Puerto Rican or Afro-descendant identity.

In addition, beyond Puerto Rico, this book advances a proposition that differs from the previously cited approach to blackness in Afro-Latin America by arguing that racialized conceptions of "black communities" can sometimes, in fact, be sustained by and accommodated to nationalist ideologies (rather than challenging them). Scripted exaltations of black heritages, I argue, can serve national elite interests and ideologies of *blanqueamiento*, especially when they bind blackness to a place and define such places (and their attributes) as exceptional, raw, and fading elements of the nation. Since Puerto Rico is a U.S. territory, I pay special attention to how such national and racialized constructs operate vis-à-vis the United States, in between the interstices of colonialism and nationalism.

Because of this last emphasis, this project is also related to a long-standing body of research comparing U.S. race relations with Latin American racial systems. Classic approaches in this body of scholarship characterize Latin American race relations as more fluid, more ambiguous, and less rigid than the U.S. model (Harris 1970; Degler 1971; Duany 2002; Skidmore 1974; Seda-Bonilla 1968; Bourdieu and Wacqant 1999; Rodríguez 1994). Other researchers recognize the difference but emphasize underlying similarities between both models, highlighting the prevalence of racist dynamics that respond more to a binary rationale of exclusion than to a fluid logic of racial mixture or upward mobility (Goldstein 1999; Skidmore 1993; Winant 1992; Sheriff 2000; Helg 1997; Telles 1999; Andrews 1992).[10] In this book, I propose a somewhat different line of inquiry. Rather than comparing one racial system to the other, I consider the contrast itself as a constitutive force in the formulation of racial nationalisms, especially for Afro-Latin American and Caribbean contexts strongly influenced by U.S. intervention. In this undertaking, I take a cue from scholars who have called for more ethnographic engagement with the everyday effects of U.S. colonialism and examination of U.S. foreign interventions as part of "American Studies" (Lutz 2006; Kaplan and Pease 1993; Desmond 2007). Hence, although the focus of the book has not been Puerto Rico's neighbor to the north, I approach the United States as "the elephant in the room"—a privileged, albeit somewhat phantasmagoric, imperial interlocutor of the dominant nationalist discourses that frame "race" in Puerto Rico.

With this in mind, I propose (1) benevolent slavery, (2) Hispanicity, and (3) race mixture as three interrelated discourses that play key roles in the process of forging a racial nationalism in Puerto Rico vis-à-vis the United States. I argue that, availed by these discourses, intellectuals, politicians, and everyday people construct Puerto Rico as a morally superior nation in contrast to the United States, with its perceived ruthless history of slavery, Anglo-Saxon whiteness, and segregated "races." Although these are not the only discourses at play, I identify them as prominent narratives that make race an explicit and visible aspect of a national identity crafted in opposition to the United States. Moreover, I argue that these discourses are particularly important for containing, "taming," or co-opting the ideological role of blackness in the process of forging that national difference. Other key arguments made in relationship to this main proposition are summarized here.

The Role of History

Constructions of nation and "black difference" previously documented are ethnographic but also inherently historical. I take this lead from Rolph Trouillot's (1995) understanding of the past as something that does not exist independently from the present. For Trouillot, "the past—or more accurately, pastness—is a position" shaped by the very conditions and pressures that influence how history is produced (15). In accordance with this proposition, I have followed a three-pronged line of inquiry, applied with different emphases throughout the chapters. First, I examined the kinds of narratives that historians, politicians, and other intellectuals tell about the Puerto Rican past in order to justify and sustain their political projects and national aspirations. Correspondingly, I asked how they validate their notions of nation and "race" (and particularly of blackness) through history. Second, I looked at particular periods in order to examine the economic and social circumstances that produce certain kinds of intellectual and racial nationalisms. Here, I asked how historical circumstances help shape the particular racialized conceptions of nation that emerge at particular times. Finally, I used ethnography to illustrate how these historically informed ideas shape scripts that are deployed in complicated and contested ways by people in the ethnographic present. Accordingly, I asked how people make sense of dominant stories told about the nation and its racialized constituents, and how their everyday practices correspond (or not) to those historically shaped discourses and stories. In answering these questions, I try to understand why certain discourses arise at certain periods, and also why evoking a particular past (i.e., slavery, Spanish occupation, abolition, U.S. colonialism) becomes more or less significant for present-day circumstances.

The Political Mobilization of Racial Scripts and Discourses

Because racial discourses are part and parcel of nation building and governing efforts (not just in Puerto Rico but in Latin American and the Caribbean), preceding chapters also have illustrated how racial discourses and scripts take on diverse emphases along political party lines. In Puerto Rico, the United States plays a key role in this process, as competing parties advocate for statehood, political independence, or more political autonomy as U.S. citizens. In this charged terrain, political parties challenge the national propositions of their contenders, selectively deploying various notions of "race" (Hispanicity, blackness, Taíno indigeneity, or race mixture) differently in debates about the status of the Island.[11]

In terms of the political mobilization of "blackness," I discuss how supporters of statehood at the beginning of the twentieth century claimed to defend the *raza de color* (colored race), arguing that Puerto Rico's permanent alliance with the United States would enable the black and *mulato* poor working classes to counteract the privileged status of national elites, bringing them economic prosperity and fair treatment. Still, as Rodríguez-Silva documents (2012), pro-statehooders and other political organizations at the turn of the century approached blackness cautiously, highlighting the class (poverty) dimensions of a black identity to bridge alliances with the labor movement, but rejecting strategies that relied on racial solidarity or a politicized black identity that could threaten negotiations with colonial authorities. The same can be said of autonomists and independence supporters, who denied the pertinence of an autochthonous black identity (including Palé's interpretation of it) in the 1930s, and of pro-commonwealth leaders like RHC, who emphasized Hispanized mixture as the mark of the nation during the 1980s.

Likewise, during my fieldwork in the 1990s, I documented how pro-statehooders placed a premium on a modernity that deemphasized blackness, while commonwealthers mobilized blackness as the traditional vestige of a blended Puerto Rican national culture in San Antón. My ethnographic exploration of these issues focused on Ponce, but politicians in the towns of Loíza (Hernández-Hiraldo 2006b) and Caguas (Lloréns and Carrasquillo 2008) have also mobilized blackness in "defense of Puerto Rican traditions" against pro-statehood contenders' rhetoric of modernity and progress.

Previous chapters also documented how political parties mobilized notions of whiteness differently. In Chapter 4, I documented how in the 1930s supporters of autonomy and independence mobilized notions of Hispanic whiteness (vis-à-vis Anglo-whiteness) to legitimize their capacity for self-government and autonomy in the face of colonial discourses that declared them incompetent. In contrast, they represented Anglo-Saxons as utilitarian, young, and impulsive. Pro-statehooders at the turn of the century, however, upheld these other whites from the north as representative of a democratic authority that could overturn Spain's backward rule of castes upon Puerto Rico.

Finally, there is the politicization of the indigenous Taíno, especially by supporters of political independence, to epitomize the defense of the motherland against the exploitive force of the U.S. colonizers (see chapters in Haslip-Viera 2001). In Chapter 7, I discussed how the mythic figure of the *Taíno* and corresponding racial scripts were also mobilized by people in San Antón to defend their land and *sucesiones* against the perceived threat of the municipal government's intention to expropriate their properties.

Notwithstanding these different racial emphases along party lines, leading figures and ideologues from *all* political affiliations mobilize the notion of racial mixture to describe Puerto Rico as a racially harmonious society. In fact, racial harmony becomes key for demonstrating the capacity for governance and political success, regardless of status preference. For example, pro-statehood leaders of the early twentieth century boosted their political credentials for local rule by emphasizing local racial harmony and by positing Puerto Ricans as mere spectators of the U.S. racial problem. The commonwealth party also presented Puerto Rico as a mixed and racially harmonious society to boost capitalist investment needed for Operation Bootstrap in the 1940s and 1950s. Similarly, supporters of political independence and the commonwealth described racism as a foreign U.S. problem that Puerto Ricans transcended, predicting that under statehood Puerto Ricans would be discriminated against as second-class citizens of the United States.

Thus, when analyzed as a whole, all political parties shared a long-standing hemispheric logic that privileged *blanqueamiento*, disregarded racism as a social-structural problem, and subordinated blackness in formulations of cultural nationalism. Additionally, U.S. colonial authorities also supported these ideas as a safeguard and justification for their development agendas and overseas investment. To the extent that blackness became a hemispheric "problem" of governance associated with political instability, all of these powerful actors—*criollo* elites, U.S. colonials, political party leaders—promoted the idea of racial harmony to lend credence and legitimacy to a successful outcome for their governing aspirations.

In unpacking how different formulations of "race" become politicized, I thus aimed to capture how people produce alternatives and try to negotiate their place in the nation without being able to completely free themselves from the racial hierarchies that those national and political discourses engender. At the same time, my ethnographic exploration illustrates that although people in San Antón adopt political discourses and their corresponding racial propositions, they do not necessarily base their life strategies on the precepts of political parties or nationalist discourses. Rather, strategies vary depending on people's position in a class/racial social hierarchy and the situational political junctures at play. Thus pro-statehooders who did not own land and lacked the means to fix the deteriorating conditions of their homes accepted the commonwealth "traditional" housing model (in spite of the party's emphasis on modernity). Similarly, there were commonwealth supporters who refused to sell their land and challenged the commonwealth rhetoric of traditions, assuming a Taíno identity to question the government's propositions.

It is clear that such dynamics of mobilizing racial scripts and discourses extend beyond party politics. Throughout the ethnographic material and in the preceding interviews, we see instances when people share a tacit and even normative commitment to a politics of conviviality or civility that rejects the potential disruptions that could happen if a more militant or autochthonous black identity were voiced. The tension is not always alleviated or avoided by suppressing race talk as Sheriff (2000), Rodríguez-Silva (2012), and others have argued. People can also evoke racial scripts to make "race" sanctioned in ways that reinforce the fiction of racial harmony. At the same time, people may adopt less sanctioned forms of race talk in other situations. In any case, the question of how and when people see fit to disrupt the scripts or not in order to promote class solidarity, regional unity, or communal conviviality is an issue that deserves further attention and theorizing.

Space, Place, and Race

Since all chapters draw on the ethnography of the housing project and the construction of a particular community as black, "space" and "place" emerged as important variables for my exploration of race. As stated in the introduction, notions of blackness are often "emplaced" via their association with regions and neighborhoods that can be characterized as dangerous, folkloric, or both (as is the case with San Antón). My analysis focuses on the folkloric scripts that characterize this emplacement of blackness. However, the role of place itself in this process is important, because "racial" dynamics of exclusion/inclusion are often made concrete and tangible through place and the spatial demarcation of social boundaries. Zaire Dinzey, for example, argues that "housing and neighborhoods frame race. If race is slippery or fugitive in language... in physical structures it is frozen" (Dinzey-Flores 2013, 134). Similarly, Patricia Price (2012) states that "race itself can be understood as a politics of location or emplacement" (801) and that although "race is a malleable social formation, it is never divorced from place and is therefore never entirely divorced from the frictions of place, nor place from the frictions of race. Race, like place, is never totally fluid" (807).

The argument is particularly relevant for Puerto Rico and other sites in Afro-Latin America, where discourses of race mixture, racial democracy, and *mestizaje* often silence and delegitimize racial identities resulting from racist dynamics of privilege or exclusion and marginalization. As racial identities such as white and black are silenced by discourses of racial mixture that claim to have erased racism and polar extremes of difference, places often become sanctioned proxies for such identities. Thus, even though people might hesitate to recognize "black" or "white" as legitimate personal identities in the mixed-race nation, the notions of black neighborhoods or neighborhoods of *blanquitos* (wealthy white people) are unequivocally recognized. In fact, people may use the name of a neighborhood or region instead of a particular racial category to describe a person's race/class position (Bonilla-Silva 2006; Wade 1993; Appelbaum 1999).

Without undermining the particular histories of communities or regions, I argue that part of the reason such emplacement of race (and particularly of blackness) is so customary is because it allows people to segregate these spaces and construct nonblackness as the normative mark of the nation. Such processes facilitate the construction of the coast as black and foreign, and the exaltation of the mountainous interior as typical and nonblack. This also happened at the municipal level as people referred to the barrio as the place where "black people" live. In fact, the mere demarcation of San Antón as a distinct community in Ponce's landscape (and residents' efforts to ensure its continuity) became inevitably entangled with discourses that equate blackness to musical folklore, "the past," and the fading properties of racial mixture.

For this same reason, the management and representation of space within the community (linear model or family bloc model) also became inextricably entangled with racial scripts and the national discourses that support such ideologies. At the same time, this spatial plan coexisted with other spatial markers, such as lampposts and architectural designs that served to designate San Antón as a historical zone of the aristocratic city.

Since people also often interpret notions of progress and traditions in relationship to Americanization and Puerto Rico's position vis-à-vis the United States, the question of how to manage the emplacement of blackness in San Antón was implicated in discourses about the community's difference or sameness with respect to Puerto Rico and the United States. In this way, space, place, and the spatial dynamics that developed during my fieldwork acted as vectors that "raised the volume" or "put a spotlight" on what are often silenced or taken-for-granted discourses of *blanqueamiento*, thereby making more evident the racial discourses and scripts I document in the present book. The fact that these scripts were not just materialized "on stage" (as in the form of a folkloric performance) but in permanent housing arrangements that affected people's everyday lives also enables me to ground these discourses, documenting their contradictory applications and people's responses to them.

Continuing Transformations in San Antón

After sixteen years of doing fieldwork, the housing initiative in San Antón continues to be a problematic development for me to examine, its current outcomes still difficult to ascertain in absolute terms. A total of forty-seven units are now aligned along the five streets that constitute the renovated section, with the last houses built in 2008. As had been agreed in 1996, residents who did not want to sell their property were not forced to move into the housing project and remained in their previous lots and houses (a population estimated at 180) outside the quadrangle of the renovated area. Hence the new "historic" housing coexists with the previous family structures and *patios* in the barrio.[12]

When I visited in 2013, most homes in the housing project looked well-kept and adorned. Marian said she likes her house and that she made the right decision in moving there. From her point of view, the wooden structure has sustained the wear and tear of the past years well, although water pipes sometimes break. Pedro is of the same positive opinion, especially because he now owns a house, whereas previously he rented. Mario, a longtime resident, was especially proud of his house and over the years made various improvements such as an eight-foot concrete fence that divided his property from his immediate neighbors' (they were not part of his family group). He also built a garage for his car, constructed a barbeque area at the back, and painted his home with his own choice of colors. Among his property assets, he mentioned a coconut palm, a mango, and an avocado tree.

A couple of streets down from Mario's home live Fabiola and Margarita, the mother and daughter of an extended family previously forced to sell their land when the Electrical Authority established itself there (prior to 1960). After the government expropriated the land of their *sucesión* to build the electrical towers, they were told they could construct new houses on the land surrounding the towers. The land they occupied during the time of my fieldwork, nevertheless, still belonged to the Authority of Electrical Energy. Now, in the new development, mother and daughter own their individual house *and* plot. This is an advantage, although their current plot is not even a fraction of what had been the *sucesión* of their ancestors, before the government expropriated it to install the electrical infrastructure.

Yet not all families thought the same. Seven families refused to move into the renovated section, even though their houses were also on land belonging to the Authority of Electrical Energy. Carmen, a member of one of these families, said she preferred to stay where she is because she is more comfortable there and has more privacy. She said that her friend Maria (whose family had always lived in San Antón) recently left the development because she could no longer bear the noise and disturbances in the house she occupied in the renovated area. Carmen, in her location, did not have such problems. However, she did not have the benefit of the new sewer system, either. All the residents who, like her, lived outside the renovated area had to rely on the same septic-tank system that was in place when I did fieldwork sixteen years earlier. But Carmen did not mind. She said in her current home she does not have to pay for electricity and her water bill is not high. Water bills in the new housing project, by contrast, are calculated with new equipment. "*Esos contadores son unos 'atletas,'*" she said, "*Corren a las millas los condenaos!*" (Those water meters are athletes. They run really fast, those suckers!)[13]

Ernesto, a musician and member of another *sucesión*, also said he wouldn't move. He said his house gets a wonderful breeze, just where it is. In the yard owned by his family he has space for parking and many trees. When I asked him where I could find Victoria, matriarch of one of the biggest *patios* in San Antón, he commented, "*Ese patio lo rompieron*" (That patio was broken up). They now lived in the renovated area. He explained that the land of their *sucesión* was still there, but the municipality had cleared the lot, and now family members were scattered throughout the renovated project.

When I found Victoria (now ninety-five years old), she was sitting in a chair in the living room of her niece's house, which was next to hers in the renovated segment of San Antón. Her eyesight was almost gone but her reasoning just fine. When I asked her what she thought of her now not-so-new house, she said she preferred her old one because "*Esa casa, mi mama luchó mucho para tenerla, vendiendo frituras, pasteles y esas cosas*" (That house, my mother struggled a lot to have it, selling fritters, *pasteles*, and those things). To my surprise, she said the municipality had not paid her for her old house or for her land. After all these years, she seemed most upset about not getting compensated for the house. "*La casa, ellos dicen que no vale mucho, como $12,000 o $13,000 . . . que esto vale poco, que lo otro es poco, poco esto, poco *lo otro, todo poco"* (They say that the house is not worth a lot, like $12,000 or $13,000 ... that this is not much, that other things are not much, everything is not much).

Future Directions . . .

While recognizing that marginalized communities have drawn on racial scripts and notions of black culture to demand recognition and rights as citizens across the Americas and that folklore is deeply felt and embodied, with this book I seek to look critically at how signs and practices associated with African heritage are selectively incorporated in state- and government-sponsored narratives that deem other, nonscripted accomplishments as *poco* (not much). In a context of assailed sovereignty, where the United States is a key player in determining "outside interests," the impetus of this relationship can encourage and buttress racial exclusions in national and multicultural discourses. In these contexts, struggles for social justice might be framed in terms of a colonial versus national dichotomy, or a national versus a U.S. way. However, an effective antiracist movement would need to come to terms with the fact that racism functions well on both sides of those equations and that "culture," "multiculturalism," or "ethnicity" are not flawless positions from which to launch an antiracist alternative.

This book stems from the conviction that questioning the political factors and ideological constraints that limit how black people and communities are incorporated as part of the "national culture" puts one in a better position to construct alternative nationalist narratives with more liberating, antiracist, and just possibilities. One can start by imagining a future in which African heritage and its legacy are not conceived as a few scattered "hot spots" and in which the contemporary effects of slavery and colonialism—as manifested in the structural and personal dimensions of racism—can be narrated as part of *"lo nacional"* (that which is national). In this future, narratives about slave resistance, about the agency of free people of color—their resilience, solidarity, and wide-ranging efforts at surviving a racist society (acquiring land!)—would be told as part of a national story, widely available, especially to those who are impacted most directly by racial inequality and the economic effects of modern-day colonialism (whether they live in the coast, mountain, or urban areas). Without ignoring regional specificities and histories, it should also be possible to recognize innovative practices and current accomplishments (in art and technologies) of black people and communities as modern *and* national—rather than dismissing them as Americanized or foreign imitations. In this future, intellect, innovation, entrepreneurship, modernity, resilience, solidarity, and knowledge of the land (including urban landscapes) could form an integral part of the repertoire of attributes Puerto Rican and other Afro-descendant people claim as part of their diasporic legacy. Such experiences, attributes, and orientations (which can also find legitimacy in history) need not be absent from the narratives one constructs to confront the effects of neo-colonialism or neo-liberalism, whether in the U.S. territory of Puerto Rico or elsewhere in Afro-Latin America. To craft alternative scripts as part of an antiracist agenda that seeks not just respect for music, dance, and spirituality, but also (as Dorina Hernández states in the epigraph) the transformation of the unequal distribution of resources, is to challenge the economic model that thrives on "othering" those who benefit less from the exploitation of their resources. The task might seem monumental, but to find the way, one only has to look closely at people's everyday struggles to find dignity in solidarity and in the sustained affirmation of their humanity.

* * *

A month prior to finishing this manuscript, a fire consumed two houses of San Antón in one of the *patios* that had not been part of the housing project. The reporter covering the story stated that a group of neighbors helped the family move the debris from the land that had been in their family's hands for almost a century. "*Todos somos dueños de los ranchitos que tenemos aquí*" (We are all owners of the small shacks we have here), stated one of the fire victims. The reporter stated the *municipio* will provide the families with materials to rebuild on the same land where their homes once stood. According to the newspaper, on the day of the fire, when the owner learned there was smoke coming from his house, he ran toward the site saying "he would rather open a tent and sleep [on his land] in San Antón than move to a public housing project" (Caquías Cruz 2013). Neighbors in San Antón organized a bingo fund-raiser two weeks later at the basketball court to help the family recuperate.

Notes

Introduction

1. As with all racial forms of identification, these terms are not free of the racial hierarchies that give them social significance, and translation is problematic. *Mulata* comes from "mule." However, the term is also used in literary, popular, and artistic works (particularly in popular music) to signal the various mixtures of people of African descent in Latin America. I use it to describe people who, like my dark-skinned aunts, were definitively not "white" but that in the Puerto Rican context would not be identified as "black" either.

2. Again, translation of this racial terminology is not simple. *Trigueño* literally means "wheat-colored" but can be used to describe a wide variety of nonwhite skin tones: black, lighter than black, or darker than white. It can also be deployed as a euphemism for *negro* (black). However, *trigueño* can also be used to describe a light-skinned person with a slightly tanned complexion (Godreau 2008c). *Jabao* can be roughly translated as "high yellow" and is used to identify a person with light skin and light eyes (blue or green) who has phenotypic features associated with blackness such as very curly or kinky hair and a wide nose or lips. *Jabao* has a more colloquial, informal use than the previously mentioned terms. *Colorá* is broadly applied and can describe people with light hair, light skin, or freckles (not necessarily people who have red haircolor). Elsewhere, I discuss how meanings attributed to these and other racial terms are context-driven and influence relationships among speakers (Godreau 2008b). For more information on racial terminology in Puerto Rico, see also Clarence C. Gravlee (2005).

3. Photographs were taken by author.

244 · Notes to Introduction

4. The chorus of a famous *plena* composition by Chago Montes confirms this reputation: "La plena que yo conozco no es de la China ni del Japón, porque la plena viene de Ponce, viene del barrio de San Antón" (The *plena* that I know is not from China or from Japan because the *plena* comes from Ponce, it comes from the barrio of San Antón).

5. The concept of "emplacement" is used in sociology and in social anthropology to highlight the fact that all social interaction happens in a particular place (Gieryn 2000) and that places are vested with social meaning, are constructed through social dynamics, and can impose meaning on social interactions. To say something is emplaced means that the interpretation, representation, and construction of "place" is a salient aspect of that process. Similarly, Hilda Lloréns (2008) refers to the practice of assigning and segregating blackness to certain neighborhoods in Puerto Rico as "geographic blackness" (204). For a specific analysis of how blackness is emplaced as folkloric or as urban in Puerto Rico, see Rivera-Rideau 2013.

6. Laura Lewis (2000) documents similar dynamics of identity in San Nicolás Tolentino, Mexico, a place recognized by outsiders as a bedrock of Afro-Mexican culture but where the majority of residents identify as *morenos* and reject the label *black* as it ethnicizes and highlights their difference vis-à-vis the Mexican nation.

7. Pabón's postmodern take on the issue of nationalism was also criticized by Luis Coss for not engaging politically with the problem of colonialism and for a pessimistic view regarding the feasibility of a politically liberated Puerto Rico (Coss 1996).

8. This was not the first time that racism was addressed by the Puerto Rican public or intellectual palestra. The pioneering work of Isabelo Zenón, José Luis González, and the group CEREP (Center for the Study of Puerto Rican Reality), as well as the performances of Sylvia del Villard, had already called attention to the systematic exclusion of blacks, or Africa more broadly, from dominant representations of Puerto Rico and Puerto Ricans (Zenón-Cruz 1975; González 1980; Ramos Rosado 1999, 40–42; Fundación nacional para la cultura popular 2012; Laureano 2010).

9. All academic texts and published materials written in Spanish are translated into English by the author, by her research assistant Sherry E. Cuadrado Oyola, or by Tomás Ayala. From this point on, when the original academic text was written in Spanish, this is acknowledged in a note. I reproduce Spanish sparingly due to length constraints.

10. The museum remained unofficially closed at different moments during 2011 and 2012. In 2012, a group of citizens organized a protest to denounce its closing (Primera Hora 2012; Trelles 2012). The Museum of the Americas, also administered by the Institute of Puerto Rican Culture, has since stated that it will relocate this museum's collections to a permanent exhibit, *The African Heritage*, which opened in October 2013 (Museo de las Américas 2013).

11. *Ley de Municipios Autónomos de Puerto Rico de 1991*. Law No. 81 of August 30, 1991, as amended (21_L.P.R.A. secs. 201 a 240). http://www.lexjuris.com/lexlex/municipio/lexlmen1.htm (accessed July 2013).

12. Rather than a top-down outcome of neoliberalism, the plan and public policy were rooted in Ponce's strong trajectory of civic engagement and middle-class participation, as the city has been a seedbed of liberal and political vanguard thought since the nine-

teenth century (Ayoroa-Santaliz 2003). For a similar treatment of the emergence of local autonomy claims in Argentina, see J. Miguel Kanai (2011).

13. Original text in Spanish.

14. Although Ponce was not the first to implement the historic revitalization of neighborhoods, the scope of the city's initiative must certainly be noted as a pioneer effort in Puerto Rico. Furthermore, the explicit and public intent to preserve the traditions of an Afro-Puerto Rican community through housing design and particular spatial arrangements is unique.

15. Kevin Fox-Gotham documents similar processes in New Orleans, where contrasting yet interconnected images represent the city as a place of love and romance, on the one hand, and of unrestrained and promiscuous sexual pleasure, on the other (Gotham 2007, 72).

16. I thank Norman Whitten and editor Janet Keller for bringing this body of literature to my attention.

17. This take has also been influenced by the earlier work of Ervin Goffman (1959) and dramaturgical perspectives developed thereafter on the normative standards that mediate social exchanges, the interpretation of body posture, clothing, gesture, and other symbolic actions at play in the everyday presentation of self.

18. The same can be said of the town of Loíza, which is simultaneously represented as both traditional and dangerously linked to contemporary crime activity. The coexistence of these constructions can be found in other sites of Puerto Rico and Afro-Latin America, and its effects deserve further research.

19. These broad categorizations are also challenged in contemporary practice. For example, the idea that *bomba* has to be performed in one particular place or on a stage is challenged by the emergence in 2000 of *bombasos*, street performances of *bomba* playing and dancing in Puerto Rico that moved from place to place, often held in a pub or bar in the metropolitan area or other urban areas (Barton 2000).

20. The Afro-Puerto Rican musical genres of *plena* and especially *bomba*, for example, were cultural practices deemed "uncivilized" and "primitive" by intellectual elites until incorporated in official and government-sponsored representations of Puerto Rican culture in the 1970s (Dávila 1997). Their inclusion in the national repertoire was the product of black people's individual and collective struggles to gain recognition of them as "Puerto Rican."

21. Voting statistics were obtained from the Web site of *La Comisión Estatal de Elecciones del Estado Libre Asociado de Puerto Rico* (the Commonwealth Electoral Commission of Puerto Rico): http://www.ceepur.org/es-pr/Paginas/default.aspx

22. For example, the threat that Haiti's revolution posed to the planter class in the Americas played a crucial role in subsequent interpretations of the institution of slavery as different and benevolent not just in Puerto Rico, but elsewhere in Latin America (Figueroa 2005; Giovannetti 2006; González Mendoza 2001). In the same way, the Dominican Republic has become an important interlocutor in hegemonic representation of Puerto Rico as "the whiter" of the Antilles (Duany 2006).

23. For related critiques on approaches to resistance, see Pyke 2010 and Brown 1996.

Chapter 1. Place, Race, and the Housing Debate

1. All interviews and field data in Spanish are translated to English by the author, by her research assistant, Sherry E. Cuadrado Oyola, or by Tomás Ayala. I reproduce Spanish sparingly due to length constraints.

2. The area marked as San Antón in the map is the main area associated with the barrio and where the housing project developed. However, there are two other, much smaller, settlements that also form part of San Antón (not shown in the map). These are located to the north of Las Américas Avenue, on the boundary with the Barrio Cuatro Calles and connecting with barrio Bélgica on the boundary with road #2.

3. When Constancia was inaugurated in the early 1960s, the cost of a house there ranged from $10,500 to $11,000 U.S. (information provided by Willie Vicens Realty).

4. My landlord's perspective calls to mind the housing reform movement of the 1940s and 1950s, which sought to equalize social differences by integrating neighborhoods. This movement responded to a New Deal philosophy that sought to avoid the creation of ghettos by placing low-income families next to affluent neighborhoods to promote integration and an example of civilized urban life (Dinzey-Flores 2013, 34–39). Of course, such policies also conferred a new set of stigmatized expectations on the places to be "integrated."

5. My Italian friends stated later that they were struck by Sonia's heavy use of makeup foundation on her face and the contrast its color made with the natural skin color of her neck. They thought that she was trying to appear whiter.

6. I believe Tavín's characterization of myself as "not black" coincided with how people in the community perceived me, although this could vary. A few times, residents referred to me as *jabá* or called attention to my hair or *nalgas* (buttocks) to make the point that I was not such an outsider or that I was welcomed. Still, overall, I believe I was perceived as a young, privileged, "off-white" outsider to the community.

7. *Trigueño* is derived from *trigo* (wheat) and literally means wheat-colored. However, it can be deployed as a euphemism for *negro* (black) to avoid the pejorative connotations derived from its association with slave status.

8. Calling someone *negro* often carries pejorative connotations, but the use of *negro* or its diminutive form *negrito* or *negrita* may communicate affection and intimacy.

9. Prior to 2000 (between 1960 and 1990), the census did not record the "race" of individuals. The local government (controlled for two decades by advocates of autonomy) eliminated the question in the 1950s. In 1992, a pro-statehood administration requested that Puerto Rico be provided with the same census form as the states of the Union. Since 2000, the Census Bureau has administered a translated version of the stateside questionnaire. Puerto Rican researchers have criticized the inadequacy of the U.S. Census's racial terminology for the Puerto Rican context (Godreau et al. 2010; Vargas-Ramos 2005; Duany 2002).

10. It is interesting, for example, that while 80.5 percent of island dwellers identified as white, only 47.2 percent of Puerto Ricans who live in the United States self-identified as white in the 2000 census, evidencing the locally specific nature of the definition of "Puerto Rican whiteness."

11. This inter-subjective dimension of how race feels, and the personal manifestations of experiencing an essentialized blackness, is not the focus of this book, but a topic that

deserves further attention. According to Karen Pyke (2010), the internalization of racial oppression among the racially subordinated has been largely ignored, reflecting an academic taboo on the subject. The recent book *Negro: Este color que me queda bonito* (2013), by Benito Massó Jr., addresses this inter-subjective dimension from the point of view of a Puerto Rican black man. Other works also discuss Puerto Rican black women's internalized racism and their perception of their bodies (Franco and Ortiz 2004; Franco Ortiz and Quiñones Hernández 2005; Santos Febres 1995).

12. Information provided by personnel of the Oficina de Ordenación Territorial del Municipio Autónomo de Ponce (phone communication).

13. Photographs of Figures 2a and 2b were taken by the author.

14. The question mark indicates the author is not sure of the date, as the pamphlet offers none. The pamphlet was in circulation and was obtained from the Tourist Office in Ponce in 1995.

15. Some people argued that the houses in this pro-statehood proposal were also wooden. However, according to Ponce's pro-statehood representative and San Antón resident Cuto Colón, the original plans were to build in cement.

16. Plan drawings were sent to the author by Ponce's Mayor's Housing Office on June 24, 1994.

17. Plan drawings were sent to the author by Ponce's Mayor's Housing Office on June 24, 1994.

18. Letter to the author, "Datos sobre San Antón solicitados durante entrevista el 15 de enero de 1995 con el Arq. Javier Bonnin Orozco," January 21, 1997.

19. Ibid.

20. Plan drawings were sent to the author by Ponce's Mayor's Housing Office on June 24, 1994.

21. According to the copy of the adopted agreement, held by the Permits Office of the Municipality of Ponce, "Autorizando Condicionado Desarrollo Preliminar para Rehabilitación en la comunidad San Antón," case number 95-63-C-563-UPGD; this building area corresponded to five plots of land that the municipal government intended to purchase, comprising a total of 3.20054 acres. Two of the biggest plots belonged to absentee landholders. The rest, however, were *patios* or *sucesiones* that had four or six housing units each.

22. Ibid.

23. All academic texts and other published materials written in Spanish were translated into English by the author, by her research assistant, Sherry E. Cuadrado Oyola, or by Tomás Ayala. From this point on, when the original academic text is in Spanish, this will be acknowledged in a note.

24. Article 549 of Puerto Rico's Civil Code, 31 LPRA section 1931, establishes the following: "Ownership and other property rights are acquired and transmitted by law, by gift, by testate or intestate succession, and, in consequence of certain contracts, by tradition. . . . It may also be acquired by prescription."

25. Two of the plots purchased by the government belonged to absentee landlords. The others belonged to families still residing in San Antón. The government subdivided and sold the new plots to residents who previously owned land. Those families who owned

property in San Antón had to sell their land to the government, divide the money among the rightful heirs, and use that amount to buy the new property. Because the project is heavily subsidized by federal funds, residents who did not own property paid monthly mortgage payments that fluctuate between $55 and $75. The government planned to compensate those who owned property (houses) so they could use part of that amount to pay the total cost of the new house. In a survey (2002), all of those making monthly payments said they considered the amount reasonable.

26. Plan drawings were sent to the author by Ponce's Mayor's Housing Office on June 24, 1994.

27. The government accomplished this by starting construction in an empty plot of land that they expropriated from an absentee owner. When the construction of the new houses was completed, they moved the first residents. Once residents moved into the new houses, their old houses were demolished and the estimated value of their property was credited toward the payment on their new house. New houses were then built in the area where the old houses were demolished, a second group of residents would then move, and so forth.

28. Original text in Spanish.

29. A letter sent to residents from the mayor's office stated: "A property title will be given to every owner for the lot and the structure which they don't have now. This title will have all the characteristics of a property title as described under the mortgage law and will be registered in the Property Register" (Cordero-Santiago 1996a; original text in Spanish).

30. This is stipulated in article 549 of Puerto Rico's Civil Code and ratified by the Supreme Court in the case *Feliciano Suárez, Ex parte*, 1986, 117 D.P.R. 402, which determined that "Succession, be it testate or intestate, is one of the ways or means of acquiring and transferring property and other rights and obligations of the deceased," meaning that formal inscription is not necessary to claim ownership. This information was shared with San Antón residents and in a public conference offered for the community of San Antón on May 15, 1996, by my father (Michel Godreau), who is a lawyer specializing in property rights.

31. Houses could have two, three, or four bedrooms and measure between 650 to 800 total square feet. Rooms had dimensions of 8.5 x 9.5 feet (Cordero-Santiago 1996a).

32. Original text in Spanish.

33. Traditional anthropological literature treated such family structure as a "different," if not deviant, aspect of Caribbean social life by pointing to the absence of male heads of household. Other scholarship interpreted aspects of black family structure as African retentions (Clarke 1957; Herskovits and Herskovits 1947; R. Smith 1957).

34. Original text in Spanish.

Chapter 2. Slavery and the Politics of Erasure

1. All interviews and field data collected in Spanish are translated to English by the author, by her research assistant, Sherry E. Cuadrado Oyola, or by Tomás Ayala.

2. Tannenbaum (1947) argued that these harmonious race relations came about as a result of certain historical processes in Spain and Portugal that entailed their previous experience with slavery; their more liberal legal traditions; and the role that Catholic religious institutions played in the integration of slaves, blacks, and Indians into the lower strata of their colonial society. His work showed how the Iberian moral and ideological conception of the slave-subject differed from that of the Anglo-Saxon.

3. All academic texts and published material written in Spanish are translated into English by the author, by her research assistant, Sherry E. Cuadrado Oyola, and by Tomás Ayala. From this point on, when the original academic text was written in Spanish, this is acknowledged in a note.

4. For a thorough analysis of this contrast in Blanco's work, see Díaz-Quiñones 1985, 42–46. For an analysis of this and other scholarship that supported the benevolent-slavery thesis, see Mayo Santana et al. 1997, 129–35.

5. Original text in Spanish.
6. Original text in Spanish.
7. Original text in Spanish.

8. Eric Williams (1957) criticized Tannenbaum for emphasizing the moral and ideological factors embedded in legal codes and downplaying the impact of economic and political factors on race relations. Harry Hoetink (1967) and Franklin Knight (1992) also questioned the distinction based on religious factors, pointing to similarities between countries of different variants in similar stages of economic development. Mintz also argued that slave regimes in Spanish colonies varied considerably among themselves, depending on the extent of the power of the planter class in the Caribbean society (Mintz 1989).

9. Puerto Rican historian Gervasio García uses the term "happy slavery" (*esclavitud alegre*) to describe such frameworks (García 1989, 49).

10. Sidney Mintz, for example, interpreted the color-blindness of forced-labor laws as a specific strategy employed by the planter class at a specific moment for the purpose of increasing production and profit; and not the manifestation of moral considerations or benevolent attitudes toward slaves (Mintz 1959). His critique, however, had more to do with supporting an economic rather than moral explanation, and was not so much targeted at denouncing racism in Puerto Rican society.

11. The majority of the articles examined were published in the main local newspaper, *El Nuevo Día*, which had the broadest circulation at the time.

12. Coverage focused primarily on racial discrimination suffered by individuals. Institutional dimensions of racism were seldom mentioned in the press.

13. The term *criollo* is usually used to identify Island-born sons of Spaniards who where white, relatively wealthy, and well educated and who aspired to lead the political destiny of the Island. For a detailed definition, see Cubano Iguina 1997, 638–40.

14. The abolitionist plaza where the kneeling statue was located was built in 1881.The statue by artist Victor Colt was installed later, in 1956 (Oficina de Desarrollo Cultural 2001).

15. The monument is placed at the Monument Park to Agüeybaná II, along Road #2 near the Plaza del Caribe commercial center in October 2008. Its plaque reads, *El Cacique*

enfrentó a los conquistadores españoles en la batalla de Yahueca en 1511 (The Indian chief confronted the Spanish conquerors in the battle of Yahueca in 1511).

16. There were also a number of legal ways in which people could buy or negotiate their social position as "whites" (see, for example, the colonial concessions called Gracias al Sacar). The Cédula came at a time when the revolutionary experience of Haiti (then Saint Domingue) had led, in the Caribbean, to a notion of independence in the Americas as something that was black (Sagrera 1973; González 1993; Trouillot 1995).

17. Loveman and Muniz also found similar strategies of "whitening," in early twentieth-century census documents, arguing that people reclassified themselves as white in the census by expanding the social definition of whiteness itself (Loveman and Muniz 2007).

18. Although smuggling continued, later treaties increased the cost of slaves, bringing Puerto Rican slave trade to a sharp decline by 1847 (Morales-Carrión 1978, 149).

19. Unlike the Spanish possessions, French and English colonies experienced a sustained trend of economic growth during the seventeenth and eighteenth centuries that was intimately tied to the metropolis's involvement in the colonial plantation economy and that depended increasingly on the steady influx of African slave labor.

20. Faced with the increasing losses in human resources during the seventeenth century, the Spanish crown offered slaves freedom if they converted to the Catholic faith. In the middle of the seventeenth century, there was a strong migration of slaves fleeing from Danish and other neighboring colonies to Puerto Rico looking for their freedom (Picó 1988, 98).

21. Original text in Spanish.

22. The term *marronage* literally refers to runaway slaves who escaped the plantation to live in retreat. However, Quintero uses the word figuratively to mean the act of living in retreat.

23. Duany later revised his postulate in his book *Puerto Rican Nation on the Move* (2002), in which he critiques the idealization of Puerto Rico's preindustrial rural past and its "white" subsistence farmers and the corresponding exclusion of African slaves, free people of color, and recent immigrants from the definition of the nation (Duany 2002, 20).

24. Original text in Spanish.

25. Spencer upheld the idea that geography and climate provoked an uneven evolution of the human species that produced different races, some of which were considered more fit and closer to civilization than others.

26. Sidney Mintz's study of Cañamelar also evidenced distrust toward blacks among lighter-skinned sugar-cane workers and the acceptance of whiteness as ideal.

27. Puerto Ricans can use the term in a pejorative way to describe someone who is shy, uneducated, or stupid.

28. An incident that points to its demise occurred in 1986, when the *jíbaro* monument was vandalized and splattered with black ink. Government officials ordered twenty-four-hour vigilance of the monument (Morales 1986, 38).

29. I asked people, "What is a *jíbaro*?," "Who is not a *jíbaro*?," and "Would you consider a black cane worker from the coast a *jíbaro*?"

30. The *seis* and the *aguinaldo* are musical forms derived from Spanish folklore, played with a guitar, a *cuatro*—a guitar-like instrument derived from the Spanish *vihuela*—and African- and Indian-derived percussion.

31. Original text in Spanish.

Chapter 3. Unfolkloric Slavery

1. All academic texts and published material written in Spanish are translated into English by the author, by her research assistant, Sherry E. Cuadrado Oyola, or by Tomás Ayala. From this point on, when the original academic text was written in Spanish, this is acknowledged in a note.

2. San Antón's population constituted about 2 percent of Ponce's total population during the latter part of the nineteenth century. Free people of color constituted the majority of the population throughout this period.

3. Sources: Ponce's Historical Archive. Box #: S54-S548, S-599. Junta de Planificación de Puerto Rico's pamphlet "Ponce y Sus Barrios."

4. Original text in Spanish.

5. All interviews and field data collected in Spanish are translated to English by the author, by her research assistant, Sherry E. Cuadrado Oyola, or by Tomás Ayala.

6. There is, however, a document listing heads of households in the barrio for that same year.

7. Source: Historical Archives of the Autonomous Municipality of Ponce, Puerto Rico.

8. For a more detailed treatment of the topic of house and land ownership in Guayama among *libertos*, and *liberto* women in particular, see L. Figueroa 2005 (151–65).

9. Original text in Spanish.

10. *Hacendados* also used certain dispositions of the abolition law that obliged *libertos* to work for them under contract for a period of three years (Ramos-Mattei 1982).

11. Labor Gómez, for example, concluded that the plantation in Puerto Rico was color-blind. Upon examining a series of forced-labor laws known as El Régimen de la Libreta (184973), which obliged unemployed freemen and landless peasants to work with slaves in plantations, he maintained that racism could not have taken hold in a society in which white peasants and black slaves worked side by side (Gómez Acevedo 1970, 101).

12. In his nineteenth-century report, the English general George Flinter also notes that "the mulattos in the colonies have a mortal dislike toward slaves, and hoping to climb to a higher sphere, they strongly adhere to whites with whom they always unite in common defense against the Negroes" (Flinter 1976[1832], 31; original text in Spanish).

13. At the time of our interview, Don Carlos lived with his son, Roberto, who looked after him. His daughter, a nurse who lived in Constancia, also helped.

14. Other documents disclose that Hacienda Matilde was owned by the *hacendado* Juan Pratz (Mayoral-Barnés 1946, 33). Unfortunately, I found no other references to corroborate that location, and these names never came up in my interviews with community elders.

252 · Notes to Chapters 3 and 4

15. According to historian Francisco Scarano, these immigrants generally combined sugar production with import–export business operations, establishing their own trading firms or acting as intermediaries for powerful merchants in Saint Thomas, the United States, and Europe (Scarano 1989, 44; original text in Spanish).

16. By 1913, Hacienda Estrella is no longer listed as owned by Franceschi, but by Saurí and Subirá, along with Hacienda Constancia (Tellechea and Rodil 1913, 171). According to Manuel Mayoral-Barnés, the sugar corporation Saurí y Subirá and its Central Constancia were still operating in 1946.

17. Free people of color in San Antón are not listed as slave owners, but there were free people of color who owned slaves in Puerto Rico.

18. Carnegie summarizes the principal features of family land as follows: "1) holdings are passed on undivided to a group of heirs collectively; 2) all the children, irrespective of where they reside, birth order or legal status, are entitled to inherit; 3) no heir is free to alienate all or any portion of the holding. Beyond these minimal common denominator of factors, however, the descriptions of land tenure in the Caribbean indicate some inexactness about just what principles the customary system upholds and how these principles work together" (Carnegie 1987, 83).

19. This "tenancy in common" is also known in Spanish as *"propiedad en común pro indiviso,"* as established by the Puerto Rican Civil Code, when the person who dies has left no will and family members inherit the property.

20. Information provided by the Oficina de Ordenamiento Territorial de Ponce in 1996.

Chapter 4. Hispanophile Zones of Whiteness

1. Rafael Hernández Colón served a previous term as Puerto Rican governor, 1972–76.

2. Plans for Ponce in Marcha are, in fact, still under litigation between the government of the Autonomous Municipality of Ponce and the government of Puerto Rico.

3. All academic texts and other published materials written in Spanish were translated into English by the author, by her research assistant, Sherry E. Cuadrado Oyola, or by Tomás Ayala. From this point on, when the original academic text was written in Spanish, this is acknowledged in a note.

4. Original text in Spanish.
5. Original text in Spanish.
6. Original text in Spanish.
7. Original text in Spanish.
8. Original text in Spanish.
9. Original text in Spanish.
10. Original text in Spanish.
11. Original text in Spanish.
12. Original text in Spanish.
13. Original text in Spanish.

14. The literary production of this generation of writers varied. While Cabral, in the Dominican Republic, developed a social poetry that addressed the problems facing black people, Palés's literary creation was more idealistic than socially engaged (Badiane 2010).

15. Original text in Spanish.
16. Original text in Spanish.
17. Original text in Spanish.
18. Original text in Spanish.
19. Original text in Spanish.

20. Reasons for Ponce's selection also have to do with RHC's personal interest in preserving his city's historic monuments, an interest he had been making public long before he came to power as governor. I was told that one of the reasons for this choice was that Ponce, unlike San Juan, had not been subjected to reconstruction up to then and was more prone to future deterioration. The architectural distinctiveness of Ponce's historic buildings also attracted the Spanish team and influenced its decision to start there.

21. Original text in Spanish.

22. In 1988, the ICI adopted the name Spanish Agency of International Cooperation (Agencia Española de Cooperación Internacional; AECI). However, because Mariana continued to refer to the agency as ICI, I use this acronym instead of AECI.

23. Pseudonym.

24. All interviews and field data collected in Spanish are translated to English by the author, by her research assistant, Sherry E. Cuadrado Oyola, or by Tomás Ayala.

25. Years later, in August 2003, Mayor Cordero favored a measure to exclude Bélgica, Claussells, and Cantera—all poor, low-income communities—from the Historic Zone (Santana 2004). Subsequent pro-statehood administrations established further changes in the methodology used to demarcate the Historic Zone, indicating that the zone would not be conceived as a holistic area but that certain structures within the designated area would be given more or less priority according to their "monumental value" as cultural patrimony (Santana 2006).

26. According to Scarano and Curtis White (2007), the practice of taking in relatives and even nonrelatives was a common adaptive strategy to deal with impoverishment in the first decades of the twentieth century. Similarly, Peter Ward and colleagues (2011) discuss the formation of high-density and irregular settlements in the form of self-built consolidated dwellings in areas that were originally peripheral settlements but that are now located in the intermediate ring of cities (like San Antón) as a common practice in Latin America.

27. Other factors were the Cédula de Gracias (see Chapter 2), conflicts in La Hispañola (particularly in Haiti), and the independence wars of Latin America.

28. Original text in Spanish.

29. The mission of Casa Ponceña Inc. was to aid and support *ponceños* in New York City and particularly to coordinate *ponceños*' participation in the Puerto Rican parade.

30. Original text in Spanish.
31. Original text in Spanish.

Chapter 5. His-Panic / My Panic

1. All interviews and field data in Spanish are translated to English by the author, by her research assistant, Sherry E. Cuadrado Oyola, or by Tomás Ayala.

2. For a detailed analysis and ethnography of fencing practices among the rich in Ponce, see Dinzey-Flores 2013.

3. According to Negrón-Portillo (1997), political organizations such as the Turbas Republicanas sustained through aggressive and violent means that the aristocratic elite should be banned from the political structures of the island.

4. All academic texts and other published materials written in Spanish were translated into English by the author, by her research assistant, Sherry E. Cuadrado Oyola, or by Tomás Ayala. From this point on, when the original academic text is in Spanish, this will be acknowledged in a note.

5. Original text in Spanish.

6. In the 1970s and 1980s, pro-statehood leader Carlos Romero Barceló (1974) argued that U.S. statehood was for the poor, who would benefit most from U.S. federal aid. This pro-statehood neopopulism coexisted with white-collar corruption and party-sanctioned violent acts of repression against supporters of independence and anyone affiliated to the political "left." Pro-statehood elites long affiliated with U.S. corporate interests backed privatization ventures supported by U.S. capital investments and neoliberal policies in the 1990s.

7. The two anthropologists were my professors from the University of California at Santa Cruz. They were able to come with me to the field because at that time (April 18–21, 1996), the American Ethnological Society was holding its annual conference in Puerto Rico.

8. María Judith had a university degree and lived in an *urbanización*. Hence, she was recommending a neighborhood settlement approach that she had not adopted herself.

9. My comment is meant to serve as a foil to the common saying "*mejorar la raza*" (improving the race), which is often said to describe the outcome of people becoming lighter (not darker) as a result of mixture. It was intended to offer an alternative interpretation to Cari's comment about the mixture that according to her had "ruined the race" for Europeans.

10. The San Sebastian Festival of La Novilla takes place every June when townspeople dress a young cow and parade it through the streets. Different *comparsas*, or chorused parades with costume, follow. Ramonita's *comparsa* is composed of a group of children who appear dressed in yellow and red and parade wearing blackface behind a huge, tall "white" doll called "la Pipina." The doll represents the mother of these "black" kids. The *choros* of the *comparsa* says: "*Los negritos estan pintao de amarrillo y colorao*" (The little blacks are painted in yellow and red tints).

Chapter 6. Flowing through My Veins

1. All interviews and field data collected in Spanish are translated to English by the author, by her research assistant, Sherry E. Cuadrado Oyola, or by Tomás Ayala.

2. Renzo Sereno (1947), for example, coined the term *cryptomelanism* to describe the constant effort to hide the existence of the color problem within the self.

3. At the time, Puerto Rico also became an important schema for African American organizations who sought to understand the limits and possibilities of a people who

had a racialized and economic position similar to that of the United States, emphasizing similarities between the Island's economy and that of the U.S. South and the second-class citizenship status of Puerto Ricans and African Americans (Alamo-Pastrana 2012).

4. The book is a landmark study of racism in Puerto Rico, yet it has been out of print for almost four decades and few reviews were published.

5. The author of this review signed as a member of the "Committee for Puerto Rican Independence."

6. All academic texts and published materials written in Spanish were translated into English by the author, by her research assistant, Sherry E. Cuadrado Oyola, or by Tomás Ayala. From this point on, when the original academic text is in Spanish, this will be acknowledged in a note.

7. Original text in Spanish.

8. Original text in Spanish. The word "*mestiza*" in brackets is part of the original text.

9. The ICP's emblem was approved in 1956. It was conceived by Ricardo Alegría and rendered by graphic artist Lorenzo Homar (Instituto de Cultura Puertorriqueña 2011).

10. Mural was commissioned by San Germán mayor Jorge Alberto Ramos Comas in 1985.

11. The *vejigante* is a masked carnival figure whose function is to be mischievous and to scare people during carnaval. The horns displayed in the masks have associations with the devil. The masks are usually painted in bright primary colors.

12. Original translation to English by the ICP. http://www.icp.gobierno.pr/quiene-somos/emblema.

13. Yolandita Monge, for example recorded *bombas* and *plenas* and the video clip for her record "*Mi encuentro*" in San Antón. Her producer believed salsa was in crisis and qualified Yolandita's move to *bomba* and *plena* as "bold and creative" (Torres-Torres 1996, 94).

14. Original text in Spanish.

15. Original in Spanish.

16. (Palés-Matos 1974, 69–70). Special credit is given to Tomás Ayala, who translated this poem by Luis Palés Matos in 1998.

17. Poem translated by Tomás Ayala.

18. *Pandero* is a handheld percussion instrument. It is similar to a tambourine but bigger and has no metal jingles.

19. In his pioneer work *Narciso Descubre su Trasero*, Isabelo Zenón Cruz launched one of the first and most public criticisms of Palés's work. Specifically, he criticized Palés's Eurocentric construction of the black man as an exotic being (Zenón 1975, 47)

20. Original text in Spanish.

21. During his conference, de Mata explained that he borrowed the term *tarcualitos* from his father, a black man, who used to say that if you were black and ugly, you had to find a woman who was lighter than you so that your offspring could come out "*tarcualitos*." The term can thus be understood as a construction of *tal-cual-clarito* (just-like-a light one). de Matta used this as an example of the black man's complex of bettering his race.

22. The conference was sponsored by Ponce's Catholic University in commemoration of the abolition of slavery.

23. In this poem, de Matta extends his criticism to black poets and black declaimers such as Juan Boria, who popularized *negroide* poetry.

24. Poem translated by Tomás Ayala.

25. Original text in Spanish.

26. For a more thorough analysis of this piece, see Arroyo 2002 and Rivero 2006.

27. Original text in Spanish.

28. Original text in Spanish.

29. Original text in Spanish.

30. A discussion of this film event was previously published in Godreau 2008a.

31. It should be noted that Patricia Fox cautions against essentializing improvisation and related skills found in wordplay, joking, and other verbal arts as existing independently of the situation. Otherwise, she states, "one can end up confining people of African descent to the category of oral, mythical, sensual, whimsical, rather than textual, inherently rational, planned or projected" (Fox 2006, 102).

Chapter 7. Irresolute Blackness

1. All interviews and field data collected in Spanish are translated to English by the author, by her research assistant, Sherry E. Cuadrado Oyola, or by Tomás Ayala.

2. The term *Afroantillana* in the title of the event broadly described the following categories of competition: *repicador de plena, bailador de bomba, quintero rumba, tumbador de rumba, chéquere, cantante de plena, cantante de rumba, bongosero,* and *declamador de poesía negroide* (plena lead drummer, bomba dancer, rumba lead drummer, rumba base drummer, *chequere* [large Cuban maraca with exterior beads], *plena* singer, rumba singer, bongo player, and person who declaims black poetry).

3. Tito refers to the practice of burying a baby's umbilical cord remnant in the place where she/he was born.

4. Internal communication to the governor, *Comunicación interna al Honorable Rafael Cordero-Santiago, alcalde. Rehabilitación integral del Barrio San Antón: Plan maestro general de acción municipal,* May 1995. All academic texts and other published materials written in Spanish were translated into English by the author, by her research assistant, Sherry E. Cuadrado Oyola, or by Tomás Ayala. From this point on, when the original academic text is in Spanish, this will be acknowledged in a note.

5. Public figures with visibly black features have also adopted celebrity nicknames such as "La Taína" (model Noris Pérez Díaz) or "El Indio" (former Major League baseball player Rubén Sierra).

6. The neo-Taíno share a notion of themselves as colonial subjects who have to struggle against the double burden of Spanish and U.S. colonialism. They critique the nationalist Hispanophile policies of a Puerto Rico commonwealth government that subordinates Taíno influence to Spanish culture and allows a *criollo* elite of Spanish ancestry to manipulate Taíno symbols and heritage. In the United States, they also seek to enhance their status as a U.S. colonized, culturally distinct minority, accommodating their plight of Taíno cultural preservation to U.S. discourses of multiculturalism (Haslip-Viera 2001).

7. The recognition of collective property rights (especially to land) achieved by Afro-Latinos was availed by constitutional and legal frameworks developed after decades of authoritarian rule and dictatorships (French 2009; Hooker 2005). In an effort to restore democratic legitimacy, different Latin American countries amended their constitutions to send a message about the state's recognition of the multicultural nature of the nation.

8. The neo-Taíno movement is an exception, yet most of these organizations are based in the United States. In the Island, the Taíno have been used more as a historic symbol of national assertion vis-à-vis the United States and not so much as the contemporary identity of an organized movement seeking indigenous rights.

9. The play performed by Taller La Brisa (see Chapter 2), in which actors did make public affirmations of their black identity and evoked the history of slavery, is an exception.

Conclusion

Chapter epigraph by Columbian community activist Dorina Hernández taken from Martínez, ed., 2014, 100.

1. All academic texts and published materials written in Spanish were translated into English by the author, by her research assistant, Sherry E. Cuadrado Oyola, or by Tomás Ayala. From this point on, when the original academic text is in Spanish, this will be acknowledged in a note.

2. Law No. 91, July 26, 2010. P. de la C. 1392 (2010).

3. Law No. 91, July 26, 2010. P. de la C. 1392 (2010), page 2. Original text in Spanish.

4. Ibid.

5. Law No. 91, July 26, 2010. P. de la C. 1392 (2010), page 1. Original text in Spanish.

6. Ibid.

7. Original text in Spanish.

8. A less flawed (though still problematic) analogy would have been to say that San Antón is to Ponce as Santurce is to San Juan (or as Loíza is to Puerto Rico).

9. As with all projects, this book's scope is limited. The questions I asked, my interests, and other shortcomings left pertinent topics such as migration, gender, violence, poverty, youth culture, and related issues, including interpersonal racism and its effects on personal subjectivities, relatively unexplored. These and other angles of pertinence remain for future explorations.

10. The exclusivity of the U.S. binary system has also been criticized by scholars, especially after considering the fluidity prevalent in African American "race talk" in the United States (Russell et al. 1992; Keith and Herring 1991).

11. In a conference sponsored by the Smithsonian Institution at the University of Puerto Rico in Mayagüez (El significado de la herencia indígena en Puerto Rico, February 20, 2013), Dr. Delgado Colón, a specialist on Taíno indigenous culture, characterized the racial discourses of the three different political parties in a humorous but telling way. During the question-and-answer period, he stated that the pro-statehood party or Partido Nuevo Progresista, the acronym for which in Spanish is the PNP, also stood for the "Partido de la

Negritud Puertorriqueña" (Party of Puerto Rican Negritude); that the pro-independence party or Partido Independentista Puertorriqueño, whose acronym is PIP, was the "Partido Indigenista Puertorriqueño" (Puerto Rican Indigenous Party); and that the commonwealth party, or Partido Popular Democrático, whose acronym is PPD, was the "Partido Peninsular De España" (Peninsular Party of Spain). The joke of course simplifies what is a much more complex reality, but it is the first time I have heard a scholar point to these important political and racial emphases, mentioned in this book and deserving of further analysis.

12. Infrastructure facilities such as sewer systems and water pipes were available only to residents of the renovated area, although the government constructed other facilities, such as a renovated basketball court and baseball park, for all community members.

13. All interviews and field data collected in Spanish are translated to English by the author, by her research assistant, Sherry E. Cuadrado Oyola, or by Tomás Ayala.

References

Abelson, Robert P.
　1981 Psychological Status of the Script Concept. American Psychologist 36(7): 715–729.
Alamo-Pastrana, Carlos
　2009 Con el Eco de los Barriles: Race, Gender, and the Bomba Imaginary in Puerto Rico. Identities: Global Studies in Culture and Power 16(5): 573–600.
　2012 Dispatches from a Colonial Outpost: Puerto Rico as Schema in the Black Popular Press, 1942–1951. Du Bois Review: Social Science Research on Race 9(1): 201–225 doi: 10.1017/S1742058X11000312
Albizu Campos, Pedro
　1974 La conciencia nacional puertorriqueña por Pedro Albizu Campos. Selección, introduccióny notas de Manuel Maldonado-Denis. México: Siglo Veintiuno Editores.
Alegre-Barríos, Marío
　1996 Ocho artistas negros alzan su voz. El Nuevo Día, May 7: 72–73.
Alegría-Ortega, Idsa E., and Palmira N. Ríos
　2005 Contrapunto de género y raza en Puerto Rico. Río Piedras, Puerto Rico: Centro de Investigaciones Sociales, Universidad de Puerto Rico, Recinto de Río Piedras.
Alexander, Jack
　1977 The Culture of Race in Middle-Class Kingston, Jamaica. American Ethnologist 4(3): 413–435. doi: 10.1525/ae.1977.4.3.02a00020
Alfonso, Omar
　1997 De fiesta los residentes del Barrio San Antón. La Perla del Sur, July 2–8: 11.

Álvarez-Curbelo, Silvia
  1993 La conflictividad en el discurso político de Luis Muñoz-Marín, 1926–1936. In Del nacionalismo al populismo: cultura y política en Puerto Rico. Sylvia Álvarez-Curbelo and María Elena Rodríguez Castro, eds. Pp. 13–36. Río Piedras, Puerto Rico: Ediciones Huracán.
Álvarez-Curbelo, Silvia, and Enrique Vivoni Farage
  1998 Crónica de una casa hispanófila: La Casa Cabassa en Ponce / The Chronicle of a Hispanophile House: The Casa Cabassa in Ponce. In Hispanofilia: arquitectura y vida en Puerto Rico, 1900–1950 / Hispanophilia: Architecture and Life in Puerto Rico, 1900–1950. Enrique Vivoni Farage and Silvia Álvarez Curbelo, eds. Pp. 207–243. San Juan, Puerto Rico: Editorial de la Universidad de Puerto Rico.
Álvarez-Curbelo, Silvia, and María Elena Rodríguez Castro, eds.
  1993 Del nacionalismo al populismo: cultura y política en Puerto Rico. Río Piedras, Puerto Rico: Ediciones Huracán.
Álvarez Rivera, Manuel
  2013 Elections in Puerto Rico / Elecciones en Puerto Rico. Accessed June 2013: http://electionspuertorico.org/home_es.html
Anderson, Benedict
  1989 Imagined Communities: Reflections on the Origins and Spread of Nationalism. London: Verso.
Anderson, Mark D.
  2009 Black and Indigenous: Garifuna Activism and Consumer Culture in Honduras. Minneapolis: University of Minnesota Press.
Andrews, George R.
  1992 Racial Inequality in Brazil and the United States: A Statistical Comparison. Journal of Social History 26(2): 229–263.
  1996 Brazilian Racial Democracy, 1900–90: An American Counterpoint. Journal of Contemporary History 31(3): 483–507.
Appelbaum, Nancy
  1999 Whitening the Region: Caucano Mediation and "Antioqueño Colonization" in Nineteenth-Century Colombia. The Hispanic American Historical Review 79(4): 631–667.
Arnedo, Miguel
  1997 The Portrayal of the Afro-Cuban Female Dancer in Cuban "Negrista" Poetry. Afro-Hispanic Review 16(2): 26–33.
Arrieta Vilá, Rubén
  1998 Se rompen las cadenas para miles de esclavos. El Nuevo Día, March 23: 26.
  2006 Historia de barbarie la esclavitud y su lucha abolicionista. El Nuevo Día, March 22: 27.
Arroyo, Jossianna
  2002 "Mirror, Mirror on the Wall": Performing Racial and Gender Identities in Javier Cardona's "You Don't Look Like." In The State of Latino Theater in the United States: Hybridity, Transculturation, and Identity. Luis A. Ramos-García, ed. Pp. 152–171. New York: Routledge.

2010 "Roots" or the Virtualities of Racial Imaginaries in Puerto Rico and the Diaspora. Latino Studies 8(2): 195–219.

Ayoroa Santaliz, José Enrique
2003 Presentación: Ponce y la acción autónoma ciudadana. In PONCE: La Capital Alterna. Sociología de la sociedad civil y la cultura urbana en la historia de la relación entre clase, "raza" y nación en Puerto Rico. Ángel G. Quintero Rivera, ed. Pp. 9–11. Ponce, Puerto Rico: Ponceños de Verdad; Río Piedras, Puerto Rico: Centro de Investigaciones Sociales, Universidad de Puerto Rico, Recinto de Río Piedras.

Badiane, Mamadou
2010 The Changing Face of Afro-Caribbean Cultural Identity: Negrismo and Négritude. Lanham, Md.: Lexington Books.

Baerga, María del C.
2009–10 Transgresiones corporales. El mejoramiento de la raza y los discursos eugenésicos en el Puerto Rico de finales del siglo XIX y principios del XX. Op. cit.: Revista del Centro de Investigaciones Históricas 19: 79–106.

Baralt, Guillermo A.
1981 Esclavos rebeldes: Conspiraciones y sublevaciones de esclavos. Río Piedras, Puerto Rico: Ediciones Huracán.

Barbosa, José Celso
1937 Problema de razas: Documentos para la historia, seleccionados y recopilados por Pilar Barbosa de Rosario. La obra de José Celso Barbosa, vol. 3. San Juan, Puerto Rico: Imprenta Venezuela.

Barton, Halbert E.
1995 The Drum-Dance Challenge: An Anthropological Study of Gender, Race and Class Marginalization of Bomba in Puerto Rico. PhD dissertation, Department of Anthropology, Cornell University, Ithaca, N.Y.
2000 A Thousand Soberaos: CICRE and the Bombazo Movement. In Caribe 2000: Definiciones, identidades y culturas regionales y/o nacionales; Caribbean 2000: Regional and/or National Definitions, Identities and Cultures. Lowell Fiet and Janette Becerra, eds. Pp. 35–47. San Juan, Puerto Rico: Sargasso/Caribe 2000–Facultad de Humanidades, Universidad de Puerto Rico.

Belaval, Emilio S.
1948 Areyto. San Juan, Puerto Rico: Biblioteca de Autores Puertorriqueños.
1977 Los problemas de la cultura puertorriqueña. Río Piedras, Puerto Rico: Editorial Cultural.

Bendix, Regina
1997 In Search of Authenticity: The Formation of Folklore Studies. Madison: University of Wisconsin Press.

Besson, Jean
1984a Family Land and Caribbean Society: Toward an Ethnography of Afro-Caribbean Peasantries. In Perspectives on Caribbean Regional Identity. Elizabeth M. Thomas-Hope, ed. Pp. 57–83. Liverpool, UK: Centre for Latin American Studies, University of Liverpool.

1984b Land Tenure in the Free Villages of Trelawny, Jamaica: A Case Study in the Caribbean Peasant Response to Emancipation. Slavery and Abolition. A Journal of Slave and Post-Slave Studies 5(1): 3–23. doi: 10.1080/01440398408574862

Bhabha, Homi
 1994 Narrating the Nation. In Nationalism. John Hutchinson, and Anthony D. Smith, eds. Pp. 306–311. London: Oxford University Press.

Blanco, Tomás
 1942 El prejuicio racial en Puerto Rico. San Juan, Puerto Rico: Editorial Biblioteca de Autores Puertorriqueños.
 1979 Elogio de la plena (variaciones boricuas). Revista del Instituto de Cultura Puertorriqueña 22(84): 39–42.

Bliss, Peggy A.
 1995 Black, White, Puerto Rican All Over. The San Juan Star, March 22: 30–31.

Bonilla Ramos, Yarimar
 2010 Guadalupe Is Ours: The Prefigurative Politics of the Mass Strike in the French Antilles. Interventions: International Journal of Postcolonial Studies 12(1): 125–137.
 2012 Nonsovereign Futures?: French Caribbean Politics in the Wake of Disenchantment. In Caribbean Sovereignty, Democracy and Development in an Age of Globalization. Linden Lewis, ed. Pp. 208–227. New York: Routledge.
 2013 Ordinary Sovereignty. Small Axe: A Caribbean Journal of Criticism 13 (3: 42): 152–65 (forthcoming).

Bonilla-Silva, Eduardo, Carla Goar, and David G. Embrick
 2006 When Whites Flock Together: The Social Psychology of White Habitus. Critical Sociology 32(2–3): 229–253. doi: 10.1163/156916306777835268

Bourdieu, Pierre, and Loïc Wacqant
 1999 On the Cunning of Imperialist Reason. Theory, Culture & Society 16(1): 41–58.

Bower, Gordon H., John B. Black, and Terrence J. Turner
 1979 Scripts in Memory for Text. Cognitive Psychology 11(2): 177–220.

Branche, Jerome
 1999 Negrismo: Hibridez cultural, autoridad y la cuestión de la nación. Revista Iberoamericana LXV (188–189): 483–504.

Briggs, Laura
 2002 La Vida, Moynihan, and Other Libels: Migration, Social Science, and the Making of the Puerto Rican Welfare Queen. CENTRO: Journal of the Center for Puerto Rican Studies 14(1): 75–101.

Brown, Jacqueline N.
 2000 Enslaving History: Narratives on Local Whiteness in a Black Atlantic Port. American Ethnologist 27(2): 340–370.

Brown, Michael F.
 1996 On Resisting Resistance. American Anthropologist, New Series 98(4): 729–735.

Candelario, Ginetta
   2000 Hair Race-ing: Dominican Beauty Culture and Identity Production. Meridians 1(1): 128–156.
   2007 Black behind the Ears: Dominican Racial Identity from Museums to Beauty Shops. Durham, N.C.: Duke University Press.
Caquías Cruz, Sandra
   2013 Fuego en San Antón por culpa de una vela. El Nuevo Día, August 6. Accessed August 2013. http://www.elnuevodia.com/nota-1566583.html
Cardona, Javier
   1998 Un testimonio para la muestra: revolviendo un oscuro asunto en la escena teatral puertorriqueña. Diálogo, April: 11.
Carnegie, Charles V.
   1987 Is Family Land an Institution? In Afro-Caribbean Villages in Historical Perspective. Charles V. Carnegie, ed. Pp. 83–100. Kingston, Jamaica: Afro-Caribbean Institute of Jamaica.
Carrasquillo, Rosa E.
   2006 Our Landless Patria: Marginal Citizenship and Race in Caguas, Puerto Rico, 1880–1910. Lincoln: University of Nebraska Press.
Carrión, Juan M.
   1993 Etnia, raza y la nacionalidad puertorriqueña. In La nación puertorriqueña: Ensayos entorno a Pedro Albizu-Campos. Juan Manuel Carrión, ed. Pp. 3–18. Río Piedras, Puerto Rico: Editorial de la Universidad de Puerto Rico.
   1996 Sobre la nación sin bordes. Diálogo, March: 41.
Cartagena, Juan
   2004 When Bomba Becomes the National Music of the Puerto Rico Nation. CENTRO: Journal of the Center for Puerto Rican Studies 16(1): 14–35.
Casson, Ronald W.
   1983 Schemata in Cognitive Anthropology. Annual Review of Anthropology 12: 429–462.
Castro-Pereda, Rafael
   1988 La adscripción a la demagogia. El Nuevo Día, June 24: 67.
CB Staff
   2013 Five Million Puerto Ricans Now Living in the Mainland U.S. Caribbean Business PR, June 27. Accessed July 2013. http://www.caribbeanbusinesspr.com/prnt_ed/five-million-puerto-ricans-now-living-in-the-mainland-u.s.-8675.html
Chatterjee, Partha
   1986 Nationalist Thought and the Colonial World: A Derivative Discourse. Minneapolis: University of Minnesota Press.
   1996 Whose Imagined Community? In Mapping the Nation. Gopal Balakrishnan, ed. Pp. 214–225. London: Verso.
Chinea, Jorge L.
   1996 Race, Colonial Exploitation and West Indian Immigration in Nineteenth-Century Puerto Rico, 1800–1850. The Americas 52(4): 495–519.

    2002 Fissures in El Primer Piso: Racial Politics in Spanish Colonial Puerto Rico During Its Pre-Plantation Era, c. 1700–1800. Caribbean Studies 30(1): 169–204.
    2005 Race and Labor in the Hispanic Caribbean: The West Indian Immigrant Worker Experience in Puerto Rico, 1800–1850. Gainesville: University Press of Florida.

Clark, Truman R.
    1973 "Educating the Natives in Self-Government": Puerto Rico and the United States, 1900–1933. Pacific Historical Review 42(2): 220–233.

Clarke, Edith
    1957 My Mother Who Fathered Me: A Study of the Family in Three Selected Communities in Jamaica. London: Allen and Unwin.

Collins, John
    2008 "But What If I Should Need to Defecate in Your Neighborhood, Madame?": Empire, Redemption, and the "Tradition of the Oppressed" in a Brazilian World Heritage Site. Cultural Anthropology 23(2): 279–328. doi: 10.1525/can.2008.23.2.279

Comisión de Derechos Civiles de Puerto Rico
    1998 ¿Somos Racistas?: Cómo podemos combatir el racismo. San Juan, Puerto Rico: La Comisión.

Convenio entre España y Puerto Rico
    1988 Proyecto de Convenio entre el Gobierno de Estado Libre Asociado de Puerto Rico y el Instituto de Cooperación Iberoamericana. Madrid.

Cordero-Santiago, Rafael
    1996a Carta dirigida a residentes de San Antón y Aclaración de Inquietudes. 9 de mayo de 1996. Estado Libre Asociado de Puerto Rico, Gobierno Autónomo de Ponce, Oficina del Alcalde. Ponce, Puerto Rico.
    1996b Carta dirigida a residentes de San Antón. 22 de mayo de 1996. Estado Libre Asociado de Puerto Rico, Gobierno Autónomo de Ponce, Oficina del Alcalde. Ponce, Puerto Rico.

Coss, Luis F.
    1996 La nación en la orilla (respuesta a los posmodernos pesimistas). San Juan, Puerto Rico: Editorial Punto de Encuentro.

Crump, David, David Stanley Caudill, and David Hricik
    2004 Property: Cases, Documents, and Lawyering Strategies. Newark, N.J.: LexisNexis.

Cubano Iguina, Astrid
    1997 Criollos ante el 98: La cambiante imagen del dominio español durante su crisis y caída en Puerto Rico, 1889–1899. Revista de Indias 57(211): 637–655.
    2006 Rituals of Violence in Nineteenth-Century Puerto Rico Individual Conflict, Gender, and the Law. Gainesville: University Press of Florida.
    2011 Freedom in the Making: The Slaves of Hacienda La Esperanza, Manatí, Puerto Rico, on the Eve of Abolition, 1868–76. Social History 36(3): 280–293.

Cultural Survival, Inc.
    2002 Quilombos and Land Rights in Contemporary Brazil. Cultural Survival Quarterly 25(4): 20.
Cuning, Elisabeth, and Christian Rinaudo
    2008 Consuming the City in Passing: Guided Visits and the Marketing of Difference in Cartagena de Indias, Colombia. Tourist Studies 8(2): 267–286. doi: 10.1177/1468797608099252
Curet-Alonso, Tite
    1988 Racismo: un "issue" sin valor alguno. El Mundo, June 21: 42.
Curet-Cuevas, Eliezer
    1976 El desarrollo económico de Puerto Rico, 1940–1972. San Juan, Puerto Rico: Management Aid Center Inc.
Dávila, Arlene M.
    1997 Sponsored Identities: Cultural Politics in Puerto Rico. Philadelphia: Temple University Press.
    2001 Local/Diasporic Taínos: Towards a Cultural Politics of Memory, Reality and Imagery. In Taíno Revival: Critical Perspectives on Puerto Rican Identity and Cultural Politics. Gabriel Haslip-Viera, ed. Pp. 33–53. Princeton, N.J.: Markus Wiener.
    2004 Empowered Culture? New York City's Empowerment Zone and the Selling of El Barrio. Annals of the American Academy of Political and Social Science: Race, Politics, and Community Development in U.S. Cities 594: 49–64.
de Certeau, Michel, Luce Giard, and Pierre Mayol
    1998 The Practice of Everyday Life. Volume 2, Living and Cooking. Timothy J. Tomasik, trans. Minneapolis: University of Minnesota Press.
de Diego-Padró, José I.
    1973 Luis Palés-Matos y su transmundo poético. Río Piedras, Puerto Rico: Ediciones Puerto Saldaña.
De Jesús Correa, Bienvenido
    2002 Re: R. de la C. 747 6 de marzo de 2001. Poncenia de Emancipación Inc. Yvacinos Comunidad la Arena Barrio Torrecilla Loiza Puertorica. Ponencias 2001–2004, Proyecto de la Cámara 0747. Accessed August 2013: http://www.oslpr.org/2001-2004/A230G9O1.pdf
De León Monsalvo, Alfredo
    2009 Sociales 3: Serie de Estudios Sociales para Escuela Elemental. Serie Huellas. San Juan, Puerto Rico: Editorial Panamericana.
de Matta-García, Juan
    1991 Prietuzcos y Tarcualitos: poemas negristas y otros poemas. Arecibo, Puerto Rico: Editores Garandú.
Degler, Carl N.
    1971 Neither Black Nor White: Slavery and Race Relations in Brazil and the United States. New York: Macmillan.

Departamento de Educación
   1992 Los municipios de Puerto Rico: Ponce. San Juan, Puerto Rico: Programa Regular de Educación, Programa Editorial.
Desmond, Jane
   2007 Legacies of 1898: U.S. Imperialism in a Multi-sited Historical Perspective. Comparative American Studies: An International Journal 5(2): 115–118.
Díaz-Quiñones, Arcadio
   1985 Tomás Blanco: racismo, historia, esclavitud. In El prejuicio racial en Puerto Rico: Obras Completas Tomo III. Tomás Blanco, ed. Pp. 15–91. Río Piedras, Puerto Rico: Ediciones Huracán.
Díaz-Soler, Luis M.
   1981 Historia de la esclavitud negra en Puerto Rico, 1493–1890. 3rd edition. Río Piedras, Puerto Rico: Editorial de la Universidad de Puerto Rico.
Dinzey-Flores, Zaire Z.
   2007 Temporary Housing, Permanent Communities Public Housing Policy and Design in Puerto Rico. Journal of Urban History 33(3): 467–492.
   2008 De la Disco al Caserío: Urban Spatial Aesthetics and Policy to the Beat of Reggaetón. CENTRO: Journal of the Center for Puerto Rican Studies 20(2): 35–69.
   2013 Locked In, Locked Out: Gated Communities in a Puerto Rican City. Philadelphia: University of Pennsylvania Press.
Domínguez, Virginia R.
   1986 White by Definition: Social Classification in Creole Louisiana. New Brunswick, N.J.: Rutgers University Press.
   2007 When the Enemy is Unclear: US Censuses and Photographs of Cuba, Puerto Rico, and the Philippines from the Beginning of the 20th Century. Comparative American Studies 5(2): 173–203.
Dorris, Michael
   1992 Noble Savages? We'll Drink to That. The New York Times, April 21: A14.
Drummond, L.
   1980 The Cultural Continuum: A Theory of Intersystems. Man, New Series 15(2): 352–374.
Duany, Jorge
   1985 Ethnicity in the Spanish Caribbean: Notes on the Consolidation of Creole Identity in Cuba and Puerto Rico, 1762–1868. In Caribbean Ethnicity Revisited: A Special Issue of Ethnic Groups International Periodical of Ethnic Studies. Stephen Glazier, ed. Pp. 15–39. New York: Gordon and Breach.
   1987 Imperialistas reacios: Los antropólogos norteamericanos en Puerto Rico, 1898–1950. Revista del Instituto de Cultura Puertorriqueña 26(97): 3–11.
   2001 Making Indians Out of Blacks: The Revitalization of Taíno Identity in Contemporary Puerto Rico. In Taíno Revival: Critical Perspectives on Puerto Rican Identity and Cultural Politics. Gabriel Haslip-Viera, ed. Pp. 55–81. Princeton, N.J.: Markus Wiener.

2002 Puerto Rican Nation on the Move: Identities on the Island and in the United States. Chapel Hill: University of North Carolina Press.
2005 Introducción: El primer estudio antropológico de una comunidad puertorriqueña por Morris Siegel. In Un Pueblo Puertorriqueño. Morris Siegel, autor. Pp. vii–xix. Jorge Duany, María de Jesús García Moreno, and Noelia Sánchez Walker, trans. Hato Rey, Puerto Rico: Publicaciones Puertorriqueñas.
2006 Racializing Ethnicity in the Spanish-Speaking Caribbean. Latin American and Caribbean Ethnic Studies 1(2): 231–248.
2010 Anthropology in a Postcolonial Colony: Helen I. Safa's Contribution to Puerto Rican Ethnography. Caribbean Studies 38(2): 33–57.

Duchesne, Juan, Chloé Georas, Ramón Grosfoguel, Agustín Lao, Frances Negrón-Muntaner, Pedro Angel Rivera, and Aurea María Sotomayor
1997 La estadidad desde una perspectiva democrática radical: Propuesta de discusión a todo habitante del archipiélago puertorriqueño. Diálogo, February: 30–31.

Dungy, Kathryn R.
2005 Live and Let Live: Native and Immigrant Free People of Color in Early Nineteenth Century Puerto Rico. Caribbean Studies 33(1): 79–111.

Edmonds, Ennis B.
2003 Rastafari: From Outcasts to Culture Bearers. New York: Oxford University Press.

Edwards, Derek
1997 Discourse and cognition. London: Sage Publications.

Emmanuelli Jiménez, Rolando
2010 Alcaldesa de Ponce: ¿La 'quejona' de Marcos Rodríguez? La Perla del Sur, July 21. Accesed April 2012: http://tinyurl.com/kcpwlqk

Fernández, M. A.
1976 Review of Narciso Descubre su Trasero, Volume I, by Isabelo Zenon (in Spanish) (Puerto Rico, Editorial Furidi, 1974). 344 pp. Race and Class 18: 104–105.

Ferrao, Luis A.
1993 Nacionalismo, hispanismo y élite intelectual en el Puerto Rico de los años treinta. In Del nacionalismo al populismo: Cultura y política en Puerto Rico. Sylvia Álvarez-Curbelo and María Elena Rodríguez Castro, eds. Pp. 37–60. Río Piedras, Puerto Rico: Ediciones Huracán.

Festival de Bomba y Plena, Ponce, PR.
2011 Festival de Bomba y Plena celebrado en Noviembre del 1994 en Ponce, Puerto Rico YouTube video, 52:06. Posted by salsero79. Accessed July 10, 2011: http://www.youtube.com/watch?v=tBjbFtQNvf8&feature=endscreen

Figueroa, Luis A.
2005 Sugar, Slavery, and Freedom in Nineteenth-Century Puerto Rico. Chapel Hill: University of North Carolina Press.

Findlay, Eileen J.
1999 Imposing Decency: The Politics of Sexuality and Race in Puerto Rico, 1870–1920. Durham, N.C.: Duke University Press.

Flinter, George D.
 [1976(1832)] Examen del estado actual de los esclavos de la Isla de Puerto Rico. San Juan, Puerto Rico: Instituto de Cultura Puertorriqueña.
Flores-Collazo, María M.
 1998 La lucha por definir la nación: el debate en torno a la creación del Instituto de Cultura Puertorriqueña, 1955. Op. Cit. Revista del Centro de Investigaciones Históricas 10: 175–200.
Flores-Collazo, María M., and Humberto García-Muñiz
 2009 To (Re)construct to Commemorate: Memory Mutations of Abolition in Ponce, Puerto Rico. In Living History: Encountering the Memory and the History of the Heirs of Slavery. Ana Lucia Araujo, ed. Pp. 134–150. United Kingdom: Cambridge Scholars Publishing.
Flores, Richard R.
 2002 Remembering the Alamo: Memory, Modernity, and the Master Symbol. Austin: University of Texas Press.
Font-Saldaña, Jorge
 1998 Palés Matos afirma una identidad nacional mulata. Diálogo, April: 10.
Fowles, George M.
 1906 Down in Porto Rico. New York, Eaton & Mains.
Fox, Patricia D.
 2006 Being and Blackness in Latin America: Uprootedness and Improvisation. Gainesville: University Press of Florida.
Franco Ortiz, Mariluz
 2010 Control de Acceso y Racismo Cotidiano. El Vocero, December 3: 32.
Franco, Mariluz, and Blanca Ortiz
 2004 Desenmascarando experiencias de racismo con niñas y jóvenes de Loíza. (Everyday racism experiences with girls from Loíza). Identidades: Revista Interdisciplinaria deEstudios de Género 2: 18–43.
Franco Ortiz, Mariluz, and Doris Quiñones Hernández
 2005 Huellas de ébano: afirmando cuerpos de mujeres negras. In Contrapunto de género y razaen Puerto Rico. Idsa E. Alegría Ortega and Palmira N. Ríos González, eds. Pp. 223–238. Río Piedras, Puerto Rico: Centro de Investigaciones Sociales, Universidad de Puerto Rico, Recinto de Río Piedras.
French, Jan Hoffman
 2006 Buried Alive: Imagining Africa in the Brazilian Northeast. American Ethnologist 33(3): 340–360.
 2009 Legalizing Identities: Becoming Black or Indian in Brazil's Northeast. Chapel Hill: University of North Carolina Press.
Freyre, Gilberto
 1977 Casa-grande y senzala: formación de la familia brasileña bajo el régimen de laeconomía patriarcal: introducción a la historia de la sociedad patriarcal en el Brasil. Caracas: Biblioteca Ayacucho.

Fry, Peter
  2000 Politics, Nationality, and the Meanings of "Race" in Brazil. Daedalus 129(2): 83–118.
Fundación nacional para la cultura popular
  2012 Biografías-Sylvia del Villard. Fundación nacional para la cultura popular. Accessed April 2012: http://www.prpop.org/biografias/s_bios/sylvia_del_villard.shtml
Fusté, José I.
  2010 Colonial laboratories, irreparable subjects: the experiment of '(b)ordering' San Juan's public housing residents. Social Identities: Journal for the Study of Race, Nation and Culture 16(1): 41–59.
García-Canclini, Néstor
  1989 Culturas híbridas: Estrategias para entrar y salir de la modernidad. Mexico City: Grijalbo.
García, Gervasio L.
  1989 Historia crítica, historia sin coartadas: algunos problemas de la historia de Puerto Rico. 2nd ed. Río Piedras, Puerto Rico: Ediciones Huracán.
  2000 I Am the Other: Puerto Rico in the Eyes of North Americans, 1898. The Journal of American History 87(1): 39–64.
Garver, Earl S., and Ernest B. Fincher
  1945 Puerto Rico: Unsolved Problem. Elgin, Illinois: The Elgin Press.
Gates, Henry Louis
  1986 "Race," Writing, and Difference. Chicago: University of Chicago Press.
Géliga-Vargas, Jocelyn A., Irmaris Rosas Nazario, and Tania Delgado Hernández
  2007–8 Testimonios Afropuertorriqueños: Using Oral History to (Re)Write Race in Contemporary Puerto Rico. Sargasso 1: 115–130.
Gieryn, Thomas F.
  2000 A Space for Place in Sociology. Annual Review of Sociology 26: 463–496.
Gil, Carlos
  1994 Intellectuals Confront the Crisis of Traditional Narratives in Puerto Rico. Social Text 38: 97–104.
Gilroy, Paul
  1987 There Ain't No Black in the Union Jack: The Cultural Politics of Race and Nation. Chicago: University of Chicago Press.
Giovannetti, Jorge L.
  2006 Grounds of Race: Slavery, Racism, and the Plantation in the Caribbean. Latin American and Caribbean Ethnic Studies 1(1): 5–36.
Girón, Socorro
  1979 La plena, la bomba y el barrio de San Antón. Anuario Quinta Feria Regional de Artesanías de Ponce. Ponce, Puerto Rico: s.n.
Giusti Cordero, Juan A.
  1994 Labor, Ecology and History in a Caribbean Sugar Plantation Region: Piñones

(Loíza), Puerto Rico, 1770–1950. PhD dissertation. SUNY Binghamton. Binghamton, NY.

1996 Afro-Puerto Rican Cultural Studies: Beyond cultura negroide and antillanismo. CENTRO: Journal of the Center for Puerto Rican Studies 8(1–2): 56–77.

Gobierno Municipal Autónomo de Ponce, ed.

1995 [¿?] Ponce: Ciudad Señorial. Ponce, Puerto Rico: Gobierno Municipal Autónomo de Ponce.

1997 Programa: Acto Oficial: Entrega de nuevas viviendas, Barrio San Antón de Ponce 3 de julio de 1997. Ponce, Puerto Rico: Gobierno Municipal Autónomo de Ponce.

Godreau, Isar P.

1999 Missing the Mix: San Antón and the Racial Dynamics of Cultural Nationalism in Puerto Rico. PhD dissertation, Department of Anthropology, University of California Santa Cruz.

2002 Changing Space, Making Race: Distance, Nostalgia, and the Folklorization of Blackness in Puerto Rico. Identities, 9(3): 281–304.

2008a San Antón for TV: Gender Performances of Puerto Rican Black Folklore / San Antón para la TV: El performance de género en el folclor puertorriqueño negro. E-misférica 5(2): //hemi.nyu.edu/hemi/es/e-misferica-52/godreau

2008b Slippery Semantics: Race Talk and Everyday Uses of Racial Terminology in Puerto Rico. CENTRO: Journal of the Center for Puerto Rican Studies 20(2): 5–33.

2008c Trigueño. In International Encyclopedia of the Social Sciences. 2nd edition. Encyclopedia.com: http://www.encyclopedia.com/doc/1G2-3045302809.html

Godreau, Isar, Hilda Lloréns, and Carlos Vargas-Ramos

2010 Colonial Incongruence at Work: Employing US Census Racial Categories in Puerto Rico. Anthropology News, 51(5): 11–12. doi: 10.1111/j.1556-3502.2010.51511.x

Godreau, Isar, Mariluz Franco-Ortiz, Hilda Lloréns, María Reinat Pumarejo, Inés Canabal Torres, and Jessica Gaspar Concepción

2013 Arrancando mitos de raíz: guía para la enseñanza antirracista de la herencia africana en Puerto Rico. 2nd edition. Cabo Rojo: Editora Educación Emergente.

Godreau, Isar, Mariolga Reyes-Cruz, Mariluz Franco Ortiz, and Sherry Cuadrado

2008 The Lessons of Slavery: Discourses of Slavery, Mestizaje and Blanqueamiento in an Elementary School of Puerto Rico. American Ethnologist 35(1): 115–135.

Goffman, Erving

1959 The Presentation of Self in Everyday Life. Harmondsworth, UK: Pelican.

Goldstein, Daniel M.

1998 Performing National Culture in a Bolivian Migrant Community. Ethnology: Special Issue: Relocating Bolivia: Popular Political Perspectives 37(2): 117–132.

Goldstein, Donna M.

1999 "Interracial" Sex and Racial Democracy in Brazil: Twin Concepts? American Anthropologist 101(3): 563–578.

Gómez Acevedo, Labor
　1970 Organización y Reglamentación del Trabajo en el Puerto Rico del siglo XIX (Propietarios y Jornaleros). San Juan, Puerto Rico: Instituto de Cultura Puertorriqueña.
González, Aníbal
　1992 Puerto Rico. In Handbook of Latin American Literature. Garland Reference Library of the Humanities, 1459. 2nd edition. David William Foster, ed. Pp. 555–581. New York: Garland Publishing.
González, José L.
　1980 El País de Cuatro Pisos y Otros Ensayos. Río Piedras, Puerto Rico: Ediciones Huracán.
　1993 Puerto Rico: The Four-Storeyed Country. Gerald Guinness, trans. Maplewood, N.J.: Waterfront Press.
González, Lydia Milagros, ed.
　1992 La tercera raíz: presencia africana en Puerto Rico: Catálogo acompañando la exposición. San Juan, Puerto Rico: Centro de Estudios de la Realidad Puertorriqueña (CEREP).
González, Lydia Milagros, and Ana Lydia Vega, eds.
　1990 El Machete de Ogún: las luchas de los esclavos en Puerto Rico: (siglo 19). Río Piedras, Puerto Rico: Centro de Estudios de la Realidad Puertorriqueña (CEREP), Proyecto dedivulgación popular.
González, Lydia Milagros, and Angel G. Quintero-Rivera, eds.
　1970 La otra cara de la historia: la historia de Puerto Rico desde su cara obrera 1800–1925 (Álbum de fotos de la clase obrera puertorriqueña, 1). Río Piedras, Puerto Rico: Centro de Estudios de la Realidad Puertorriqueña (CEREP).
González, Mirerza
　1995 De cara a San Antón. Suplemento: Ponce una perla en el sur. El Vocero, May 8: S-4–S-5.
González Mendoza, Juan R.
　2001 Puerto Rico's Creole Patriots and the Slave Trade after the Haitian Revolution. In The Impact of the Haitian Revolution in the Atlantic World. David P. Geggus, ed. Pp. 58–71. Columbia: University of South Carolina Press.
González Olán, Julio A.
　2009 Ponce es Ponce y lo demás es parking. Slideshare Presentation. SlideShare. Accessed April, 2012: http://www.slideshare.net/lodemasesparking/ponce-es-ponce
González Tejera, Efraín
　2001 Derecho de Sucesiones: Tomo 1: La sucesión intestada. Río Piedras, Puerto Rico: Editorial Universidad de Puerto Rico.
Gotham, Kevin Fox
　2007 Authentic New Orleans: Tourism, Culture, and Race in the Big Easy. New York: New York University Press.
Gravlee, Clarence C.
　2005 Ethnic Classification in Southeastern Puerto Rico: The Cultural Model of "Color." Social Forces 83(3): 949–970.

Grosfoguel, Ramón
    2003 Colonial Subjects: Puerto Ricans in a Global Perspective. Berkeley: University of California Press.
    2008 Recolonization or Decolonization?: The Neocolonial Project of the United States in Puerto Rico. ReVista: Harvard Review of Latin America: Puerto Rico: The Island and Beyond (Spring): 3–7.
Grosfoguel, Ramón, Frances Negrón-Muntaner, and Chloé S. Georas
    1997 Introduction: Beyond Nationalist and Colonialist Discourses: The Jaiba Politics of the Puerto Rican Ethno-Nation. In Puerto Rican Jam: Rethinking Colonialism and Nationalism. Frances Negrón-Muntaner and Ramón Grosfoguel, eds. Pp. 1–38. Minneapolis: University of Minnesota Press.
Guerra, Lillian
    1998 Popular Expression and National Identity in Puerto Rico: The Struggle for Self, Community, and Nation. Gainesville: University Press of Florida.
Guss, David M.
    1993 The Selling of San Juan: The Performance of History in an Afro-Venezuelan Community. American Ethnologist 20(3): 451–473.
Hale, Charles R.
    2002 Does Multiculturalism Menace? Governance, Cultural Rights and the Politics of Identity in Guatemala. Journal of Latin American Studies 34(3): 485–524.
    2005 Neoliberal Multiculturalism: The Remaking of Cultural Rights and Racial Dominance in Central America. PoLAR: Political and Legal Anthropology Review 28(1): 10–28.
Hall, Stuart
    1980 Race, Articulation, and Societies Structured in Dominance. In Sociological Theories: Race and Colonialism. Unesco, ed. Pp. 305–345. Paris: Unesco.
Hanchard, Michael G.
    1994 Orpheus and Power: The Movimento Negro of Rio de Janeiro and Sao Paulo, Brazil, 1945–1988. Princeton, N.J.: Princeton University Press.
Handler, Richard
    1988 Nationalism and the Politics of Culture in Quebec. Madison: University of Wisconsin Press.
Handler, Richard, and Eric Gable
    1997 The New History in an Old Museum: Creating the Past at Colonial Williamsburg. Durham, N.C.: Duke University Press.
Harris, Marvin
    1970 Referential Ambiguity in the Calculus of Brazilian Racial Identity. Southwestern Journal of Anthropology 26(1): 1–14.
Hartigan, John, Jr.
    1999 Racial Situations: Class Predicaments of Whiteness in Detroit. Princeton, N.J.: Princeton University Press.
Harvey, Edwin R.
    1988 Legislación cultural: legislación cultural puertorriqueña, legislación cultural comparada. San Juan, Puerto Rico: Instituto de Cultura Puertorriqueña.

Haslip-Viera, Gabriel, ed.
　2001 Taíno Revival: Critical Perspectives on Puerto Rican Identity and Cultural Politics. Princeton, N.J.: Markus Wiener.
Healey, Mark A.
　2000 Disseram que voltei americanisada. Bourdieu y Wacquant sobre la raza en Brasil. Apuntes de investigación del CECyP 5: 95–102.
Helg, Aline
　1997 Race and Black Mobilization in Colonial and Early Independent Cuba: A Comparative Perspective. Ethnohistory 44(1): 53–74.
Helms, Mary W.
　1977 Negro or Indian? The Changing Identity of a Frontier Population. In Old Roots in New Lands: Historical and Anthropological Perspectives on Black Experiences in the Americas. Ann M. Fescatello, ed. Pp. 157–172. Westport, Conn.: Greenwood Press.
Hernández, Tanya Katerí
　2013 Racial Subordination in Latin America: The Role of the State, Customary Law, and the New Civil Rights Response. New York: Cambridge University Press.
Hernández-Colón, Rafael
　1988a España, San Antón y el ser nacional. El Nuevo Día, June 6: 53.
　1988b Mensaje del Gobernador del Estado Libre Asociado de Puerto Rico en ocasión de acto ofrecido en su honor por el Secretario de Estado para la cooperación internacional y para Iberoamérica y Presidente del Instituto de Cooperación Iberoamericana, excmo. Sr. Don Luis Yañez-Barnuevo. Madrid, España, 17 de mayo.
Hernández-Hiraldo, Samiri
　2006a Black Puerto Rican Identity and Religious Experience. Gainesville: University Press of Florida.
　2006b "If God Were Black and from Loíza": Managing Identities in a Puerto Rican Seaside Town. Latin American Perspectives: Struggle and Change in Puerto Rico: Expecting Democracy 33(1): 66–82.
Herskovits, Melville J., and Frances S. Herskovits
　1947 Trinidad Village. New York: Alfred A. Knopf
Hinton, Devon E., David Howes, and Laurence J. Kirmayer
　2008 Toward a Medical Anthropology of Sensations: Definitions and Research Agenda. Transcultural Psychiatry 45(2): 142–162.
Hobsbawn, Eric, and Terence Ranger
　1983 The Invention of Tradition. New York: Cambridge University Press.
Hoetink, Harry
　1985 Race and Color in the Caribbean. In Caribbean Contours. Sydney W. Mintz and Sally Price, eds. Pp. 55–84. Baltimore, Md.: Johns Hopkins University Press.
　1967 The Two Variants in Caribbean Race Relations: A Contribution to the Sociology of Segmented Societies. London: Institute of Race Relations and Oxford University Press.

Hoffnung-Garskof, Jesse
    2011 To Abolish the Law of Castes: Merit, Manhood and the Problem of Colour in the Puerto Rican Liberal Movement, 1873–92. Social History 36(3): 312–342.
Hooker, Juliet
    2005 Indigenous Inclusion/Black Exclusion: Race, Ethnicity and Multicultural Citizenship in Latin America. Journal of Latin American Studies 37(2): 285–310.
Instituto de Cultura Puertorriqueña
    2011 Emblema/Emblem. Instituto de Cultura Puertorriqueña. Accessed July 2012: http://www.icp.gobierno.pr/quiene-somos/emblema
Jackson, Richard L.
    1976 The Black Image in Latin American Literature. Albuquerque: University of New Mexico Press.
Jiménez-Román, Miriam
    1996 Un hombre (negro) del pueblo: José Celso Barbosa and the Puerto Rican "Race" Towards Whiteness. CENTRO: Journal of the Center for Puerto Rican Studies 8(1–2): 8–29.
    2001 The Indians Are Coming! The Indians Are Coming!: The Taíno and Puerto Rican Identity. In Taíno Revival: Critical Perspectives on Puerto Rican Identity and Cultural Politics. Gabriel Haslip-Viera, ed. Pp. 101–138. Princeton, N.J.: Markus Wiener.
Jolee, Edmondson
    1994 An Elegant City in Puerto Rico That Time Almost Forgot. Smithsonian 25(5): 64.
Joplin, Carol F.
    1988 Puerto Rican Houses in Sociohistorical Perspective. Knoxville: University of Tennessee Press.
Junta de Extremadura Consejería de Cultura y Patrimonio
    1998 La Gráfica Política del 98. Cáceres, España: CEXECI.
Junta de Planificación de Puerto Rico
    1953 Ponce y sus barrios: memoria suplementaria al mapa de límites del Municipio y sus barrios. Ponce, Puerto Rico: Imprenta Gobierno Municipal de Ponce.
    1992 Plan territorial de Ponce. Santurce: La Junta.
Kaiser, Rudolf
    1987 Chief Seattle's Speeches: American Origins and European Reception. In Recovering the World: Essays on Native American Literature. Brian Swann and Arnold Krupat, eds. Pp. 497–536. Berkeley: University of California Press.
Kanai, J. Miguel
    2011 Barrio Resurgence in Buenos Aires: Local Autonomy Claims amid State-Sponsored Transnationalism. Political Geography 30(4): 225–235.
Kaplan, Amy, and Donald E. Pease, eds.
    1993 Cultures of United States Imperialism. Durham, N.C.: Duke University Press.
Keith, Verna, and Cedric Herring
    1991 Skin Tone and Stratification in the Black Community. American Journal of Sociology 97(3): 760–778.

Kennedy, Philip W.
    1971 Race and American Expansion in Cuba and Puerto Rico, 1895–1905. Journal of Black Studies 1(3): 306–316.
Khan, Aisha
    1993 What Is "a Spanish"?: Ambiguity and "Mixed" Ethnicity in Trinidad. In Trinidad Ethnicity. Kevin A. Yelvington, ed. Pp. 180–207. Knoxville: University of Tennessee Press.
Kinsbruner, Jay
    1996 Not of Pure Blood: The Free People of Color and Racial Prejudice in Nineteenth-Century Puerto Rico. Durham, N.C.: Duke University Press.
Klak, T., and G. Myers
    1998 How States Sell Their Countries and Their People. In Globalization and Neoliberalism: The Caribbean Context. T. Klak, ed. Pp. 87–110. Lanham, Md.: Rowman and Littlefield.
Knight, Franklin
    1992 Introduction. In Slave and Citizen: The Classic Comparative Study of Race Relations in the Americas. Frank Tannenbaum, author. Pp. v–xiv. Boston: Beacon Press.
La Biblioteca, ed.
    2002 Somos Puerto Rico: El país, la patria. San Juan, Puerto Rico: Editorial La Biblioteca.
Lancaster, Roger N.
    1991 Skin Color, Race, and Racism in Nicaragua. Ethnology: An International Journal of Cultural and Social Anthropology 30(4): 339–353.
Laó-Montes, Agustin G.
    1997 Islands at the Crossroads: Puerto Ricanness Traveling between the Translocal Nation and the Global City. In Puerto Rican Jam: Rethinking Colonialism and Nationalism. Frances Negrón-Muntaner and Ramón Grosfoguel, eds. Pp. 169–188. Minneapolis: University of Minnesota Press.
    2008–9 Cartographies of Afro-Latina/o Politics: Political Contests and Historical Challenges. Negritud: Revista de Estudios Afro-Latinoamericanos 2(2): 237–262.
Laureano, Bianca
    2010 LatiNegr@s Project: Sylvia del Villard. Latino Sexuality. Accessed April 2012: http://latinosexuality.blogspot.com/2010/02/latinegrs-project-sylvia-del-villard.html
Lauria-Pericelli, Anthony
    1989 A Study in Historical and Critical Anthropology: The Making of the People of Puerto Rico. PhD dissertation. New York: New School for Social Research.
Lewis, Laura A.
    2000 Blacks, Black Indians, Afromexicans: The Dynamics of Race, Nation and Identity in a Mexican moreno Community (Guerrero). American Ethnologist 27(4): 898–926.
Lind-Ramos, Daniel
    1996 Un planteamiento personal en torno al problema racial. El Nuevo Día, June 6: 148–149.

Lloréns, Hilda
    2008 Brothels, Hell and Puerto Rican Bodies: Sex, Race and Other Cultural Politics in 21st Century Artistic Representations. CENTRO: Journal of the Center for Puerto Rican Studies 20(1): 192–217.

Lloréns, Hilda, and Rosa E. Carrasquillo
    2008 Sculpting Blackness: Representations of Black-Puerto Ricans in Public Art. Visual Anthropology Review 24(2): 103–116.

López, Ramón
    1986 ¿Poesía negroide? Claridad. February.

Loury, Glenn C.
    2002 The Anatomy of Racial Inequality. Cambridge, Mass.: Harvard University Press.

Loveman, Mara
    1999 Is "Race" Essential? American Sociological Review 64(6): 891–898.

Loveman, Mara, and Jeronimo O. Muniz
    2007 How Puerto Rico Became White: Boundary Dynamics and Intercensus Racial Reclassification. American Sociological Review 72(6): 915–939.

Low, Denise
    1995 Contemporary Reinvention of Chief Seattle: Variant Texts of Chief Seattle's 1854 Speech. American Indian Quarterly 19(3): 407–421.

Lutz, Catherine
    2006 Empire Is in the Details. American Ethnologist 33(4): 593–611.

Maldonado Denis, Manuel
    1988 Ni hispanófilos ni hispanófobos: puertorriqueños. El Mundo, June 13: 54

Marazzi, Rosa
    1974 El impacto de la inmigración a Puerto Rico 1800–1830: análisis estadístico. Revista de Ciencias Sociales 18(1–2): 1–41.

Martínez-Alier, Verena
    1974 Marriage, Class and Colour in Nineteenth-Century Cuba: A Study of Racial Attitudes and Sexual Values in a Slave Society. New York: Cambridge University Press.

Martínez-Vergne, Teresita
    1992 Capitalism in Colonial Puerto Rico: Central San Vicente in the Late Nineteenth Century. Gainesville: University Press of Florida.

Martínez, María I., ed.
    2012 El despertar de las comunidades afrocolombianas: relatos de cinco líderes, Dorina Hernández, Libia Grueso, Carlos Rosero, Marino Córdoba, Zulia Mena. Introductory essay by Ángel G. Quintero Rivera. Houston, Tex.: LACASA.

Martorell, Antonio
    1988 Corte, colonia y color. El Nuevo Día, June 10: 67.

Massó, Benito, Jr.
    2013 Negro: este color que me queda bonito. Autoetnografía y memorias de mis vivencias y proceso de sanación como hombre negro. Puerto Rico: Divinas Letras, Literatura para Sanar.

Matory, J. Lorand
 2006 Tradition, Transnationalism and Gender in the Afro-Brazilian Candomble. In Cultural Agency in the Americas. Doris Summer, ed. Pp. 121–145. Durham, N.C.: Duke University Press.

Mayoral-Barnés, Manuel
 1946 Ponce y su historial geopolítico- económico y cultural, con el árbol genealógico de sus pobladores. Ponce, Puerto Rico: Editorial Promisión del Porvevir.

Mayo-Santana, Raúl, Mariano Negrón-Portillo, and Manuel Mayo-Lopez
 1997 Cadenas de esclavitud y de solidaridad: esclavos y libertos en San Juan, siglo XIX. Río Piedras, Puerto Rico: Centro de Investigaciones Sociales, Universidad de Puerto Rico.

Meléndez, Edgardo
 1993 Movimiento anexionista en Puerto Rico. Río Piedras, Puerto Rico: Editorial de la Universidad de Puerto Rico.

Michaels, Walter B.
 1992 Race into Culture: A Critical Genealogy of Cultural Identity. Critical Inquiry 18(4): 655–685.

Mignolo, Walter D.
 2000 Local Histories/Global Designs: Coloniality, Subaltern Knowledges, and Border Thinking. Princeton, N.J.: Princeton University Press.

Milanich, Nara
 2007 Review Essay: Whither Family History? A Road Map from Latin America. The American Historical Review 112(2): 439–458.

Millán-Pabón, Carmen
 1995 Sagradas las raíces. El Nuevo Día, June 16: 5.

Mills-Bocachica, Wanda Ivelysse
 1993 La revitalización del barrio histórico de San Antón. MA dissertation. Río Piedras, University of Puerto Rico.
 1998 Identity, Power and Place at the Periphery. Development 41(2): 38–43.

Mintz, Sidney
 1959 Labor and Sugar in Puerto Rico and in Jamaica 1800–1850. Comparative Studies in Society and History 1(3): 273–281.
 1978 The Role of Puerto Rico in Modern Social Science. Revista/Review Interamericana 8(1): 5–16.
 1989 Caribbean Transformations. New York: Columbia University Press.

Moore, Robert J.
 1999 Colonial Images of Blacks and Indians in Nineteenth Century Guyana. In The Colonial Caribbean in Transition: Essays on Postemancipation Social and Cultural History. Bridget Bereton and Kevin A Yelvington, eds. Pp. 126–158. Kingston, Jamaica: The University Press of the West Indies.

Morales-Carrión, Arturo
 1978 Auge y decadencia de la trata negrera en Puerto Rico (1820–1860). San Juan, Puerto Rico: Centro de Estudios Avanzados de Puerto Rico y el Caribe; Instituto de Cultura Puertorriqueña.

Morales, José Ramón
    1986 Ultraje a la patria. El Mundo, September 19: 38.
Morris, Nancy
    1995 Puerto Rico: Culture, Politics and Identity. Westport, Conn.: Praeger.
Moscoso, Guillermo
    1988 Puerto Rican Regardless of Race. The San Juan Star, June 27: 16.
Moya Pons, Frank
    1996 Dominican National Identity: A Historical Perspective. Punto 7 Review: A Journal of Marginal Discourse 3(1): 14–25.
Municipio de Ponce
    2010a Atracciones Turísticas. Visit Ponce. Accessed March 2010: http://www.visitponce.com/atraccionesTuristicas.aspx
    2010b Walking Tour. Visit Ponce. Accessed July 7, 2013: http://www.visitponce.com/walkingTour.aspx
Muñoz Marín, Luis
    1985 La personalidad puertorriqueña en el Estado Libre Asociado. In Del cañaveral a lafábrica: cambio social en Puerto Rico. Eduardo Rivera Medina and Rafael L. Ramírez,eds. Pp. 99–108. Río Piedras, Puerto Rico: Ediciones Huracán.
Museo de las Américas
    2013 Salas Permanentes: Herencia Africana. Museo de las Américas. Accessed August 2013, http://www.museolasamericas.org/salas-permanentes/herencia-africana.html
Negrón-Muntaner, Frances
    1997 "English Only Jamás but Spanish Only Cuidado: Language and Nationalism in Contemporary Puerto Rico." In Puerto Rican Jam: Rethinking Colonialism and Nationalism. Frances Negrón-Muntaner and Ramón Grosfoguel, eds. Pp. 257–286. Minneapolis: University of Minnesota Press.
Negrón-Muntaner, Frances, and Ramón Grosfoguel, eds.
    1997 Puerto Rican Jam: Rethinking Colonialism and Nationalism. Minneapolis: University of Minnesota Press.
Negrón-Portillo, Mariano
    1997 Puerto Rico: Surviving Colonialism and Nationalism. In Puerto Rican Jam: Rethinking Colonialism and Nationalism. Frances Negrón-Muntaner and Ramón Grosfoguel, eds. Pp. 39–56. Minneapolis: University of Minnesota Press.
Negrón-Portillo, Mariano, and Raúl Mayo Santana
    2007 La esclavitud menor: la esclavitud en los municipios del interior de Puerto Rico en el siglo XIX: estudio del Registro de esclavos de 1872, segunda parte. San Juan, Puerto Rico: Centro de Investigaciones Sociales, Universidad de Puerto Rico, Recinto de Rio Piedras.
Ng'weno, Bettina
    2007 Turf Wars: Territory and Citizenship in the Contemporary State. Stanford, California: Stanford University Press.

Nieto-Phillips, John
  1999 Citizenship and Empire: Race, Language, and Self-Government in New Mexico and Puerto Rico, 1898–1917. CENTRO: Journal of the Center for Puerto Rican Studies 11(1): 50–74.
Nistal-Moret, Benjamin
  1984 Esclavos prófugos y cimarrrones: Puerto Rico 1770–1870. Río Piedras, Puerto Rico: Editorial de la Universidad de Puerto Rico.
Nuñez-Miranda, Armindo
  1998 Conversación con Alegría. Diálogo, October: 14–15.
Oficina de Desarrollo Cultural, Municipio de Ponce
  2001 Ponce: Ciudad Museo 2001. Proyecto auspiciado por la Secretaría de Arte y Cultura del municipio de Ponce, la Fundación Puertorriqueña de las Humanidades, la National Eddowment for the Humanities (NEH) y la Pontificia Universidad Católica de Puerto Rico, Recinto de Ponce. Ponce, Puerto Rico: Oficina de Desarrollo Cultural.
Olivares, José de
  1904 Our Islands and Their People. St. Louis: N. D. Thompson.
Omi, Michael, and Howard Winant
  1986 Racial Formation in the United States: From the 1960s to the 1980s. New York: Routledge.
Ortiz, Joselyn
  1994a Municipio de Ponce detalla plan de revitalización. La Perla del Sur, May 18–24: 12.
  1994b San Antón . . . arduo camino de revitalización. La Perla del Sur, May 18–24: 14.
Ortiz Lugo, Julia C.
  2004 [1995] De Arañas, Conejos y Tortugas: Presencia de África en la Cuentística deTradición Oral en Puerto Rico. San Juan, Puerto Rico: Centro de Estudios Avanzados de Puerto Rico y el Caribe.
Pabón, Carlos
  1995 De Albizu a Madona: para armar y desarmar la nacionalidad. Bordes 1: 22–40.
  1996 Nación ¿Quién la define? Diálogo, February: 18.
Palés-Matos, Luis
  1974 Tuntún de pasa y grifería: Poemas Afroantillanos. San Juan, Puerto Rico: Biblioteca de Autores Puertorriqueños.
Partido Popular Democrático de Ponce
  1996a Ponce: Un pueblo con la voluntad de resistir. Rafael "Churumba" Cordero Alcalde. 1996–2000. [Brochure]. Ponce, Puerto Rico: Partido Popular Democrático de Ponce.
  1996b Ponce: Un pueblo con la voluntad de resistir. Rafael "Churumba" Cordero Alcalde. 1997–2000. [Flyer]. Ponce, Puerto Rico: Partido Popular Democrático de Ponce.

Paschel, Tianna S.
  2009 Re-Africanization and the Cultural Politics of Bahianidade. Souls: A Critical Journal of Black Politics, Culture, and Society 11(4): 423–440.
  2010 The Right to Difference: Explaining Colombia's Shift from Color Blindness to the Law of Black Communities. The American Journal of Sociology 116(3): 729–769.
Pattullo, Polly
  1996 Last Resorts: The Cost of Tourism in the Caribbean. Kingston, Jamaica: Ian Randle Publishers.
Pedreira, Antonio S.
  1992 Insularismo. Obras completas de Antonio S. Pedreira, Tomo 3. Río Piedras, Puerto Rico: Editorial Edil.
Pérez, Louis A.
  2008 Cuba in the American Imagination: Metaphor and the Imperial Ethos. Chapel Hill: University of North Carolina Press.
Pérez, Silverio
  1988 El hábito no hace al monge. El Mundo, August 11: 54.
Pérez-Vega, Ivette
  1988 El cielo y la tierra en sus manos: los grandes propietarios de Ponce, 1816–1830. Río Piedras, Puerto Rico: Ediciones Huracán.
Picó, Fernando
  1977 Documentos en torno a una intervención del Conde de Mirasol en una causa promovida por un esclavo. Anales de Investigación Histórica 4(1–2): 81–91.
  1988 Historia General de Puerto Rico. Río Piedras, Puerto Rico: Ediciones Huracán.
  1997 Las construcciones de lo español entre los militares norteamericanos en Puerto Rico,1898–99. Revista de Indias 57(211): 625–635.
  2007 Cayeyanos: familias y solidaridades en la historia de Cayey. Río Piedras, Puerto Rico: Ediciones Huracán.
Pinho, Patricia de Santana
  2010 Mama Africa: Reinventing Blackness in Bahia. Durham, NC: Duke University Press.
Price, Richard
  1998 The Convict and the Colonel. Boston: Beacon Press.
  2012 Race and Ethnicity: Latino/a Immigrants and Emerging Geographies of Race and Place in the USA. Progress in Human Geography 36(6): 800–809.
Primera Hora
  2008 La bomba y la plena salvaron al barrio San Antón. Primera Hora, July 17. Accessed August 2013: http://tinyurl.com/qb4hplk
  2012 ICP desmiente desmantelación del Museo Nuestra Raíz Africana. Primera Hora, March 21. Accessed July 2013: http://tinyurl.com/pql5e6r
Pyke, Karen D.
  2010 What Is Internalized Racial Oppression and Why Don't We Study It? Acknowledging Racism's Hidden Injuries. Sociological Perspectives 53(4): 551–572.

Quijano, Anibal
   2000 Coloniality of Power and Eurocentrism in Latin America. International Sociology 15(2): 215–232.
Quintero-Rivera, Ángel G.
   1987 The Rural–Urban Dichotomy in the Formation of Puerto Rico's Cultural Identity. New West Indian Guide 61(3/4): 127–144.
   1988 Patricios y plebeyos: burgueses, hacendados, artesanos y obreros. Las relaciones declase en el Puerto Rico de cambio de siglo. Río Piedras, Puerto Rico: Ediciones Huracán.
Rahier, Jean Muteba
   1998 Blackness, the Racial/Spatial Order, Migrations, and Miss Ecuador 1995–96. American Anthropologist 100(2): 421–430.
Ramírez, Rafael L.
   1978 Treinta años de antropología en Puerto Rico. Revista/Review Interamericana 8(1): 37–49.
Ramos-Mattei, Andrés A.
   1982 El liberto en el régimen de trabajo azucarero de Puerto Rico, 1870–1880. In Azúcar y esclavitud. Andrés Ramos Mattei, ed. Pp. 91–124. Río Piedras: Editorial de la Universidad de Puerto Rico.
   1988 La sociedad del azúcar en Puerto Rico, 1870–1910. Río Piedras, Puerto Rico: Universidad de Puerto Rico, Recinto de Río Piedras.
Ramos Rosado, Marie
   1999 La mujer negra en la literatura puertorriqueña. Río Piedras, Puerto Rico: Editorial de la Universidad de Puerto Rico.
Ramos-Zayas, Ana Y.
   2003 National Performances: The Politics of Class, Race, and Space in Puerto Rican Chicago. Chicago: University of Chicago Press.
   2007 Becoming American, Becoming Black? Urban Competency, Racialized Spaces, and the Politics of Citizenship among Brazilian and Puerto Rican Youth in Newark. Identities: Global Studies in Culture and Power 14: 85–109.
Resto, Aixa M.
   1995 Ponce en el Mapa del Mundo. Suplemento: Ponce una perla en el sur. El Vocero, May 8: S-6.
Restrepo, Eduardo
   2004 Ethnicizatioin of Blackness in Columbia: Toward De-racializing Theoretical and Political Imagination. Cultural Studies 18(5): 698–715.
Rivera-Bonilla, Ivelisse
   2003 Divided City: The Proliferation of Gated Communities in San Juan. PhD dissertation. Department of Anthropology, University of California, Santa Cruz.
Rivera-Ramos, Efren
   2001 The Legal Construction of Identity: The Judicial and Social Legacy of American Colonialism in Puerto Rico. Washington, D.C.: American Psychological Association (APA).

Rivera, Raquel Z.
　2003 New York Ricans from the Hip Hop Zone. New York: Palgrave Macmillan.
　2007 Will the "Real" Puerto Rican Culture Please Stand Up?: Thoughts on Cultural Nationalism. In None of the Above: Puerto Ricans in the Global Era. Frances Negrón-Muntaner, ed. Pp. 217–231. New York: Palgrave Macmillan.
Rivera-Rideau, Petra R.
　2013 From Carolina to Loíza: Race, Place and Puerto Rican Racial Democracy. Identities: Global Studies in Culture and Power 20(5): 616–632.
Rivero, Yeidy M.
　2005 Tuning Out Blackness: Race and Nation in the History of Puerto Rican Television. Durham, N.C.: Duke University Press.
　2006 Channeling Blackness, Challenging Racism: A Theatrical Response. Global Media and Communication 2(3): 335–354.
Rodó, José Enrique
　[1962(1900)] Ariel. Buenos Aires: Editorial Kapelusz.
Rodríguez, Christopher
　2008 Statistical Genocide in Puerto Rico. VidaAfroLatina.com. Posted on June 26, 2008. Accessed January 2012: http://vidaafrolatina.com/Statistical_Genocide_in.html
Rodríguez, Clara E.
　1994 Challenging Racial Hegemony: Puerto Ricans in the United States. In Race. Steven Gregory and Roger Sanjek, eds. Pp. 131–145. New Brunswick, N.J.: Rutgers University Press.
Rodríguez-Castro, María E.
　1993 Foro de 1940: las pasiones y los intereses se dan la mano. In Del nacionalismo al populismo: cultura y política en Puerto Rico. Sylvia Alvarez-Curbelo and María Elena Rodriguez Castro, eds. Pp. 61–106. Río Piedras, Puerto Rico: Ediciones Huracán.
Rodríguez Cruz, Juan
　1965 Las relaciones raciales en Puerto Rico. Revista de Ciencias Sociales 9(4): 373–386.
Rodríguez-Silva, Ileana M.
　2006 Review of Sugar, Slavery, & Freedom in Nineteenth-Century Puerto Rico. Journal of Colonialism and Colonial History 7(2). Doi: 10.1353/cch.2006.0039
　2012 Silencing Race: Disentangling Blackness, Colonialism, and National Identities in Puerto Rico. New York: Palgrave Macmillan.
Rodríguez-Vázquez, José J.
　2004 El sueño que no cesa: la nación deseada en el debate intelectual y político puertorriqueño, 1920–1940. San Juan, Puerto Rico: Ediciones Callejón.
Rogler, Charles C.
　1944 The Role of Semantics in the Study of Race Distance in Puerto Rico. Social Forces 22(4): 448–453.
　1946 The Morality of Race Mixing in Puerto Rico. Social Forces 25(1): 77–81.

Roland, L. Kaifa
  2006 Tourism and the Negrificación of Cuban Identity. Transforming Anthropology 14 (2): 151–162.
Romero Barceló, Carlos
  1974 La estadidad es para los pobres. 2nd revised edition. San Juan, Puerto Rico: s.n.
Rosaldo, Renato
  1989 Imperialist Nostalgia. Representations: Special Issue: Memory and Counter-Memory 26: 107–122.
RoseGreen-Williams, Claudette
  1993 The Myth of Black Female Sexuality in Spanish Caribbean Poetry: A Deconstructive Critical View. Afro-Hispanic Review 12(1): 16–23.
Roy-Féquière, Magali
  1996 Negar lo negro sería gazmoñería: Luis Palés Matos, Margot Arce and the Black Poetry Debate. CENTRO: Journal of the Center for Puerto Rican Studies 8(1–2): 82–91.
  2004 Women, Creole Identity, and Intellectual Life in Early Twentieth-Century Puerto Rico. Philadelphia: Temple University Press.
Rumelhart, David E., and Donald A. Norman
  1988 Representation in Memory. In Stevens' handbook of experimental psychology: Vol 2, Learning and Cognition. 2nd edition. Richard C. Atkinson, Richard J. Herrnstein, Gardner Lindzey, and R. Duncan Luce, eds. Pp.511–587. New York: Wiley.
Russell Kathy, Midge Wilson, and Roland E. Hall, eds.
  1992 The Color Complex: The Politics of Skin Color among African Americans. New York: Harcourt Brace Jovanovich.
Sagrera, Martín
  1973 Racismo y política en Puerto Rico: la desintegración interna y externa de un pueblo. Río Piedras, Puerto Rico: Editorial Edil.
Sánchez, Celeste
  2001 Geografía e historia de Puerto Rico. Madrid: Ediciones SM.
Sanjek, Roger
  1971 Brazilian Racial Terms: Some Aspects of Meaning and Learning. American Anthropologist, New Series 73(5): 1126–1143. doi: 10.1525/aa.1971.73.5.02a00120.
Santana, Mario
  2004 Revitalización por ley. El Nuevo Día, February 12: 73.
  2006 Cambios en las normas en busca de repoblar. El Nuevo Día, June 9: 61.
Santiago, David
  1995 Bobareyto: cuento, poesía, teatro. San Germán, Puerto Rico: Centro de Publicaciones Universidad Interamericana.
Santiago de Curet, Annie
  1985 La reacción de Ponce a la ocupación americana, 1898. Revista del Instituto de Cultura Puertorriqueña 24 (90): 9–17.

Santiago-Valles, Kelvin A.
- 1994 "Subject People" and Colonial Discourses: Economic Transformation and Social Disorder in Puerto Rico, 1898–1947. Albany: State University of New York Press.
- 1995 Vigilando, administrando y patrullando a negros y trigueños: Del cuerpo del delito aldelito de los cuerpos en la crisis del Puerto Rico urbano actual. Bordes, 2: 28–42.
- 1996 Policing the Crisis in the Whitest of all Antilles. CENTRO: Journal of the Center for Puerto Rican Studies 8(1–2): 42–57.
- 2003 Some Notes on "Race," Coloniality, and the Question of History among Puerto Ricans. In Decolonizing the Academy: Diaspora Theory and African-New World Studies. Carole Boyce-Davies, Meredith Gadsby, Charles Peterson, and Henrietta Williams, eds. Pp. 217–234. Trenton, N.J.: Africa World Press.
- 2005 Colonialidad, trabajo sexualmente racializado y nuevos circuitos migratorios In Contrapunto de género y raza en Puerto Rico. Idsa E. Alegría Ortega and Palmira N. RíosGonzález, eds. Pp.187–214. Río Piedras, Puerto Rico: Centro de Investigaciones Sociales, Universidad de Puerto Rico, Recinto de Río Piedras.
- 2007 "Our Race Today [Is] the Only Hope for the World": An African Spaniard as Chieftain of the Struggle against "Sugar Slavery" in Puerto Rico, 1926–1934. Caribbean Studies 35(1): 107–140.

Santos-Febres, Mayra
- 1995 Blackness Exposed. The San Juan Star, October 15: 20.

Scarano, Francisco A.
- 1984 Sugar and Slavery in Puerto Rico: The Plantation Economy of Ponce, 1800–1850. Madison: University of Wisconsin Press.
- 1989 Inmigración y estructura de clases: los hacendados de Ponce, 1815–1845. In Inmigracióny clases sociales en el Puerto Rico del siglo XIX. Francisco A. Scarano, ed. Pp. 21–66. Río Piedras: Ediciones Huracán.
- 1992 Haciendas y barracones: azúcar y esclavitud en Ponce Puerto Rico, 1800–1850. Río Piedras, Puerto Rico: Ediciones Huracán.
- 2000 Puerto Rico: cinco siglos de historia. San Juan, Puerto Rico: McGraw-Hill.

Scarano, Francisco A., and Katherine J. Curtis White
- 2007 A Window into the Past: Household Composition and Distribution in Puerto Rico, 1910–1920. Caribbean Studies 35(2): 115–154.

Schank, Roger C., and Robert P. Abelson
- 1977a Scripts, Plans, Goals and Understanding. Hillsdale, N.J.: Lawrence Erlbaum Associates.
- 1977b Scripts, Plans and Knowledge. In Thinking: Readings in Cognitive Science. Philip N. Johnson-Laird and Peter C. Wason, eds. Pp. 421–432. Cambridge, UK: Cambridge University Press.

Scher, Philip W.
- 2011 Heritage Tourism in the Caribbean: The Politics of Culture after Neoliberalism. Bulletin of Latin American Research 30(1): 7–20.

Seda-Bonilla, Eduardo
  1961 Social Structure and Race Relations. Social Forces 40(2): 141–148.
  1968 Dos modelos de relaciones raciales: Estados Unidos y América Latina. Revista de Ciencias Sociales 12(4): 569–597.
Segal, Daniel
  1994 Living Ancestors: Nationalism and the Past in Post-Colonial Trinidad and Tobago. In Remapping Memory: The Politics of TimeSpace. Jonathan Boyarin, ed. Pp. 186–221. Minneapolis: University of Minnesota Press.
Sereno, Renzo
  1947 Cryptomelanism: A Study of Color Relations and Personal Insecurity in Puerto Rico. Psychiatry: Journal for the Study of Interpersonal Processes 10(3): 261–269.
Sheriff, Robin E.
  2000 Exposing Silence as Cultural Censorship: A Brazilian Case. American Anthropologist, New Series 102(1): 114–132. doi: 10.1525/aa.2000.102.1.114
Siegel, Morris
  1953 Race Attitudes in Puerto Rico. Phylon (1940–1956) 14(2): 163–178.
Skidmore, Thomas E.
  1974 Black into White: Race and Nationality in Brazilian Thought. New York: Oxford University Press.
  1993 Bi-racial USA vs. Multi-racial Brazil: Is the Contrast Still Valid? Journal of Latin American Studies 25(2): 373–386.
Smith, Moira, and Paul Yachnes
  1998 Scholar's Playground or Wisdom's Temple?: Competing Metaphors in a Library Electronic Text Center. Library Trends 46(4): 718–731.
Smith, Raymond T.
  1957 The Family in the Caribbean. In Caribbean Studies: A Symposium. Vera D. Rubin, ed. Pp.67–74. Seattle: University of Washington Press.
Spengler, Oswald
  1934 La decadencia de Occidente: bosquejo de una morfología de la historia universal. 4ta edición. Manuel García Morente, trans. Madrid: Espasa Calpe.
Stark, David M.
  2007 Rescued from their Invisibility: The Afro–Puerto Ricans of Seventeenth- and Eighteenth-Century San Mateo de Cangrejos Puerto Rico. The Americas 63(4): 551–586.
Stepan, Nancy L.
  1991 The Hour of Eugenics: Race, Gender and Nation in Latin America. Ithaca, N.Y.: Cornell University Press.
Steward, Julian H., et al.
  1956 The People of Puerto Rico: A Study in Social Anthropology. Urbana: University of Illinois Press.
Streicker, Joel
  1997 Spatial Reconfigurations, Imagined Geographies, and Social Conflicts in Cartagena, Colombia. Cultural Anthropology 12(1): 109–128.

Sued-Badillo, Jalil, and Angel López-Cantos
    1986 Puerto Rico Negro. Río Piedras, Puerto Rico: Editorial Cultural.
Tannenbaum, Frank
    1947 Slave and Citizen: The Negro in the Americas. New York: A. A. Knopf.
Tellechea, Joaquín, and F. J. Rodil
    1913 Album guía de Ponce. Ponce, Puerto Rico: Liga Progresista de Ponce.
Telles, Edward
    1999 Ethnic Boundaries and Political Mobilization among African Brazilians: Comparisons with the US Case. In Racial Politics in Contemporary Brazil. Michael Hanchard, ed. Pp. 85–93. Durham, N.C.: Duke University Press.
Thomas, Deborah A.
    2004 Modern Blackness: Nationalism, Globalization and the Politics of Culture in Jamaica. Durham, N.C.: Duke University Press.
Thompson, Lanny
    2007 Nuestra isla y su gente: la construcción del "otro" puertorriqueño en Our Islands and Their People. 2nd edition. Río Piedras, Puerto Rico: Centro de Investigaciones Sociales, Universidad de Puerto Rico.
    2010 Imperial Archipelago: Representation and the Rule in the Insular Territories under U.S. Dominion after 1898. Honolulu: University of Hawaii Press.
Tió, Salvador
    1988 Adscripción biológica. El Nuevo Día, June 15: 46.
Torres, Arlene
    1998 La Gran Familia Puertorriqueña "Ej Prieta de Beldá" (The Great Puerto Rican Family Is Really Really Black). In Blackness in Latin America and the Caribbean, vol. 2. Norman E. Whitten Jr. and Arlene Torres, eds. Pp. 285–306. Bloomington: Indiana University Press.
    2006 Collecting Puerto Ricans. In Afro-Atlantic Dialogues: Anthropology in the Diaspora. Kevin A. Yelvington, ed. Pp. 327–349. Santa Fe, N.M.: School of American Research Press.
Torres-Gotay, Benjamín
    1996 Puerto Rico no es ni ha sido nunca una nación. El Nuevo Día, January 21: 16.
Torres-Martinó, J. A.
    1996 Artes plásticas y el racismo. El Nuevo Día, May 16: 94–95.
Torres-Torres, Jaime
    1996 Al ritmo de la bomba y la plena. El Nuevo Día, September 15: 94–95.
Trelles, Luis R.
    2012 Se muda la colección del Museo de Nuestra Raíz Africana. El Nuevo Día, March 23. Accessed July 2013: http://tinyurl.com/pah8frm
Trouillot, Michel-Rolph
    1995 Silencing the Past: Power and the Production of History. Boston: Beacon Press.
Tugwell, Rexford Guy
    1972 Dignidad and Its Implications. In Portrait of a Society: Readings on Puerto

Rican Sociology. Eugenio Fernández Méndez, ed. Pp. 311–315. Río Piedras: University of Puerto Rico Press.

Tumin, Melvin M., with Arnold S. Feldman
 1961 Social Class and Social Change in Puerto Rico. Princeton, N.J.: Princeton University Press.

Turnbull, David
 1840 Travels in the West: Cuba, with Notices of Porto Rico and the Slave Trade. London: Longman, Orne, Brown, Green, and Longmans.

U.S. Census Bureau
 2000a Table P003 RACE [71]. Universe: Total Population. Census 2000 Summary File 1 (SF1) 100-Percent Data. Geography: Ponce Municipio, Puerto Rico. Geography Filters: Block 1001–1045, Block Group 1, Census Track 720, Ponce Municipio. Block 4006,4007, 4009, 4011, 4014, Block Group 4, Census Tract 719, Ponce Municipio, Puerto Rico.
 2000b Table: QT-P5 Race Alone or in Combination: 2000. Census 2000 Summary File 1 (SF1) 100-Percent Data. Geography: Puerto Rico.
 2000c Table: QT-P5 Race Alone or in Combination: 2000. Census 2000 Summary File 1 (SF1) 100-Percent Data. Geography: Ponce Municipio, Puerto Rico.
 2000d Table: QT-P5 Race Alone or in Combination: 2000. Census 2000 Summary File 1 (SF1) 100-Percent Data. Geography: San Antón barrio, Ponce Municipio, Puerto Rico.
 2000e Table: QT-P5 Race Alone or in Combination: 2000. Census 2000 Summary File 1 (SF1) 100-Percent Data. Geography: United States.
 2011 Table: B03001 Hispanic or Latino Origin by Specific Origin. Universe: Total Population. 2011 American Community Survey 1-Year Estimates. Geography: United States.
 2013 Table: Pepannres: Annual Estimates of the Resident Population: April 1, 2010, to July 1, 2012. 2012 Population Estimates. Geography: Puerto Rico.

Vaiá, Duilió
 1980 Plantation Tokens of Puerto Rico: Reference Listings of Haciendas and Tokens Used (1800–1900). New York: Vantage Press.

Vanclay, Frank, and Gareth Enticott
 2011 The Role and Functioning of Cultural Scripts in Farming and Agriculture. Sociologia Ruralis 51(3): 256–271.

Vargas-Ramos, Carlos
 2005 Black, Trigueño, White . . . ?: Shifting Racial Identification among Puerto Ricans. Du Bois Review 2(2): 267–285. doi: 10.1017/S1742058X05050186

Vasconcelos, José
 1925 La raza cósmica: misión de la raza iberoamericana: notas de viajes a la América de Sur. Madrid: Agencia Mundial de Librería.

Vázquez, Blanca
 1996 Race and Identity. Special Double Issue of CENTRO: Journal of the Center for Puerto Rican Studies 8(1–2): Spring 1996.

Velasquez Runk, Julie
    2012 Indigenous Land and Environmental Conflicts in Panama: Neoliberal Multiculturalism, Changing Legislation, and Human Rights. Journal of Latin American Geography 11(2): 21–47.

Vivoni-Farage, Enrique, and Silvia Álvarez-Curbelo
    1998 Hispanofilia: el revival español en la arquitectura y la vida en Puerto Rico, 1898–1950 / Hispanofilia: The Spanish Revival in Architecture and Life in Puerto Rico, 1898–1950. Catalogue of an exhibition sponsored by the Archivo de Arquitectura y Construcción de la Universidad de Puerto Rico.

Vizcarrondo, Alicia
    1992 Puerto Rico es nuestro país. Estudios Sociales. Nivel Elemental. Santo Domingo, Dominican Republic: Editorial Sentenario.

Vizcarrondo, Fortunato
    1976 ¿Y tu agüela, a'onde ejtá? In Dinga y mandinga: poemas. 3 ed. Fortunato Vizcarrondo. Pp. 17–18. San Juan de Puerto Rico: Instituto de Cultura Puertorriqueña.

Wade, Peter
    1993 Blackness and Race Mixture: The Dynamics of Racial Identity in Colombia. Baltimore: Johns Hopkins University Press.

Ward, Peter M., Edith R. Jiménez Huerta, Erika Grajeda, and Claudia Ubaldo Velázquez
    2011 Self-Help Housing Policies for Second Generation Inheritance and Succession of "The House that Mum & Dad Built." Habitat International 35(3): 467–485.

Whitten, Norman E., Jr., and Arlene Torres
    1998 General Introduction: To Forge the Future in the Fires of the Past: An Interpretive Essay on Racism, Domination, Resistance, and Liberation. In Blackness in Latin America and the Caribbean, vol. 1. Norman E. Whitten Jr. and Arlene Torres, eds. Pp. 3–33. Bloomington: Indiana University Press.

Wierzbicka, Anna
    2005 In Defense of "Culture." Theory & Psychology 15(4): 575–597.

Wikipedia contributors
    2013 Monumento a la abolición de la esclavitud. Accessed July 7, 2013: http://tinyurl.com/lthegvs

Williams, Eric
    1944 Capitalism and Slavery. Chapel Hill: The University of North Carolina Press.
    1957 Race Relations in Caribbean Society. In Caribbean Studies: A Symposium. Vera Rubined. Pp. 54–60. Jamaica: Institute of Social and Economic Research, University College of the West Indies.

Winant, Howard
    1992 Rethinking Race in Brazil. Journal of Latin American Studies 24(1): 173–192.

Yelvington, Kevin A.
    1997 Patterns of "Race," Ethnicity, Class, and Nationalism. In Understanding Contemporary Latin America. Richard S. Hillman, ed. Pp. 229–261. Boulder, Colo.: Lynne Rienner.

2006 The Invention of Africa in Latin America and the Caribbean: Political Discourse and Anthropological Praxis, 1920–1940. In Afro-Atlantic Dialogues: Anthropology in the Diaspora. Kelving A. Yelvington, ed. Pp. 35–82. Santa Fe, N.M.: School of American Research Press.

Yelvington, Kevin A., Neill G. Goslin, and Wendy Arriaga
2002 Whose History?: Museum-Making and Struggles over Ethnicity and Representation in the Sunbelt. Critique of Anthropology 22(3): 343–379. doi: 10.1177/0308275X02022003762

Zenón-Cruz, Isabelo
1975 Narciso descubre su trasero: El negro en la cultura puertorriqueña, vols. 1 and 2. Humacao, Puerto Rico: Editorial Furidi.

Index

abolicíon, 76
abolition: abolitionism, 75; abolitionist movement, 79; commemoration of, 73–74, 78; historical implications, 81, 94, 96, 104, 250n14; law, 251n10; post-abolition narrative, 94–96, 98; and San Anton, 94–96, 98; statue of, 76, 250n14. *See also* emancipation, slavery
abolitionists, 74
adscripción retórica (rhetorical ascription), 127, 129, 132–34, 138
Africa, 5, 66, 89, 96, 122, 126, 131, 185–86, 215, 244n8
African Americans, 7, 14, 17, 155, 180, 219, 254–55n3, 257n10
African ancestry, 37, 80, 88, 110, 169
African descent, 79, 81, 85, 129, 200
African heritage, 1, 4, 8, 20, 82, 96, 153, 183, 198, 230, 241; as backward, 122, 125, 169; biological, 201, 231; in the blood, 125, 130, 189–90, 195, 198–89, 230; contributions, 79, 177, 185–86, 201; culture, 48, 70, 128, 132, 189–90; embodied, 189–90, 194; in Loíza, 207, 211; in Ponce, 40–41, 91; in San Antón, 4, 11, 29, 47, 56–57, 59, 189; scripted, 14–15, 20, 29, 173, 229, 241

African identity, 131
Africanization, 167
African music, 128, 187, 189, 251n30
African race, 23, 73, 81, 166, 185, 230
African rhythms, 96, 136, 185, 189
Africans, 75, 155, 158; belittled, 38, 126; erased, 127; as first Puerto Ricans, 72; free, 79, 102; as slaves, 80, 81, 230, 250n19, 250n23; Taínoized, 219; undermined, 180, 186
African traits (survivals), 5, 78, 84, 106, 189–90, 211, 243n33
Afro-Antillana, 132, 190, 204, 207, 209–10, 213–14, 256n2
Afro-Brazilian identity, 14
Afro-Caribbean, 190–92
Afro-Colombian, 223
Afro-descendants, 4, 8, 219, 222–24, 241–42; identity, 233; militancy, 9
Afro-Diaspora 18, 189, 219, 232, 241–42
Afro-Latin America, 5, 29, 200, 231, 233–34, 238, 242, 245n18
Afro-Latino culture, 211, 226
Afro-Latino difference, 222
Afro-Latino folklore, 211;
Afro-Latinos, 20, 221–23, 257n7

Afro-Mexico, 205
Afro-Puerto Rico (*Afropuertorriqueño*): communities, 19, 245n14; culture, 11, 16, 19, 187–88, 192–93, 200, 202, 215; culture, as natural, 189, 198–99, 207, 214; culture, as scripted, 215; folklore, 4, 19–20, 212, 224, 228; heritage, 11; identity, 39, 233; mixed race, 177; and nation, 19, 20, 189; religion, 18; traditions, 4, 11, 187, 207, 212, 232; words, 191
agency, 17, 76, 241
aggression: as scripted 18, 38, 201
agriculture: in history, 32, 105, 178–79; reform, 211; represented in national emblem, 186; subsistence, 82–83; workers, 91, 107, 179
Alamo-Pastrana, Carlos, 20, 26–27, 180, 188, 255n3
Albizu Campos, Pedro, 125–26
Alegría, Ricardo, 183, 255n9
Americanization, 3, 10, 16–17, 35, 85, 125, 166–68, 187, 230, 239, 241
Americas: demands for equality in, 241; ethnic bocks within, 232; historic sites, 141; inequality in, 39, 72; racial democracy in, 24; racism in, 69, 85, 185, 230; Spain in, 127, 130; transitions from slavery in, 79
American Studies, 234
ancestors (ancestry), 38, 101–2, 110–11, 116, 217, 240; African, 37, 88, 110, 162, 169, 186; foreign, 73; Hispanic (Spanish), 158, 163–64, 256n6; Latin, 169; "living," 184; slave (and black), 212, 231; Taíno, 215, 219, 221
ancestral cultures, 222
ancestral groups: in constitution, 182; mural of, 184
Anglo-Saxon: actions against Native Americans, 225; masculinity, 166; race, 167; as scripted, 230, 236; slave subject, 249n2. *See also* whiteness
annexation (annexationists): Barbosa, 149–50; to United States, 12, 29, 151, 153
anti-Americanism, 85, 124, 147, 231
anticolonialism, 150, 170, 173
antidiscrimination, 8
anti-Haitianism, 169
anti-Hispanic (anti-Spanish), 126, 148, 164. *See also* Hispanophobia
anti-imperialism, 13

Antilles (Antillas), 76, 190–91, 96, 127, 131–32, 245n22
anti-nationalism, 232
antiracism, 211, 224–26; activists (activism), 18–19, 68, 224; alternatives, 241–42; movements, 7, 185; organizations, 8; policies, 9
anti-United States, 126
antiwhite, 85
architects: lack of flexibility, 116; liberal, 46, 229; and *patios,* 46, 56; for Ponce's Historic Zone, 134–37; for San Antón's project, 11, 47–48, 56, 137, 140, 229
architecture: Castillo Serrallés, 171, 189; class and race in, 16, 170–73; European elements of, 139–41; lampposts as aristocratic, 138, 238; in Loíza, 157; in Ponce, 40, 121–22, 171, 189; Pueblerino script, 139–40; in San Antón, 122, 140, 238–240
aristocracy, 254n3
Aristocratic City, 1, 9–10, 40, 91, 121, 142; priority for funding, 134. *See also* Ponce
arrabal, 35, 51
arrimados, 107–8, 114
artesanos, 117. *See also* artists
artisans, 45, 83, 142, 149; skilled workers, 107, 151, 213
artists: designer of national emblem, 183; everyday, 27; plastic, 128, 197–98; in political alliances, 151; on racism, 8, 197; in San Antón, 4, 45, 50, 60, 107, 141; for TV, 199
arts: black themes, 198; Caribbean, 132; cartoons, 165, 167; European influenced, 132; folk, 16, 42, 182–86, 212; and nationalism, 183, 241; Negroide, 192, 194–98; plastic, 8, 182; poetry, 131, 191; rendering blackness passive, 75; San German's mural, 184; sculpture, 228, 250n14; Taíno, 186; verbal, 256n31
assimilation: to contain African influence, 122; into Hispanic culture, 128, 130, 132; to national culture, 222; in Puerto Rican diaspora, 20; in Puerto Rico, 127; resistance to, 232; to U.S. interests, 167–68
authenticity, 8, 55, 97–98
autochthony, 86; and black identity, 235, 237; culture, 187, 224; vegetation, 186
Autonomist Party. *See* Partido Autonomista
autonomist politics, 75, 123, 127, 151, 170, 179, 235–36

autonomous livelihoods, 81, 83
autonomy, 170, 172; cultural, 127; historically, 12, 71, 91–92, 104, 142, 170, 235, 246n9; in Latin America, 221; of maroons, 233; for Puerto Rico, 10, 12; regional, 10; of slaves and *libertos,* 91–92, 104

Banchs Cabrera, Maria Judith, xi, 34–35, 38–39, 39, 111, 153–55, 199, 201–2, 205, 254n8
Barbosa, José Celso, 125, 149–51, 155
Bejuco Blanco, 95, 100–101
Belaval, Emilio, 84–86, 125
benevolent "happy" slavery: Catholic, 69; challenged, 68, 71–74, 94; discourses or scripts of, 26–28, 61, 85, 128, 225–26, 231, 234, 249n4; and erasure, 123, 225; in history, 69; political implications, 26, 225–26, 231, 234; and whitening, 123
biology: of blackness, 29, 124, 132, 178, 231; in colonial discourse, 164; in national discourse, 123, 125, 129, 184, 201; in race mixing, 69, 123, 177, 201; of whiteness, 129, 132
black: artists, 8, 194–99; docile identity, 75–76, 194; folk and Spain, 158–61; *jíbaros,* 88–89; political movements, 8, 211–12, 223–24; pride, 38, 59, 67–68, 153–54; as racial term (*negro*), 81, 84, 89, 105, 184, 190, 196, 243; "sad color," 59; as slave, 80–81; undesired identity, 36–37, 59, 155, 246n7, 246n8; women, 8, 17, 57, 192–94, 204
blackness: affirmation (celebration of), 38, 41, 59, 67–68, 131–33, 194–97, 212; in the body, 188–91, 193; as constructed (contested), 5, 11, 198, 202, 206, 210–12, 224–25; denial of, 4, 37–39, 59, 86, 144–45, 224; destabilizing nationalism, 71–72, 132, 150, 173; diluted (*see also blanqueamiento*), 70–71, 78–79, 129–30, 167, 230; emplaced, 16–17, 36–39, 81–85, 89–90; emplaced in the coast, 82–85, 229, 237–39; emplaced in Loíza, 156–57, 207, 211; emplaced in San Antón, 4–5, 91, 97, 192, 199–202, 244n6, 245n18; as ethnicity, 221–26, 232; exceptional (nonnormative), 28–29, 61, 82, 84–85; and folklore, 17–21, 29, 40, 148, 211, 221–26; improvised or spontaneous, 190, 200–201, 214, 256, 256n31; and indigeneity, 215–26; in *mestizaje,* 155, 178, 186, 189; and multiculturalism in Latin America, 221–26; and nationalism, 5–7, 14, 19, 25–26, 72, 180–81, 231–34, 241–42; and party politics, 11, 14, 29, 55, 211, 235–37; and poverty, 153, 157, 235; primitive or backward, 173, 184, 193; and racism, familial, 161–64; and racism, personal dimensions, 35, 38, 58–59; racism and slavery, 67, 80–81; and racism toward San Antón or Loíza, 144, 151–52, 157; scripts of, 14–16, 19, 230–32; scripts of, fading, 68, 78, 81, 225–26; scripts of, limiting, 30, 215–16, 241–42; scripts of, in San Antón, 55–57, 189–90, 199–202, 213; silenced, 19, 151, 172, 222, 232, 237–38; state promoted, 14, 27, 198, 207, 241; and the United States, 25–26, 148–49, 156–57, 184–85, 233; urban, 16–18, 33, 35, 49, 136–37; vis-à-vis Aristocratic City, 1, 128, 136, 144–45, 228–29. *See also* racism, scripts
Blanco, Tomás, 4, 28, 69–70, 125–26, 249n4
blanqueamiento, 16, 91, 97, 164, 231, 239; challenged, 233; as erasure, 69, 78, 123; evidenced in census, 37; ideology, 37, 39, 56, 233; scripted, 73; valued, 20, 230, 236. *See also* whitening
bomba, 96, 136, 188, 209, 212–13, 245n9, 256n2. *See also bomba* and *plena*
bomba and *plena:* African origins, 185, 189, 190; challenging racism, 188–89; festivals (*fiestas*), 41, 74, 128, 153, 188–89, 201–5, 228; folkloric, 18, 96, 186, 196; ignored, 98, 141, 214; in national culture, 186–89; political significance, 217, 228; positioned in past, 55, 98; racialized, 4, 36, 56, 96, 136, 146–48, 189, 220; rhythm and blood, 189; significance for housing project, 11, 45, 55, 60, 116, 137, 231; and slavery, 96, 185; symbolic of San Antón, 4, 11, 137, 189, 199, 209, 227; touristic, 10, 56, 58, 204; traditions, 36, 55, 116; and youth, 55–56, 206–7
Bonilla Ramos, Yarimar, ix, x, 13, 77
bourgeoisie, 70, 83, 106, 112, 136, 166, 170
Brau, Salvador, 125
Brazil (Brasil): black movement in, 223; and land titles, 211–12, 221–22; militancy, 9; race mixture, 24, 130; racial democracy in, 24; racism in, 19; roots tourism, 14; and slavery, 69; and Vargas, 181

Cabrera, Judith, xi, 38, 41
Caguas, 11, 75, 236
Candelario, Ginnetta, 13, 81, 167, 169, 219
cane (sugar), 29, 84, 98–99, 104–6, 213; black cane workers, 88–99, 105, 136; of Constancia, 32–33, 101; *jíbaro* (white) cane cutters, 104, 106, 172, 250n26; in Ponce, 29, 100; in San Antón, 108–10, 116, 160
capitalism, 13, 21, 25, 114, 148, 153, 167, 179, 236, 254n6
Cardona, Javier, 196, 198
Caribbean, 1, 5, 36, 40, 57, 69, 71–73, 81, 105, 171, 187; anticolonialism, 150; art, 132; English, 25, 28, 46, 69, 71, 128, 185, 230; French, 71, 185, 230; Hispanic, 46, 72, 78–79, 81, 131, 164; kinship and family land, 57, 114, 248n33, 252n18; migrants, 94; race in, 14, 19, 71, 79, 122, 128, 84, 141, 196, 234, 250n16; racial discourses, 13, 164, 235; and slavery, 249n8; socioeconomic conditions, 21; sovereignty in, 13, 53; tourism in, 9
Carrión, Juan Manuel, 7, 24, 125
caseriós, 16–17, 33, 228
Catholicism: implications for slavery, 28, 69–70, 72, 74–75, 249n2, 250n20; linked with Spain, 159, 230; in Puerto Rico, 18, 32, 34, 121–22, 126, 142
Catholic sacraments, 86
Cayey, 82, 186
Cédula de Gracias, 79, 93, 112, 250n16, 253n27
cement, 3, 32, 35, 41, 52; controversy over, 42, 48, 53, 147–48, 156; and federal funding, 48, 59; in Ponce, 148; in San Antón, 42, 51, 53–55, 137, 247n15; scripts and status of, 31, 59. *See also* housing
Central America, 219
Centro Histórico (Office of Historic Preservation), 11
Chatterjee, Partha, 22–23, 26
cities: *criollo* control of, 136, 142; race mixing in, 91–92; racialized, 31, 137; zoning, 137. *See also municipio*, urban centers, *urbanizaciones*
citizenship, 22, 57, 79; metropolitan, 21; multicultural, 221; second class, 180, 236, 254–55n3; struggles for, 20, 224, 232; United States, 6, 10, 12–13, 17, 21–22, 150, 235–36
class, 1, 3, 7, 16, 26, 28, 31, 34–35, 38, 73, 79, 81, 83, 86, 91–92, 102, 105–7, 140, 145, 147, 150–53, 156, 160–61, 163, 166, 172, 179, 224, 235, 237–38; equality, 156; *hacendado,* 112; planter, 72, 81, 245n22, 249n8, 249n10; second, 180, 236, 255n3; solidarity, 237; upper, 137, 143, 148; white Spanish, 166. *See also* middle class, working class
coast: and blackness, 87–89, 193, 215, 230–31, 238; and sugar, 113
coastal-highland dichotomy, 81–82, 89, 91, 104
coastal-rural dichotomy, 18, 83–88. *See also* urban-rural dichotomy
colonial (and anticolonial) discourses, 5, 164, 167, 169, 170, 173, 231, 236
colonialism, 13, 21, 22–23, 25, 28, 69, 79–80, 122; challenged, 7, 122, 189, 194, 219, 226. *See also* Puerto Rico, United States
colonial subjectivity, 97, 256n6
color: sad, 59; skin (and eye), 2, 36–38, 90, 105, 127, 132, 149–50, 154–55, 160, 166–67, 179–80, 184–85, 197, 243n2, 246n5, 246n7, 247n11
color-blind, 73, 181, 249n10, 251n11
comadrona (midwife), 115
Comité Pro-Defensa, 52, 54, 60, 156, 203–4, 209, 214, 216, 218, 224
commonwealth party. *See* Partido Popular Democrático
commonwealth status, 10, 13, 18, 21, 26, 182
Constancia, 31–32, 39, 41–42, 139, 246n3, 252n16
Cordero-Santiago, Rafael "Churumba," 10, 13, 45, 57–58, 83, 116, 121, 143, 248n29, 248n31, 253n25
counterplantation culture, 83
criollos: defined, 249n13; European roots, 123; intellectuals, 123; and racism, 123, 136, 151; and slavery, 74; vis-à-vis Spain, 123, 170; vis-à-vis the United States, 170
Cuba, 88, 131, 141, 168, 191, 205, 256n2; and blackness or slavery, 5, 71, 79, 107, 122, 150, 168; as Catholic, 69; history, 80, 167–69; plantation economy of, 85; race missing in, 167–68; racial democracy, 24–25
cultural capital, 210–11
cultural difference, 223
cultural legislation, 182
culture: as basis for rights, 23, 222–24, 226, 228, 241; carried by blood, race, 23; as im-

Index

prisoning, 1, 20; modern, 23; spiritual, 23. *See also* Ponce, Puerto Rico, San Antón
culturetos, 209–10, 212
Curet-Alonso, Tite, 129, 132
Cuto Colón, Juan Luis, xi, 34, 49, 147, 151–53, 156–57, 247n15

Dávila, Arlene, 7, 9, 14, 22, 42, 49, 183, 185–87, 219, 226
decolonization, 179
De Diego-Padró, José, 132
del Valle Atiles, Francisco, 125
de Matta-Garcia, Juan, 195–98, 255n21, 256n23
democracy, 23, 53, 181, 223. *See also* racial democracy
development: of civilization, 86; cultural and social, 4, 9–11, 83–84, 87, 96, 129, 131, 178, 185, 228; economic and political, 10, 42, 49, 87, 93, 100, 141, 157, 179–81, 214, 249n8; historic, 227; housing, 10, 28, 44, 47–48, 57, 116, 139–40, 156–57, 229, 240
Díaz-Quiñonez, Arcadio, 70, 125, 249n4
Díaz-Soler, Luis, 28, 70–71
dignity (*dignidad*), 35, 40, 57, 59, 96, 121, 126, 142, 159, 165, 171, 242
"discovery" of America: commemorated, 133–34, 197
discrimination, 14, 38, 131, 163, 179–81, 194, 197, 222–23, 249n12
Dominican Republic, 25, 141, 167, 169, 245n22; blackness in, 71, 131, 219; Catholic, 69; race in, 81, 107, 131, 167, 169, 185
Duany, Jorge, 7, 22, 42, 80, 84–85, 105, 179–80, 185–86, 219, 233, 245n22, 246n9, 2550n23

elections, 4, 11, 13, 51, 121, 133, 141, 144, 179, 210
electricity, 41, 46, 99, 102, 108, 211, 239–40
el fanguito, 99
elites, 7, 20, 55, 124–25, 148–51, 170, 221, 224–25, 229, 235, 254n3; anti-American, 85; *criollo*, 17, 67, 71, 75, 107, 122–24, 136, 141, 169–70, 229, 231, 237, 256n6; culture, 130–31; interests and values, 169, 182, 233, 254n6; in Latin America, 130; and liberalism, 71, 75, 131; and racism, 83, 85–86, 156, 158, 194, 245n20; "white," 169–70

El Museo de Nuestra Raíz Africana, 8
emancipation, 76, 79, 108, 117, 157; Caribbean, 114; in Jamaica, 71; in Latin America, 24; in San Antón, 94, 96, 98, 102–4
emplacement, 5–6, 12, 16–17, 30, 36, 59, 229, 237–39, 244n5
English language, 13, 17, 133
environment, 157, 219
environmentalist: and indigeneity, 217, 219; proscriptions for development, 156–57
erasure, 37, 55, 68–69, 73, 78, 81, 92, 94, 96–97, 111, 116–17, 123, 231
Estado Libre Asociado (Free Associated State, ELA), 13, 179, 185
eugenics, 83, 130
Europe: influence in Antilles, 132; influence in Puerto Rico, 133; linked to nationalism, 70, 130; and racial mixing, 155, 254n9; and self government, 70, 130; and whiteness, 70, 79–80, 122, 130, 146, 172, 185

family, 2–6, 46, 58, 60–61, 99, 103, 111–13, 117, 154, 159–60, 178, 200, 204, 215, 231, 242; African influenced, 56, 248n33; extended, 44, 47–48, 56–57, 114; land, 46, 54, 57, 99, 104, 108, 114, 213, 218, 242, 252n18; matriarchy, 56–57, 154, 231, 240; networks, 41, 56–57, 228; nuclear, 35, 228; patios, 42–44, 46, 54, 56, 108, 115–16, 154, 205, 216, 218, 239–40; and race, 1–2, 37–38, 106, 161–64, 181
fieldwork, ix-xi, 3–4, 6, 239
folklore, 18, 20–21, 182–83, 186, 205, 241, 244n5, 251n30; Afro-Puerto Rican, 4, 186, 224, 228; and black women, 193; Caribbean, 196; challenging domination, 19, 20, 98, 228; characteristic of San Antón, 17, 28–29, 202, 206, 210, 212, 213; contested, 29, 202, 206, 210; elite uses of, 55, 58; ignored, 203–4, 221; as model, 202; national, 186, 188; pre-modern, 91; scripted, 18–20, 28–29, 41, 96, 238–39
folkloric culture (traditions, music), 49, 55, 205, 227, 238
folkloric leaders, 158, 187, 205–10, 212, 214
folklorization: of blackness, 14, 17–18, 20–21, 206, 211, 217, 225, 228–89; of *indigeneity*, 211
Franceschi, Juan, 54, 113
Freyre, Gilberto, 24, 69

García, Gervasio, 72, 169, 249n9
gender, 7, 18, 26, 46, 56, 73, 193, 257n9
Giusti Cordero, Juan, ix, 191–93, 196, 215
Grosfoguel, Ramón, 7, 13. 21, 25
Guerra, Lillian, 39, 85–86

hacendados (haciendas), 66–67, 70, 73–74, 91, 98, 100, 102–4, 108, 110, 111–13, 117, 124, 149, 159–60, 251n10
Hacienda Estrella, 101
Haiti, 25, 71–72, 77, 81, 88–89, 122, 150, 167, 191, 219; 245n22, 250n16, 253n27
Haitians, 107, 219
Haitian voodoo, 136
harmonious synthesis, 128, 181
Hernández, Dorina, 227, 242, 257 unnumbered note
Hernández-Colón, Rafael, 9, 127–28, 130, 252n1
Hernández-Hiraldo, Samiri, 18, 20, 38, 156–57, 207, 211, 236
hierarchy: ethnic, 21; labor, 103, 105–6; racial, 86, 158, 185–86, 221, 237; social, 39, 182, 237
highlands, 81–84, 89–91, 231
Hispanic *criollos,* 123
Hispanic culture, traditions, heritage, 84, 124–28, 130, 132, 170, 173, 185, 230–31
Hispanicity, 20, 26–29, 61, 125–26, 197, 231, 234–35
Hispanic race, 123
Hispanic Week, 187
Hispanophilia, 29, 122–24, 126–27, 132–34, 141, 163, 172, 226
Hispanophobia, 29, 124, 126, 146–47, 151, 164, 172
historical archives, x, 95, 97, 100–101, 251n7
historic housing, 227, 239
historic sites, 29, 126, 135, 141, 231
history: of the everyday, 20, 242; and ideology, 5; nonscripted, 28, 242; racialized, 5, 27, 81, 91–92, 97, 117, 172, 228, 231, 235; as selective interpretation, 5, 15, 55, 95, 140, 172, 228, 234; and tradition, 55. *See also* Puerto Rico, San Antón, slavery
Hoetnik, Harry, 37, 72, 79
housing: alleys of, 138; family-bloc model, 60, 238; historic, 239; middle class, 39, 139, 228; nuclear-family model 228; styles, 139–40, 170; wooden, 2–3, 31–33, 42, 45, 48, 51–53, 55–56, 59, 61, 101, 108, 137–40, 157, 209, 239, 247n15. *See also* cement, Comité Pro Defensa
housing, controversy over housing in San Antón, 4, 11, 42–44, 47–48, 52–55, 58, 60–61, 126, 147, 152–54, 156–57, 214, 228, 247n15; residential engagement, 50–52, 54, 59, 65, 116–17, 248n30; resistance, 55, 58–59, 65–67, 94; uses of indigeneity, 54, 156, 215–21, 223–26, 236
housing, project for San Antón, 4, 9–11, 41–42, 48, 122, 214–15, 228–29; and conceptions of family, 47–48, 56–57; exalting heritage, 45, 177; funding, 138; "History" in, 140; influenced by Hispanophilia, 134–38, 141; lampposts, 138; and land or property, 49, 116, 122, 248n25; outcomes, 239–42; preservationist agenda, 41, 49, 58, 138–40; role of *patios,* 46–48, 55–56, 240; as romantic, imperialist nostalgia, 55–56, 58, 172
hybridity, 78, 125, 130

Ibero-American race, 125
identity: black (Afro-descendent,) 4, 17, 38–39, 41, 68, 150–51, 153–54, 197–98, 222–24, 233, 235, 237; civilized, 56; and colonialism, 22, 134; *jibaró,* 84, 86–87, 89; *loizeño,* 207; politics, 4, 125, 219–21, 224, 226, 241; in Ponce, 50, 225; Puerto Rican cultural, 6, 23, 56, 170–71; Puerto Rican national, x, 3, 6, 19, 24, 26, 28, 56, 68, 83–84, 86, 89, 117, 127, 129–31, 159, 180–81, 183, 219, 233–34; racial, 38, 81, 87, 151, 198; in San Antón, 39, 206, 223; and slaves, 114; white, 33, 79, 89, 134, 158, 170–71, 182, 224, 226
Ilé, 8
immigrants, European, 1, 17, 40, 79, 94, 142, 155, 252n15
imperialist nostalgia, 56
independence (as political status), 6, 12, 18, 21, 26, 42, 68, 70, 126, 250n16; supporters of, 72, 235–36, 254n6
indigeneity, 8, 20, 82, 127–28, 132, 186, 211, 215–16, 219–20, 221–23, 25, 230, 232, 236
indigenista discourse, 219
indigenous rights, 219, 221, 223, 257n8

Indio Antón, 215–18, 220, 225
indios, 81, 99, 177, 184, 219–20, 222, 256n5
industrial economy, 32, 88
industrialization, 35, 84, 87, 178–79, 181, 183
Industrial Revolution, 79
industrial worker, 105
Institute of Puerto Rican Culture, 8, 11, 129, 134, 178, 182–83, 187, 227, 244n10
Instituto de Cooperación Iberoamericana (ICI), 127, 134–36, 253n22
intellectual imperialism, 24
intermarriage, 79
IPERI, 8

Jamaica, 71, 80, 191
jíbaro, 83–91, 104–6, 133, 185, 215, 250n28, 251n29
Jiménez-Román, Miriam, 149–50, 184–85, 219–20, 224, 226
jornaleros, 89, 102
Junta de Comunidades, 10, 153
Junta de Planificación, 10, 95, 100, 251n3

labor: coastal, 82, 89; dignity of, 165; effaced, 172; history, 12, 73, 79, 83–84, 91, 103–5, 108–10, 136, 179; movement, 150–51, 235; in San Antón, 45, 57, 93–94, 109; skilled, 4, 94, 102, 104, 107; slave, 71, 73, 93–94, 114, 230, 249n10, 250n19, 251n11; unions, 149–50
labrador, 105, 113
la generación del treinta, 126, 130, 132, 182, 190–91
la gran familia puertorriqueña, 181, 183
land: 81, 213, 215, 241–42; attachments to, 213, 215, 221–22; claims, 221–22; communal tenancy, 46, 57, 114, 211, 215, 218, 221, 252n19; cultivation, 84, 87–89, 215; expropriation, 41, 52, 54, 56, 67–68, 99, 217, 228, 236, 239; family, 46, 108, 218, 252n18; indigenous or native, 217, 232, 237; individual tenancy, 47, 57; the landless, 83, 104, 105, 108, 136, 237, 251n11; and *libertos*, 104; ownership (tenure), 46–47, 49–50, 52–54, 57, 61, 98–99, 102, 104, 108, 112, 114–16, 148, 166, 215, 248n25, 251n8; recognition, 211–12; reforms, 179, 221; rights, 8, 94, 211, 221–22, 257n7; of San Antón, 100–104; and slavery, 94, 97–98, 141; titles, 46, 211, 221. See also *patio, hacendados, arrimados*
La Tercera Raiz, 8, 197
Latin America: black movements, 224; culture, 125, 130, 224; denial of racism, 24–25; discourses of race, 13, 19, 36, 130, 233, 235; folklore, 211; hierarchy in, 31, 180, 253n26; militancy, 8; neoliberal tendencies, 9; race relations, 24, 69, 232–33; racial mixing, 14, 24, 69; reforms, 46, 221–24, 257n7; and slavery, 69, 72; ties to Puerto Rico, 122, 127, 181; ties to Spain, 122, 134, 141. See also Afro-Latin America
liberal movements, 12, 142
liberal parties, 107
liberal positions, 23, 79, 126, 148–50, 155, 178, 228, 244–45n12, 249n2
liberto, 76, 78, 80–81, 91, 93, 103–7, 117, 251n8, 251n10
Loíza, 5, 16–18, 38, 156–57, 207–8, 211–14, 227, 229, 236, 245n18, 257n8
Los Guayacanes de San Antón, 33, 128, 158, 187, 217

Majestad Negra, 190–91
marronage, 72, 83, 250n22
Martorell, Antonio, 128–89
memory, 15, 110, 217
mestizaje, 79, 223, 233; in Afro-Latin America, 29; discourses of, 8, 222, 238; and nationalism, 14, 232–33
mestizo: of nations, 8, 78, 184, 224; of persons, 125, 191, 232. See also race mixture
middle class, 2, 20, 32–33, 144–45; 151, 244–45n12; consumption, 178; housing, 39, 139, 228; neighborhoods, 42
Mintz, Sidney, x, 71–72, 79–80, 114, 180, 249n8, 249n10, 250n26
miscegenation, 130
modern, 17, 36, 124, 170–71; aesthetic, 11; *arrabal* (slum), 51; blackness, 14, 18, 49, 56, 91; city or urban area, 18, 49, 52, 58, 75, 139; colony, colonialism, 21, 53, 56, 241; national culture, 23; nationhood, 39, 125, 131, 184, 241; neighborhoods and urbanizaciones, 42, 52, 156; nonmodern, 41; premodern, 3, 17, 86–87, 91; standard of living, 4; vis-à-vis traditions, 55–56; world system, 21

modernity, 14, 16, 35, 56, 61, 146, 148, 152, 157, 170, 172, 218, 225, 236–37
modernization, 32, 87, 130, 164, 178, 181–83, 228, 230, 241
monuments, 73, 75–76, 253n20
mulatos (mulattos), 72, 80, 81, 91, 95, 106–7, 117, 119, 129, 251
multiculturalism, 8–9, 221, 223, 241, 256n6
municipio (municipality or county), 1, 9–10, 50, 82, 94, 156, 207, 229, 244n11, 247n12, 251n7, 252n2. *See also* Ponce
Muñoz Marin, Luis, 24, 87, 178, 181–82

Naranjito, 86–88, 90–91
nation, 22, 28, 53, 55, 122, 130, 169, 179, 211, 221, 224, 234, 257n7
nation, of Puerto Rico, 6, 7, 16, 26, 39, 56, 123–25, 128, 164, 235, 237; and blackness, 6, 19–20, 78, 145, 231–34; as mixed, 5, 14, 59, 125, 172, 184, 226, 231, 238; nonsovereign, 6, 11, 22, 55; and race, 26, 28, 125–26, 128, 132, 231, 235, 237–38, 250n23; vis-à-vis the United States, 26, 130, 179, 233
nation, of the United States, 6, 12, 123–24, 131
national emblem: aboriginal element of, 183–84, 186; African element of, 183–84, 186; Spanish element of, 183–84, 186
nationalism, 14, 22–23, 130, 244n7; colonial, 25–26, 42; debates, 6–7; nostalgic, 56; political, 25, 28, 70, 234–35; racialized, rural, 83; traditional, 42. *See also* Puerto Rico cultural nationalism
nation-state, 7, 13, 23
Native Americans (American Indian), 7, 29, 127, 129, 217, 220, 225. *See also* Taíno
natural selection, 123, 132
Negroid aesthetics, 190–99, 202–3. See also *Majestad Negra*
Negroid poetry, 195–96
Negrón-Portillo, Marino, 82, 149, 254n3
neoliberalism, 8–9, 14, 19, 57, 96, 157, 242, 244n12, 254n6
North America: as barbaric, 182; distinguished from Puerto Rico, 23, 42, 73, 85, 131, 182, 226; Indian reservations in, 53; influence or presence in Puerto Rico, 39, 85, 139, 159, 181, 226; in Puerto Rican history, 85, 110, 149, 158–59, 166, 171, 181, 226; racism in, 226; standards of "Otherness," 85
nostalgia, 19, 28, 55–56, 142–45. *See also* imperialist nostalgia

Office of Art and Culture, 205, 209
Operation Bootstrap, 179, 236
oppression, 24; internalized, 39, 247n11; resistance to, 196, 226

palero, 108
Palés-Matos, Luis, 125, 131–32, 190–92, 195–96, 252n14
pardos, 80, 91, 95, 102, 105, 107–8, 114
Paréntis: Ocho artistas negros contemporaneous, 8, 196–97
Partido Autonomista (Autonomist Party), 12, 142, 144
Partido Independentista Puertorriqueño (pro-independence party, PIP), 12, 21, 236, 258n11
Partido Nuevo Progresista (pro-statehood party, PNP), 11, 42, 151, 153, 257n11; and blackness, 11, 18, 157, 158, 235; and Hispanophobia, 124; history of, 151, 236; housing proposals, 41–42, 44, 124, 156, 247n15; leadership, 6, 34, 121, 128, 143–44, 151–52, 156, 187, 205, 246n9, 253n25, 254n6; support in San Antón, 52–53, 146, 156; and whitening, 153
Partido Popular Democrático (commonwealth party, PPD), 10–11, 21, 41–42, 178, 183, 187, 258n11; and blackness, 18, 152, 236; challenging statehood, 42, 44, 127, 133–34, 143, 146, 153, 236–37; and culture, national pride, 11, 42, 87, 144, 146, 231; and education, 87; Hispanophilia, 42, 127, 133–34, 146, 256n6; history, 179, 181; housing proposals, 36, 42, 44–45, 147–48, 153, 156, 237; leadership, 10–11, 121, 143, 146, 179–80, 205–7; and racial democracy, 181, 236; support in San Antón, 52, 156
Partido Republicano (Republican Party), 12, 148–51
Partido Socialista (Socialist Party), 12, 148–49
Partido Union (Union Party), 12

Paschel, Tianna, 8–9, 14, 20, 221–23, 232
Pedreira, Antonio, 125–26
pelo malo, 36–37, 196
The People of Puerto Rico, 180
Pinho, Patricia, 1, 14, 20, 30
place: and history, 54, 94, 96, 111, 143; linked to scripts, 15–17, 55, 59, 136; racialized, 5, 14, 17, 28, 49, 55, 58, 132, 156, 163, 185, 206, 212, 232–33, 238–39; and slavery, 113; and stigma, 34–35; and tourism, 49–50
Plan de Ordenación Territorial, 9, 247n12
plena, 4, 65–68, 188–89, 200, 203, 206, 209, 213, 217, 227–29, 244n4, 245n20, 256n2. See also *bomba* and *plena*
Plena Libre, 199, 202
Ponce: aristocratic, 3, 67, 143–48, 152, 157; aristocratic history, 91, 144; as Creole, 141; culture of, 40, 49, 129, 141, 209; deterring urban sprawl, 10; European influenced, 40, 121, 142–43, 146, 171, 230; greater urban area, 39; as Hispanic, 141; Historic Center (Historic Zone, Zona Histórica), 10–11, 39, 100, 121–22, 134–35, 144; history of, 40, 91, 94, 111, 134–35, 144–45; modern, 75; municipality of, 9–10, 99, 101, 205; *municipio* (county), 1; revitalization, 121–22, 126, 134–41, 145; and surrounding barrios, 2–3, 10, 91, 102, 136, 147, 210, 251n2, 257n8; as urban, 39, 91, 102, 135, 141; urban center, 134–36, 139–42; urban growth, 4; zoning and Hispanophilia, 134–35. See also Aristocratic City, *municipio*
Ponce, municipal government of, 6, 11, 40, 43, 45, 47, 50, 60, 76, 95, 101, 116, 143, 153, 209, 225, 227–28, 238, 247n21; autonomy of, 10–11; letter from The Indian Antón, 216, 225; role in heritage celebration, 207–9; role in San Antón's housing project, 11, 29, 42, 44, 48–50, 52, 60, 65, 116, 121, 126, 135, 137, 153, 214, 228–29, 236, 238, 240, 242
Ponce en Marcha, 9, 121, 143–44
ponceño, 9, 50–51, 127, 142–45, 216, 253, 253n29
populism, 177–78, 181, 254n6
Portugés River, 94, 142
postmodern, x, 244n7

poverty, 16–17, 103, 166; conflation with blackness, 153, 157, 235; signaled by housing and character of development, 3, 152, 156
pro-independence movement, 52–53
pro-independence party. See Partido Independentista Puertorriqueño
pro-statehood party. See Partido Nuevo Progresista
Protestantism: implications for slavery, 28, 69, 71–72, 230; in Ponce, 142; of the United States, 69–70
Puerto Rican diaspora, 7, 17, 20, 24, 178–79, 188, 219, 224
Puerto Rico: and colonial nationalism, 25, 42; constitution, 13, 179, 223; cultural nationalism in, 7, 12, 16, 19, 21, 27, 49, 111, 117, 146, 156, 185, 188, 215, 225; European roots, 80, 133; as Hispanic, 72–73, 124, 128, 133, 164–65, 182; history of, x, 22, 50, 54, 71, 97, 177, 232, 169; lack of sovereignty, 6, 19, 22, 241; national emblem, 183–86; sovereignty, aspired to, 6, 181; sovereignty, imagined, 23, 26; Spanish colony, 12, 71, 74–75, 81, 83, 95, 106, 122, 128–29, 133–34, 141–42, 146, 149, 169, 172–73, 186, 230, 248n2, 248n8; U.S. citizenship in, 13, 22, 150, 235; U.S. colony (*see also* colonialism, United States), 6, 12, 13, 21, 53, 56, 95, 122, 129, 133–34, 225. See also identity, race
Puerto Rico, culture of, 6, 8, 11, 19, 22, 42, 45, 48, 55–56, 69–70, 82, 84–85, 87, 123, 127–28, 130–31, 157, 181–82, 187, 207, 222, 232, 236, 241, 245n20; and biology or race, 123, 129, 130, 178, 182–86, 189, 193, 196, 214, 224–25, 230; black (African, Afro-Puerto Rican), 16, 19, 125, 128, 130, 132, 188, 198, 200, 202, 207, 212–13, 221–22, 224, 233, 241; *jíbaró,* 87; in opposition to U.S. culture, 23, 225, 231; paternalistic, 130; rural, 84; Spanish or Hispanic influenced, 29, 122–23, 125, 130, 132, 134, 173, 230, 256n6; Taíno, 183–86, 219, 224, 256n6, 257n11; urban, 141

quilombo, 211–12
Quintero-Rivera, Ángel, 72, 83, 86, 91, 142, 233, 250n22

race, 5, 8, 17, 26, 238; African (black), 73, 166, 189, 224, 255, 235, 255n21; Anglo-Saxon, 123, 167; and blood, 23, 189–90; in categorization for workers, 73; and class, 16, 26, 28, 31, 86, 106, 145, 147, 150, 152–53, 156, 160, 172, 179, 224, 238; cosmic, 125; and culture, 123, 130, 224; discourses and scripts of, 13, 19, 25, 234, 237; emplaced, 36–39, 238; euphemisms of, 37; harmonious relations, 25, 69, 128, 160, 172, 249n2; Ibero-American, 125; internalized, 247n11; Latin, 165; Latin American relations, 233; prior research, 8, 31, 69–70, 73, 179–81, 233, 249n8; in Puerto Rican identity, 6–7, 15, 23–24, 28, 31, 89–90, 126, 129, 132, 147, 151, 155, 157, 170, 177, 180, 224–25, 234–35, 237, 246n9; silenced, 19, 24, 69, 237; Spanish (Hispanic), 123, 163–64, 235; Taíno, 183–86, 235; three races of Puerto Rican identity, 23, 128, 182–84, 186, 224, 230; in the United States, 25–26, 69, 126, 234, 257n10; white, 83–84, 123, 166, 184. *See also* color

race mixture: and blackness, 231; continuum model, 24; debated, 235; discourses or narratives of, 26–27, 29, 61, 173, 185, 224, 226, 234; in eugenics, 130; harmonious, 23–24, 75, 126, 128, 132, 150, 172–73, 180–81, 185, 198, 230, 236–37; and nation, 14, 16, 69, 97, 177–78, 184, 224; in politics of erasure, 69, 184–85, 198, 238; and whitening, 167–68, 230. *See also mestizaje*

racial democracy, 14, 24, 69, 161, 166, 179, 181, 185, 238

racial terminology, 2, 36–37, 59, 81, 89, 243, 246n1, 246n2, 246n7, 246n8; *jabá (jabao)* 2, 36–37, 129, 161, 196, 243n2, 246n6; *raza de color,* 235; *rubia,* 2, 36, 155; *trigueño,* 2, 37–38, 59, 102–3, 243n2, 246n7. *See also* black, *mulato,* white

racism (discrimination, prejudice): and *adscripción retórica,* 127–30; and "benevolent slavery," 69–73, 249n10, 251n11; denied, 70, 150, 179–81, 197–98, 223, 225–26, 236; denounced, 7–8, 20, 151–52, 156–57, 188, 194–99, 223, 225–26, 255n19; familial, 161–64, 248n33; internalized, 27, 35, 38–39, 247, 247n11, 254n2; and multiculturalism, 222–24, 241; in nationalism, 14, 24, 89, 125, 180, 223, 236, 241; personal dimensions of, 58–59, 74, 180–81, 249, 249n12, 257n9; silenced, 19, 86, 132–33, 150–51, 160; and Spaniards, 158–60; in studies about Puerto Rico, 180–81, 255n4; toward San Antón or Loíz, 144, 151–52, 157; vis-à-vis the United States, 24–25, 59, 69, 70, 73, 152–53, 180, 185, 224

radical statehood, 7

regional characteristics, 9, 31, 84

regional identity, 50

regional pride, 143

regions: racialized, 5, 82, 90, 97, 131, 163, 230–31, 233, 237–38; and scripts, 81–82, 85, 89, 97, 237; vis-à-vis space, 5

Rivera, Danny, 199–202

Rodríguez-Silva, Ileana, 17, 19, 39, 68, 71, 73, 81, 83, 91, 104, 107, 125, 136–37, 149–51

Romero Barceló, Carlos, 6, 128, 254n6

rural nationalism, 83

rural-urban dichotomy. *See* urban-rural dichotomy

San Antón: architecture, 122, 136; attitudes toward Spain, 158–60; barrio of, 1, 3, 32, 48, 68, 93, 121, 136, 214, 227, 246n2; as *caserío,* 17; channeling of the river, 67, 99; cohabitation in, 105–8; cradle of *bomba* and *plena,* 11, 227–29; culture of, 11, 30, 44, 48–9, 54, 59, 96, 128, 153, 193, 203–13, 227, 228–29, 236, 244n4; foreign settlers, 112–14; heterogeneous, 4, 11, 20, 52, 116–17, 147–48, 152–54, 237; as historic site, 138, 227, 231, 238; history of, 4, 28–29, 32, 41, 44, 46, 48, 54, 58, 66, 92–99, 100–104, 136–37, 160–61, 216, 228, 231, 252n17; land ownership and *patios,* 114–16; locally produced history, 98–100, 108–12; national identity, in 233, 236; racialized, 3, 5–6, 12, 15–17, 28, 35–38, 57–59; 90–92, 97, 144–45, 151, 189, 193, 199–202, 230–32, 238–39; as scripted or stereotyped, 4, 5, 17–19, 28, 31, 33, 36, 39, 49, 55, 91–92, 96, 225–26; and slavery, 28, 68, 91–92, 94–98, 111–12; struggles, 53–54, 97, 128–29; and tourists, 48–50, 56, 58, 96, 152; as urban, 1, 10–11, 32, 39, 47, 49, 58. *See also bomba* and *plena,* cement, housing, *urbanizaciones*

San Germán, 82, 184, 255n10

San Juan, 1, 9–10, 82–83, 88, 103, 134, 142–43, 146, 151, 161, 182, 196, 229, 253n20, 257n8
Santiago-Valles, Kelvin, 8, 16, 25, 33, 68, 71, 82, 125–26, 136, 149–50
Sarabanda, 192
Scarano, Francisco, 12, 56, 73, 79, 82–83, 112, 252n15, 253n26
scripts: aesthetic elements of, 16, 138; African heritage in, 15; of Afro-Puerto-Rican culture, 96, 232; alternative, 242; architectural, 29, 138, 140, 231, 239; contested, 28–29, 41, 232; defined, 15–18, 55, 61, 78, 81, 92, 124; dynamic use, 27, 235–37; folkloric, 21, 28, 190, 238; national, 68, 73, 215–16, 225, 229–31; of place, 82, 85, 231, 238; and political parties, 235; power of, 19, 83, 98, 236; racial (*see also* blackness), 25–27, 29, 30, 173, 213, 225–26, 239; and slavery, 96; transcended, 213, 221, 225
Seda-Bonilla, Eduardo, 180
self-government, 12, 70, 85, 122, 142, 167, 236
sexuality and beauty: European, 193–94; Negroide, black or African, 49, 136, 184, 194–95, 204, 232
slavery: abolition of, 66, 71, 73–79, 81, 94–96, 98, 104, 111–12, 255n22; and blackness, 68, 81, 107; "correct" form of, 75; docility in, 71, 73; European influenced, 69, 74, 80; exaggerated, 28; and freedom, 1, 28, 72, 79–81, 83–84, 91–92, 94–97, 102, 104–8, 110, 113–14, 141, 196, 215, 231, 241, 250n23, 251n11; history of, 28, 69, 74, 79–81, 94–95, 97, 110, 113, 117, 234, 241, 257n9; labor, 71; monuments to, 75–76; politics of erasure, 68–69, 71–73, 81–82, 96, 231; in Ponce, 1, 75, 91; in Puerto Rico, 68–69, 71, 74, 79, 97, 110, 117, 231; in Puerto Rico's interior, 82, 231; resistance to, 72, 76, 97, 114; scripted (*see* benevolent slavery), 26–28, 61, 72–74, 85, 96–97, 231, 235; soft vs. harsh or brutal, 26, 68–72, 85, 123, 128, 225–26, 231, 234, 249n4; stigma of, 105–7; trivialized, 28, 68, 71–72; in the United States, 26, 69, 234. *See also* abolition, benevolent slavery, San Antón
social Darwinism, 83, 85, 123
social harmony, 25, 28, 56, 69, 71–72, 125, 133; contested, 164

socialism, 68, 150
solidarity, 38, 203, 206
space: cohabitation, of 92; communal or public, 60–61, 203; gendered, 46; and history, 33; and privacy, 46, 58; racialized, 5, 16, 83, 90, 137, 172, 231, 237–39; state-controlled, 100; and tourism, 49, 58
Spain: antidemocratic, 29; as backward, 29, 124, 164–65, 173, 236; history with Puerto Rico, 12, 22, 28, 69, 71–73, 75, 79, 84, 122–25, 126–28, 130–31, 133, 142, 148, 186, 249n2, 257–25n11; and Ponce's revitalization, 134, 141, 145, 253n20; and San Antón, 158–59, 163–64; and slavery, 70, 74, 79–80, 113, 250n20; and U.S. colonialism in Puerto Rico, 12, 29, 71–72, 126–27, 147–49, 164–66, 170–72, 219, 236. *See also* benevolent slavery, Hispanicity, Hispanophilia, Hispanophobia, slavery
Spaniards: advisors for Ponce's revitalization, 134; colonialists in Puerto Rico, 110, 125, 129, 142, 149; essentialized as ethnicity, 81, 165, 173, 186; as *hacendados,* 112, 159; immigrants, 40; in national emblem, 183–90; privileged, 72; and race mixing, 69, 112, 178, 184–85, 230; and slavery, 230; and U.S. colonialism, 149, 158, 166; white, 79, 81, 85–86, 88, 108, 166
Spanish: advisors, 136, 253n20; ancestry, 158, 162–65, 169, 171, 220, 256n6; anti-, 148; architecture, 121–22, 126, 170; colonialism, 12, 39, 75, 79, 83, 106, 124–25, 128, 142, 146, 148–49, 166, 219, 230, 235, 249n8, 256n6; in contrast with Puerto Rican developments, 83; crown, 93; culture, 127–28, 130; disdained, 148, 164, 169; government initiatives, 134; heritage, 70, 74, 122, 124, 127, 132, 141, 158, 161, 183, 186, 189, 251n30; influence, 165, 185; language, 13, 78, 122, 127–29, 133, 161, 183, 186; military, 141, 182; policies, 137; race, 23, 26, 123, 177, 184, 219; race mixing and intermarriage, 69, 79; and slavery, 80; Spanish American intellectuals, 130; traits (referents), 84, 182, 219; whiteness, 26, 73, 123, 166. *See also* Hispanicity, Spaniards
"Spanish first" legislation, 133
Spengler, Oswald, 85–86, 130, 132

statehood option, 6, 11, 18, 21, 26, 52, 124, 127, 133, 151, 155, 170; challenged by commonwealth party, 124, 127, 133–34, 143, 149; history of, 148, 151; and progress or modernity, 42, 146, 148, 151, 153, 156–57, 236; sought by competing parties, 157, 235; undermined 133

sucesión, 46–47, 52, 57, 59–60, 114, 116, 236, 239–40, 247n21

Taíno, 29, 54, 75, 78, 129, 155, 177, 186, 189, 215–16, 219–26, 230, 232, 235–37, 256n6, 257n8, 257n11
Taller La Brisa, 65–68, 94, 97, 207, 257n9
Tarcualitos, 195–96
Third World, 53
tiempo muerto, 104
Tió, Salvador, 129–32
Torres, Arlene, 5, 82, 232–33, 185
Tricoche, Valentín, 113
tristes de color, 59
tropics, 84–86
Trouillot, Rolph, x, 55, 95–97, 234, 250n16
tutelage, 164, 168

UMUPUEN, 8
underdevelopment, 3, 164
United States: admired, 123, 170; as ally, 27, 169–70; capitalism, 148, 153, 178–79, 254n6; colonial (imperial) regime in Puerto Rico (*see also* Puerto Rico), 7, 12–14, 21–25, 29–30, 42, 55, 70–71, 85–86, 123–26, 130, 142, 147, 149–50, 153, 164–67, 169–73, 184, 223, 225, 233–37, 241–41; colonial (imperial) regime in Puerto Rico, challenged, 126, 189, 194, 219, 226, 244n7; in contrast to Puerto Rico, 3, 6, 13, 16, 20, 24–27, 69, 72, 75, 80, 122–24, 127, 130–32, 151–55, 158, 231, 234, 239, 241; essentialized, 26; and indigeneity, 219, 223, 225, 256n6, 257n8; influence, 6, 13, 22, 25, 40, 55, 126, 168, 178–79, 226, 241, 212; intervention, 21, 169, 234; labor organizations, 149; as materialistic, utilitarian, 130–31; military, 124, 143, 148–49, 159, 169, 178, 233; nation, 6, 124; presence, 23; and progress, 87, 148; in Puerto Rican politics, 7, 10, 12, 42, 53, 70, 85, 123, 127, 133, 148–51, 156–57, 164, 166, 168, 178–79, 182, 184, 233, 235–36, 254n6; and race, 17, 24–25, 28, 37, 59, 69–70, 73, 85, 117, 126, 133, 146, 149, 153, 168–70, 172, 179–80, 184–85, 197, 224, 230–31, 234, 236, 246n10, 255–56n3, 257n10; and slavery, 69, 74, 117; sugar corporations, 70, 125, 151; territories, 6, 13, 166–67, 216, 233, 142

urbanizaciones, 16; history of, 32; privileged, 34–35, 41–42; variation among, 35; vis-à-vis San Antón, 34–36, 38, 41–42, 115, 126, 144–45, 154, 227–28
urban-rural dichotomy, 83, 91
urban spaces: complexity of, 16–17, 83, 91, 94, 107, 125, 149, 223, 246n4; culture, 206; margins, 149; policies for, 16, 33, 126; racialized, 16–17, 33; as scripted, 18, 33; vis-à-vis coast, 18, 83, 88, 91
U.S. Congress, 13, 179
U.S. federal government, 13, 50, 217
U.S. federal laws and regulations, 13, 48, 59, 137, 179
U.S. federal transfers, 151

vejigantes, 10, 196–97, 202
Velázquez, Edwin, 197
Vélez Franceschi, Carlos "Cao," xi, 33, 187–88, 206, 210, 228–29
Vizcarrondo, Fortunato, 74, 191–92

West, 23, 85; assimilation to, 130, 132
Western culture, 70, 129
Western domination and hierarchy, 21, 23, 25; resistance to, 225
Western hemisphere, 12, 25
Westernization, 114
white (*blanco*): elites, 67; habitus, 31; race, 70, 83–84, 91, 123, 166, 169, 184; in scripts, 21, 26, 83; as term, 2, 81, 90, 105; in the United States, 17, 126
white *hacendados*, 160
white identity, 33, 79, 89–91, 158, 184, 225, 238, 246n10, 250n17; *criollo*, 145; in the Dominican Republic, 169; Hispanic, 108, 117, 130–32, 158–59, 166; *jíbaro*, 84–91, 105–6, 215; and nation, 83, 85; as privileged, 124, 157; in Puerto Rico, 123, 129, 155, 189; in San Antón, 113, 172

white immigration, 79
white man: letter to, 216–17, 220, 225
white model, 228
whiteness: Anglo-Saxon, 26, 123–24, 146, 172, 231, 234, 236; in architecture, 16, 138–40, 170–73; biological, 129, 132; in the Dominican Republic, 169; elasticity of, 79; European, 70, 146, 172, 185; Hispanic (Spanish, cultural), 26, 29, 117, 123–24, 128–34, 145–46, 158, 161, 170, 172, 231, 236; *jíbaro,* 85–91; in nationalism, 25, 56, 71, 185, 231; and political parties, 236; and racism, 161–64; scripts of, 20, 122; as status, 107, 155, 170, 250n26
whitening, 16, 20, 37, 78; as assimilation, 167–69; and colonization, 169–70; and eugenics, 130; in highlands, 82, 86; in history, 71, 79, 82, 126, 128, 178; for the nation, 123, 167; in Ponce, 90–92; for pro-statehooders, 153; and race mixing, 79, 82, 97, 123, 167–68, 185, 230–31; and racial harmony, 173; resistance to, 38; in scripts, 26, 56, 85; for self government, 70–71, 85; in terminology, 38. See also *blanqueamiento*
white poetry, 131
whites (*blancos*): and blacks, 70, 80, 84, 89, 106, 155–56, 132, 160, 181; in census, 37, 79, 94–95, 105–6, 113–14; coastal, 84; *criollos,* 67, 74, 151, 169, 194; in the Dominican Republic, 81; Hispanic (Spanish), 79, 83, 85, 108; in Ponce, 37, 71; as privileged, 53–54, 106, 137, 161, 226, 250n16; in Puerto Rico, 37, 73, 80, 105, 129, 131, 169, 195–96, 236; in racism, 59, 81, 86, 156, 224, 251n12; in San Antón, 38, 89–92, 94–95, 97, 152, 160; "superiority" of, 84, 123, 194
white tourist, 152
white women, 144, 164, 193–201
working class (popular sectors), 19, 29, 68, 85, 143, 169; bias against, 17, 124, 172–73; and *criollos,* 122, 136, 151; and development, 121, 137, 139; Hispanophobia of, 164; movements, 150; Puerto Ricans in the United States, 20; of San Antón, 4; and U.S. interests, 148–49, 151, 164, 178, 235

zafra, 104, 106, 110, 190
Zenón, Isabelo, 89, 180–81, 185, 193, 244n8, 255n19
zoning, 9, 16, 29, 134, 137

ISAR P. GODREAU is a researcher at and former director of the Institute for Interdisciplinary Research at the University of Puerto Rico at Cayey.

The University of Illinois Press
is a founding member of the
Association of American University Presses.

Composed in 10.5/13 Marat Pro
by Lisa Connery
at the University of Illinois Press
Manufactured by Sheridan Books, Inc.

University of Illinois Press
1325 South Oak Street
Champaign, IL 61820-6903
www.press.uillinois.edu